THE IDENTITY OF AMERICA'S
MOST ELUSIVE SERIAL KILLER REVEALED

UNMASKED

ROBERT GRAYSMITH

BERKLEY BOOKS, NEW YORK

ZODIAC UNMASKED

A Berkley Book / published by arrangement with
the author

PRINTING HISTORY
Berkley hardcover edition / April 2002
Berkley mass-market edition / March 2003

ISBN: 0-425-18943-0

BERKLEY®
Berkley Books are published by The Berkley Publishing Group,
a division of Penguin Putnam Inc., 375 Hudson Street,
New York, New York 10014.
BERKLEY and the "B" design
are trademarks belonging to Penguin Putnam Inc.

PRINTED IN THE UNITED STATES OF AMERICA

10 9 8 7 6 5 4 3 2 1

TO JANE

ACKNOWLEDGMENTS

All the material in this book is derived from official records or interviews I've conducted over a thirty year period in my search for Zodiac. My heartfelt thanks to Inspector Dave Toschi, Detective George Bawart, and the editorial, legal, and production staff of this book: Gary Mailman, Liz Perl, Hillary Schupf, Heather Conner, Jill Boltin, Pauline Neuwirth, Esther Strauss, and especially, Natalee Rosenstein, my editor.

Zodiac in Costume by Robert Graysmith.
Author's line-cut illustration of Zodiac in costume at Lake Berryessa.

INTRODUCTION

ZODIAC'S UNMASKED FEATURES first came into focus one blazing summer day upon the crystal face of a watch. The detectives inside the cramped office studied the large, expensive timepiece on the wrist of their prime suspect with dread. Such a commonplace object should not arouse fear—yet it did. It had taken them almost three years to winnow 2500 suspects down to a handful, among them a man named Starr. Now they saw Starr's broad, smiling face reflected in that watch and they knew. The watch had been a catalyst for murder. Its stark black and white markings had inspired an unprecedented reign of terror. Its logo had given the killer his symbol, a crossed circle, like a gun sight, and his name—Zodiac.

After Jack the Ripper and before Son of Sam there is only one name their equal in terror: the deadly, elusive, and mysterious Zodiac. Since 1968 the hooded murderer had terrified San Francisco and the Bay Area with a string of cold-blooded killings. He hid his true features beneath a black homemade executioner's hood, emblazoned in white with his symbol. Zodiac, in taunting letters sent to newspapers, provided hidden clues to his identity with cunning codes. "This is the Zodiac speaking," he began as always. "By the way have you cracked the last cipher I sent you? My name is—" His cryptograms defied the greatest code-breaking minds of the FBI, the CIA, and NSA.

To terrify the public, Zodiac employed arcane terminology and purposely misspelled words. Sometimes he forgot himself and spelled a word correctly within the same letter. He used mispunctuation and un-grammatical language in his letters, yet understood subtle grammatical usages such as "shall" and "will." "I shall no longer announce to anyone when I comitt my murders," Zodiac printed in blue felt-tip pen in November 1969. "They shall look like routine robberies, killings of anger, & a few fake accidents, etc. The police shall never catch me, because I have been too clever for them." And Zodiac was clever, wearing glue on his fingertips to keep from leaving prints, and changing bizarre weapons with each attack. Among his weapons were a gun that projected a beam of light so he could hunt people at night, electronic bombs in his basement (targeted for school children), a homemade knife in a decorated scabbard, and guns of every caliber. We were all afraid. Single-winged planes trailed school buses manned by armed guards, a reaction to Zodiac's threat to "pick off the kiddies as they come bouncing out." With each whispered phone call and cryptic message, each bloody scrap of victim's clothing mailed to the *San Francisco Chronicle,* where I worked as a political cartoonist, a resolve grew within me to uncover his true face.

What made Zodiac so irresistible to the human imagination was not only that he offered so many hints to his true identity, but that he was always just out of reach. Who could forget the phone receiver, still damp with sweat and swinging from its cord, that Zodiac had used only moments before? He had brazenly called police from a booth four blocks from their headquarters. Directly after an attack, he was compelled to gloat, heartlessly calling his victims' families, breathing silently into the phone—as if he were about to speak his name.

We knew Zodiac, whoever he was, as a man of many parts— cryptographer, criminologist, chemist, artist, engineer, bomb-builder, poet, weapons master, and above all a practioneer of the rope, the gun, and the knife. The tension grew as Zodiac, unquenchable in his blood lust, hinted at previously concealed murders. Had he made a past mistake that might reveal his true face? "They are only finding the easy ones," he wrote. "There are a hell of a lot more down there." Zodiac may have been referring to the October 30, 1966 murder of a Riverside, California coed. Zodiac was drawn to attack or write on holidays—the Fourth of July, Thanksgiving, Columbus Day, Christmas, Halloween, and Labor Day. In Southern California a double murder on a beach on Whit Monday, a Virgin Island holiday, may have been his first, a rehearsal for a double stabbing at a lake six years later. Zodiac had connections to the Virgin Islands, as did one of his victims.

Though highly intelligent, Zodiac was not an original man. He had stolen his image and method of murder from a watch, movies, comic strips, and a short story. His M.O. had been laid out in advance on the pages of his favorite adventure tale. Obsessed with the idea of hunting men as game, Zodiac stalked young couples "because man is the most dangerous animal of all to kill." His rampages occurred on weekends at dusk or at night under a new or full moon. He cloaked himself in astrology (though that may have been a sham) and apparently cast his own horoscope to determine when he struck. Or was Zodiac only "moon mad," affected by the moon as the tides are?

Almost all the homicides attributed to him involved students killed in or around their cars near bodies of water and places named after water. Water always figured in his crimes somewhere. Possibly Zodiac was a swimmer, boatman, or sailor. Whatever he was, he knew Vallejo, a Navy town where the Northern California murders began, intimately. I was convinced Zodiac was a longtime Vallejo resident who knew his victims and had stalked two for a period of time, one in particular.

Zodiac still walked among us from the 1960s into the 1990s. He was not at work elsewhere. His massive ego and easily identifiable methods would have made him known instantly. He intended to play his game of "outdoor chess" to the death and on home turf. Surviving victims and horrified witnesses fled into hiding. Investigators themselves were fearful. In their hearts they knew there was no defense against the compulsive, random killer. Some eyewitnesses were never interviewed by the police or recontacted to be shown photos of suspects. I only found them decades afterward. One had seen Zodiac unmasked and could identify him. Others had seen him cloaked in darkness, or in his hood, or at a distance. All of the witnesses had untapped and important information to give. The prime suspect had unique body language and, unbidden, the eyewitnesses all commented on Zodiac as "lumbering like a bear," "clumsy," "not very nimble."

Included in this book is an in-depth analysis of the two films that inspired Zodiac's costume and M.O. and the short story that obsessed him. Popular culture and the face of a watch may have inspired him, but Zodiac himself inspired not one, but three copycat murderers—in New York, Vallejo, and Japan. Beginning in 1986, I set out to tell the end of Zodiac's chilling story—using the complete FBI file on Zodiac, confidential state and police files and internal and intradepartmental law enforcement memos, psychological and parole officer files, psychiatrists' sessions with the chief suspect, lie-detector tests, never-published newspaper stories, unused reporter's notes, and outtakes from television interviews. I have tried to make this book as accurate an account as thirty years of research can provide.

Most importantly, in this book, for the first time, are *all* the Zodiac letters and envelopes previously unreproduced. Quoted are copycat letters and possible Zodiac letters mailed anonymously to me. Automatic writing done under hypnosis by Starr's sister-in-law indicates she saw Zodiac ciphers in his hand before they appeared in the press. Starr had bragged to friends, long before there was such a person as Zodiac, that he would hunt couples with a gun that projected a beam of light, taunt the police in letters, and call himself Zodiac. As one detective said, "If this story is true, then he almost has to be Zodiac." Recorded interviews with detectives and witnesses I conducted almost thirty years ago took on new meaning as I incorporated hundreds of facts never revealed in print before.

The long pursuit and lure of the case, its mystery, tragedy, and loss, ruined marriages, derailed careers, and demolished the health of a brilliant reporter. Zodiac's story began with obsession, but its ending was a study in frustration. Police were beaten back time and again. Would the most elusive killer in history, a cerebral, modern-day Jack the Ripper, escape them? Or would the dedicated teams of detectives and amateur sleuths all over the world uncover the final secret of Zodiac? It was a toss-up whether or not police could ever prove that Starr, their brilliant and physically powerful chief suspect, was their man. Zodiac's murders had taken place in different counties and, due to interdepartmental jealousy (Zodiac was the biggest case of all), each police agency withheld vital information from the others. Not only that, but sexual sadists like Zodiac (who achieve pleasure through the pain they cause others) become amazingly proficient at concealing their identities.

We begin unmasking Zodiac on a sultry July Fourth, and conclude on another, more lethal, Fourth of July. In between we learn of murders unsuspected, a lonely man in his basement home, and a shadowy figure who might be Zodiac's accomplice. But it had all begun with a watch. In that stifling room on that summer day the cops kept reminding themselves, "It's only a watch." But they were still afraid. That watch was the stuff of nightmares.

—Robert Graysmith
San Francisco
July 2001

1

ZODIAC

STARR'S face was everywhere. Across the illuminated show-room, his round face was reflected in the brass compass, duplicated in the shiny varnished sides of the Chris Craft, reflected in the deep and highly polished floor, mirrored in the brass work around him, and copied in a hundred polished shaft bearings. His stocky form was reproduced full length in the floor-to-ceiling show window. Finally, the showroom closed, the holiday sale ended, the lights were extinguished, and Robert Hall Starr departed. He lumbered toward the lot, an immense shape against the summer night. As he went, he fished for keys to one of his many cars. Keys to cars he did not own jangled in his pocket.

At the end of the lot, Starr was a hazy blur—momentarily visible in the flash of the Volvo's interior lights. He slid behind the wheel, gunned the engine, and expertly merged into freeway traffic. Soon, he reached Vallejo, a town typical of many other small California towns baking in a sultry summer night. Black skeletal derricks flashed by; battleships and three-tiered warehouses crouched in silhouette. Mare Island loomed as a shadowy mass across the straits, and sailboats fleeted as oily smudges on San Pablo Bay. Skyrockets flared briefly above. The staccato *pop-pop-pop* of firecrackers was like gunfire. The smell of gunpowder was in the air. San Francisco towered thirty miles away, Oakland less than twenty, and to the north the fertile Wine Country stretched through sun-drenched Napa and Sonoma counties.

The town was ideal for a man with so many vehicles. Interstate 80, the main coast-to-coast route of the West, neatly bisected the suburb. California 29 and 37 and Interstate 680 twisted veinlike to its heart. Vallejo occupied a strategic position between San Francisco and the capital—right where the river snaked down from Sacramento to greet the Bay Area—right where salt water embraced fresh. Here, a deepwater channel for seagoing traffic linked the Sacramento and San Joaquin River ports. Surrounded by water on three sides, Vallejo was a water town—home for Zodiac, a water-obsessed killer—a sailor of the knife, a mariner of the gun and of the rope.

Starr braked at a chestnut-colored stucco two-story house slouching on the east side of Fresno Street. Spanish tiles traced the rooflines of the low-pitched dwelling. At the rear, a modest chimney peeked over a field of weathered shingles. Left of the entrance stairs, a portico shrouded a conventional stile-and-rail door. From a brilliantly lit picture window, a woman's lean shadow stretched to grotesque lengths across the sunburned lawn. Bernice glowered at her son. Frequently, he stood for hours at the same Venetian window, motionless as if at the length of a chain.

Years ago he had been a trim athlete, a potential Olympic swimmer, a former lifeguard at "The Plunge." Now weight had swollen a face once lean and sun-bronzed from innumerable days of sailing and swimming. His light-colored hair, reddish in the summer, had thinned perceptibly, and a noticeable paunch disrupted the line of his athletic torso. Bernice considered his increasing girth a dreadful failing. Soon he would be nearly unrecognizable. She was a tall woman, almost as tall as her son. Starr's health, splendidly robust in his youth, had perceptibly faltered. His hunter's eyes had dimmed. His flat feet and injured leg made any activity but swimming and trampolining difficult. Aimless hours spent guzzling Coors beer from quart jars had taken their toll. He frequently parked in secluded rural areas, legs curled against the dash, until he cramped and could sit and drink and watch no more. His violent outbursts terrified Bernice. Squabbles between mother and son had always been fierce, but since his father's death last March their dinner table skirmishes had escalated. She often observed her son at the open trunk of his car, peering intently inside. Little eyes looked back. "Damn chipmunks," she thought.

In his spare time Starr, a crafty and silent Sagittarius, stalked chipmunks with a bow and arrow. Sometimes he used a .22, and at other times set traps. The tiny squirrels he snared alive were popular with the neighborhood children. On weekends kids circled him gleefully, flags flying behind their two-wheelers. Disregarding their parents' warnings, the offspring flocked to see the

"Chipmunk Man." They adored feeding peanuts to his pets.

Now Starr slammed the trunk lid shut and strode to the northeast side of the house. He trudged down a driveway to where a white Mercedes glowed luminously in the dusk. The darker silhouette of a detached two-door garage skulked further back. A black shroud of ivy cascaded over the fence.

A creak at the side screen door alerted Bernice, and she hastened to fix supper. Wriggling chipmunks squealed, clinging to Starr's broad swimmer's shoulders. Giving his mother's back a disdainful look, and still wearing his living-fur wrap, Starr dropped down into his cellar room. Bernice was most fearful of what her son stored in that basement. In that dreary tomb ticked something he had once called his "death machine."

IT HAD BEEN almost two years since Zodiac had murdered a taxi driver in San Francisco—longer than that since he shot and stabbed the others. But in all that time Homicide Inspectors Bill Armstrong and Dave Toschi (pronounced Tahs-kee) had not forgotten the elusive Zodiac. Twenty-nine minutes away from the turbulent household on Fresno Street, past the lonely Emeryville mudflats and just across the Bay Bridge, they continued to labor at the Hall of Justice. On the street below, the red-neon "OK Bail Bonds" sign flashed twenty-four hours a day. "Zodiac actually set out a challenge," Inspector Toschi recalled. "'I'm better than you,' he taunted us. 'Smarter than you,' he said. 'Catch me if you can.' We intended to do just that."

As Zodiac terrorized the Bay Area, inundating local papers with his chilling letters with bizarre references to popular culture, he invariably belittled the SFPD for failing to halt his string of murders. Zodiac had made it personal, tantalizing them with masterly cryptograms—some so unbreakable that they baffled the brightest code-breakers the FBI, NSA, and CIA could field. All but two homicides attributed to him involved couples—young students killed in or around their cars on weekends. He hinted at unknown murders, past and present.

"Zodiac struck out in savage rage," speculated one psychiatrist, "against those who flaunted an intimacy he craved with an intensity only the deeply frustrated human can imagine." Sex was never a factor in his motiveless attacks. Sadism was; the more pain he caused, the more pleasure he felt. Directly after an attack, Zodiac was compelled to gloat, pitilessly writing or phoning his victims' families, breathing silently into their ears—a sound like the rushing of wind. He used a different weapon each time, and when possible took something from each victim—car keys, a bloody shirt, a wallet—trophies. He still had them somewhere. Now if only Toschi and Armstrong could find them.

Zodiac's rampages occurred at dusk (when he sometimes wore a grisly executioner's costume) or at night under a new or full moon. Bodies of water and places named after water drew him as metal to a lodestone. Perhaps Zodiac was a sailor, swimmer, or boatman. Whatever he was, he knew Vallejo intimately—its back lanes and pebbled shortcuts, its black country roads and echoing quarries. Toschi was convinced he was a longtime resident of Water Town.

And so Toschi and Armstrong developed new facts and shuffled yellow sheets under the burning fluorescent lights of their fourth-floor office. They watched the minute hand of the big clock jerking intermittently, like a barely beating heart. At times it hardly seemed to move. Toschi leaned back in his swivel chair, its springs complaining loudly. "What we need now," said Toschi, looking across at Bill Armstrong, "is a good snitch." Between the ticks of that clock something happened—the detectives were about to come up with their most important lead yet in Zodiac's seemingly endless reign of terror. It would arrive by letter, the killer's chosen medium.

THURSDAY, JULY 15, 1971

MANHATTAN Beach is northernmost in a succession of all-American beach towns running south from LAX to the Palos Verde Peninsula. It roosts some twenty miles southwest of downtown Los Angeles. Scores of wealthy white Angelenos inhabit the rows of pastel cottages hugging its shores. The town's main drag is Highland, and at 2:50 P.M. bronzed surfers were catching the best waves of the day as an unmarked cop car hurtled south along the broad avenue. Detective Richard Amos and his partner, Art Langstaff, were following up a tip that had originated in Pomona. Two Torrance men had information about Zodiac.

The skies were smog-tinged, the air muggy, but traffic was light. Amos sped east on Artesia, then spun onto lengthy Hawthorne Boulevard. A red light halted them. Impatiently,

Amos drummed the wheel. The car idled, pumping exhaust onto the shimmering asphalt. He considered Zodiac—uncaught and insubstantial as vapor. Years of effort, and yet no one seemed able to lay a hand on him.

Both informants were waiting in front of Science Dynamics, a computer bookkeeping business, as Amos pulled to a stop. Santo Paul Panzarella, "Sandy" to his friends, was a Lawndale resident and owner of the company. His employee and college roommate, Donald Lee Cheney, was the more anxious of the pair. The South Bay investigators had no sooner climbed out than Panzarella and Cheney got to the point—they knew the identity of Zodiac.

Out of the stifling heat, they named their man—Robert Hall Starr. They had known Starr almost ten years, since 1962, known him while attending Cal Poly in Pomona with Starr's brother, Ron. Cheney had last seen Starr on a day as cold as today was blistering. Though Panzarella had made the call that had summoned them, it was Cheney who told them the story.

"It was New Year's Day afternoon," Cheney said. "I was living in the Bay Area then—I drove to Starr's home on Fresno Street in Vallejo. I'm positive my visit was not later than January 1, 1969, because I moved to Southern California on that day. I remember specifically it was the New Year's after Starr was fired from Valley Springs School up near the Mokelumne River. That had been in the early summer. As to Starr's reason for leaving Valley Springs, he hemmed and hawed more than he said anything, and gave me some kind of lame excuse about it, but I never heard the straight story. I helped him move back to Fresno Street. On New Year's Day I came over to his house because my wife and I had been arguing and I just had to get out of the house.

"We had gone to his apartment—at this time it was a one-car garage that had been converted into a room. You didn't step down, the basement lair came later. You just walked in at ground level. It had three exterior walls—a window in the front, a window in the side, a small window in the back. There was a bathroom at the rear which had a window which let some light in there. The other part of the house was fairly well isolated from that room. I don't remember ever hearing activity unless the mother was cooking. It was early afternoon."

Starr read a lot of science fiction. On the table that day lay the August 1967 *Fact and Amazing Science Fiction* open to Jack Vance's 15,000-word story, "The Man from Zodiac." On their last hunting trip Starr had talked about science fiction with Cheney. On several previous occasions he and Cheney had gone hiking and hunting in the woods northeast of San Francisco. In the twilight, rifles lowered, Starr had shared long, sometimes unsettling, discourses with him—talks about death. He was a huge silhouette in the dark, and his eyes glittered in the firelight as he expounded bizarre theories. "With Starr," said Cheney, "you just get into conversations about 'What if this?' and 'What if that?' He had a way about him."

On their final hunting trip Starr had abruptly changed the subject from science fiction to something totally unrelated. He first mentioned hunting, then guided the conversation to an adventure story he had read in the eleventh grade—"The Most Dangerous Game." Richard Connell's taut, classic tale concerned the hunting of men in a forest with bows and arrows and guns.

"Have you ever thought of hunting people?" said Starr.

"What?" said Cheney. Cheney recalled other weird conversations with his friend before, and took this one in stride. He was well acquainted with Starr's way of drawing people into his own interior fantasy world.

"It would be great sport to hunt people," Starr elaborated in the night, using personalized expressions such as "If I did this" or "If I did that . . ." At times he cast his remarks in the form of a novel he intended to write someday. He was a powerful man, gesticulating in the dark.

"Beneath that fat," said Cheney, "was steel."

That day Starr's eyes strayed to the unique watch he had gotten on his birthday only days before. "He showed me the watch first," Cheney told the detectives. "I remember the unusual logo symbol just above the pinion in the dial. When he showed the watch to me, it was pretty much like he wanted an opinion about the quality of the watch. 'I don't think this is a very good watch,' he said. 'Well, it's a fine Swiss watch,' I told him. 'That's a quality watch.'"

Starr began talking about his career. "It's time to look for a new job," he said. "I'm thinking about becoming a private eye, a private investigator like 'Mike Hammer.' That would be fun and interesting. I'm looking for something I can do on my own without having to be hired."

Cheney thought this was because he was having problems getting hired. "You don't really have the training," said Cheney.

"And you really don't have a base of people who know who you are that you can get business from." Cheney was not so much amazed at Starr's idea, but honestly concerned that his friend was ill-equipped for such a job. Starr seemed to read his thoughts.

"Well, maybe I can create my own business by being a criminal," said Starr, "And if I was, here's what I'd do."

Starr suggested he might go to a lovers' lane area to seek out victims at night—attach a flashlight to a gun barrel and shoot them. "I would use the light as an aiming device," he said, "enabling me to walk up and gun down people in total darkness. As the shootings would be without motive, imagine how difficult such murders would be for the police to solve. They would never catch you. You could then send confusing letters to the police"— he might have said "authorities," Cheney amended in an aside to Amos and Langstaff—"letters to harass and lead them astray.

"And I would sign them 'Zodiac.' "

" 'Zodiac,' " said Cheney. "Why that? Why not something else? That's stupid." Cheney paused and said to the investigators, "I might have used the phrase 'childish.' I don't remember exactly. Whichever word I spoke, it had a remarkable effect on him. He became emotional, very emotional, and I was sorry I had said anything at all."

"I don't care what you think," Starr had snapped. "I've thought about it a long time. I like the name 'Zodiac' and that's the name I'm going to use. Yes, I would call myself 'Zodiac.' "

As Starr queried him about methods to disguise his handwriting and makeup to disguise himself, Cheney's eyes roved over Starr's room—to the disheveled piles of papers and maps, and the rows of books on aviation and sailing lining the walls, the stacks of *Mad* magazine. In the shadowy room, among the clutter, he observed Starr's Ruger single-six and Harrington Richards long-barrel. "The Harrington Richards was kind of old and battered and had the nine-shot cylinder," he recalled. "That was his arsenal as far as I knew, though he did come up with a rifle for deer hunting from somewhere, that and a pair of .22-caliber revolvers."

On December 20, 1968, twelve days earlier, Zodiac had used a .22-caliber semiautomatic J. C. Higgins Model 80 to murder two teenagers out on Vallejo's lonely Lake Herman Road. These were his first known Northern California murders. The killer utilized .22-caliber Super X copper-coated long-rifle Winchester Western ammo—the same brand used in double murders south of Lompoc in 1963. "Earlier in the day," added Cheney, "he took me out Lake Herman Road and pointed out a roadside turnout. He didn't signify its importance, but I think that's where the two kids had recently been killed."

Starr discussed shooting the tire off a school bus and picking off "the little darlings." He would shoot them as "they came bounding out" of the bus. Cheney doubted his friend would actually be doing these things. "It was like we were talking about a plot for a book or something in that order," he told the detectives. "It was not quite as if we were talking about real events. He kind of slipped in and out of the present. We were having that kind of conversation. It gave me the shivers a little bit. Even then. That was the last time I ever saw him. I knew it was in my mind that I wasn't going to see him again."

When Cheney got home that night, he told his wife, Ann, his friend was "acting strange." "I moved quite shortly after that," Cheney concluded. "I had the opportunity for a job in Los Angeles. It didn't have to do with him. It had to do with me finding work."

There was silence. His words seemed to the detectives to be reasonable enough, the kind of things an honest man might say. The afternoon had waned. The detectives had spent over an hour with the men. Both Cheney and Panzarella cautioned Amos and Langstaff as they left. "He is a very intelligent man, but also a very impatient person. We think he carries a weapon at all times."

Returning to their headquarters on 15th Street, the detectives asked Criminal Identification and Investigation (CI&I) in Sacramento to expedite Starr's "yellow sheet," a record of previous arrests, to them by Teletype. While they waited they had time to think. When Starr had made the remarks to Cheney was crucial. By Amos's calculations those words were uttered only days *after* the first known Northern California Zodiac murders. Additionally, all letters in which the murderer identified himself as Zodiac had been mailed *after* Starr and Cheney's New Year's Day discussion. Not until August 4, 1969 (though Toschi and Armstrong's files said August 7) had Zodiac baptized himself in a three-page letter to Bay Area papers. Until then the phantom had no shape, no name, only a crossed circle scrawled at the bottom of three letters and ciphers delivered at the end of July. There was no way around it. Panzarella backed up Cheney's story, and both seemed upstanding, astute, credible. Their words had the ring of

Gospel. If what they said was true, then Robert Hall Starr *had* to be the notorious Zodiac.

Amos and Langstaff assessed what motives the two local men might have to lie. The length of time it had taken them to come forward puzzled the detectives. Zodiac had been a menace for years. A previous headline ("ZODIAC LINKED TO RIVER-SIDE SLAYING") spanning the *Los Angeles Times*'s front page on November 16, 1970, had not flushed the friends out. For some reason a more recent letter had galvanized them.

Four months before (March 13, 1971), the "Cipher Slayer" had written the *Times* from Pleasanton, a small, sleepy town in Alameda County across the Bay from San Francisco. As was his practice, Zodiac affixed excessive postage—two inverted six-cent Roosevelt stamps. As was his rule, he exhorted in block printing: "Please Rush to Editor." The words "AIR Mail" took up a third of the envelope. Zodiac was a highly impatient maniac. His letter covered most of the *Times* front page—big black head-lines, bold as a declaration of war.

> "This is the Zodiac speaking," he began as always. "Like I have always said I am crack proof. If the Blue Meannies are evere going to catch me, they had best get off their fat asses & do something. Because the longer they fiddle & fart around, the more slaves I will collect for my after life. I do have to give them credit for stumbling across my riverside activity, but they are only finding the easy ones, there are a hell of a lot more down there. The reason that I am writing the Times is this, They don't bury me on the back pages like some of the others." He had signed the letter with a box score: "SFPD-0" and "[Zodiac's symbol: a crossed circle]-17+."

Something about the recent communication, possibly a telling phrase, may have rung a bell with Cheney and Panzarella. Zodiac had used the term "Blue Meannies," meaning, Amos surmised, the cops. Music-hating "Blue Meanies" had terrorized the Beat-les in a 1968 animated film, *The Yellow Submarine.* Starr had once wanted to be a submarine sailor, so that made a little sense. "Fiddle & fart around," an odd, crude expression, was spoken re-gionally in Missouri, Pennsylvania, and Lubbock, Texas. Marines and sailors said it. Maybe Starr, an ex-Navy man, used it too. Cheney said no, but recalled his friend often used the phrase

"Do my thing," a popular phrase Zodiac had used in a letter. Initially, Zodiac had concealed his murderous connection with Southern California (belatedly capitalizing on it). Until now he had been predictable—governed by a daily horoscope he wanted police to believe he cast himself, and drawn to water-related sites to murder. Afterward, he unfailingly wrote the *San Francisco Chronicle* to boast of his atrocities and taunt the police. But by writing an L.A. paper Zodiac had broken his pattern. For what reason? Possibly he had made a mistake down south. Perhaps he intended his *Times* letter as a warning to people who still remembered him there. If he did, the letter had had the opposite effect.

It alerted Cheney instead, attracting him for the first time to a composite drawing and written physical depiction of Zodiac. Of course, all of this was speculation. Something had delayed Cheney in coming forward with his fears. Was it possible that Cheney had a motive in fingering Starr and that there was ill will between the two? This was not the case with Panzarella, who knew what had alerted him. "All of a sudden," Panzarella said, "Zodiac was writing letters to the *Times* near where we were living. It didn't bother me, though I suspected Starr was the author, but it bothered Cheney a lot. Starr fits everything I ever thought about Zodiac. He is incredibly intelligent and has a great deal of problems with any type of authority figure." Panzarella had told the detectives that Starr was "a very intelligent man, but also emotional-type person." As far as Panzarella could tell, Starr matched the descriptions in every respect. Ten days after the *Times* letter, Zodiac had resumed his old ways. He dispatched a four-cent postcard to the *Chronicle,* affixed with a stamp of Lincoln, his head lowered in mourning. On the opposite side was a drawing of a man digging in a snowy, wooded encampment. The phrase "Don't bury me" implied someone in Zodiac's life had died. By May, the maniac was cynically pleading for help by phone—begging to be stopped before he killed more.

The staccato clatter of keys and the insistent ringing of the Teletype bell interrupted the detectives' theorizing. Amos laid the CI&I report next to the old black phone that had unleashed them on the scent scant hours ago. The printout provided basic facts: File #131151/Social Security #576-44-8882; date of birth, December 18, 1933—unmarried—living with his mother in Northern California. Langstaff noted job application entries running from 1958 through 1964, among them "NON/CERT Personnel, Watsonville Public Schools." They found one arrest: "6-15-58 Vallejo P.D. 60278, D.P. [disturbing the peace], dismissed on 7-8-58." There were no wants. Gradually, Amos added to the data by phone. The suspect's family, he learned, had some money and his father, a Navy flier of some note, had passed away in March—just when Zodiac had broken a five-month-long letter-writing dry spell.

And Starr might be placed down south for the murder of a coed in Riverside, just east of Pomona, where he visited his brother, Ronald, and Cheney and Panzarella at college. Robert Hall Starr had attended Cal Poly San Luis Obispo in the late 1950s and early 1960s while studying to become an elementary school teacher, had even taught at Atascadero State Hospital for the Criminally Insane just to the north of the university. Langstaff assembled some new information, drafted a letter, and sent it flying up to the San Francisco Bay Area—where Starr lived, worked, and hunted.

MONDAY, JULY 19, 1971

LANGSTAFF'S letter containing Panzarella and Cheney's suspicions arrived at Armstrong and Toschi's Bryant Street Headquarters. In contrast to the summer sun, the Hall of Justice was a chilly structure, and massive—750,000 square feet, 885 rooms. The morning light glinted on gold lettering carved into the facade— "EXACT JUSTICE TO ALL . . ." The messenger carried the letter past the metal detector and armed guard and into an elevator to the fourth floor—Homicide and Sex Crimes Detail. He paused at black hand-painted lettering on frosted glass, which read, "Room 454." A handmade sign above the door read, "City Zoo." He saw that the room beyond was huge, with polished floors, gray file cabinets, and wooden desks. Finally, the letter landed on San Francisco Homicide Inspector John McKenna's desk.

McKenna, an intelligent man, well read, a former banker, had already been alerted by an earlier phone conversation with Detective Amos. He scanned the letter avidly, then rang up Cheney. "We want you to attempt to obtain samples of Starr's handprinting," he said. "Any specimens acquired and any new disclosures should be sent directly to Inspector Toschi." The following day, Toschi's partner, Bill Armstrong, opened a second letter from the

Manhattan Beach police. It provided more details—fascinating details. Pulses began to race. The old black clock on the wall ticked faster.

WORLD-FAMOUS ATTORNEY Melvin Belli returned late from the theater and unlocked his opulent Montgomery Street office. His broad face, lit by the warm glow of a Tiffany lamp, was pensive. He sat at a magnificent desk, gazed out his sidewalk picture window, and for long moments rubbed his brow. "The King of Torts" was thinking of Zodiac and his friend Inspector Dave Toschi. Toschi had never forgotten his first meeting with the lawyer. "The elevator door opens and a dozen or so TV people and reporters are there," Toschi recalled. "And here Belli comes with a black hat slanted very low over his right ear and this long, black cashmere coat draped over his shoulders. I never saw a scarf so long. It must have gone down to his knees because it was wrapped around his neck half a dozen times. You could barely see his face. His wife, dressed in a beautiful tan fur, towered over him. I told the assistant D.A., 'The Great One has arrived.' It was Belli's show and after he entered the packed courtroom, it must have taken him a couple of minutes to unwind that amazing scarf."

Zodiac had written the silver-maned solicitor just before Christmas, 1969. "School children make nice targets," he threatened. "I think I shall wipe out a school bus some morning." "In 1969," Belli recalled, "the San Francisco papers were full of a one-man crime wave called the Zodiac killer, a real loony who'd attacked three couples in lovers' lanes in the Bay Area and a cabdriver, killing five of them, and leaving his mark [a crossed circle like a gun sight] at the scene. On October 13, 1969 [twenty-two months after Starr's discussion with Cheney], the Zodiac had threatened to shoot the tires out on a school bus and 'pick off the kiddies as they come bouncing out.' The police were guarding the school buses and some parents were driving their kids to school in their own cars. The public was frantic, and the police were under a good deal of pressure to find the Zodiac."

For some reason Zodiac not only mentioned Belli in his letters, but phoned him more than once. In some twisted way he either admired Belli's flamboyant courtroom bravado (a bravado second only to his own) or presumed that Belli might offer a lifeline to him. The attorney had defended both Mickey Cohen and Jack Ruby. Now Belli climbed a hard rope ladder to the unique bed he kept fifteen feet up in his living room. He slept fitfully, unable to escape the thought that he actually possessed a clue that might solve the case.

THURSDAY, JULY 22, 1971

THE San Francisco detectives failed in their attempt to get Cheney to obtain samples of Starr's handprinting. "I didn't have any source for that," Cheney told me much later. "Armstrong kind of hinted around: Would I write a letter to him to try and get some response out of him? If I had been a single man at the time I would have done anything they wanted, but I had a wife and two little kids and I didn't want to open any doors. He could have found me by just looking in the phone directory."

Next, the Department of Justice requested samples of Starr's handprinting from Dr. Frank English, District Superintendent of Valley Springs Elementary School, where Starr had once taught. Dr. English complied immediately, and exemplars of Starr's handprinting were rushed to the SFPD. By car Toschi hand-delivered the blockprinted applications to CI&I's Mel Nicolai in Sacramento. Nicolai quickly submitted the samples to Sherwood Morrill, the state agency's crack documents examiner. The scholarly analyst compared them to Zodiac's letters and reported to Nicolai the following Thursday. A. L. Coffey, Chief of the Bureau and Nicolai's boss, wrote the SFPD the same day.

"Enclosed are the exemplars for Robert Hall Starr," Coffey stated. "Mr. Sherwood Morrill . . . has compared the printing on the submitted documents with the printing contained in the Zodiac letters and advised they were not prepared by the same person." Agents returned Starr's original applications, and they were replaced in his employment file with no one the wiser. In spite of this setback, the San Francisco detectives were not deterred. Zodiac was the most intelligent criminal in their experience. He would know a way around Morrill and how to fake handprinting. That had to be the answer. They rushed on, heedless in their excitement.

SATURDAY, JULY 24, 1971

In 1970 Detective William Baker joined the Major Crimes Unit of the Santa Barbara County Sheriff's Department and was assigned to several unsolved cases. One was the tragic double murder on a remote beach of two Lompoc High School seniors, Robert George Domingos and Linda Faye Edwards. "I picked up the case seven years after it occurred," Baker told me. "Several of the investigators on the case were still active, so I took every available opportunity to bug them about it." One morning Baker came across a Halloween card Zodiac had written to the *Chronicle* on October 27, 1970. The killer had drawn an arcane "Sartor Cross," accomplishing this by crossing two words—"Slaves" and "Paradice." However, Zodiac had printed other words on both sides. These riveted Baker's attention. The killer had neatly painted, "By ROPE, By GUN, By KNiFE, By FiRE." Rope, gun, knife, and fire had been part of Baker's unsolved case.

"I immediately sent out a statewide Teletype asking for similars," he said. "I was soon called, in succession, by Bill Armstrong and Mel Nicolai. To make a long story short, both told me that just on the basis of the description I offered them, there was a good possibility Zodiac was responsible and our cases might be linked. However, inconsistent with the other cases attributable to Zodiac, our victims were killed on a Monday. It is unknown if the murders occurred at dusk or later, but it's unlikely, judging by how the victims were dressed—in swimsuits." At every possible opportunity Baker worked the Domingos and Edwards case. A long road lay ahead. He began traveling to speak with most of the detectives in most of the precincts where the crimes were attributable to Zodiac.

MONDAY, JULY 26, 1971

Inspector Armstrong was traveling too. The handsome, silver-haired investigator, sharp-featured and strong-jawed, arrived in Torrance and reached Cheney and Panzarella at Science Dynamics. "Down comes this guy," Panzarella recalled, "a poster guy for the FBI, but very sensitive for a cop." Armstrong heard essentially the same story that Amos and Langstaff had. Cheney unerringly re-created the conversation he'd had with his friend. But Armstrong, not satisfied, began to probe. "Mr. Cheney," he asked, "could you have read some news accounts about the Zodiac killings and associated those articles with your conversation with Starr?"

"That's not the case," he replied. "I can recall the conversation and the date. I can recall my responses to what he said. I could testify to the same under oath in court." Armstrong could not shake him on the date of the conversation. A background investigation revealed Cheney, born in Bakersfield on April 25, 1934, had attended Cal Poly Pomona from fall 1959 until winter 1964 while studying to become a mechanical engineer. Currently he lived in Pomona with his wife and children. He had no criminal record.

Armstrong spoke next to Sandy Panzarella, Cheney's boss and longtime friend. He too had studied at Cal Poly Pomona—from fall 1961 until his graduation in spring 1964 with a degree in electronic engineering. Panzarella characterized Cheney as a "very solid person not given to exaggeration or the telling of falsehoods. He's a very methodical, logical thinker." Later on Starr's sister-in-law and brother confirmed Cheney's reliability. "If Don Cheney said that to you," Starr's brother, Ron, said, "I would believe the same to be true." Armstrong promptly returned to San Francisco to bring Toschi up to speed.

He and Toschi painstakingly searched for an ulterior motive on Cheney's part. "Why would he make such a statement to the police if it were not true?" asked Toschi. For Starr to call himself Zodiac, to lay down the method of procedure, the M.O. of the murders, long before Zodiac named himself, was highly incriminating. Unlike Jack the Ripper, who had, in all likelihood, gotten his name through the ingenuity of a London reporter, Zodiac had chosen the sobriquet by which he was now known. The homicide detectives felt that if that conversation were true, then Starr *had* to be Zodiac. And what had accounted for the long delay in Cheney coming forward to the police? Sometime later Cheney explained how he had come to recall the conversation he had with Starr that fateful New Year's Day 1969.

"When I left college," Cheney told me, "I got a job at G. J. Yamas in San Francisco. I was there a couple of years. Then, when I lived in Concord, I had an unsuccessful period trying to sell life insurance, and moved back to Pomona to start working at the Fluor Company. Fluor was an engineering company, but primarily they were in refineries and chemical plants. At one time

...lor and Parsons were all partners—they built the ...gether.

...ning Ron and Karen, Starr's brother and sister-in-law, we... ...y house in Southern California for dinner. We were sitting around the kitchen table chatting, and Karen told us about Starr going to a painting party in his suit. Ron was on the guest list. Ron and his brother were at the party and Starr was the guy in the suit. She was using that as an example of him being unadjusted to social things. She was ragging him on that. She was a little afraid of her brother-in-law because she recognized he was not squared away with the world at all. With her education in social work she had been exposed to such things.

"One morning I was having breakfast in the new cafeteria at Fluor in what they called the Task Force Center. I had been at the company about three months or four months then. My brother-in-law, Ron Ebersole, had a newspaper and he was pointing to a composite drawing. 'That looks like your buddy,' he said. And I looked, and that composite was a picture of Starr—except for the hair and absence of glasses. Ron was the only guy at Fluor who could have recognized him from a prior time. I said, 'Yes, that looks like him,' but I didn't think much of it."

What was unique about the sketch was that it was not the round-faced composites from Zodiac's attacks at Lake Berryessa or in San Francisco, but a profile that Toschi and Armstrong had never seen. "My brother-in-law passed me the paper and I read the article," Cheney continued. "Up to this moment I had forgotten the crucial details of my conversation with Starr—that he was going to call himself Zodiac. I hadn't remembered even when I had seen the occasional stories about Zodiac. That sketch was a coincidence, I thought, but a few months later [November 16, 1970] I saw Zodiac's threat in the *Times* about shooting out the tires of a school bus and shooting kids as they came bouncing out, something Starr had said to me. I knew it couldn't be a coincidence. I couldn't ever get over that. That's when it absolutely clicked. Then I remembered everything he had said.

"It was another year before I called the police. I was at Fluor in 1969 and 1970. We finished a big contract and they had had major layoffs, so I had about a year where I was working at a big paper mill in Laverne, which was just a few miles up from my house. I didn't talk to the San Francisco police about it right away, I sat on it a while and just thought about it. I just couldn't get around the fact that it couldn't be chance. That was too specific a quote. The 1971 killings in the Grass Valley area had also brought my suspicions to a focus.

"I went to the Pomona police station since I was living in Pomona at the time, and had an interview with an officer. I spent an hour there and I thought that might execute my responsibility on the business, but nothing ever happened. Apparently what I told him was never reported because they were getting hundreds of tips. Then Sandy Panzarella asked me to come down and work for him in 1971 at Science Dynamics. We were always good friends. After college, Sandy had become an electronic engineer and worked at that for a few years. Then he went into this computer bookkeeping business on his own and did very well. He had the magic touch. He got his foot in the door and soon was doing billing for medical practices and hospitals—that sort of thing.

"I was the operations manager at Science Dynamics—hiring and firing, managing the keypunch department and twelve girls, two couriers that made all our pickups and deliveries in Los Angeles County, and three or four boys in the mailroom to handle the logistics of the paper. I was responsible for all the material logistics. We had another team that ran the computer part of the business. Of course I've used computers in structural analysis and pipe stress, but was never a computer guy. Then one day the subject of Starr came up again and I finally told Sandy of my suspicions.

"Later, Ron came down to Torrance and we all talked over our apprehensions. Once we got on that discussion, we decided to do something about it. 'I can see that the police have basically ignored you,' said Sandy. He was a real 'take-charge guy.' I had never spoken to Manhattan Beach police, but for some reason that's who responded to Science Dynamics in Torrance that afternoon."

"Don kept telling me the story," Panzarella told me later. And he said, 'No policeman will answer my call.' I said, 'Bullshit! Let's get on the phone here.' And that's how it got started. Don was trying and no one took him seriously. He was not an aggressive guy. There was a Torrance policeman named Amos, and I knew if I called him that would get things going. 'I know you guys get a lot of crank calls about who the Zodiac killer may be,' I told him. Amos then called up to San Francisco, asked who was on the case, and they referred him to Inspector Bill Armstrong. Armstrong advised, 'Get the local P.D. to send us a report.' And then Amos called me back. 'Come on over and talk to us,' I said.

Meanwhile in Vallejo, another investigator was fast becoming an expert on Zodiac—Detective George Bawart (Bow-art), a stocky, powerful man, relentless as a bloodhound. "Cheney had already talked to Panzarella about his suspicions," Bawart told me later, "and at that time Cheney still was friends with Starr. Then he became non-friends. There was an inference that Starr may have become too friendly with his daughter, and Cheney broke off the relationship because of that. And I was concerned that was the reason he might be making up a story.

"I don't really trust polygraphs to any great degree, but that was one of the reasons we afterward ran Cheney on a polygraph up in the state of Washington. The Washington state police ran Cheney on a poly and he came out clean. *He was telling the truth.* I tend to agree with the results of that because Panzarella claims and Cheney claims that before the falling-out occurred, he had alluded to this incident to Panzarella."

In mid-1967 Starr and Cheney and his wife and daughter, who was two or three at the time, went camping and fly-rod fishing up near Valley Springs in the Mokelumne. The daughter came up and said, 'Daddy, Uncle Bob touched my bottom.' Cheney, noting his daughter wasn't upset or hurt, had no reason to believe that his friend had really done something like that. However, from that point on when Cheney was around his friend, he didn't have his family. "He stayed friends with Starr for a year and a half after that," said a source. "Of course the daughter couldn't communicate very well. If Cheney was upset he wouldn't have stayed friends afterward for so long, right? They were pals long after that."

TUESDAY, JULY 27, 1971

LIEUTENANT Ellis of SFPD Homicide relayed Armstrong and Toschi's findings to Vallejo Police Sergeant Jack Mulanax, alerting him the two inspectors would soon pay a visit. At the time Mulanax inherited the Blue Rock Springs murder case (and with it the Zodiac investigation), his chief, Jack E. Stiltz, had made a comment. "Zodiac keeps putting out clues for us," Stiltz lamented, "taunts us and doesn't indicate in any way that he suffers from the slightest feeling of remorse. He is a thrill killer and the most dangerous person I've ever encountered in all my years of law enforcement." Mulanax agreed. Mulanax was also a man known to get white hot about a suspect, and once he scanned what the SFPD had learned so far, his temperature rose. His first order of business was to learn as much as possible about Zodiac's true physical appearance and compare it to the new suspect's.

"Now where was that description of Zodiac?" he thought. The two-year-old circular, No. 90-69, case No. 696134, buried under more recent wants, was still pinned to the bulletin board. The wanted poster showed not one, but two composite drawings of Zodiac. That in itself was unusual, thought Mulanax. Some new information had caused the police to alter the description. The three teenagers who had witnessed the murder of Yellow Cab driver and student Paul Lee Stine near San Francisco's Presidio had at first estimated Zodiac to be "a white male with reddish or blond crew-cut hair, around twenty-five or thirty years of age and wearing glasses."

"Supplementing our Bulletin 87-69 of October 13, 1969," read the second flier. "Additional information has developed the above amended drawing of the murder suspect known as 'Zodiac.'" An adjusted written description now placed Zodiac's age at thirty-five to forty-five years old. He was of "heavy build, approximately five-foot, eight-inches tall. Short brown hair, possibly with a red tint." Mulanax checked Starr's physical statistics. He was a White Male Adult, with light brown hair and clear brown eyes, thirty-seven years old, and weighing between 230 and 240 pounds. Mulanax noted Starr was five-eleven and three-quarter inches tall—almost six feet—and four inches taller than the circular's estimate. Mulanax took into account that the kids were peering down from a second-floor window. The children had observed Zodiac waste precious time ripping off a portion of the cabbie's shirt and squander more time walking around the cab, coolly rubbing the vehicle down and apparently drenching the fabric in blood.

Zodiac must have been covered in blood himself. "In a head wound," Toschi explained, "the person may or may not bleed profusely. When a person does not, it's because the swelling brain has plugged the bullet hole. In the case of Paul Stine, the path of the bullet tore the vessels badly and destroyed one main blood vessel along the top of his head. He was killed with a contact wound [barrel against the skin] in front of his right ear. This type of wound usually destroys many blood vessels in the head and brain, causing extensive bleeding. From witnesses' observations, Stine's head was laying on Zodiac's lap as he searched him, so when Zodiac made his escape he *had* to have extensive blood on his person."

Two Richmond District patrolmen, Donald A. Fouke and Eric Zelms of Richmond Station, got a better look that wild night, Columbus Day, October 11, 1969. Zodiac always earmarked holidays for his most vicious actions.

FOUKE AND ZELMS chanced upon Zodiac in the shadows as he "lumbered" north toward the heavily wooded Presidio. He later claimed he glibly sent the officers roaring off in the wrong direction, then sprinted through Julius Kahn Playground, vanishing near Letterman Hospital. Zodiac's narrow escape permanently enraged him toward the SFPD—a fury approaching that of a rebuffed suitor. Days later the two officers realized they had passed Zodiac. "I felt so bad for Officer Fouke," Toschi said. "He was afraid he was going to be reprimanded and that's why he waited so long. 'Why would they reprimand you?' I reassured him. 'No, you did the right thing in reporting it.' This would have come out eventually because we heard the transmission tape and we were trying to find out which Richmond Station unit was circling the area. We wanted to talk to them and find out if they had touched the cab. We had to know who was in the area. And finally, they came forward quite some time after. It was kind of frustrating.

"Transmission to radio cars that night was halting. Lots of pauses. Units circling the area kept saying, 'How many suspects? How many suspects?' Communications wasn't responding. They were telling officers, 'Stand by—we're dealing with youngsters— stand by!' These kids were scared stiff and they were all trying to talk on the phone at once, and Communications were trying to get a true picture of a suspect or how many suspects. They were relaying the location . . . 'Victim appears to be DOA . . . ambulance responding . . . we're trying to get a description of suspect . . . ' And they said that several times. 'We're dealing with youngsters.' And the officers in the radio car, trying to make an arrest, asked, 'What's the description . . . we're responding . . . we're close . . . we're on Arguello [Avenue] . . . what's the description?'

"And finally, the misidentification of an African American by someone over the airwaves threw Fouke and his partner off. There was so much chatter going on because everyone figured it was a sloppy cab stickup gone wrong. The killer was supposedly seen on foot, and unfortunately a couple of words came over unintelligible and BMA blurted out when it should have been WMA. They are now assuming it's a black suspect. Then—'Correction . . . we now have further information . . . a Caucasian . . . short hair, glasses, husky, potbelly, black or blue windbreaker jacket . . . baggy pants . . . armed with a handgun . . . use caution, very dangerous, use caution if approaching.' But in the meantime we were losing seconds and minutes. It was very exciting. I remember it as if it were last weekend.

"Afterward, I decided to go talk to the fellow who took the call. He says, 'Damn it, Dave. I got two or three kids who sound like teenagers and they're screaming in the background. First I thought they were being hurt. I was trying to talk quietly. They kept saying, 'Our parents are coming home . . . the driver looks like he's dead in the cab and there's a light on in the cab and they were fighting. Oh, please come, please come!' I kept telling them, 'Stay in the house.' Which they did. You know how fast those black and whites need the radio information. We do our best, but when you're dealing with children . . . I've got my own and I know . . . they're scared to death and they know something's wrong and they can see this body of the cabbie laying over on the side with the door open.'

"There were Richmond units and Park Station units all responding. They all knew that Julius Kahn Playground is there and that's part of the Presidio. If he goes in there, we're probably going to lose him. From Arguello, Fouke and Zelms would have to make a right going north, then onto Washington. They were probably the only unit there and I'm convinced that they actually saw the Zodiac. Fouke was more of a veteran officer than Zelms. As senior officer, he was driving and got the better view of the stranger. Apparently Zelms didn't think it was anything. And Fouke would have had the radio conversation. Things happened so quickly. And then you have no idea that three days later you realize you're dealing with the most dangerous serial killer in the country.

"That cab was out of there long before the Fire Department arrived. All we wanted from them was a special smoke-eater unit for searchlight only. Coming up the hill from Arguello was an Army unit with large searchlight trucks. We had gone over everything and I told [Jim] Kirkendall and [Bob] Dagitz, 'Get the cab out of here. The body's gone.' Neighbors were kind of leaning in.

I had to ask two or three uniform guys, 'Don't let anybody near the taxi, guys, please.' I had Dagitz follow the tow to the Hall of Justice. They put the cab in the impound room and started work on it in the morning."

The officers' modified second sketch made Zodiac fuller-faced, older. But an amended written description, including details in an important interdepartmental memorandum submitted by Fouke a month after the shooting, November 12, 1969, was never added to the wanted circular. Fouke's more accurate depiction languished within SFPD's eight drawers of files on Zodiac. It is crucial enough to quote in full:

"Sir: I respectfully wish to report the following, that while responding to the area of Cherry and Washington Streets a suspect fitting the description of the Zodiac killer was observed by officer Fouke," he wrote, "walking in an easterly direction on Jackson street and then turn north on Maple street. This subject was not stopped as the description received from communications was that of a Negro male. When the right description was broadcast reporting officer informed communications that a possible suspect had been seen going north on Maple Street into the Presidio, the area of Julius Kahn playground and a search was started which had negative results. The suspect that was observed by officer Fouke was a WMA 35–45 Yrs about five-foot, ten inches, 180–200 pounds. Medium heavy build—Barrel chested—Medium complexion—Light-colored hair possibly greying in rear (May have been lighting that caused this effect.) Crew cut—wearing glasses—Dressed in dark blue waist length zipper type jacket (Navy or royal blue) Elastic cuffs and waist band zipped part way up. Brown wool pants pleeted [sic] type baggy in rear (Rust brown) May have been wearing low cut shoes. Subject at no time appeared to be in a hurry walking with a shuffling lope, Slightly bent forward. The subjects general appearance—Welsh ancestry. My partner that night was officer E. Zelms #1348 of Richmond station. I do not know if he observed this subject or not. Respectfully submitted. Donald A. Fouke, Patrolman, Star 847."

"I remember Officer Fouke telling us the composite drawing was not nearly as accurate as we originally thought with the children," Toschi told me. Within the homicide division the wanted poster was changed to read "five feet eleven inches" tall. "That Zodiac was rounder-faced, bigger. When you think back to Fouke's verbal description the word 'lumbering' sounds like a gorilla, for God's sake." As years passed, Fouke altered his estimate of Zodiac's weight upward to 230–240 pounds and calculated his height at six feet or six feet one. He eventually recalled the low-cut shoes as engineering boots and the jacket as "dirty." "Zodiac," he said to a television producer, was "walking toward us at an average pace, turned when he saw us, and walked into a private residence [on Jackson Street]."

Toschi disagreed. "Zodiac disappeared," he said. " 'Into the brush, somewhere in the park,' is what Fouke said, not into a residence, not whatsoever. Fouke clocked the encounter at no more than five to ten seconds. We felt that Zelms and Fouke had stopped Zodiac, and did everything we could to keep it quiet so they wouldn't be hurt by the police commission or embarrassed. I remember I talked to Don [Fouke] on the side. He was all teary-eyed. 'Jesus Christ, Dave, my God, it was the guy,' he said. I said, 'Yeah, it was, Don, but he could've killed you so easy. If you had gotten out of your vehicle, unassuming, he could have blown you and Eric [Zelms] away. You gotta consider that.' We had them do a sketch, sent our sketch artist out there, and got the composite."

"I interviewed the one surviving member of that duo there in the 1990s," George Bawart told me later. "One guy was dead and the other was still working for SFPD. He was working Juvenile or something and he wasn't real happy about being interviewed. It was not the high point of his career and he didn't want to talk about it. Who could blame him."

Vallejo Detective Sergeant John Lynch too was obsessed with how close Zodiac had come to being captured. "The way I heard the thing," he told me, "is that when they were talking to him a call came on the radio that they were looking for a black man, and [they] let this guy go and he disappeared into the Presidio. I don't believe he was covered with blood. You know, in the murder of a cabdriver you can almost bet your boots the cops came out of that squad car with their guns in their hands. You'd have to. They waited so long to tell their chief because they were probably shook up over that."

Twelve days before, there may have been a dry run for the Stine shooting. At 11:00 P.M., September 30, 1969, Yellow Cab driver Paul Hom snagged a fare at the Mark Hopkin's Hotel. The passenger asked to be driven to Washington and Locust Streets, three blocks before Washington and Cherry Streets. At the destination, he asked Hom to continue along Washington to Arguello Boulevard, then proceed north into the Presidio for several hundred yards. Abruptly, he pulled a long-barreled revolver and robbed Hom of $35 in cash. The cabbie, forced into the trunk, pleaded with the robber to spare his life. Later he was released, unharmed, by M.P.'s. After Stine's murder, Captain Marty Lee, basing his conclusion on an "amazing similarity of M.O. between criminals in two cabby cases," said he believed the robber to have been Zodiac. The *Chronicle* thought so too. "One of the luckiest men alive," it reported, "taken for a ride by Zodiac, but lived to tell about it." One discrepancy could not be explained. Hom's robber was only twenty-four, "135 pounds with black hair and eyes," and dressed in "blue denim jacket and dark slacks." But Zodiac was undeniably a stocky, older man. Did he have a young accomplice who had scouted out the scene for him, rehearsing the Stine killing? Was that where the answer lay?

MULANAX WOULD NEVER see Fouke's internal SFPD communication and upward estimate of Zodiac's height and weight. Virtually no one did. He replaced the wanted poster with a mistaken conception of the killer's appearance and an uncomfortable sense it did not entirely fit their new suspect. The Vallejo detective also never knew that Starr had an odd way of striding. "When walking he was terribly lumbering," Starr's friend told me later. "He had a funny hip [his leg was lacerated so badly in August of 1965 that plastic surgery had been required]." One common link was the description of Zodiac as an unusually round-faced man. "Could Zodiac's round, bloated face be indicative of fluid retention from a developing health problem?" I asked a nurse. "Such as failing kidneys?" she answered. "Yes, very definitely."

Mulanax next learned that the suspect had been arrested June 15, 1958, for a violation of 415 P.C., disturbing the peace. It was a minor blip in his record, but one that had disastrous ramifications later on. As Mulanax put away the file folder, he saw that Starr had been a victim or a witness to several other incidents. Additionally, suspicions existed about his improper relationships with children.

"Not a nice boy," Mulanax thought.

The detective wanted to be prepared before the arrival of the "Zodiac Twins"—as the papers had dubbed Armstrong and Toschi. He phoned CI&I for a more detailed rap sheet, then buzzed the Department of Motor Vehicles for a photo. "Susan, that's California Driver's License #B672352," he repeated for Susan Raspino. While she processed his request, Mulanax left the office to check out the residence Starr shared with his widowed mother. It was cooler that day. Prevailing winds through the Golden Gate kept the town's climate a little warmer in winter and a little cooler in summer than other Bay Area cities. Mulanax turned off Tennessee Street and swung by Fresno Street.

Starr's home, hunched on the east side of the street, was sun-bleached brown and shone pinkish-gray where diagonal slashes of light cut across it. The numerals "32," affixed in a metal frame on the facade, stood out stark black against white. A 1957 blue and white Ford sedan, parked in front and hooked to a boat trailer, caught Mulanax's eye. He slowed and jotted down the license number—LDH 974. DMV verified it was registered to Starr, who also owned a two-seat Austin Healey, a VW, and a white Buick. A driveway led back to a detached two-door garage where a white 1965 Mercedes 220SB was parked. Mulanax had already learned that the suspect had formerly been employed as an attendant at Harry Wogan's Service Station. An auto repair job such as that would have made many cars left overnight for repair available to Starr.

The sergeant reached the end of the block, made a U-turn at Illinois Street, and cruised back by the house. He took one last critical look, then spoke with Wogan. The service station owner told Mulanax that Starr had left his employment in 1970. "He said he was thinking of returning to school at Sonoma State College in Cotati," replied Wogan. This was true. Starr had begun working toward a degree in biology in the fall of 1970. Though Starr, according to his former boss, had been an efficient worker, he had shown too much interest in small children. Wogan had three small children himself and they sometimes came around the station. "That worried me," he said. "I wasn't sorry to see him go." That seemed to be the way with Starr's many employers. "They had him working at a school as some sort of custodian," Mulanax told me later. "I was infuriated because I felt he should have been arrested."

At the start of summer, Starr had dropped by Wogan's home

and picked up his thirteen-year-old daughter. "How would you like to go for a ride with me on my boat?" he had asked. The youngster had accepted without her parents' consent. The girl returned to relate that Starr had made "improper advances" toward her. After this, Wogan had not seen his employee again or wanted to.

Sergeant Mulanax believed much of the interest pedophiles had in small children came from having absolute power over another individual, reducing them to objects—a trait Zodiac and almost every serial killer shared. "When Zodiac had hog-tied his victims at Lake Berryessa," he told me, "he had had complete power, had reduced them in his mind to mere objects, and especially wore his homemade executioner's costume for the occasion." Perhaps Zodiac had hoped someone might glimpse his frightening outfit and incite more terror in an already terrified community. But he could hardly have hoped his victims would survive to tell the tale. Had he shown himself to someone else, as yet unknown?

Zodiac's threats to blow up school buses and shoot children inspired as much fear as his costume. Mulanax recalled armed sentinels—off-duty teachers, drivers, and firemen, riding shotgun on school buses. Napa P.D., the jurisdiction of the Berryessa stabbings, assigned more than seventy police units to follow the buses, and fixed-wing guard planes trailed hawklike behind them. People peeked behind their doors and gave second, even third glances to cars gliding along the freeways and back roads at night. Zodiac was the twentieth-century version of the Bogeyman.

To obtain more samples of Starr's handprinting, Mulanax drove to 1660 Tennessee Street, where Starr maintained a checking account at Crocker-Citizens Bank. He arranged to get photostats of recent canceled checks connected to account #546-1685-48. He had considered borrowing the originals (since Starr had ordered the bank not to return them), but decided against it. He saw one draft was to a man named Phil Tucker. Another, dated July 20, 1971, was a $9.00 check to R. G. Blackwood for a 44-gallon cooler. A third showed a June 4 payment made out to Tall Trees Trailer Court. The notation said: "Storage Rental." Mulanax dispatched all three samples to Morrill for analysis without giving much consideration to what Starr might be storing in a trailer court. He had many trailers.

At 1:30 P.M., Inspectors Armstrong and Toschi, like travelers

into a foreign land, crossed into Solano County for their appointment with Mulanax. Since 1969 they had examined hundreds of
suspects, were, in fact, weary. However, Starr was beginning to
look serious, beginning to look very good. Toschi, with his mass
of tight, curly black hair, was wearing his trademark bow tie. A
smile broadened his remarkably expressive face. They had
brought along Mel Nicolai, and Toschi was beaming at being
among such good company. He had a high opinion of Nicolai.
"Very professional," he told me later. "Mel enjoyed a good laugh
and was a very, very good law enforcement officer. With his crew
cut and glasses, he looked like a professor. Nicolai, as a State Department of Justice CI&I agent, put cases together when multiple
counties were involved. He was a middle guy. We could contact
him and he could get us information out of Sacramento."

As for Mulanax, he was a man's man, a rugged outdoorsman,
a hunter like Zodiac. "After I see Starr in person, I'll contact you
guys to come back," he assured them as the meeting concluded.
Mulanax was the kind of man you could count on. Toschi knew
he would come back with the goods.

MONDAY, AUGUST 2, 1971

MULANAX continued his circumspect investigation into Starr's
past, gathering as much background information as he could before making personal contact with the suspect. He noted, as others had, that Starr's birth date was December 18—two days shy
of the December 20 date of the Lake Herman Road double murders. Mulanax knew some serial killers struck on dates that held
significance for them. So far, Zodiac had shot or stabbed couples
on the Fourth of July, near Halloween, Columbus Day, and a few
days before Christmas. However, a few VPD investigators believed Zodiac had only taken responsibility for the Lake Herman
tragedy to enhance his rep and further confuse the police. "Mulanax told me," said Toschi, "that one day when Starr wasn't
home, he went to Starr's house and his mother was there. He
kinda just walked around and searched a little bit."

If Mulanax spoke conversationally with Starr himself that day
(not a questioning in any respect), no record has survived. Mulanax saw the open door to Starr's basement room yawning before him, and observed it was painted the same "near-neutral

green" as the kitchen, though a shade lighter. Was Starr down there now, peering up at him? Bernice, catching his eye, said, "It was a bedroom for both my boys for many years." The mailbox was a slot in the corner of the basement room. "All letters must drop into that hideaway," thought Mulanax, thinking of the mail-obsessed killer. And Zodiac had said in a letter he had a basement and bombs there. Starr had moved from an upstairs room back to the basement for more privacy. Mulanax was tempted, but caution prevented him from advancing a step further. He retreated, but was still thinking over the substance of his visit and a few of Bernice's vague remarks as the weekend ended and he prepared to confer again with the San Francisco detectives.

TUESDAY, AUGUST 3, 1971

MANY along Fresno Street had known Starr since he was a boy, knew how devoted he was to his mother. But that mutual affection existed only as smoke and mirrors—neighbors often overheard shouting matches between the two. "His mother was a little on the stern side," said Cheney. "Yeah, she was tough. She was a tall woman, almost as tall as Starr. Both parents were tall and slender like Ron. Unlike his brother, Ron got along with everybody." The main bone of contention was that Bernice held Starr's younger brother, Ron, in higher regard than him.

"There was a big rivalry between Ron and his older brother," Panzarella told me later. "Ron got more girls. He could be more charming and the mother used to favor him, much to Starr's disdain. She adored Ron who was a nice-looking kid. And Starr at this time had already gotten fat. I spent the weekend in the home with the dad and the mom. Starr came over. He was living in his trailer at the time and I saw how unassuming the father was. He had been wounded in an airplane wreck over Oklahoma in the late fifties or early sixties and he was never the same after that. He was a draftsman now and we drove him to work, dropped him off and picked him up later. Nice man, but very meek. He wasn't always that way. Ron told me it was the accident that made him that way. After the accident Ethan could no longer keep his son in line. He became—how should I say this—quiet. The mother was totally the dominant personality. They were always arguing and bantering. He'd really cuss her up and down, screaming at her. I know if I had spoken to my parents that way, they would have killed me. Starr called her a 'c—' and stuff like that. It was awful and this was at the dinner table."

Cheney elaborated on this. "Starr's father was a decorated jet pilot," he told me. "I don't know if he got shot down or he had a wreck, but he had an accident and was injured pretty badly and was medically discharged. I didn't know him from the days when he was still in the Navy. He was still active, but apparently had lost some of his fire. He wasn't the hot jet pilot he had once been. He still went to work and still was a draftsman on Mare Island. He wasn't bummed up. He could walk all right and all of his functions were normal. He was a nice guy. The family had commissary privileges and had I.D. cards so they could shop on military bases. The Wing Walker shoes he wore probably came from Mare Island. They were made for pilots and crewmen."

From the street Mulanax idled his car and observed the smudged, practically ground-level window to Starr's disordered basement apartment, and tried to imagine what it must be like. He still yearned to have a peek. Starr's mother had described her son's inner sanctum as stacked with books. Starr was quite the student, "a professional student," his brother said. "After summer vacation," Bernice had explained, "he intends to return to college at Cotati for the fall semester." Mulanax thought back to 1969 and to another summer vacation—tumultuous times, violent times for Vallejo.

Starr had been a student then too and Zodiac had been at his boldest, grasping Water Town in a grip of fear. With the intimate knowledge of a Vallejo resident, he capitalized on a citywide police and firemen's strike. Throughout the walkout there were only two dozen California Highway Patrolmen to cruise about and enforce traffic laws for a city of 72,000. On July 21, negotiators almost had the strike licked, but Apollo 11 delayed a settlement meeting when Governor Reagan declared a moon-flight holiday.

So far summer vacation 1971 had been less turbulent, thought Mulanax. Vallejo had a highly efficient law enforcement team in place and Starr had a job with Union Oil of California to keep him occupied. Returning to headquarters just before lunch, Mulanax rang the Union Oil refinery at Pinole and spoke with Mc-Namara in Personnel. He confirmed Starr was employed as a junior chemist in their lab, had been since September 8, 1970. But Starr could not have been very happy at Pinole. Last April

20, the overqualified man had applied for employment at a Union 76 garage in nearby Rodeo. "His summer hours at the refinery are from 8:00 A.M. until 4:00 P.M.–4:30 P.M.," continued McNamara, "and that's each weekday."

"I'd like to interview him during working hours," Mulanax explained.

"That's a bit out of the ordinary," said the personnel chief, "and bound to cause some disruption." Disruption was exactly what Mulanax had in mind. "Well, we can provide my private office for your purposes," McNamara agreed.

"Good," said the detective. "Just don't let on that we intend to interview him prior to his being brought to the office." Most definitely Mulanax wanted to surprise Starr and put him off balance. He hung up, noted the appointment on his pad, then dialed Toschi and Armstrong and informed them of the meeting. Famished after a busy morning, he went to lunch.

Armstrong and Toschi had been busy too. Toschi studied two pages of scribbled notes, munching animal crackers and dunking them in a cup of Instant Folgers. He had just learned that Starr, though born left-handed, had been compelled as a child to write with his right hand—a possible cause of serious psychological problems.

After lunch, Morrill got back to Mulanax in Vallejo about Starr's canceled checks. "I've compared them to Zodiac lettering," Morrill said, "and they come up negative." What were they missing? wondered Mulanax. If Starr was Zodiac, had he devised a way to disguise his printing? Or had a confederate written them? Right to the end that shadowy second man would be a worrisome element in the hunt for Zodiac.

WEDNESDAY, AUGUST 4, 1971

TOSCHI, Armstrong, and Mulanax sped south from Vallejo along Interstate 80 and rattled across the Carquinez Bridge into Contra Costa County. Tracing the shore of San Pablo Bay, they swept past Selby, Tormey, Rodeo, and Hercules. To the west Hamilton AFB shimmered across clouded green water. The previous January two Standard Oil Company tankers had collided just outside the Golden Gate, spilling almost two million gallons of black gummy crude into the Bay. Shortly before 10:25 A.M. the detectives halted at the chain-link gate of a vast oil refinery. The Pinole installation was impressive. By night, when it was twinkling with a million diamond lights, great clouds of roiling steam made it otherworldly; by day fingerlike black towers shot hundreds of feet upward like the barrels of guns.

The gate slid back and, three or four blocks later, the detectives climbed out. Toschi craned his neck upward, where processing towers boiled crude oil to 750 degrees. The heating procedure separated molecules, converting them into propane, gasoline, butane, kerosene, diesel fuel, lubricating oil, even road tar and wax. Starr was a chemist and the refinery itself no more than a giant chemical lab. Complex conduits twisted into overlapping tunnels, funneling raw petroleum into mammoth storage tanks, catalytic units, and vacuum distillation units.

Sudden shrill whistles alerted Toschi. High above, men scrambled on gantries and towers. An unctuous mist like soot showered down on them and made Toschi queasy. His breakfast this morning and for many mornings prior had been a few aspirins washed down with cold coffee. They entered McNamara's office and watched as he phoned a lab to summon the unsuspecting assistant chemist. "It'll be a minute," he said. Starr's records were spread out like a fan on McNamara's desk. Bill Armstrong took the time to thumb through them since he would be in charge of the questioning.

The investigators did not hear the suspect in the hallway—only the elevator doors opening with a "whoosh." Starr walked softly for a big man and was wearing padded shoes of some sort. At last they would see him face to face. Toschi sat rigid in his seat. He half rose. After so many suspects, after so many years and disappointments, was Zodiac finally here—within their grasp? Toschi held his breath. The door opened. Starr's physical presence was all Toschi thought it would be and all that he knew Zodiac's was.

2

ROBERT HALL STARR

STARR filled the doorway. His bold, almost hairless head swiveled from face to face as the trio of detectives identified themselves. Starr seemed surprised and a little nervous that they were policemen. "I realized that he was afraid he was going to get fired," Toschi told me later, "and that alone might have accounted for his apprehension." Twenty-five hundred Zodiac suspects had surfaced over the years and been painstakingly checked out. Since so many counties, jurisdictions, and unincorporated areas were involved, cops did not always compare notes or even names. Starr was not their first good suspect. He was not their last. Conveniently, alarm bells should have resounded in the investigators' minds. They didn't. Only after the conference, when their heads were cool and time allowed them to consider what Starr had said, so much of it unbidden, did their pulses begin to race. Back at Homicide that stark black clock seemed to tick faster.

As Mulanax had done, Toschi took in the suspect's physical presence—Starr had blue-brown eyes and short light brown hair that was graying in the back. Hadn't Officer Fouke mentioned something about Zodiac having "light-colored hair possibly graying in the rear," recollected Toschi, "and the curve of Zodiac's skull had shone through his sparse hair the night he shot the cabdriver." The late sixties were a period of protest when people rebelled against the shorter hair of the fifties and wore their hair long. In 1969, Zodiac had worn his short—like a military man. However, during a previous attack at Lake Berryessa, Zodiac presumably sported a healthy head of straight brown hair beneath his hood.

"I remember a kind of greasy forehead . . ." the surviving

Berryessa victim told me later. He thought the perpetrator had dark brown hair—a lock had shown through dark glasses covering narrow eyelets. Beneath those glasses, the wounded boy conjectured, were a second pair of glasses. The killer, in complete costume—a black executioner's hood with a white circle and cross on the chest—had appeared almost magically in the twilight on September 27, 1969. Zodiac had traveled north to Napa County and targeted the student and his young girlfriend, stabbing them with a foot-long, inch-wide bayonet with a taped wooden handle. He had decorated the haft, carried at his belt in a handmade scabbard, with brass rivets. "I don't know how tall Zodiac was, maybe five foot eight or six feet, somewhere in there. I'm a pretty poor judge of height because of my height," said the lanky student.

Starr's wide brow had breadth enough for a second apple-cheeked face; his neck was thick; high-set ears flew out like horns. His broad-shouldered, six-foot-tall bulk was intimidating. "Everybody that I ever saw that met Starr underestimated his height," Cheney later explained. "He had that fearsome look in his eyes. Thick thighs and a big butt and a belly and strong shoulders and chest." Yes, Starr was a heavy man, but then so was Zodiac. The surviving Berryessa victim estimated Zodiac's weight at between 225 and 250 pounds. "I described this guy as being really fat," he said. "I don't know, he could have been moderately heavy and wearing a thickly lined windbreaker." But there was another way to tell.

Detective Sergeant Ken Narlow of the Napa County Sheriff's Department had done a compaction test on Zodiac's unique footprints. He had a deputy sheriff weighing 210 pounds walk alongside them. "He didn't sink down as deeply as Zodiac had," Narlow told me, "In order to put that print so deeply into the sand we figured the Zodiac weighed at least 220 pounds. Clear prints at the heel had indicated that Zodiac was not running when he left." Morrill, the handwriting examiner, as conservative with the compaction test as with handprinting, told me, "It depends on how the sand was at the time too. If the guy was taking big loping steps or mincing along. They were guessing at the size from the indentation he made. Suppose the sand the day before was different. Suppose there had been water in it."

But the ground had been dry and he had been striding leisurely. The prints were firm and especially clear at the heel. Napa cops arrived almost immediately because Zodiac had boldly phoned them from a booth within four and one-half blocks of their headquarters. "He was bound to have some blood on him," Narlow told me. "To come in from Berryessa and hit that particular telephone he had to pass, I figure, some twenty to twenty-one telephones. He came in close enough to hear any possible sirens rushing out of the city of Napa. He could call in from the lake, but he would be trapping himself up there. It's a twenty-five-minute drive down. The booth was twenty-seven miles from the crime scene. If we had found out he was calling from the lake we could have sealed the area off."

At the lake there was further proof that Zodiac's considerable weight was not padding. He had impressed unique marks deeply into the earth. A circle on the sole reading "SUPERWEAR" showed clearly in Narlow's plaster moulages. Zodiac's military motif, suggested by a black holster at his belt containing a blue-steel semiautomatic military .45, was enhanced by the identifying logos of his shoes—black boots used primarily by the Navy. Wing Walker shoes were worn almost exclusively by aircraft maintenance crewmen for walking the wings of jets. Narlow discovered that, but only after his men culled 150 shoe boutiques with names like "The Spinning Wheel" and "Willow Tree."

In 1969, 103,700 pairs of Wing Walkers had been shipped to Ogden, Utah. The Weinbrenner Shoe Company of Merrill, Wisconsin, had manufactured them per a 1966 government contract for one million pairs total. The last pairs were distributed to Air Force and Naval installations on the West Coast. Only active-duty personnel or former active-duty personnel, or their dependents, could have purchased such shoes. These personnel were required to present an I.D. card that carried a thumbprint and photo to enter any base exchange and make any purchases there. Vallejo, its economy directly related to military operations, served as home for many skilled employees with Navy or Air Force ties. They toiled at Travis AFB, north of Vallejo near Fairfield, or at Hamilton, Mather, and McClellan Air Force Bases, nearby Mare Island, Alameda Naval Station, and Treasure Island. The FBI believed in the military connection.

"UNSUB [unknown subject of an investigation] may have military background," the FBI file said, "inasmuch as UNSUB used bayonet and two separate 9mm weapons and one of the surviving victims observed UNSUB to be wearing military-type boots."

Not only were these unusual-looking chucker-type boots available only through a limited outlet, but police had their size. Zodiac wore a size 10½ Regular shoe, which indicated a tall man, as did his long stride.

Toschi, recalling Zodiac's unusual homemade costume, later told me: "We sent our artist to Napa County [on October 24, 1969]. Surviving victim Bryan Hartnell described the Zodiac's hood as black and sleeveless, the white circle and crosshair in the middle of the chest. The hood looked well made and well-sewn [the corners had been stitched and there was neat stitching around the flat top] with clip-on sunglasses over the eye slits." And Starr could sew (he had been a sailmaker). But the police in that cramped refinery office scarcely wondered about the suspect's sewing skills or paid much attention to his shoes—they were studying his face. Beyond his strength and the build of a potential Gold Medal swimmer gone to seed was a highly intelligent mind. Starr's I.Q. was 136.

"We're investigating the Zodiac murders in San Francisco and Vallejo," said Armstrong, "and we have some questions for you." The detective pulled out a chair for the chemist. Toschi noticed barely perceptible droplets beaded on Starr's wide forehead. "An informant has notified us that you made certain statements approximately eleven months prior to the first Zodiac murder," continued Armstrong. "If these are true, then they are of an incriminating nature." Armstrong, though referring to Cheney's recollected dialogue with the suspect, did not mention his name. "Do you recall having such a conversation with anyone?"

"I don't recall such a conversation," Starr said mildly. Oddly, he failed to ask with whom he had reportedly conversed. He seemed already to know. "Others are quick to react to what you say and do," his horoscope had read in that morning's *Chronicle*. "Choose your words carefully."

"Have you ever read or heard of Zodiac?"

"I read about the Zodiac when it first appeared in the newspapers," said Starr. "I didn't follow up on it after those first reports."

"Why?"

"Because it was too morbid."

But Starr, later in the interview, made other statements that were in direct conflict with this remark. First, though, he volunteered this: "A Vallejo police sergeant questioned me after the Zodiac murders at Lake Berryessa."

All three investigators were stunned.

"We weren't aware you had ever been questioned by the police before," said Armstrong.

"I told him," said Starr, "that on that particular weekend [Saturday, September 27, 1969] I had gone to Salt Point Ranch near Fort Ross to skin-dive. [Salt Point Ranch lay in the opposite direction from Lake Berryessa.] I went alone, but I met a serviceman and his wife who were stationed on Treasure Island. I don't recall his name, but I have it written down somewhere at home. I got back to Vallejo about 4:00 P.M."

Armstrong, Toschi, and Mulanax listened intently. Outside, a steam whistle blew and a foreman barked orders. Inside, Starr's voice droned in the heat. They could almost hear wheels turning in his head. A palpable tension choked the little office. "I recall speaking to a neighbor shortly after I drove into my driveway," Starr went on. "I guess I neglected to tell the Vallejo officer when he questioned me about being seen by this neighbor."

"And what was the neighbor's name?" asked Armstrong.

"[William] White. But he died a week after I was questioned so I never bothered to contact the police." That was very convenient. Suddenly, Starr made a bizarre leap in subject matter—one so strange that Toschi caught Armstrong's attention with a quizzical raising of his eyebrow. Without any questioning about a knife such as Zodiac had used in the Berryessa stabbings, the suspect made an astonishing statement:

"The two knives I had in my car had blood on them," he said. "The blood came from a chicken I had killed."

The day Zodiac stabbed two college students at Lake Berryessa, Starr was to have been there shooting ground squirrels and had told his sister-in-law so. His new story was that he had gone scuba diving instead—elsewhere. Starr both skin dived and scuba dived. To explain why Zodiac chose sites near lakes, a theory had circulated that Zodiac was a diver who hid his weapons and souvenirs in watertight containers underwater. And that's why the killer had a paunch—a weighted diving belt around his waist. To Toschi, that hypothesis now looked considerably less farfetched. Starr was not only a boater, but an avid skin diver and spear fisherman.

"Starr thinks we have some information regarding a knife," thought Armstrong. "He thinks we know more than we do, but knowledge of that bloody knife is information we don't possess."

All the detectives could fathom was that someone had glimpsed the stained knives or knife on his car seat and Starr knew they had. Did he think that his neighbor, William White, had observed a bloody blade when he returned home that day and mentioned it to someone? More than likely, thought Toschi, Starr's brother, Ron, or sister-in-law, Karen, were the ones who had spied the bloody blade. Starr was hedging his bets and explaining away in advance any information that the police *may* have received.

"Were you in Southern California in 1966?" asked Armstrong.

Once again, Starr volunteered startling specifics without prompting.

"You mean about the Riverside killing?" he said. "Yes, I was in Southern California at the approximate time as the Riverside murder in which Zodiac is a suspect."

The information about a Zodiac stabbing in Riverside had been made public only ten months earlier. Phil Sins, a southern resident, had seen parallels between a local murder and Zodiac's Northern California activities. The break ran in the *Chronicle*. But hadn't Starr just stated he had long before ceased reading articles about Zodiac? The headline story suggested Zodiac had killed a Riverside College coed, Cheri Jo Bates, just before Halloween Night 1966. The writer of the handprinted Riverside notes had also been fond of writing taunting letters to the press ("BATES HAD TO DIE THERE WILL BE MORE") and using too much postage. A squiggled signature on three letters was either a "2" or a "Z." Most importantly, Morrill had identified Zodiac as the author of the Southern California notes.

"I admit I'm interested in guns," Starr continued, "but the only handguns I own are .22-caliber. I don't have and have never owned an automatic weapon."

"Have you ever owned a 1965–66 brown Corvair?" asked Armstrong. Zodiac was driving such a vehicle the night of his Fourth of July murder.

"No." Starr folded his arms. He was dressed in a short-sleeved white shirt, his forearms as massive as "Popeye's."

Toschi noticed a big watch on Starr's wrist. "It was a rugged man's watch," he told me later. "It's the kind of watch a man would buy to be seen—'Look at what I've got on my wrist.' And I spotted it instantly—the word 'Zodiac.' I asked him specifically to show it to me. 'That's a nice watch you've got there,' I said. 'Oh, I've had it awhile,' he said. 'Do you like it?' I said. 'Oh, yeah,' he said. And you can see the letters Z-o-d-i-a-c. I still re-member seeing that watch. And he wanted people to see what he had on his arm. He wore it in defiance. I couldn't take my eyes off it. When we saw the watch we were amazed—and the brother and sister-in-law afterward mentioned to Armstrong and I that, 'He even wears a Zodiac watch.' "

"May I see that?" said Armstrong. He gestured toward Starr's wrist. He had also noticed their suspect was wearing an unusual-looking watch. A ray of light through the blinds made the crystal face sparkle. Above the watchmaker's name, in the center of the face, was emblazoned a bold emblem. It froze the officers in spite of the heat. There, glowing stark white on black, was a circle and crosshairs—*Zodiac's symbol.*

The expensive watch on Starr's wrist had been manufactured by Zodiac Astrographic Automatic, LeLocle, Switzerland/New York, a company whose roots stretched back to the nineteenth century. Now Mulanax saw it too. Neatly printed across the bot-tom, in upper and lower case, was the word "Zodiac." The name and symbol were exactly like those used as a signature on Zo-diac's letters.

"Only in Zodiac's letters had the name 'Zodiac' and the killer's crossed-circle symbol ever appeared together in the same place," Toschi thought. He knew because he had searched every-where for that crossed circle. To this moment, he had assumed it represented a gun sight. Starr turned the watch on his wrist as if admiring it. "It was a birthday gift," he said to Armstrong. "This watch was given to me by my mother two years ago."

Mulanax counted back in his mind. "Let's see—exactly two years back from today is August 4, 1969. On August 4, 1969, the killer had used the name 'Zodiac' for the first time in a three-page letter to the *Examiner*. The paper had buried his note in the late edition at the top of page 4. Only five days before, Zodiac had in-troduced his crossed circle symbol to the papers." Though a later CI&I report stated Starr had gotten the watch in August 1969, his brother, Ron, contradicted that. He said that Starr "received the watch from his mother as a Christmas gift in December 1968." Starr's thirty-fifth birthday had been December 18, 1968, just two days before Zodiac's first known Northern California murders.

Starr would own a second Zodiac watch later. The manufactur-ers of the "World Famous Zodiac Watches" manufactured a Zo-diac Clebar Skin-diver Underwater Chronograph in 1969: "It's a stop watch! Aviator and skin-diver's watch. Tested for 20 atmospheres (comparable to 660 feet underwater)." Starr was, by then, both an aviator and skin diver. Like its brother, a logo in the lower right-hand corner of the watch was a crossed circle on a dark background above the word "Zodiac." It was quiet in the office. The Zodiac watch, mention of a bloody knife, Starr's volunteered information had dazed them all. What was coming next?

"I'm willing to help you in the investigation in any way possible," the suspect said, licking his lips. He coughed and cleared his throat. Starr apparently wanted to interpose a high note, one with some humor, reconciliation, and good fellowship all round. "I can't wait until the time comes when police officers are not referred to as 'pigs,' " he said with a sad shake of his head. Some antiwar protesters and students of the period commonly called police "pigs." Zodiac used the same epithet. "I enjoy needling the blue pigs," he had taunted. "Hey blue pig I was in the park."

"Can you recall anyone whom you might have had a conversation with regarding Zodiac?" interjected Mulanax.

"I might have had a conversation with Ted Kidder and Phil Tucker of the Vallejo Recreation Department when I was working there, but I'm not positive." Starr continued answering questions before they were asked. In this way he might defuse any damaging evidence against him in their minds. What had they heard? He had no way of knowing which of many acquaintances had turned him in as a killer. He said some very strange things in private. He liked to talk and he talked loud and his remarks made him the center of attention. Suddenly, Starr paused—he realized who had sent the police!

" 'The Most Dangerous Game,' " he said.

"What?" said Toschi.

Out of nowhere, Starr had mentioned the title of a short story he had read in the eleventh grade, a tale that, by his own admission, had made a deep and lasting impression on him. Toschi recalled Langstaff's Manhattan Beach report and recognized "The Most Dangerous Game" as the same story Starr had rhapsodized over a full year before the murders began. Toschi smiled inwardly—Starr had finally figured out who had ratted him out.

"It was called 'The Most Dangerous Game,' " Starr elaborated. "It was the best thing I read in high school." Zodiac had given "The Most Dangerous Game" as his motive in a cunning, almost unbreakable three-part cipher. But Salinas schoolteacher Don

Harden had cracked it on August 4, 1969, exactly two years ago today, though Harden's solution was not made public until August 12. Encrypting mistakes and all, the bizarre solution read:

"I LIKE KILLING PEOPLE BECAUSE IT IS SO MUCH FUN IT IS MORE FUN THAN KILLING WILD GAME IN THE FORREST BECAUSE MAN IS THE MOST DANGEROUE ANAMAL OF ALL TO KILL SOMETHING GIVES ME THE MOST THRILLING EXPERENCE IT IS EVEN BETTER THAN GETTING YOUR ROCKS OFF WITH A GIRL THE BEST PART OF IT IS THAE WHEN I DIE I WILL BE REBORN IN PARADICE AND THEI HAVE KILLED WILL BECOME MY SLAVES I WILL NOT GIVE YOU MY NAME BECAUSE YOU WILL TRY TO SLOI DOWN OR ATOP MY COLLECTIOG OF SLAVES FOR AFTERLIFE . . ."

Roughly, the short story by Richard Connell dealt with the son of a military officer hunting humans with a rifle and bow and arrow for sport in the forest. Aptly, Starr, the son of a military man, hunted in the woods with a bow and arrow. Mulanax summarized the story in this manner: "This book was made into a movie and concerns a man shipwrecked on an island and being hunted by another man 'like an animal.' " It might be important to study that brief story in depth for clues, thought Mulanax, learn if it had been a movie or dramatized on television, learn where Zodiac might have stumbled across it and when.

"Starr mentioned 'The Most Dangerous Game' during that questioning," Toschi told me later, "and his brother afterward confirmed that he felt that man was 'the most dangerous game, not shooting game.' " The precise words Starr had used, verified by another witness than Cheney, were: "I think of man as game." The adventure story might have been the flash point, no less a catalyst than the re-forming process Starr performed daily as an assistant chemist.

The informal cross-examination ended.

Less than an hour had passed since those elevator doors had opened, but it seemed longer. As an interview it had been mild. Though Starr had been isolated, a true interrogation would have been more focused, the setting bleaker, the intimidation more intense. Pointedly, the trio escorted Starr back to his lab, then left.

Inwardly, the chemist boiled at being taken out, humiliated, and "questioned like a thief." Toschi admitted that he found Starr "a dangerous animal," and though armed, had some fear of him in close quarters. Starr's ears were crimson; his face flushed. He could barely control his anger and he had never been a patient man. Men all around him, in their lab coats, paper booties over engineering boots, were staring and whispering. He sat at his work station. "You don't know what it's like," mumbled Starr to a coworker, his eyes fixed on his desk. "Everything is fine—going good. Then somebody calls you to the office. And they suggest terrible things about you. You just can't know—terrible things. And all the time I'm racking my brain to figure out who sent them. They make you sweat, then take you through the halls—in front of everyone—like a child! I can't forgive that." The next time Starr met Toschi and Armstrong, he would claim not to remember them.

Ignoring the buzz of his coworkers, Starr began scanning test results. He might be in a predicament—he was Zodiac's weight, height, age. He had the same color and length of hair. He crossed his legs and removed the paper booties over his shoes. Absently, he surveyed the unusual-looking chucker-type Wing Walker boots he was wearing. Like Zodiac, Starr wore a size 10½ Regular. Two women he knew had seen him in those shoes and could testify to that. But in the end, perhaps he was only a man who liked people to think he was Zodiac.

Outside, the investigators climbed back into their car. Their unanimous consensus was that the investigation of Starr should continue and in greater depth. "Absolutely," said Toschi with feeling. "But what I really want to know is who the hell questioned him just after the murders?"

Mulanax had absolutely no idea. "God, that was over two years ago," he said. He made a mental note to fine-comb the Vallejo files regarding any questioning of Starr as a Zodiac suspect and any previous reports about a bloody knife or knives on a car seat.

3

ARTHUR LEIGH ALLEN

SOMEONE had desperately wanted us to know such a thing as a Zodiac watch existed. I studied the neatly penciled letter in my hand. At the *San Francisco Chronicle,* where I worked as an editorial cartoonist, everyone wondered about Zodiac. His terrifying letters had irrevocably linked him to the newspaper. Gradually, a determination grew within me to disentangle the killer's clues and unmask his true identity. Failing that, I intended to present every scrap of evidence available to ensure that someone might recognize Zodiac and resolve the missing pieces of the puzzle.

At the window I contemplated the long shadows stretching across wide Mission Street. On Fifth Street, strangers milled about the Pickwick Hotel (Hammett's "Pickwick Stage terminal" where the Maltese Falcon had been stashed). Transients huddled in front of the Chronicle Hotel, and well-dressed men with briefcases stood on the marble steps of the indestructible Old Mint. Zodiac could be any of them. He was a watcher. The first letter in which he christened himself "Zodiac" carried a different watermark than three earlier letters (Monarch-cut bond, imprinted with an "Eaton" watermark). The new watermark was "FIFTH AVENUE," an imprint of Frank Winfield Woolworth's national chain. A huge Woolworth's stood just a block away from the *Chronicle,* at the cable car turntable at Fifth and Market and Powell. In the basement, next to the goldfish, Woolworth's sold blue felt-tip pens and paper exactly like Zodiac used. What if he bought his paper and blue felt-tip pens there? What if he spied from the shadows as his letters were delivered?

Last March Zodiac had been writing industriously, casting his net wide; spreading his word southward. After the oil refinery interview with Starr, the flow of words halted abruptly. Nonetheless, *Chronicle* reporter Paul Stuart Avery optimistically left standing orders with the city desk. "We can probably expect to receive a new Zodiac communication any day now," he said brightly. "As usual, every effort should be made to prevent any *Chronicle* employee's fingerprints from getting on the letter." The letters had been handled by a lot of the staff—Carol Fisher, Brant Parker . . . Toschi had already fingerprinted all the copy people.

Sometimes Zodiac attempted to sneak letters into print. Since Letters Editor Carol Fisher retained all reader submissions as hedges against libel, this anonymous letter from November 1970 had been on file.

> "Dear Sir," the note read. "In reading a recent issue of 'Playboy' magazine I noticed an advertisement for 'Zodiac' watches. The trademark on the face of the watch is identical to that used by the notorious killer. Since I've always read in the press that the crimes have been interpreted as some sort of astrological thing. The fact that such a singular hyrogrific [sic] effect is in fact a watch brand emblem seems somehow interesting."

Had a gloating Zodiac slyly called attention to the inspiration for his name and symbol? After "a Vallejo cop" had cleared him, Starr must have felt secure. He had gone on wearing his Zodiac wristwatch, at least until Toschi, Armstrong, and Mulanax surprised him. I visualized a tantalizing sequence of events—Starr, obsessed with "The Most Dangerous Game" since high school, received a Zodiac watch from his mother on December 18, 1968, and began wearing a second birthday gift, a ring with a "Z" on it. Thirteen days later, he had a conversation with Cheney, much like earlier discussions in which he mentioned putting a light on the barrel of his gun and hunting couples. He spoke of calling himself "Zodiac" and shooting out the tires of a school bus. This chronology set down a definite time frame for Zodiac's choice of name, symbol, and M.O.—sometime between December 18, 1968, and January 1, 1969, after which Cheney moved to Southern California to work for a new company. Starr had revealed a monumental secret about himself on New Year's Day, but then Zodiac always chose holidays for his most important crimes and revelations.

Cheney's visit, the symbol on the watch, its exotic trademark, the ring, his favorite story from his youth—all must have been bubbling in Starr's head. The first two murders occured on December 20, two days after Starr's birthday. On August 4, 1971, two years after the killer had first signed his name "Zodiac," he told Armstrong he had received the Zodiac watch "exactly two years earlier"—August 4, 1969. Either scenario presented a fascinating sequence of events and explained the killer's choice of name and symbol.

Police, during their manhunt for Zodiac, zealously guarded the prime suspect's real name. If his name was never publicized, this ensured any subsequent tip about Starr would be valid. As for myself, I made a practice of never writing, until now, Starr's true name.

His real name was Arthur Leigh Allen.

Almost a decade after the oil refinery questioning, I finally located the "Vallejo cop" who had questioned Allen so early in the case. Detective Sergeant John Lynch talked to me at his home on Carolina Street in Vallejo. A slender, solid older man with penetrating eyes, he began speaking the instant we sat down at his dining room table. The room was almost completely dark. I had just mentioned Allen. "Oh," he said, "Lay Allen." He pronounced "Leigh" as "Lay." I realized because of the different spellings Lynch thought that "Leigh" and "Lee" were two different suspects in the case. "Lee" was not a new name in the case—just before Zodiac shot a couple out at Blue Rock Springs on the Fourth of July, an unknown man named "Lee" had already been an object of speculation.

"I talked to Leigh at great length several times," said Lynch. "He was up the coast at Bodega Bay [where he had a trailer] . . . he's a skin diver; on that Fourth of July, 1969, he said he was with three or four other guys."

"When did you speak to him—in 1971?" I asked, at first thinking Lynch had been following up Panzarella and Cheney's tip to Manhattan Beach P.D.

"Long before that," he answered. "Within one or two months. Leigh was employed as a janitor at that time at one of the schools here. I went up to the school—I don't know how I got his name in the first place. You know the way things were going then, there were so damn many people to talk to and we were getting so many phone calls and letters and clues. I got so I almost looked at the guy and said, 'That's not him,' to myself. And when I saw this Leigh Allen. He was bald-headed and he's a great big guy. Have you seen him?"

"Yes," I said. Linda Del Buono, Blue Rock Springs victim Darlene Ferrin's sister, had prepared a composite drawing for the Vallejo P.D. "They compared Linda's composite to another Zodiac composite, and told me, 'Everything but the chin was right.' This was supposed to be a profile of a guy named 'Lee' who hung out at Darlene's painting party, the same guy Linda observed harassing her sister while she was waitressing at Terry's Restaurant. Did you ever speak to this 'Lee'?"

"Leigh Allen?"

"I don't know. All Linda knew was the name 'Lee.'"

"No," he said. "Anyway, I was positive it wasn't Allen. The minute I looked at him, I said mentally, 'That isn't Zodiac.' [Vallejo Lieutenant Jim] Husted liked Allen best. I liked him least. I only typed in five to six lines on the report—only in order to get Allen's name in. Checked his car and he had his scuba gear in the back of the car. Real old dirty car."

Lynch explained that on Monday, October 6, 1969, he sought out Allen about the stabbings at Berryessa ten days earlier. Allen, then thirty-five and an occasional student, worked part-time as a custodian at Elmer Cave Elementary School. At 4:05 P.M., Lynch turned south off Tennessee Street onto Vervais. He reached the school at 770 Tregaskis and immediately saw Leigh across the playground. For his report he scrawled this description: "241 pounds and almost six-foot-one." As Lynch observed a few children playing tether ball, an intuitive thought about child molesters entered his head. Allen had been suspected of such crimes and Lynch, and later Mulanax, would wonder if they had missed any obvious signs. Lynch turned his attention from the kids back to the suspect—single, unmarried, and living with his parents. He was well educated and not only a custodian at Cave School, but a janitor at Benjamin Franklin Jr. High School at 501 Starr Avenue, very near a Zodiac victim's home.

They chatted. According to Allen, he had gone skin diving on Salt Point Ranch on September 26, 1969, stayed overnight, and returned to Vallejo on September 27 at approximately 2:00 to 4:30 P.M. "For the remainder of the day," Allen said, "I stayed at home. I don't recall whether my parents were home on that day or not."

"Someone thought you might be the Zodiac killer and reported you," said Lynch matter-of-factly. "Is that a fact," Allen said with a laugh as if such an accusation was an everyday occurrence. He placed his broom against the wall. Lynch looked him up and down. "Well, Zodiac had curly hair," Lynch said, thinking of Linda's description, "and you obviously don't. So that's it."

Had Lynch's visit been a flash point?

Five days after Leigh's reassuring interview with the easygoing Lynch, Zodiac drove to San Francisco, shot Yellow Cab driver Paul Stine, and fled into the Presidio, police dogs nearly at his heels. He ran in the direction of the huge Letterman Complex. There, at a new ten-story Army Medical Center, future Zodiac victim Donna Lass was working that night. She and her roommate, Jo Anne Goettsche, had been in the practice of going flying with two men from Riverside who lived in the San Francisco area. Leigh, of all the suspects, was a pilot.

Seven days after Lynch's questioning, Zodiac dropped the *Chronicle* a line. He enclosed a bloody swatch of the cabbie's shirt to provide irrefutable proof he had murdered Stine. Police speculated Zodiac had switched to a bigger city to garner bigger headlines. But wasn't he simply distancing himself from Vallejo where things had suddenly gotten too hot? Zodiac's intimate knowledge of Vallejo's back roads and lovers' lanes branded him as a longtime resident. Thanks to that bloody swatch Zodiac was now forever identified as a San Francisco killer.

Eighteen days after Leigh spoke with Lynch, William Langdon White, Allen's seventy-three-year-old neighbor, died of heart failure at 9:55 P.M., just after seeing his doctor. White, California-born and a twenty-one-year resident of Vallejo, had lived seven houses down from Leigh's at 45 Fresno. He had been Leigh's alleged alibi for the Berryessa stabbings. "I recall speaking to a neighbor shortly after I drove into my driveway," Leigh had said. "I guess I neglected to tell the Vallejo officer. . . ."

White had also been a possible witness of a bloody knife on Allen's car seat. As a longtime business representative for Butchers' Union Local 532, White logically might have paid attention to any knife. Coincidentally, William White's birthday, December 20, was also the date of the Lake Herman Road shootings. White shared a last name with Sergeant William White, the second ranger to reach the couple Zodiac stabbed at Lake Berryessa.

All through October 1969, Ranger White had been highly visible in a series of television interviews about Zodiac.

"Yes, I talked to [Allen] at great length *several* times," Lynch recalled. "I spoke to him within one or two months of one killing." He now recalled a typed three-by-five card addressed specifically to himself had arrived at the Vallejo P.D. on August 10, 1969. It had gone to the FBI, and he could not recall if it had been returned or not. "Dear Sgt. Lynch," it read. "I hope the enclosed key will prove beneficial to you in connection with the cipher letter writer. [signed] Concerned Citizen." At that time only a Vallejo resident would have known Lynch was handling the then-embryonic Zodiac case. "Concerned" had included a valid key to Zodiac's three-part cipher. The key bore handprinted letters and symbols beginning "A-G-backwards S-L." The FBI reported, "It was a substantially accurate key for decryption of the three-part-cipher mailed by Zodiac." A solution to the cipher was not published in the *Chronicle* until two days later.

In a letter to the *San Francisco Examiner* a week earlier, Zodiac explained he did not leave the scene "with squealling tires and raceing engine as described in the Vallejo papers." This was another indication Zodiac was a Vallejo resident who read the limited circulation local paper. So was his instant reply to Vallejo Police Chief Stiltz's August 1 entreaty for "more details." It would be a considerable time after the oil refinery questioning before Lynch's 110-word report on Allen would be found—sandwiched between FBI Flyers #59 and #4316, and a local tip that went nowhere.

"Another example of a lack of coordination," Vallejo Police Captain Roy Conway lamented many years later. "Sergeant Lynch, a good personal friend of mine who was assigned to the case for a long time, died in the last couple of years. He has a police report that says on a particular date he interviewed Arthur Leigh Allen about his whereabouts on the day of the Berryessa homicide. Which is all well and good, but he doesn't have any recollection whatsoever what information he had that made him interview Arthur Leigh Allen.

"Arthur Leigh Allen told him at that time—it's just one little paragraph in the police report—it doesn't say why he went to see him, what caused him to see him, what conclusions he reached—nothing. Just that 'I interviewed him about what he was doing the

day of the Lake Berryessa killing.' Coincidentally, Leigh had told
Lynch, 'I was on the way to Lake Berryessa that day to go fishing, but I changed my mind and went to the coast.' "

Detective Bawart also agreed with Conway in hindsight.
"There's a lot of instances that occurred in this case that happened in one area and the other area didn't know about it," he
said. "The Vallejo Police Department interviewed Arthur Leigh
Allen in 1969 about the stabbings at Lake Berryessa. The sergeant who did that interview went down and talked to him as he
had talked to probably a hundred other people. Asked him where
he was the day of the Berryessa slaying. He said he had not gone
to Berryessa but up the coast instead. Now we get back and look
at this years later and we go back to this Lynch, a lieutenant retired then—'I don't remember why I was talking to the guy,' he
says. 'Somebody must have called his name in.' He steps back
and says, 'No, I just don't recall.' If we knew who called his
name in, that person must have had some reason for suspecting
that Arthur Leigh Allen was responsible, had something to do
with the case."

County Sheriff's Detective Sergeant Les Lundblad had also
questioned Allen. Someone had tipped him too. This interview
apparently was unknown to the VPD because the Vallejo Sheriff's and Police Departments were separate and independent
forces. The third week after the teenagers out on Lake Herman
Road had been murdered by Zodiac, Lundblad went to see Allen.
The stocky man had an alibi for that Zodiac attack too, one considerably similar to that he would give Lynch. "I was out at Fort
Point near Big Sur scuba diving," he said. After each Zodiac murder, Arthur Leigh Allen had been sought out. He was not such a
new suspect after all. Someone out there knew something, and
who that person was, was as much a mystery as Zodiac's true
identity.

WEDNESDAY, AUGUST 4, 1971

DIRECTLY after speaking with Allen at the refinery, Toschi and
Mulanax decided to follow up on Ted Kidder and Phil Tucker—
the men Allen mentioned he might have shared conversations
with about Zodiac. "I think Allen initially assumed Kidder and

Tucker had tipped the police," Mulanax said. "That's why he volunteered their names so promptly."

"Yeah," said Toschi. "I think you've pegged it. It just took him a bit longer to realize he should have been thinking of Cheney and Panzarella." But a lead was a lead, so the detectives hustled over to the Greater Vallejo Recreation District, where Kidder and Tucker worked. If Allen had predicted Zodiac's coming to Cheney, maybe he had done the same with Kidder or Tucker. Mulanax slid into a spot right in front of 395 Amador Street, and they went inside looking for Kidder. Tucker might be the General Supervisor for the Recreation District, but Kidder was his boss.

"Do you know Arthur Leigh Allen?" Toschi asked Kidder. Kidder's name had appeared on teacher's applications Leigh filed with the Calaveras Unified School District on December 23, 1965, and June 18, 1966.

"Sure," he said.

"Has Leigh ever mentioned the Zodiac case?"

"To my knowledge, I never discussed the case with him. He was formally employed by the Recreation District as a lifeguard and trampoline instructor." Cheney confirmed that sometime later. "Allen was going around teaching kids on the trampoline. He liked that. He was very adept on the trampoline and a remarkable swimmer and diver—a champion on the diving board. He was superb at any athletic activity that did not involve walking or running—Allen was not good at running. At that time, well into his thirties, he was still active, at least with the trampoline, while he was in Valley Springs. He would set it up in the front yard and he loved getting a bunch of kids and coaching them."

Allen left GVRD for the same reason he had left Wogan's station—his inappropriate actions toward small children. "I had received numerous complaints from concerned parents about acts he had made toward their children," said Kidder. "But no formal complaint was ever lodged to the police about Allen's actions, no *formal* complaint anyway. As recently as three weeks ago, Phil Tucker and I had a discussion about Allen being a suspect in the Zodiac murders. This talk came about primarily because of Allen's suspected possibility of being a sexual deviate. That and his physical description. We both considered Allen a loner type."

Had either Kidder or Tucker been the original informant to Lynch and Lundblad? Tucker had reportedly gone to school with

Allen at Cal Poly at San Luis Obispo. He would know more. Toschi asked for Tucker to be summoned to Kidder's office so they could ask him the same questions. Tucker related that he had known Allen about five years. Lieutenant Husted of the VPD later told me more about Tucker. "Tucker and Allen often talked with each other about death and about murder for sale," he said. "I have a 1971 application filled out by Allen for a job as a Rodeo [California] service station attendant, Tucker's name on it. Tucker's name is on all of them. I found it in the margins of one application. Very reliable guy, Tucker."

Tucker confirmed to Toschi that Leigh was equally proficient with both hands and ambidextrous as an adult. This skill with both hands might explain why Leigh's handprinting did not match Zodiac's. Zodiac, a born leftie, was writing with his right hand. "His handwriting is not real good," said Tucker, "and so he prints most things."

"So, Leigh could write and shoot with both hands?" said Toschi.

"Yes," Tucker admitted, then added, "For the last two years, Allen has brought up the Zodiac case in conversation. I feel he has an interest in the case." He sat back and thought. "I remember on one occasion he had told me that police considered him a suspect."

"To your knowledge, did Allen have an interest in guns?" Toschi asked Tucker.

"He said he did have. He owned two handguns. One was a revolver, the other some type of automatic. I don't know the calibers because I don't have much of a knowledge of guns myself. I think the guns in his home might be .22-caliber revolvers, and I saw at least one automatic. I recall that he discussed having a special light attached to a gun barrel so that a person could shoot accurately at night. On more than one occasion he admitted to shooting with special sights for firing in the dark."

Toschi rubbed the back of his neck. Another portion of Cheney's story had been corroborated. It was even hotter.

"Another time, about eighteen months ago," continued Tucker, "my wife and I visited Leigh in his home. He made a remark that he had something he would like to show us. 'I only show this particular thing to very certain people,' he said. Or something to that effect. He then took a paper from a gray metal box he had gotten from his bedroom. This paper was handprinted and contained several pages of legal terminology and several pages of letters which had symbols or codes or cryptograms on them. He said they pertained to a person who had been committed to Atascadero for molesting a child. This paper rambled on and on in language of a legal nature, that sort of terminology, this and that. It was about this person having been betrayed by his attorney. I noticed in this script there were various symbols used by Zodiac in his coded messages."

Toschi nodded. He didn't find it unusual that Tucker could recognize the symbols as Zodiac-like. The killer's three-part cipher had been widely reprinted. On June 29, 1970, the approximate time of Tucker's visit, the *Chronicle* had published a new Zodiac two-line cipher. "I only expressed polite interest in the paper," said Tucker, "but my wife showed genuine interest. She found the symbols or codes or cryptograms unusual. She asked him if she might borrow the paper to study it, but he refused to allow her to take the paper. He did promise to have a copy made to give her."

"And did he?" asked Toschi.

"No, he never did."

"Do you know if Allen has ever owned a 1965–'66 brown Corvair?"

"Not to my knowledge," he replied.

"I see," said Toschi.

"But I did," said Tucker.

"You did?" said Toschi, wheeling. "You owned a 1965 brown Corvair?"

"Yes."

"Did you ever loan this car to Allen?"

"No, I haven't. At the time I had two cars, the Corvair and the Pontiac. I let him use my Pontiac on occasion. I was living in Berkeley at that time. In the summer of 1969 I left the Corvair parked at the Richfield Service Station at Nebraska and Broadway [in Vallejo] for about two weeks. I was trying to sell it. I left the keys at the station and at this particular time Allen was employed as an attendant at that station."

"Exactly when in the summer did you leave your car?"

"I can't recall the exact time, but it was mid-summer of 1969."

Tucker recollected that three weeks prior, Karen, Leigh Allen's sister-in-law, had visited and wanted him to speak to Allen on her behalf. "The family had gotten another complaint about his recent involvement with a child," Tucker said. "I went to Allen's home and spoke to him about resuming psychiatric treatment. However, I was unsuccessful and so I washed my hands of him. I told him, 'I don't want you to come around my home in the future. Our association is at an end.' "

Toschi studied his Timex, anxious to compare notes with Armstrong. He visualized his partner equally anxious to get on his motorbike and take to the suburban dirt trails, the warm sun in his face. The rugged trail would rattle the cobwebs from his head. On weekends, as a diversion from stress, Armstrong focused on salvaging his perpetually wilting backyard garden. As for Mulanax, he was as fired up as he had been days ago. Now he was interested in contacting Mrs. Tucker as soon as possible. He wanted to see what she recalled about the printing inside the gray box. He rang her from Kidder's office, and learned she was working the graveyard shift at an Oakland hospital. That meeting would have to be postponed. Instead, Mulanax decided to speak with Allen's sister-in-law, Karen Allen, a twenty-six-year-old former schoolteacher. Mulanax phoned Karen at her job and arranged to have her come into the Vallejo P.D. She arrived promptly at 2:00 P.M. and took a seat.

"Let me tell you why I asked you in," Mulanax said. On the surface, Karen seemed surprised that her brother-in-law was suspected of being the long-sought Zodiac killer, but offered to give whatever help she could. Mulanax wondered if she could be the original tipster. He confirmed that Karen knew of Allen's preoccupation with children. She stated another thing positively—her brother-in-law hated women. "He has never had a serious relationship with a female of his own age," she said. Sandy Panzarella had voiced similar remarks. "Leigh just pretended to be interested in women," he said. "Eventually he gave up even that slender pretext." Various women Leigh had dated afterward voiced the same opinion—their relationship with him had only been platonic. In most cases sexual psychopaths have few social or sexual affiliations, and might never have experienced normal sexual intercourse. In these uncommon individuals, for reasons unknown, aggressive and sexual impulses intertwine early in childhood. Ultimately, these confused feelings find expression in vicious sexual assaults and sadistic murders. Lacking a conscience, Zodiac had no remorse for the pain he inflicted on others. Their pain brings him pleasure.

Karen disclosed that, after her marriage to Ron, it became apparent that Leigh viewed her as an intruder. He believed she had come to separate him from his brother, and actually made threats against her. "He was spoiled and pampered by his mother," she said with a trace of bitterness. "She does his cooking, washes his clothes, cleans up after him, and gives him money. She even paid for his two cars and two boats." It was odd that Allen intensely disliked his mother no matter what she did for him, and even stranger that he had expressed such feelings to Karen, whom he viewed as an interloper.

As for Bernice Allen, she had never forgotten her son's squandered Olympic potential. Leigh had been a talented diver. "She's always ragging me about my weight," he had snarled to Cheney and Panzarella. A competition photo of him in a Vallejo paper depicted a slender, almost handsome young man with blondish hair. Other pictures from the 1960s showed how much he resembled the younger, unamended San Francisco Zodiac composite drawing. If Leigh had not been steadily gaining weight, he would have been a dead ringer for the sketch. Allen's altered appearance reminded Mulanax of a line Zodiac had written:

> "I look like the description passed out only when I do my thing, the rest of the time I look entirle different. I shall not tell you what my discise [disguise] consists of when I kill."

Mulanax passed copies of Zodiac's bizarre notes to Karen. She studied them and said she had noticed a paper with similar printing in her brother-in-law's hand in November 1969. "What is that?" she had asked. "This is the work of an insane person," Leigh replied. "I'll show you later." As with the Tuckers, he never did. However, while the printing on the Zodiac letters was not familiar to her as being that of her brother-in-law, some phrases were. Leigh had used the expression "trigger mach" instead of trigger mechanism. Finally, she thumbed to a copy of an authenticated Christmas card Zodiac had mailed to attorney Melvin Belli during a period when the master criminal wanted to give himself up.

An FBI report, December 31, 1969, noted the note had "not been written as freely as the other threatening letters in this matter." However, an enclosed blood-blackened portion of a victim's shirt validated it. Zodiac's handwriting *was* subject to change and in the space of months. At 1:59 P.M. the following day, a man identifying himself as Zodiac called the switchboard operator at FBI headquarters in Sacramento, then hung up after beginning to name someone he had just killed. " 'Happy Christmass,' " Karen read aloud from the photostat. "I definitely recall having received a card at Christmas from my brother-in-law," she said. " 'Happy Christmass' was spelled exactly the same way."

Karen, like Tucker, confirmed Allen was left-handed. "His elementary school teachers attempted to make him right-handed," she said. "He learned to write that way, but soon reverted to writing with his left hand." While Morrill believed the letters were written right-handed, he suspected that Zodiac was naturally left-handed. The obscuring effect of a felt-tip pen and a left-handed man printing firmly and unnaturally with his right hand might explain the difficulty in matching handprinting to any suspect. Sergeant Mulanax was hungry to learn more.

"Could I drop by tonight when your husband will be home?" he said. "We want to ask him some questions too." Ronald Gene Allen, a thirty-two-year-old landscape engineer, was currently attending Berkeley College. He had attended Cal Poly from fall 1960 until fall 1968, when he attained a bachelor of science degree. "He'll be late," she said, but agreed that 8:00 P.M. would be convenient. After she left, Mulanax contacted Armstrong and Toschi and asked them to rendezvous with him at 216 Aragon Street in Vallejo that night. An already long day was growing longer.

Mulanax reached the home first. It was just off Columbus Parkway, which led directly into Blue Rock Springs to the north. He suspected Zodiac had used the parkway as an escape route after the July Fourth shootings. Mulanax stood in the deep shadows of the pleasant tree-lined cul-de-sac. Somewhere in his cozy little town, the most cunning criminal he had ever come across was waiting. A cool wind blew in from San Pablo Bay. He scanned the hedges and fences, unable to shake thoughts of a watcher. Fifteen minutes later, Toschi and Armstrong reached Ron and Karen's home and found Mulanax already inside and glad to be in the light.

As Karen had done, Ron offered to help in the investigation if he could. Mulanax believed his offer to be sincere. "But I can't believe my brother is a serious suspect in the case," he said. At first, he offered little on either side of the scale as to his brother's guilt or innocence. "I am well acquainted with your source of information." So, thought Toschi, the informants, Cheney and Panzarella, had spoken with Ron before the Manhattan Beach P.D. He did not know that Cheney and Ron had been roommates in college. "They are responsible people," the brother admitted. "They wouldn't have made such statements if they were not true." He also explained that he had received a complaint from one of the informants that Allen had made improper advances toward one of his children. "He has a definite problem as far as children are concerned and he does drink to excess." Though Ron didn't say so outright, Mulanax reserved the possibility that a personal motive might be behind some of the accusations against Allen. That would explain many things and it would mean they were on the wrong track. Few serial killers drank to excess. It had something to do with the lack of control.

Ron confirmed that Allen's two revolvers were .22-caliber. Zodiac had used a .22-caliber automatic pistol during the Lake Herman Road homicides, but from then on had used various 9-mm automatics, a .45-caliber weapon, and even a knife. Though Ron had never seen any of the handprinting Tucker had mentioned, he had observed the gray box. At one point it, he recalled, had been kept in his old room.

"Ron and his wife were very cooperative," Toschi said later. "What I heard is that he [Allen] was not close to his mother, that he just lived in the house, that's the only place he had. Allen, we learned afterward, had many weapons and, like the brother said, was very familiar with the roads and side roads all around the area. Later, Karen just felt that her brother-in-law was the one we were looking for and that Vallejo P.D. kind of just kissed him off, and that disturbed me. We had to work with these other detectives, and it bothered me that they felt we were the big-city detectives when in fact we never came across that way at all."

The three policemen left. Ron followed them out and promised again to do anything he could to assist. He was as helpful as his big brother had been at the refinery that morning. Toschi looked back. Ron appeared a lonely and worried figure under the porch light. It was now 10:00 P.M. Toschi reached his Sunset District home soon after, kissed Carol good night, looked in on his three daughters, Linda, Karen, and Susan, and crawled into bed. Every bone in his body ached and cried for sleep, but he tossed and turned all night. He could not get that watch out of his mind. And a neighbor had seen a bloody knife, dying only days after glimpsing the blade.

WEDNESDAY, AUGUST 11, 1971

AT 11:00 A.M., Mulanax got hold of Bob Luce, owner-operator of the Arco station at 640 Broadway in Vallejo. Mulanax told Luce, "I'm conducting an investigation on a former employee." He did not tell him why right off.

"Leigh worked for me on a part-time schedule for about half a year," Luce explained, "but tended to be undependable. And there were those complaints about him and children . . . he seemed too interested in small girls. In April [1969] he came to work drunk again—once too often for me. I fired him." Mulanax wondered if the job loss had precipitated the July 4, 1969, Blue Rock Springs shootings by Zodiac. Mulanax laid his cards on the table. This was unusual. "I knew Mulanax pretty well," Bawart told me. "Mulanax was a kind of a close-to-the-vest guy."

Mulanax brought up the possibility that Allen might have used Phil Tucker's car to commit a Zodiac murder. "Tucker had his car here all right, but it wasn't for as long as two weeks," Luce said. "No, that's not right." Tucker himself hadn't kept a record of the dates, and Mulanax badly needed Luce's repair invoice. In spite of a diligent search, they could not uncover the exact days the Corvair had been left overnight at the station. On the July 4, 1969, date of the Blue Rock Springs shootings, Allen was no longer working at the Arco station, and so the repair record didn't matter—unless Leigh had kept a set of keys to the station or made his own.

At 5:00 that evening, Mulanax contacted Tucker's wife, Joan, at her home. Joan substantiated her husband's story about the gray box and the papers tucked inside. "I had been very interested in the content of the papers," she said, "since I was preparing for a college psychology exam. Leigh explained he had received these papers from a patient at Atascadero, and I said my interest was directed toward the working of this person's mind. I was impressed by the neatness and exactness of the printing and of the arcane symbols."

The detective showed her Zodiac ciphers clipped from three Bay Area papers. Joan identified numerous symbols as being the same as those on papers Allen had showed her. Her recollection was that these were drawn with a felt-tip pen. At 5:30 Tucker returned from work and Mulanax showed him the same cryptograms. He too thought certain symbols looked the same as those Allen had shown him.

"And we still haven't been able to track down the exact date you left your Corvair at the Arco station," said Mulanax.

"I didn't have any luck either," Tucker said, "but I do remember that when my car was not sold, I left it parked in front of my father-in-law's house for a considerable period of time. It's possible that Allen could have driven the car during this period, but I don't know if he did. My in-laws are in Europe now, and when they get back I'll ask them if they know." The in-laws knew Leigh Allen as a friend of their son-in-law, and would not have thought it strange to see him around the Corvair. Tucker began to speak more freely of his former employee.

"Leigh is a schizophrenic personality," Tucker said. During Leigh's therapy five different personalities had been found. "At times he actually seems to live the part of whatever literature he's reading. He can tell a lie and actually believe what he is telling is the truth." Mulanax's eyebrows went up. This was a very interesting talent—one that might stand a lie detector on its head. Once more Mulanax heard that Allen truly hated women and had said so on many occasions. No one hated women as much as Zodiac. The only victims that had managed to survive had been men.

THURSDAY, AUGUST 12, 1971

IN the morning Mulanax typed up his reports and studied the various stories related to him about the best Zodiac suspect yet. Physically, Leigh matched Zodiac—from hair coloring to weight to height to wearing the exact size of the killer's unique flight-line Wing Walker boots. Circumstantial evidence was compelling: Leigh had predicted he would call himself "Zodiac" and shoot couples in lovers' lanes long before there was a Zodiac. He had spoken of an "electric gun sight" and "picking off kiddies," used phrases like "Happy Christmass," and "trigger mach" before Zodiac had. Allen wore a Zodiac wristwatch and kept Zodiac-like symbols in a gray box. Like Zodiac, he was enamored of "The Most Dangerous Game." He had been headed for

Lake Berryessa the day of the stabbings and been seen with a bloody knife. Mulanax did not know that Allen and his former friend, Don Cheney, had often fly-fished at Clear Lake and Grass Valley, and once at Berryessa. "We fished in a stream below the lake and fifty yards from where we parked," he later told me. "It was crowded the one time we went." Not only did Leigh have friends in those areas, a man and a woman at Clear Lake, for instance, but there had been a recent murder at all three.

Meanwhile, at the refinery, Allen was in a rage—because of the questioning, he was certain he would be fired from his job at Union Oil. When McNamara had called him into his office, Leigh had known his days there were numbered.

FRIDAY, AUGUST 13, 1971

AFTER the two authenticated letters in March, all correspondence from Zodiac had ceased. Police in four counties speculated Zodiac might have been arrested for another crime, institutionalized, or died. Nonetheless, Mulanax continued to plow through the files. For just over a week he had been seeking a record of any officer questioning Leigh Allen back in 1969. Sergeant Lynch had not yet recalled questioning Leigh. His meeting at Cave School with the skin-diving chemist consumed only two paragraphs in the center of a single page. As the towering sheaves of paper became an avalanche, that page was buried in an ever-increasing snowbank. Manpower stretched to the breaking point, and everyone feared Zodiac might strike again.

WEDNESDAY, SEPTEMBER 1, 1971

THE SFPD fared scarcely better than Vallejo. Armstrong and Toschi, routinely working six murders simultaneously, felt at times that the Bay Area held a franchise on homicidal maniacs. Toschi, in spite of once being a fitness instructor, was subject to bouts of illness from stress. He was a contradiction—he was modest, but enjoyed the limelight. Some nights he slipped on his all-weather raincoat and Hush Puppies, then strolled, head down, through his Sunset neighborhood. Other nights he took long drives down the coast highway, or slumped in his easy chair listening to Big Band 78s in stereo. As he desperately tried to sort it all out, he recalled that exactly eleven years ago today Chief Tom Cahill had signed his transfer to the Bureau of Inspectors. It had been the second happiest day of his life.

FRIDAY, SEPTEMBER 17, 1971

ARMSTRONG and Toschi later ascertained from Ron Allen that his brother spent at least two days a week at their mother's home. Allen's mother, Bernice, traveled abroad frequently, her trips spanning many weeks. These excursions, arranged through the Vallejo Travel Club, were financed by pension money from Leigh's recently deceased father. During his mother's absence, Allen would reside alone at the family residence. Though the upstairs was free to him, he still clung, leechlike, to that dank, unkempt basement bedroom where the secret box had been stored. It was as if he were guarding a fortress.

However, Bernice had been ill and remained home. Out of respect for her, the police held back from searching her home. Allen was, after all, only one of nearly three thousand Zodiac suspects. "We were always concerned about his elderly mother who was not well," Toschi told me. "The family had mentioned it several times and asked us not to go in. The brother is telling us, 'I can search the basement myself. I know where he keeps things especially when he's away.' Jack Mulanax never wanted to talk seriously about a search warrant. He had been turned down on handprinting and on fingerprints. He just said, 'He sure looks good, but I don't even know if I could get a search warrant.'"

"We did not search the residence of his mother at 32 Fresno Street in Vallejo," wrote Armstrong later. "We relied on his brother, Ron, who was cooperating with the investigation, to look through Allen's room in the basement of this residence. . . . Ron had informed us that he had observed some cryptogram-type materials, but was unsure if they were related to Zodiac. No further action was taken regarding a search of 32 Fresno and the basement there."

Whoever Zodiac was, he had a cellar where he did his secret and devilish work. "What you do not know," he said in a November 9, 1969, letter to the *Chronicle*, "is whether the death machine is at the sight or whether it is being stored in my basement for further use." Police, dumbfounded by the bizarre threats of the "death machine" letter, said at the time, "We have reason to believe he's a maniac. It appears to us that he's killing just for the thrill of killing." On April 20, 1970, Zodiac complained he had been "swamped out by the rain we had a while back." Rain might flood a basement room. A burst pipe or water heater would cause a similar inundation. No one checked to see if the house on Fresno Street had been flooded. But what if Zodiac had not meant a proper basement? Mobile-home dwellers call the area beneath the trailer a "basement." While it is illegal to store things there, it is done all the time. Sometimes a rain puddle on the road becomes a swamp under a trailer. Leigh had a trailer off-wheels in another county, and for over a year had been squirreling away things under it. The problem was that Toschi and Armstrong were not only unaware of the trailer's location, but its existence.

"Allen's got to have someplace where he can stash and hide things and be certain no cop will ever know where he has everything," Mulanax told Toschi.

"What he's going to show us is just things on the surface," replied Toschi. "And we know that he's laughing at us on the inside."

Mulanax nodded.

MONDAY, NOVEMBER 22, 1971

LEIGH was approved for his Red Cross Certificate for Standard First Aid. Since he was constantly boating in a sailing club, and considering taking up air jumping over water, it was a useful skill. Meanwhile in San Francisco, Toschi and Armstrong had made scant progress in the three and a half months since the questioning at the oil refinery. "Apparently," Toschi told me, "Allen's family still harbored grave misgivings about him. The brother and sister-in-law were very concerned because they see that Allen is still walking around and don't know how thoroughly the Vallejo Police Department went into the investigation. What we didn't know was that they were building up courage to speak to us.

"I could always tell Ken Narlow was a little disturbed because San Francisco was getting all the big play in the media. We were getting more work too. Which we didn't need. But it was because

Armstrong and I were getting so much media attention that Ron and Karen later felt right in calling us. And it put me in a very precarious position. I didn't want anyone thinking we were trying to monopolize the case. My God, we had enough work to do on our own without making more work out of another jurisdiction. We were getting so many tips and phone calls just from San Francisco. People calling him 'the *San Francisco* Zodiac killer,' when there're multi-counties involved. Zodiac came to us for more attention. He wanted to see his name there." More than once Toschi wondered, "Why?"

The situation was worse than on the surface. Every three weeks Toschi and Armstrong also had a load of brand-new homicides to crack. Unknown to them, at that time, Allen was no longer in Vallejo. The morning of November 22, he had traveled south to Torrance, where Don Cheney lived, perhaps for a confrontation. Long after, I asked Cheney, "Do you have any idea why Leigh visited Torrance on November 22, 1971?" There was a gasp of surprise. "If I had known about it at the time, it would have worried me," Cheney said. "And yet, though I was always listed down in Southern California, I never got one crank phone call or threat after police interviewed Leigh."

TUESDAY, NOVEMBER 23, 1971

PANZARELLA never realized Allen was in Torrance. Even if he had, it wouldn't have mattered. Panzarella was a cool customer. He hadn't been scared when Zodiac wrote the *L.A. Times,* even though he suspected Allen was the author. While he was in town, Leigh got into enough mischief on Hawthorne Boulevard to be arrested for disturbing the peace. Cheney still considered Zodiac's connections to unknown murders in Southern California as possible and Zodiac's connection to Allen as "very probable." Though Allen had ties to the area, most of his movements down south were a mystery, at least to the police.

WEDNESDAY, NOVEMBER 24, 1971

AT times the Vallejo P.D. had a sense that the SFPD was trying to freeze them out and collar Zodiac all by themselves. "Vallejo is small potatoes compared to San Francisco," Detective Bawart told me, "but when you take a look at the homicide division in San Francisco, they're like anything else in police work. They divide up all the murder cases. One homicide detective there is working about the same amount of cases as one homicide detective in Vallejo. It's grueling."

And in San Francisco, Toschi was equally unsure he was getting everything Vallejo knew. "My thoughts were," he explained, "when they would say, 'Well, we talked to this person and that person,' my mind was always like a minute ahead. I was saying to myself, 'Did you really?' Because when I said I talked to somebody, you can bet all your good money on it I did. I would never lie about that." He began to fear the Zodiac information highway might be a one-way street. And that was just the way Zodiac liked it. The killer preferred to strike in zones of confused jurisdiction—different counties, on borderlines, and in unincorporated wilderness areas. He counted on adjoining departments working against each other, not sharing information—the more the merrier. It was a big case, a competitive investigation. Everyone wanted a piece of it and whoever solved it would be the Ace of Detectives. Zodiac, with his huge ego, counted on the egos of policemen to allow him to continue his deadly work.

Armstrong and Toschi could not get Leigh Allen off their minds, and sought to jump-start their investigation. They needed another tip. After such a promising beginning, Toschi studied the growing face of the moon. He could almost hear Zodiac's laughter—the laughter of Satan. And the rustle of that terrible black costume.

4
ARTHUR LEIGH ALLEN

ARTHUR LEIGH ALLEN, born in Honolulu, Hawaii, December 18, 1933, was a Sagittarius (November 22–December 21). His zodiac sign was The Archer, and he became an expert with a bow and arrow. While Zodiac wore glasses, possibly as a disguise, Leigh rarely did (though the DMV required he wear lenses to drive). In 1964 Leigh weighed 185 pounds, but within three years his weight had ballooned drastically. The photo on his driver's license [#3B672352], taken on October 13, 1967, depicted a moonfaced thirty-three-year-old whose weight now yoyoed between 230 and 250 pounds. Allen, in 1967, listed his address simply as a post office box in Burson.

As for Leigh's checkered educational record, he truly was a "professional student." He attended Vallejo Senior High School, which shared the same building on Amador Street as the junior college. Across the street at 801 Nebraska Street stood The Plunge, a Vallejo community swimming center also shared by high school and junior college students. There, a slender, good-looking Allen, a member of the wrestling team, toiled at the pool as a popular lifeguard from 1950 through his graduation in 1951 and a short time after. "Leigh was a hell of a diver," one student recalled, "and drove a Cadillac." Allen, during this period, became intensely jealous of his friend, Robert Emmett, who was not only captain of the Vallejo High School swimming team, but Leigh's diving coach.

"I knew Leigh my last two years of high school and part of my junior college year," his close friend, Kay, told me. "I lived in Carquinez and my folks, about that time, bought a house in town and I became a 'townie.' My dad worked as a fireman, then at Mare Island. Leigh started offering me a lift to and from school and soon was taking any number of our friends in his Cadillac. In fact, I learned to change my first tire on that car. Leigh came out of the house one time from visiting. He says, 'Kay, have you ever changed a flat before?' 'No,' I said. 'Well, there's no time like the present,' he said, then sat and supervised.

"Other times we'd go to the pool. Leigh going up the ladder for a high dive would cause laughter because he was built sort of pear-shaped and he would go up the ladder like a woman would. There would be a lot of snickering in the crowd. And so he would walk to the end of the board like he was going to make his dive. He called it a 'Change Your Mind Dive.' He would go up, hit the board, turn and do a back flip, landing back on the board as if he had had second thoughts. Then he would suddenly shoot up in a two and a half forward somersault, cutting the water below without a ripple. That gymnastic dive got the crowd's attention fast. They didn't laugh anymore! He could also start a front dive, do it backing up from the board and end up doing a back dive, but that was really hard and he missed that quite often.

"Leigh cut quite a figure with his Cadillac, his trick dives, his white dog, Frosty, and Petunia, a skunk who was *not* de-scented. What he really liked to talk about with me was music and plays, anything from comedy to farce, mysteries to Gilbert and Sullivan." Kay assumed Leigh was gay as he rarely dated. When he did go out, he brought along his father. "Leigh would give a call and we'd take off to the movies together," she recalled, "Leigh's father was very gracious and took me to symphonies and plays with them. I knew the father from '53 through '56, a very, very gentle man. I met Leigh's mother only a couple of times. She never made herself visible. I saw her at swim meets. I liked to go and look at the guys. Leigh was extremely intelligent, almost scary sometimes. He was a bright fellow, but his brother Ron was the golden boy. His mother wouldn't have much to do with Leigh. I wasn't ever privy to the fights, but I was privy to the cold shoulders. Commander Allen would ask her if she wanted to go along with us and she'd snap, 'Why?' Sometimes Ron went with us and I would have thought she would have been glad to go. Sometimes Leigh spoke of a girl named Bobbie who had 'broken his heart.' Bobbie was Leigh's first big love, and he used to just talk in glowing colors about her. She was the love of his life."

Bobbie's daughter later told me of her mother's friendship with Leigh Allen. "She was a diver whose picture often appeared in Vallejo papers in the sports section between 1952 to 1957," she said. "Sometimes Allen's picture was alongside hers in the paper.

I think he was a platform diver and a wrestler. Very clumsy walk when walking down the diving board, he looked terrible until he left the board and dove. Then he was very graceful. But when walking he was terribly lumbering. He had a funny hip. In case you don't already know." Harold Huffman, Leigh's childhood friend, thought Leigh's fluctuating weight caused the limp.

Leigh attended Vallejo Junior College, majoring in the liberal arts, and became All-American Diving Champ there. On September 18, 1954, he enrolled at California Polytechnic State University at San Luis Obispo. During the 1950s and 1960s Cal Poly San Luis Obispo was affiliated with Cal Poly Pomona, where Don Cheney, Sandy Panzarella, and Leigh's brother, Ron, studied. Leigh's pal, Harold Huffman, was already down there attending USC and coaching every sport he could. For awhile Leigh had difficulty choosing between an engineering or physical education major. Since his math skills proved too meager for engineering, he decided to focus on physical education. Ultimately, he settled on elementary education as his major. On June 16, 1956, at the end of his term, he used his summer break to enlist in the Navy.

He received his associate of arts degree from Vallejo Junior College in 1957. He returned to Cal Poly from January 1959 until June 13, 1959, and excelled. He became the State College Trampoline Champion for Central California and Central California Spear Fishing Champ. On July 27, 1959, Allen applied at the State Department of Education in Sacramento for a position, but by January 4, 1960, was back studying at San Luis Obispo. He remained until June 1960, when he began work at Hemet Mental Hospital only twenty miles from Riverside. One good thing had resulted from his brief Navy stint—he was able to study on the G.I. Bill at Cal Poly from January 1961 until March 1961.

On June 19, 1961 he applied at the State Personnel Board in Sacramento as a psychiatric technical trainee, Department of Mental Hygiene, and briefly became a psychiatric teacher at Atascadero. There he became friendly with a convicted murderer who had been jailed for several years. He later said they exchanged samples of code. Allen graduated from Cal Poly with a bachelor's in education (B.E.) on December 15, 1961. Only six units shy of a master's degree, he seemed unable to finally sever his ties with college life. During this time, he owned hunting rifles, at least two .22-caliber pistols, and, true to his Zodiac sign of Sagittarius, a hunting bow and arrows.

From 1959 to 1963, Leigh, still in the process of obtaining his teaching credentials, had various jobs. He taught fourth grade and P.E. at Santa Rosa School in Atascadero just north of Cal Poly. "I really enjoyed teaching elementary school kids," he said. "My kids did well—one little girl in the third grade knew tenth-grade math by the time she graduated. My entire class could read at seventh-grade level. I sure loved working with elementary school kids."

Meanwhile, Panzarella, Cheney, and Leigh's brother, Ron, were attending the Cal Poly campus in Pomona together. Panzarella's major field of study was electronic engineering, Cheney's was mechanical engineering, and Ron's, landscape architecture. They shared a rented house to cut costs. "In 1961–1962," Cheney afterward told me, "we all were living in a four-bedroom house with two students named Bill and Joe. We had two guys in the one larger bedroom—Ron and I slept there. Those were good times.

"Ron had a good sense of humor, he was entertaining and a fun guy. Everyone liked him. He was a very easygoing guy and a notorious underachiever. He was very well laid back. He was brilliant in his landscape architecting work at school, but he didn't keep his grade point average up. He passed some courses, but not with flying colors, so he had to stay at Cal Poly for quite a while so that he could get his average up to graduate. He would do very well in other courses, but he could never get around to taking the final. He dragged on and on. He never made it to early morning classes. He had an alarm clock—one of those Big Bens with the great big gongs on the top of it—that thing would ring, would run down and stop ringing, and he wouldn't twitch.

"Cal Poly Pomona was about two miles away to the west, and I rode a bike to school each day. Sandy graduated in the spring of 1964, but I never actually graduated. I should have graduated in the winter of 1964. I finished up and had a problem with my senior project and I wimped out on that, didn't do it.

"That house is where Sandy and I first met Leigh. It was 1962. I was still single then, and married Ann later that year. I remember that one time especially. Leigh had just rolled in there from Riverside. He had been attending sports car racing. He went every year for the big race they held down there in the early summer. I went with Ron and Leigh together one time. In fact, the only sporting events Leigh and I went to together were road racing. He frequented Laguna Seca, Vacaville, and Riverside. He was a student there. Leigh owned an Austin Healey and used to go to a driving school in Riverside; after taking those lessons he kept commuting down there for the races."

FRIDAY, MAY 30, 1963

LEIGH Allen paid an unexpected visit to the house in Southern California. "I remember Leigh came down to visit us," Panzarella told me. "Leigh was not living in the Pomona area, but had just come down to Pomona that weekend. I thought it was odd at the time. And he had a machete in the car. For no particular reason, he walked in without a word and slammed it into the counter and tried to scare everybody. One of my roommates, Joe Dandurand, was there. My ex-wife was there when it happened. Ron was somewhere in the house. That was just before I left at the end of the semester and Ron and I went and got a place together in Walnut. I still think about Leigh coming to Pomona to visit just before the boy and girl were murdered. That's creepy."

MONDAY, JUNE 3, 1963

IN the morning, Leigh curtailed his visit and started back to Atascadero, where Santa Rosa Elementary School was closing for the summer. He intended to pack up, then return to Vallejo that day. Heading north on Highway 101, on a direct line to Atascadero, he climbed from Ventura to Santa Barbara, passing Goleta, then El Capitan Beach, and closing on Refugio Beach. The Santa Ynez Mountains loomed to the northeast, and further east and far beyond—Los Padres National Forest. Sand blew across the divided blacktop and gulls wheeled in the sky. In places the north and south lanes were neighborly, running side by side with each other, but in spots they widened away. A gray mist swept in from the sea. "They've got me searching my memory for blank spots, for lapses," Allen would say years later. Ahead he saw a turnout, just at the point where 101 leaves the beach. His eyes strayed over the divide to 101 southbound. Beyond was the beach. He was now three miles south of the Gaviota Tunnel.

5
ROBERT DOMINGOS AND
LINDA EDWARDS

MONDAY, JUNE 3, 1963

THREE miles south of the Gaviota Tunnel, an attractive teenage couple, Robert George Domingos and Linda Faye Edwards, swung onto an oak-lined turnout just off southbound 101. Domingos pulled his gray Pontiac over and the laughing couple piled out, radiant in their youth and promise. They had left home, ostensibly for a Lompoc High School seniors' "Ditch Day" graduation party. Instead, the couple intended celebrating at the seashore. Thick bushes hid their car from passing northbound traffic. However, any auto cruising southbound could spot the vehicle, an indication someone was down on the isolated beach.

Robert was the eighteen-year-old son of a well-to-do Lompoc rancher; Linda was to be eighteen in three days. For both it had been a day of farewell and anticipation as they looked forward to their nuptials in October. The teenagers were roughly twenty miles west of Santa Barbara and three miles from El Capitan Beach. Robert dug a large blanket from the trunk, and the couple crossed the highway and over railroad tracks running between them and a low bluff. From the bluff, one of the chain of unstable sea cliffs tracing the shoreline, they had a view of the mile-and-a-half-long state beach below. Beyond stood the Channel Islands—San Miguel, Santa Rosa, and Santa Cruz. Robert and Linda commenced down a steep, partially hidden path to the beach, running the last twenty yards. Banana palm trees lining Refugio Creek gave the area a tropical atmosphere. Where the creek flowed into the ocean, a freshwater lagoon had formed.

Robert and Linda reached an isolated spot frequented only by the occasional local fisherman. They saw evidence of recent activity. Long ago this beach had been the chief *contrabandista* port on the coast, visited by genteel smugglers and ferocious pirates. At the mouth of the canyon, buried in the sand, lay traces of an ancient adobe foundation. In early California days a grand rancho, La Nuestara Señora del Refugio, stood there. It faced the sea boldly until the French pirate Hyppolyte de Bouchard—by gun, by knife, by rope, and by fire—put an end to that. His buccaneers wounded the servants, cut the throats of the horses, tied up the Ortega family, and burned their impressive hacienda.

The teenagers spread out their blanket on the sand near the rocky shoreline. The day before, at just the same spot, a man with reddish hair had been shooting at seagulls with a rifle. Rich tide pools, swarming with life, moved with each surge of salt water. Spray exploded against black rocks, and the sharp tang of sea air filled the teenagers' lungs. Sailboats danced in Santa Barbara Channel, and in the sky aircraft droned lazily—an airport was nearby. The laughing pair lounged in their swimsuits at the surf line as the day passed and the sky clouded over. Of all transitional domains, those between sea and land are the most disparate and prone to alteration. Robert and Linda grew drowsy, barely aware of the boom of the waves and wavelets rustling eel grasses at the sea edge. The crack of a twig on the path made them start. The lowering sun flashing off the water and gusts of sand blinded them. They drew back as a squarish shadow fell upon the sand. Peering up, they saw a man leveling a .22-caliber rifle at them.

By Rope—He barked orders. First came fumbling attempts to tie them—the man had brought along precut lengths of narrow cotton clothesline. First he coerced Linda to bind Robert. She had tied a loosely knotted length around his wrist, and was still clinching a rope in her hand when the stranger knelt. With trembling fingers, he began to finish the tying himself—first with a few granny knots and then marline hitches, a knot not commonly used by laymen. In the midst of this, Robert and Linda leaped to their feet and plunged into the steep creek bed leading uphill from the blanket. The couple tried to run in the soft sand of the creek bed. They lurched in the general direction of a shack, which had been barely visible from the blanket.

By Gun—The interloper thundered after them, firing on the run. Slugs ripped into the young man first, hitting him in the back as he ran screaming for help. There was no one to hear them. The bullets were closely grouped, astonishing accuracy for shooting while moving. Robert dropped face down. The stranger then swung the rifle toward Linda, firing into her back. He approached slowly until he stood over the couple. He pumped more bullets into the boy's back, striking him in all eleven times. Linda had fallen onto her back, and so a fusillade of bullets penetrated her chest. Altogether, she was hit eight times.

The killer's viciousness had not abated as he continued to inflict injuries upon the corpses. Dragging Robert face down by his legs away from the shoreline, he left welts and abrasions just above the boy's surfer's trunks. Rocks scraped his chest and face, leaving deep contusions. The stranger was sweating by the time he completed the first part of his gruesome task—hiding the corpse in the woodpile shelter by the nearly dry creek bed. The primitive structure lay halfway between the shore and the railroad embankment. Almost lost among dense shrubs and trees, it was used mostly by transients.

By Knife—He returned to the woman, cut down the front of her swimsuit with a knife, and exposed her breasts. He slashed her body, the wounds describing a curved river. Next, he dragged her feet-first to the shack, and because Linda was supine, all the abrasions were to her back and buttocks. After pulling her inside the lean-to, he ripped off her swimsuit and tossed it callously over her fiancé. Then he draped Linda's body, face up, over the boy.

By Fire—Now the stranger looked around for things to burn. He gathered up his leftover lengths of rope and empty cartridge boxes and tossed them into the shack. Smashing the lean-to, he ignited it with wooden matches he had brought along. A funeral pyre would hide all traces of his crime. Although he tried several times, the structure refused to catch, or he might have returned to his car on the road above believing that everything behind him was blazing.

TUESDAY, JUNE 4, 1963

WHEN Linda and Robert failed to return, Domingos's father filed a missing persons report. The Santa Barbara Sheriff's Department issued an all-points bulletin. The father, along with other family members, joined the search party, and that night located the missing boy's car in the turnout. A Highway Patrolman took the trail to the beach below to look further. The lean-to shack was so concealed it took searchers thirty hours to discover the teenagers. Tracks and postmortem marks on the bodies showed they had been dragged there. That there were no usable latent prints meant the killer had likely worn gloves. It was an incomparably evil crime.

No sexual attack had taken place, and that was uncommon. At least there was no presence of semen, though the relatively primitive forensic techniques of the time might have missed it. Still, that was doubtful. The board-certified forensics pathologist who performed the autopsies was highly qualified, having been trained at the L.A. Coroner's Office.

A contingent of jail inmates roved the crime scene. Prisoners had been bused there to scour the brush and comb a three-mile section of desolate beach for evidence. The lead sheriff's detective, William Baker, feared they might have compromised the integrity of the crime scene. "You have an inkling of what I am up against," Baker told me, "as I strive to resurrect from the ashes the reality of the case. You have to figure it was 1963. We'd go out with either Search and Rescue, or sometimes get other explorers. This time they had trustees out there going on searches for cartridge casings or whatever else they could find. I shudder when I think about it, but that's the reality. And they did find some casings, quite a few, expended along the victims' flight path—a dry creek bed that led from the blanket near the beach up towards the shack where the kids were actually found. Two distinct points where more casings were located served to pinpoint where the victims were initially dropped."

One convict spotted twenty .22-caliber shell casings glimmering in the canyon creek bed. Detectives spied something too— shoe tracks cut deeply into the light sand and sparse grass leading to and from the ragged shelter. The tracks came from a Navy or Air Force shoe similar to Wing Walkers. Both the ammo and shoes were sold through base exchanges. Vandenberg Air Force Base, a SAC unit, lay near Lompoc, and was only an hour's drive from the murder site.

"And since this was an early experience for the killer," Baker noted, "he may have held onto his weapon and even the same ammo to use again." The murderer had used Winchester .22 ammo, long-rifle—the same brand and caliber Zodiac would use five and a half years later on dark Lake Herman Road just outside Vallejo. "The location where Domingos and Edwards chose to spend 'Ditch Day' was isolated," Baker said, "and not a site where one would expect to find young couples, even with the presence of the victims' car at the turnout. Given that, the killer, armed with a firearm and knife, along with precut lengths of rope and wooden matches, descended upon our victims with apparent murderous intent. Were they followed there? Had he selected his victims beforehand and was there a way to find a connection between the victims and the killer?"

Though Baker could not name them, he suspected items were missing from the crime site. In his studies, he scanned six eight-by-ten-inch police glossies. One showed the arson attempt upon the lean-to, the male victim in situ within the shack. Another photo showed Sheriff James W. Webster, Chief of Detectives Charles Taylor, and a local TV anchorman by the lean-to. The newsman was posed with his hand on the shack and a cigarette in his mouth. Baker studied three pictures of Robert on the autopsy table showing contusions and abrasions on his knuckles. The discoloration on the knuckles of his right hand (Baker could not see the left in the pictures) led him to suspect Robert had fought with his attacker. "Those abrasions on his face were perimortem or postmortem when he was dragged face down by his feet to the shack," said Baker. "I suspect the same thing would have happened to the Berryessa victims if they had broken loose from Zodiac. Zodiac would have dropped his knife and gunned them down. As for the red-haired man [seen the day before], police found him and determined to their satisfaction that he wasn't involved. Other circumstances didn't lead me to give it any particular emphasis. As for Riverside, I felt Zodiac had only taken credit for that murder. But the attack had occurred in Southern California and Zodiac talked about there being a lot more of them down here. He might have meant our case."

WEDNESDAY, JUNE 5, 1963

EDWARDS and Domingos had just been killed and were in everyone's thoughts. Certainly the tragedy occupied Panzarella and Cheney's minds. They had discussed the murders at length. Because of that, they were able to accurately recall the exact weekend Allen appeared suddenly at their door. In Lompoc the high school graduations ceremonies were still held, but conducted around two empty seats. Above those lonely chairs, a flag fluttered at half-mast. Six months passed as the terrible and motiveless murders remained unsolved.

MONDAY, DECEMBER 9, 1963

ALLEN, still qualifying for his teaching credentials, continued to apply for various positions at the Department of Education in Sacramento. While he was waiting, his scholastic record and military background allowed him to teach school at Travis AFB in Fairfield, not far from Vallejo. Though he preferred elementary classes, he settled for instructing seventh- and eighth-graders in spelling, health, and P.E. He was permitted to shop at the base exchange, purchasing goods at discount—everything from ammo for his hunting trips to boots. However, Wing Walker shoes were not sold there until two years later when the Weinbrenner shipment was dispersed. After a year at the Travis school, he was fired for habitually leaving an assortment of deadly weapons lying about his car in plain sight.

"The thing that got me," recalled Panzarella, "was that when Leigh lost a teaching job, he came down in his Austin Healey sports car and tried to convince us guys that he lost the job because they had a security check and he was carrying a revolver. But the real reason was child molesting. He used the phrase that it made him so angry that he wanted to 'kill the little kiddies as they came bouncing off the bus.' That stuck with me all my life. And that's the phrase that was later used by the Zodiac killer."

In 1964, Leigh taught at Watsonville, north of Salinas, and heard a strange story. In the San Bernardino area at Pacific High School, a young student in dark-framed glasses with a black elastic band strode unannounced to the front of the classroom. The teacher had not yet arrived. "In very large letters, he wrote ZODIAC on the blackboard," said a student there, "along with a few codelike symbols I cannot recall."

In August 1965, Leigh lacerated his leg in an accident that required plastic surgery, and though his mishap hobbled him well into 1966, he still sent out feelers for a new teaching job. "The injury," he wrote on December 23, 1965, "put me out of commission until recently." But he was reportedly able to work a little for his friend Glen Rinehart's brother, Dale, at an airfield in Texas, where he got his pilot's license. His weight was now 220 pounds.

SATURDAY, JUNE 18, 1966

CLAIMING a state credential in General Elementary and four years' teaching experience, Allen applied by mail to the Calaveras Unified School District in San Andreas for work. "I also enjoy the country," he wrote, "and I can't *stand* smog." He listed the grades he wanted to instruct in order of preference—"4, 5, 6, 7, and 8." "I can teach physical education and art and music, but not too well." The elementary school subjects that most interested him were "athletics, science, nature study, and music appreciation." He gave his height as six feet, altered his weight to reflect another ten pounds gained because of his incapacity, and mentioned membership "until this year" in two professional organizations—the NEA and CTA. Leigh exaggerated the time he had actually taught, and claimed a present salary of $300 per month. He quickly altered the figure to $400. "When can you come in for an interview?" he was asked. "Mondays or Tuesdays would be best as I am involved in recreation on other days," he answered.

He began honing his teaching skills at a school called Mountain Town in the Sierras and at Valley Springs Elementary School in Valley Springs, a Northern California town just west of San Andreas. On the Valley Springs application he wrote down Ted Kidder as a reference. Leigh taught his first year of grade school at Valley Springs uneventfully, but soon old problems arose—his improper attentions toward children and poorly concealed hatred of women.

"Leigh sent out a lot of resumes," Cheney told me, "and worked hard to find a teaching job. But I didn't know about the teaching jobs that he had had. He didn't speak about that. I knew he taught at Travis, but I didn't see or visit him while he was there. He looked a lot like Dan Blocker, 'Hoss' Cartwright on the *Bonanza* television show, so in the sixties, when Leigh used to go to a big sporting event or there were a lot of people around, he had a big white cowboy hat he would wear. He wanted people, especially kids, to think he was Dan Blocker. As for that cowboy hat, Leigh had that before I met him, and probably had been pulling that deception since the show came on the air in 1959." Leigh would smile and say, " 'Hoss' is Scandinavian for Good Luck."

SUNDAY, OCTOBER 30, 1966

LEIGH Allen, wearing his white cowboy hat and "Big" Dan Blocker smile, traveled to Riverside to attend the Los Angeles International Grand Prix. That autumn afternoon, he watched the race along with approximately eighty thousand people. At 6:10 P.M. Cheri Jo Bates, an eighteen-year-old Riverside City College freshman, set out along Magnolia to the RCC library. The library closed between 5:00 and 6:00 P.M. In order to realize her ambition to become an airline stewardess, Cheri Jo had to meet education and age requirements. She would qualify by the end of her sophomore year and had contacted many of the major airlines. Cheri Jo had just visited her fiancé of two years, Dennis Earl Highland, at San Francisco State University. Inexplicably, she told two girlfriends, "I'm going to the library to meet my boyfriend." However, Highland was at that moment playing football in San Francisco at S. F. State. Police later conjectured that she had meant a former suitor.

A friend observed the strikingly attractive, blond cheerleader speed by in her lime-green VW. A 1965–66 bronze Oldsmobile followed closely behind. She parked, leaving the right passenger window partially down. Ten minutes later Cheri Jo checked out three books from the local college library. Though her friends were at the small, cramped library between 7:15 and 8:57 P.M., none recalled seeing her there. At 9:00 P.M., when the archives closed, she returned to her car to discover the engine would not catch. And here she had been working part-time at the Riverside National Bank just to pay for the vehicle. Parked behind her car was a Tucker Torpedo that had not been there before.

In her absence, someone had gained access to the engine, yanked out the distributor coil and condenser, and disconnected the middle wire of the distributor. As Cheri Jo ran the battery down, a man approached from the shadows and stepped to the partially rolled-down right-side window. "Having trouble?" he said. "Let me take a look at the engine." After failing to start the auto, he said, "My car is over in the parking lot. Come on, I'll give you a lift." She left her books on the seat and keys still in the ignition. Did she know the man, or had he forced her to accompany him?

The unlit gravel road to the parking lot was long, dark, and silent. The pair walked approximately two hundred feet away and paused in a dirt driveway midway between two vacant frame houses at 3680 and 3692 Terracina. Their conversation was later detailed in a typed "confession letter" sent to the police. "It's about time," he said. "About time for what?" she asked. "It's about time for you to die." A knife was in his hand. Between 10:15 and 10:45 P.M. a female neighbor heard an "awful scream." At 10:30 another heard "two screams." After a couple of minutes of silence, an old car started up. In that time the killer, trailing drops of blood, had gone back to search for something he had dropped.

MONDAY, OCTOBER 31, 1966

A groundskeeper discovered Cheri Jo at 6:28 A.M. From the forty-two stab wounds, estimates were the knife blade was approximately three and one-half inches long and one and one-half inch wide. The motive was mystifying—she was fully clothed and had not been sexually attacked or robbed. During a ferocious, earth-churning battle, Bates had scratched her killer's face and ripped a paint-spattered Timex watch from his wrist. The black band, broken away from one side of the watch face, measured seven inches in circumference. The Timex had been purchased at a military base exchange. The B.F. Goodrich heel prints found near Bates's body indicated a size-8-to-10 Wing Walker–like shoe manufactured for the military by Leavenworth prisoners and sold by military exchanges. Just outside Riverside city limits lay March Air Force Base, a SAC base. A number of greasy finger and palm prints were discovered on the left door of the victim's car. Four workmen had been seen across the street from where Bates's car was parked on Terracina. The prints were sent to Washington and the Timex to CI&I.

At 8:30 A.M. Leigh Allen called in sick. For the first time, he missed a day of work at Valley Springs School. The next day, he filled out an absence form and signed it. No one recalled scratches on his face, but Allen said he was in Pomona when he heard Cheri Jo Bates was killed. He had served as a painter in the Navy. That might explain paint specks on the base exchange Timex, but that was a long time ago.

"I was at the Riverside City College library the night Cheri Bates was murdered," an RCC student told me. "I had the same kind of car that she had and I was parked in front of her. I normally left the library when it closed, as she did, but I left earlier that night. The point is that I always felt [the victim] could have been me because of the timing and that I must have been in the library with him that night. Bates was a cheerleader and my best friend."

A transient, with a knife in his possession, was discovered sleeping in his nearby car, questioned, then released. A local mother found a kitchen knife missing and told police she suspected her son might be the killer. After questioning Cheri Jo's friends, police turned to questioning fifteen military men from the nearby air base. Fourteen days after Bates's murder, Riverside police, under command to "drop everything and work this case until solved!" ordered the sixty-two students, two librarians, and one custodian who had been at the library that fatal night to return for a reconstruction. "Wear the same clothes you did two weeks ago."

SUNDAY, NOVEMBER 13, 1966

DETECTIVE Dick Yonkers and Detective Sergeant LeRoy Gren coordinated the library reenactment. The two stage managers lifted the curtain at 5 P.M. just as six motorcycle officers under traffic sergeant Al Fogarty were stationed at Terracina and Riverside, Fairfax and Riverside, in the alleyway parallel to Magnolia near Terracina, and at the alley exit onto Fairfax.

Detective Earl Brown and D.A.'s investigator Loren Mitchell, working from a master list, questioned and tape-recorded each student as they entered. "What vehicle did you notice parked in front of you?" asked Brown. "A '47–'52 tan-gray Studebaker with oxidized paint," came one answer. After the initial interview, each student was given a card with an assigned letter and checked off personally by Captain Irvin Cross, head of the detective bureau, as they completed the reenactment. Cross fingerprinted and snipped a lock of hair from each student. "Is there anybody you recall seeing here that night who isn't here tonight?" he asked each. "Give me a name and description." The curtain fell at 9:00 P.M., the time when the library usually closed on Sunday nights. Only two people hadn't returned—a woman and a bearded, heavyset young man, five feet eleven and a half inches—Allen's height.

Agent Mel Nicolai later placed Allen in Riverside that dreary Sunday. "He wasn't working or going to school at the college," he said. "He would just go down every weekend from Calaveras County because he was involved in a car club down there. He was definitely there that weekend."

MONDAY, NOVEMBER 14, 1966

HEADLINE in the *Press-Enterprise*: "City police hunt bearded man after staging scene in murder. A heavy-set man with a beard is being sought." Sergeant Gren said police are "very interested" in talking to this man. The implication was that the killer had worn a beard as a disguise. Did Zodiac disguise himself with various wigs—pompadour, black hair, crew cut? What sort of man relies on a hairpiece to look different? A man without hair.

TUESDAY, NOVEMBER 22, 1966

A nineteen-year-old University of California at Riverside coed, walking west on Linden, became aware of a car creeping slowly alongside her. Looking around, she observed a man offering her a ride. "No, thanks," she said. "Well, after all, I'm not Jack the Ripper," replied the driver. "Don't you recall? I gave you a ride three weeks ago." Three weeks ago Cheri Jo had been murdered. The girl smiled, vaguely remembering him, opened the car door, and slid in. The ride went smoothly. He dropped her off at a local pizza parlor. When her boyfriend failed to meet her, she started back toward the UCR library. The same man rolled alongside again and picked her up, but instead of taking her home, drove rapidly up a dark road to Pigeon Pass. "There are a lot of kooks running around," he said as the car slowed. "You heard about that girl at City College, didn't you?" Frightened, the girl leaped from the car. Racing along the road's edge, she fell. "I'm not going to kill you," he shouted as she scrambled to her feet. "If I wanted to kill you, I could just hit you in the head with this piece of wood." She returned to the car, but instantly his hands closed around her throat. "Now if I wanted to kill you, I could just snap your neck," he said. "Shall I kill you now, or are you going to take off your clothes?"

As he grabbed her sweatshirt, she wriggled free and bolted into the woods. The stranger gave up searching for her and roared off with her purse and books. Sobbing, covered with scratches and burrs, she staggered to the Highgrove area. When police responded, she described the suspect as "thirty-five, five feet nine inches tall with a chunky, protruding stomach." Later descriptions of Zodiac mentioned "a slight potbelly" and that his "stomach hung over his trousers."

TUESDAY, NOVEMBER 29, 1966

BATES'S killer (or someone pretending to be her murderer) mailed two unstamped letters from a rural mailbox to the police and *Riverside Press-Enterprise*. The typed confession letters, re-peating what he and Cheri Jo had spoken to each other in the dark, were blurry fourth- and seventh-generation carbon copies. The original was never mailed, making a match to a specific typewriter difficult. The writer had used a portable Royal type-writer, Elite-type, Canterbury shaded.[1] Leigh's mother had given him just such a portable. The length of the paper was unknown since the author had torn off the bottom and top of a strip of Tele-type paper. Oddly, he had folded back both bottom corners. The writer claimed to have phoned the *Press-Enterprise,* but probably did not. Some of the language was Zodiac-like. "I AM NOT SICK. I AM INSANE. BUT THAT WILL NOT STOP THE GAME." Zodiac wrote: "why spoil our game!"

---

[1]The FBI believed the typewriter to be a Royal Merit Pica provides 508. Pica provides ten characters to the vertical inch. Elite provides twelve. The anony-mous writer, working with multigenerational copies, used the larger font.

WEDNESDAY, NOVEMBER 30, 1966

ALLEN received his first critique at Valley Springs School. "It might be better to refrain from drinking soda pop in the classroom," his evaluator suggested, "and voice loudness needs to be refined." Leigh's personal characteristics were judged "satisfactory," as were his classroom control and management. "Very excellent in use of Audio-Visual materials . . . needs to react with pupils so they can distinguish between friendliness and familiarity."

FRIDAY, MARCH 10, 1967

THE Valley Springs administrator delivered his second appraisal. "Leigh accepts criticism and suggestions easily, is open-minded and adaptable to new ideas," it read. "I would suggest he take more care in his dress."

But Leigh would sometimes, when the black mood was upon him, lower his head to his desk in the classroom and murmur the word "Titwillow" over and over. This and his unwelcome advances against the eleven- and twelve-year-old girls in his classes caused great fear. He would have the more developed girls bounce for him on his trampoline, then make unwelcome remarks. Two of the girls caught him spying on them at their grandmother's house across the freeway from Allen's home.

It was morning, March or early April 1968, and classes at Valley Springs had already started, when the mother of one of Allen's pupils stalked into the principal's office. "Yesterday," she said, "Mr. Allen had his hands all over my daughter right at his desk." The principal, already suspicious, believed her immediately. He called and got a substitute teacher. When the substitute arrived, he called Allen out of his class and fired him on the spot. Allen started crying and sobbing. "Yes," Leigh said, "I did it. I don't know why I did it. I don't know what's wrong with me." As far as the principal was concerned, this was a "great big act." Within days, Ron and Karen Allen drove to the school to apologize for Leigh's behavior. They had been amazed he had gotten a job there in the first place.

The official reason for Leigh's termination was given as "improper conduct" and an "exaggeration of his teaching credentials." Leigh filed his resignation and moved on, continuing to work with children.

SUNDAY, APRIL 30, 1967

SIX months later, in response to an article in the Sunday morning *Press-Enterprise,* Zodiac cruelly wrote the victim's father, the *Enterprise,* and the police. His three handprinted letters, on lined, three-holed school paper of poor quality, measured eight inches wide. Standard writing paper was eight and one-half inches wide. His letters, like Zodiac's letters, carried double postage, and like Leigh Allen's personal letters to children, were in pencil.

FRIDAY, AUGUST 25, 1967

"IN the summer of 1967 Leigh and I went on a deer hunt north of the Bay Area," Cheney told me. "I used to be an avid hunter, but I don't hunt anymore. That was when I was growing up and that was what we did then. I didn't go hunting with him often because I really didn't think he was a superior hunting partner. I went a couple of times with him on a major deer hunt where we went and spent two or three days. A few other times we just went out for the day to hunt small game. He was all right to fish with, if you didn't have to hike. He wasn't that good on his feet. His feet hurt him. He had flat feet and was overweight; sometimes he had gout. As for weapons, I had a Winchester Model 88, .308 NATO cartridge, but I don't remember what gun Leigh had. I didn't have another large rifle to loan him at that time, and so he dug something up on his own. He got it from somewhere.

"Just a couple blocks away from his house, nestled at the bottom of Fresno Street, was a pancake house. After the hunting trip, we were going someplace for an outing when we saw a girl there, a waitress. Leigh indicated that he was interested in her and asked what did I think of her. He thought he might make some headway with her. In all the time I had known him this was the only female he had ever mentioned, the only time I'd seen him show interest in a particular woman. He liked women, but they just didn't like him. The waitress was young, pretty, with brown hair. I don't remember her name and it was the only time Leigh mentioned her, the only time he mentioned a specific woman. That stuck in my mind."

MONDAY, SEPTEMBER 4, 1967

ALLEN began teaching at Camp La Honda YMCA at La Honda Gulch, never missing a day of work until Monday, February 5, 1968, when he skipped three days in a row. "Personal business," he scrawled on his absentee slip, then thought better of it and altered it to read "school business" instead.

FRIDAY, JUNE 7, 1968

ALLEN left La Honda and for the next year toiled sporadically at Harry Wogan's as a mechanic, at the Franklin School as a janitor, and at a host of other jobs in menial positions. He still found room for good times. "Ron and Leigh went to Mexico," Cheney told me. "I heard this story secondhand from Ron. 'Nasty Norm' might have been along. They called him 'Nasty Norm,' a school nickname, because he had dark curly hair, a French look, kind of a low forehead, dark hair on his arms, sort of ape-looking guy. He was perfectly civilized, but he had that appearance. He and Leigh were skin-diving buddies, and I did a little skin diving with them when we visited Norm at Morro Bay on one trip and in Monterey, on another. At that time Leigh had a catamaran, a Catalina Cat, and he had a small awkward boat. In Mexico, Ron, Leigh, and possibly Norm caught some lobsters and talked a Mexican couple they met on the beach into cooking a big feast for them on the shore." By October 6, 1969, Leigh was laboring part-time as a custodian at Elmer Cave School. It was there that Sergeant Lynch, dispatched by some still-unknown informant, questioned him as a suspect in the Zodiac murders.

MONDAY, OCTOBER 20, 1969

RIVERSIDE Police Chief L. T. Kinkead and Detective Sergeant H. L. Homsher contacted Napa Sheriff Earl Randol and Captain Donald A. Townsend: "This letter is in reference to our telephone conversation of 10/17/69 regarding the similar M.O. of your 'Zodiac' suspect and the suspect of our homicide File No. 352-481:

"One month after the homicide, letters were received at the *Press* and our department written by the suspect of our homicide. The suspect used a black felt pen to address the envelopes and had used upper case print. The confession letter was typed. There are numerous errors in spelling, punctuation, etc., as you will notice. The person who wrote the confession letter is aware of facts about the homicide that only the killer would know. There is no doubt that the person who wrote the confession letter is our homicide suspect. There are numerous similarities in your homicide and our Inv. 352-481. I thought you should be aware that we are working a similar-type investigation."

When the murderer disabled Bates's car, he might have left prints. Unidentified latent prints were lifted off the vehicle and sent to the FBI, which marked the file #32-27195, Latent Case #73096. The SFPD rushed copies of their latents from the cab to the FBI for comparison. However, the partial prints did not match anyone in the case, and there had been innumerable suspects.

Fear on the RCC campus had escalated. More open space had been cleared and bright lights installed. Joseph Bates secured a loan on his house to finance a reward for the capture of his daughter's killer.

TUESDAY, OCTOBER 21, 1969

SAN Francisco newsmen still struggled to make sense of the case. "In all three cases," a *Chronicle* interoffice Zodiac memo to reporter Mike Grieg read,

"When there was a boy and a girl—Zodiac tried to kill both, got the girl all three times, but got the guy only the first time. There were 197 days between the first pair of killings and the second attempt; 84 days between the second and third tries; and 14 days between the last tries—they're getting closer. Zodiac seems to strike exclusively on Fri. and Sat. nites—which makes it questionable how he's going to get a school bus. Any pattern I have tried to draw is broken at least once. Horoscopes (at least those in the Chron) offer no clue. Capricorn is

vaguely applicable except for the first murder. . . . I have been
unable to find any statistical or numerological pattern here in
about 2–3 hours work. . . . [Lake Berryessa victim] was
stabbed more than 20 times with a 12-inch butcher's knife, in
the chest, back and abdomen—with many of the stabs coming
in pairs, making Zodiac's cross-hair mark.—[Marshall]
Schwartz."

The last was not true.

Over at the SFPD, professorial, pipe-smoking Bill Hamlet was
hunched over a makeshift desk in the hallway. "We put a little
partition around him so he wouldn't be bothered," said Toschi.
"We were getting prints from all over the Bay Area and Northern
California. He's got his magnifying glasses on, he's working off
three-by-five cards. That's all he was working on. If you get too
many guys examining prints, you lose something." But that cab
print never matched anyone.

WEDNESDAY, DECEMBER 31, 1969

ZODIAC'S periods of violent activity mirrored school-year vacation time and holidays—summertime, Columbus Day, Halloween, Thanksgiving, Christmas, and the Fourth of July. Leigh
Allen's revelations to Cheney had been imparted on New Year's
Day. Most of his time-consuming letters and codes were mailed
during school vacations. Few occupations outside an elementary
schoolteacher's offered holidays off, plus an additional three
months' vacation. Zodiac's activities fit the school year and
hardly anything else.

Zodiac had threatened to shoot children as they dashed from a
disabled school bus. He promised to plant bombs that targeted
the buses by their height and number of windows and detonated
along school bus routes. "I feel that the odds are substantial that
the killer is a public employee, possibly working for one of the
schools," theorized an expert. "His possible connection with a
school or university, even if only as an area maintenance man, is
open to speculation."

Though Leigh, at this time, was showing those closest to him
cryptograms he kept concealed in a gray metal box, he never

spoke of codes with Cheney. "No, absolutely not," said Cheney. "Leigh never talked about codes, didn't even work crossword puzzles, and at no time evidenced any interest in astrology. He liked to make up rhymes, however."

FRIDAY, JANUARY 30, 1970

FOUR Cal Poly at San Luis Obispo students provided a tip to the local police, who passed it on to the FBI Identification Division. Their information was that a graduate of their university closely resembled the composite of Zodiac. "He owns 9-mm and .22-caliber handguns and frequently travels alone in San Francisco and frequently remote areas of the state," they said. "He was absent from Cal Poly the weekend of the last murder." During the time Zodiac was penning letters and committing a string of brutal murders, Allen was well settled in the Bay Area. However, if it was Leigh the four students were pinpointing, then he might still be making frequent southbound trips to his old alma mater. He tended to rove the Golden State, large blocks of his time unaccounted for, and this left his family wondering.

MONDAY, MARCH 23, 1970

AT 3:00 A.M, forty minutes after she escaped from her kidnapper, Kathleen Johns filed a report with Stanislaus Sheriff's Deputy Jim Ray Lovett. The pregnant woman and her baby girl had been abducted en route to Petaluma from her Compus Way, San Bernardino home. As with Bates, the interloper had gimmicked her Chevrolet wagon to trick her into his car. He conveyed Johns on a terror ride until she and her baby leaped from the moving car and hid in a field. He searched for them until the timely arrival of a passing trucker. Deputy Lovett later located her blazing auto on Highway 132, about one-quarter mile west of the Delta. The abductor had taken the time to replace a sabotaged tire, drive the car elsewhere, and torch it.

The kidnapper drove a tan late-model vehicle, wore glasses, a dark ski jacket, and navy-blue bell-bottoms. Johns had recognized him as Zodiac from a wanted poster tacked to Lovett's wall. He was thirty, stood five feet nine inches, and weighed

160—too light for Zodiac. "It was twenty-eight years ago," Johns recalled recently, "and I perhaps wouldn't know him now. . . . The calm voice—I remember it like it was yesterday. I don't think you could live through something like that and forget."

FRIDAY, JULY 24, 1970

ZODIAC belatedly claimed responsibility for the Johns abduction in a letter not published until October 12. On June 26 he had claimed to have shot SFPD Officer Richard Radetich, and *that* was a downright lie. It made Toschi wonder about his claims of a Riverside murder.

6
AVERY AND THE
DARK ALLEY

SATURDAY, OCTOBER 24, 1970

THE Zodiac case was already affecting *Chronicle* reporter Paul Avery's health. It would eventually destroy it. In the early morning hours he drove his car onto narrow little Mary Street. Mary lay in the shadow of the *Chronicle* and continued on northwest, running behind the Old Mint. Avery parked where Mary intersected Minna, the dank alley separating the *Chronicle* from the *Examiner.* It was a rough area and Minna at the time held a dubious honor. It was the site of more murders than any other place in the city. He was not gone long—from 12:40 A.M. until 1:40 A.M., but long enough. During that time he traversed a long, dimly lit corridor into the city room. The *Chronicle* was a huge three-story barnlike building with a tower at the Mission and Fifth Street corner. The quality of light was yellow-greenish at best. Beneath his feet Avery felt the tremble of tremendous presses grinding out an early morning edition. Teletype keys rattled nervously in a little room to his left—a ghost was on the line. Lines of rubber-cement pots, rows of battered old Smith-Coronas, and stacks of used photo zincs, copper-backed and etched with acid, crowded desktops.

Avery filed a story, then returned to his car. The right vent window was smashed—the mark of an experienced booster. Only a few things were missing. His Wells Fargo checkbook, containing checks numbered 118 to 125, had been taken. His expensive Sony cassette tape recorder, which held an interview with a Zodiac tipster—a man with a muffled voice—was gone. Avery was concerned enough to call the police. Officers Gerald Derham and William Thiffault reported.

It was then Avery noticed that his large gray briefcase, emblazoned with his initials, "P. A.," had been stolen. He had stuffed that briefcase with a complete clipping file on Zodiac. He looked up and down the darkened street. It began to dawn on him how close the killer was. He seemed to be privy to reporter's notes and Sunday features before they were published; he used newspaper Teletype paper and supplies that might had been purchased from Woolworth's down the street. What if Zodiac were getting into the building late at night? The paper was a twenty-four-hour operation, but manned by a skeleton crew at night. Security in the building consisted of a guard at a tall desk on the Fifth Street entrance, but there were two sets of back stairs and two elevators that led to the editorial floor. Additionally, there was a passage between the *Examiner* and *Chronicle* that spanned Minna Street and allowed people to walk from one paper to the other. Zodiac was not just watching the hunters; he might be entering the paper at night.

A *Chronicle* printer believed Zodiac actually worked there. "Many of the Zodiac cipher symbols are also printer's proofreading marks," he told me. "The Zodiac symbol itself is a proofreader's mark used to line up corrections on a tissue overlay and for color registration. His method of numbering pages is also the printer's method: 1/6, 2/6, one of six, two of six, etc. . . . to alert the typesetter and proofreader to follow the flow of copy. The arrows used on the bus diagrams are also printer's arrows. Not just a line with an inverted 'V,' but with the 'V' filled in.

"When Zodiac began writing his letters, the paper was attempting to enter the electronic age with a computer system known as the 'Braegen.' Rather than generating tape-punched copy for the Linotype machines on Fairchild TTS machines, copy was typed on IBM typewriters, then single-sheet-fed into scanners, which in turn generated tape sent to the Linotypes. The paper used for typing was narrow fan-fold cheap bond such as Zodiac used. Blue felt-tipped pens were provided to us (they would not reproduce on copy fed through the scanners) and used by the copy cutters for instructions and the typesetters for notes questioning spelling, continuity, and so on."

Chronicle editors eventually cast a jaundiced eye upon two former employees. The editors went over their employment records to see if any days off corresponded with Zodiac crimes and letters. One worker, suffering bouts of severe depression, had disappeared during the night shift, leaving behind a note for four years' sick leave. The other vanished, leaving behind four payroll checks he never picked up.

MONDAY, OCTOBER 26, 1970

IN North Sacramento, two days after Avery's files were stolen, twenty-eight-year-old court reporter and juvenile court aide Nancy M. Bennallack failed to show up at work. Friends discovered her bloody body, throat slashed, in her second-floor flat. The unknown killer had entered by a sliding glass door Miss Bennallack had left open so her cat could get in. She was engaged to be married on November 28. She had not been sexually assaulted. Her apartment was a half mile from Nurse Judith Hakari's apartment. Hakari, twenty-three, had been kidnapped from in front of her North Area apartment after leaving her job at a local hospital. Her badly beaten body was found in a shallow grave in a remote section of Placer County. She too had not been sexually assaulted. Like Miss Bennallack, she was engaged to be married.

TUESDAY, OCTOBER 27, 1970

THE next afternoon Zodiac mailed "Averly" a garishly decorated Halloween card signed "Your Secret Pal." My comparison of an unaltered card demonstrated Zodiac had done considerable redrawing. He had carefully cut out and pasted a skeleton and an orange pumpkin to the card, painted staring eyes, and skillfully added brush lettering. It had taken him at least a day to prepare. "You can see how Zodiac must have taken delight in putting his own markings on the card," Toschi told me. "Also, the 'PEEK-A-BOO' and the added printing on the card. All done by Zodiac." The card, illustrated with a smiling skeleton giving Avery the high sign, was signed "Your Secret Pal." Zodiac had painted a small number 14 on the skeletal right hand. Inside, he claimed victim "4-TEEN." News of Bennallack's death would not appear in the *Chronicle* until the following morning.

Avery wrote Chief Al Nelder:

> "Due to the death threat mailed me by the so-called Zodiac killer, I wholeheartedly agree with the advice I have received from Armstrong and Toschi that discretion is the better part of valor and that I should carry a gun in order to protect myself should need arise. Therefore this is my formal request that your office issue me on a temporary basis a permit to carry a concealed weapon."

Nelder concurred, not only granting Avery authority to pack a .38-caliber revolver, but permission to practice on the police target range. Nelder's consideration got Avery in hot water immediately. Around 9:45 P.M., patting the reassuring weight of the .38 in a concealed holster under his jacket, he waved good night to Night City Editor Steve Gavin. Avery retrieved his car from the multistory lot on Fifth Street and turned onto Minna. At the corner of Sixth Street, twenty derelicts, peering from dark doorways and gloomy barroom entrances, watched intently. Avery's headlights illuminated a one-sided struggle. Only ten feet away, two men were grappling. The first, making hard, thrusting motions from the waist, was armed with a hunting knife. The second, wounded in his chest, had doubled his belt around his fist as a shield and was backing up, warding off blows with his arms.

Avery frantically honked his horn, but the fight continued. Worried about his own safety, he made a quick U-turn to the opposite side of Sixth. The knife man moved in as his victim finally toppled into the street. Avery, still honking and yelling, observed a drunk lurching up Sixth, supporting himself close against the dirty building fronts. As the wino weaved by, the knife man wheeled, rushed the drunk, and stabbed him too. In a pathetic attempt at self-defense, the drunk folded his arms over his heart. Anyone who crossed the knife man's path was in peril.

"Someone is going to be killed," Avery thought, and slipped from his car, drawing his weapon as he crept closer. Halfway across Sixth Street, he shouted, "Drop the knife and get against the wall!" The knife man froze, then faced Avery. He raised his arms above his head and took a few halting steps in the reporter's direction, fixing him with a glassy stare as he came. Avery repeated his command, locking eyes with him and leveling the gun until he heard, rather than saw, the bloody knife land at his feet. The knife man placed his palms against the front of 125 Sixth Street, a hotel. Avery yelled into the lobby to the desk clerk: "Call the cops!" In a minute a relatively well-dressed pensioner tottered to the door and said, "The police are on the way." For the next five minutes Avery kept well back from his prisoner. Finally he heard the wail of a siren, a police car appeared, and two officers climbed out.

"This guy just stabbed a couple of people—will you take over?"

"Whose gun do you have?" said the senior officer.

"It's mine," said Avery, producing his special police star. He explained the circumstances leading up to authority being granted for him to carry a gun. "You can check this out by giving the chief a call," he said.

"Oh, yeah. I'm supposed to call Chief Nelder at ten o'clock on a Sunday night."

"Why don't you call Armstrong or Toschi?"

"You do it," said the cop.

Toschi vouched for Avery and everything was fine, except that the two victims had limped away into the night.

"No victims," said the cop, shrugging. "The best we can do is book him for brandishing a knife in a rude and threatening manner. Just misdemeanors." No one was questioned and, since Avery ended up being the only witness, he signed a citizen's complaint. Next morning, he got to the Hall of Justice by 10:30, but the knife man, sentence suspended, had already been released. "I didn't exactly enjoy the role of policeman," he told Nelder. "I'm worried how close I came to killing the guy. I kept looking at him and thinking if he comes at me with a knife, if it comes down to it, if it's a matter of survival, I'm going to have to pull the trigger. I don't think I ever really paused to consider before that by carrying a gun, I was putting myself in a position where sooner or later I'd have to use it. I'm going to get rid of it, Chief. The weight of that gun has gotten too heavy." When Avery returned to his houseboat in Marin County, he hauled down the sheet of steel plate he had installed in the one window that faced a shadowed Sausalito street next to Gate 5. He felt sick and Zodiac had made him that way. Over time his lungs began to fail.

7

ARTHUR LEIGH ALLEN

FRIDAY, NOVEMBER 13, 1970

A San Rafael graphologist analyzed Zodiac's handprinting. "He is five feet eleven and one-half inches tall, sharp but not creative," she speculated. "His hair is sparse and he may sometimes wear a wig or false beard. He may wear lenses on occasion. He may have a malformation or fault such as finger damage on his right hand. He puts himself under self-hypnosis consciously or unconsciously, and may know something of this in actual fact. He always believes that he is drowning, either by emotional pattern or literally by water or being overwhelmed by unpremeditated circumstance. May have boat or houseboat. Has probably scuba dived. Brain damage. Tissue damage from oxygen lack at birth or later, maybe from diving too long and running out of oxygen . . ." Zodiac had written, "Please help me I am drownding."

In the fall Leigh had begun attending Sonoma State University in Rohnert Park, and rented a slot for his trailer in Santa Rosa. On Friday the thirteenth, Allen had a motorcycle accident while returning from Sacramento where, earlier in the day, someone murdered Santa Rosa resident Carol Beth Hilburn. She had last been seen at the Zodiac, an after-hours club on West Capitol Avenue frequented by members of motorcycle gangs. She had been wearing a jacket with the large yellow letters SANTA ROSA on the right side. Hilburn had been staying in Santa Rosa with her sister while studying to be an X-ray technician. On the left side of her slick, hip-length black jacket was her name, CAROL. She was the third attractive young woman to be killed in less than a year in Sacramento. Her nude, severely bludgeoned body was found in an isolated field near Dry Creek on the city's northern edge. A car had dragged her into a field and left her face up. Her throat was then cut and she was beaten so savagely she was unrecognizable.

That afternoon, both Paul Avery and Detective Sergeant Dave Bonine requested Sherwood Morrill conduct a comparison between handwriting samples from Zodiac and the Riverside printing received in the Bates case.

SUNDAY, NOVEMBER 15, 1970

OVER the years a white Chevy Impala would make many appearances in the Zodiac case. A victim's baby-sitter saw a round-faced watcher on Wallace Street in an "American made sedan, white with large windshield and out of state plates." Three women at Lake Berryessa the day of the stabbings observed a suspicious man in a Chevrolet, "silver blue or ice blue in color, 1966, two-door sedan, full size car, quiet, very conservative, with California plates." The Impala showed up again in Santa Rosa on November 15, 1970. At 4:00 A.M. a woman driver saw "a 1962–63 White Chevrolet" following her from a Santa Rosa post office. Shortly after, a "white Chevrolet Impala, sedan 1964," followed a second woman on Mendocino Avenue and Chanate Road. At 5:10 A.M. a "white Chevy, 1963–64" tailgating a woman on Fourth Street was stopped by police and tried to speed off. The driver, a twenty-five-year-old Vallejo man, said he was lost and looking for a way out of town. The officer escorted him out of town. The next day came a break in the case.

MONDAY, NOVEMBER 16, 1970

MORRILL found a match, linking Zodiac's printing with three "BATES HAD TO DIE" letters and a wavering blockprinted poem discovered in the Riverside College Library. Zodiac had carved a ghastly verse into a plywood-board study desktop with a blue ballpoint pen. The poem was probably written as early as January 1967, when the desk was stored in an unused college basement. "Sick of Living . . ." it began. Beneath the gory poem were the incised lower-case initials "R H." Morrill checked over six thousand handwriting samples searching for a killer with those initials. "Most of those exemplars came from the Riverside

College and military installations," he told me. "They were all on microfilm, blown up, and I had a magnifier that I just slipped them under one after another. Now this is the weak link in the case—some of those registration certificates were typed." Captain Cross was encouraged. "Well, it looks like we're in business," he said. The hunt for Zodiac was now statewide.

In the early evening of November 16, Allen stood in the doorway of his trailer nursing his wounds, physical and emotional, past and present. He listened. The roar of traffic on Santa Rosa Avenue filled his head. He put on his white hat and locked the door to his trailer. He limped to his car and started the dusty old clunker. Night was falling.

At 6:00 P.M. an employee at the Los Guilucos School for Girls, about eight miles from Santa Rosa, returned from shopping. She slowed for heavy oncoming traffic at the corner of Pythian Way and two-lane Sonoma Highway. Approaching the narrow road for her turn, she flicked on her turn signal, slowed, and waited for two cars at the corner. As the second car passed by, a hand shot from the bushes. It fastened on her door handle. A face glared at her from the brush. It looked familiar. The features resembled the Zodiac wanted poster. "My impression was of light-colored hair, somewhat receding, though not bald," she recalled. "He was dressed in a navy-blue jacket and I judged him to be about thirty-five and wearing dark-rimmed glasses." She stepped on the throttle, executed a sharp left turn, and raced another quarter mile to the apartment complex where she lived. "I feel," she said, "that the man at the corner and the man sketched in the paper are one and the same."

THURSDAY, NOVEMBER 19, 1970

THE Riverside P.D. held a secret Zodiac conference. While Armstrong remained behind, Toschi, Narlow, and Nicolai flew southward. "Sometimes we split up," said Toschi. " 'Do you want to do this?' Armstrong would ask me, and we would take turns in order to accomplish different tasks at the same time." Toschi was shocked to discover Avery on the same plane to Riverside. "We saw him right away. He had his name stenciled on the back of his carry-on. Narlow and Nicolai looked at me, and I said, 'Hey, I don't know anything about this!' They thought Bill or I might have told him. I asked Avery, 'Paul, how did you know we were going down? You have to tell me. These guys think I'm a snitch.' Avery said, 'Captain Cross told me.' After we landed and were waiting for our Rent-A-Car, Avery had the balls to ask to ride with us to headquarters. Of course the answer was no. I liked Avery and had been able to trust him on cases where a lot of guys thought he was a little sneaky. He was never that way with me at any time."

As Avery drove alone to the meeting, he thought back three days earlier to an incident on Berkeley's Telegraph Avenue. A stocky stranger, "between twenty-five and forty-five years old" had approached two girls and offered them a ride. "No, thanks," they said, gesturing to a VW at the curb, "we've got our own." They ate at a snack bar, returned forty minutes later, and discovered their car wouldn't start. Suddenly, the same stranger was at their side, extending his aid. A passerby noticed the man helping a young girl push a Volkswagen, the other girl behind the wheel. When he offered to help, the stocky man, enraged at the intrusion, ran off. The second Good Samaritan checked the engine. "The middle distributor wire has been ripped out," he told Avery later. "The girls filed a report with the local police that may contain the stranger's license plate number," the man added. Twelve hours afterward, the *Chronicle* received an anonymous call. "City desk, don't bother with general rewrite," the voice said. "This is the Zodiac and it's the last time I am going to call." Avery thought it odd that Zodiac knew newspaper lingo. Berkeley cops searched their files, but could not find the plate number.

Avery was actually quivering. The pressure was tremendous and he had been increasingly "freaked out" over Zodiac's threat against him twenty-four days earlier. Ten days ago, when Avery first visited Riverside, he had begged the city desk to call him if any letters came while he was away.

"Zode—as I call him," wrote Avery in a memo, "is something like the Viet Cong. [Avery had spent three years in Vietnam as a war correspondent.] You don't know who he is, where he is, or when or where he might strike next. I am getting cross-eyed from trying to keep one eye directed ahead and the other over my shoulder. I really doubt he intends to come after me, but I am being careful."

"I wasn't pleased with the Riverside visit," Toschi told me. "I tried to be friendly as the meeting got under way, introduced myself by giving my name, spelling it T-O-S-C-H-I, and saying (as I always do), 'That's Italian.' I'm very proud of my heritage—I spoke Italian before English because my mother was Piemontese and my father Toscano. We spent the whole day in their office and had lunch. We thought we were going to get more information. We got minimal. I was truly disappointed that we weren't getting a heck of lot of anything. With the exception of [Detective] Bud Kelly, who was always up front with me, we never got much cooperation with Riverside. These Riverside guys aren't telling us anything. It's so obvious that they're holding on to everything for themselves like we're here to purse-snatch. And that was not the case. We were there to share information.

"They had confiscated the Riverside desk and kept it in a special evidence room at police headquarters. That desk really got my attention . . . that lettering was so obviously by Zodiac. Later, after we got the tip about Allen, Riverside never even bothered to check on him having been in the region—and I asked, 'Did you know Arthur Leigh Allen?' 'Did you arrest him?' 'Has he ever been cited in the area?' 'Can we connect him to RCC?' They were kind of leaning against the fact that it could have been our killer, Zodiac. From that moment on, they developed tunnel vision to any other suspects. Riverside thought they knew who had committed the Bates murder."

Captain Irv Cross of the Detective Bureau said, "We are not ruling out the possibility that the killer may have been a local youth."

Back in San Francisco, an anonymous typed letter arrived at the *Chronicle*—"It both angers me and amazes me," I read, "that a wanton killer like the Zodiac has escaped detection and justice for so long.

"It is my personal opinion Zodiac has spent time in some type of institution—either prison or mental hospital. . . . Zodiac would not be married. He is unable to function in a relationship with a woman, either sexually or emotionally. . . . The hunt for the Zodiac killer has been a tragic comedy of errors. . . . I know this: every act of horror such as mass killers beginning their ugly business has a starting point which is ignited by what I choose to call a trigger. The beast within them lies quietly most of the time, but then something triggers it or sets it off. In the case of Zodiac I speculate it was due to two things: an episode in his life at the time of the first killing, traumatic to the person known as Zodiac, but not necessarily to anyone else. He seems to have a real hatred for police and enjoys needling them in their failure to catch him. Possibly an encounter with police at that particular time. I don't personally believe he does his killing according to some astrological timetable. I think he kills on holidays and week-ends simply because he doesn't work then. I suggest in all probability he has a job which is a forty hour work week and five consecutive days. . . . I shall remain anonymous. I hope you will not stop in your efforts to find this fiend. I wish you good health and good hunting. [signed] Armchair."

In the unusual letter "Armchair" mentions he never heard of a mother shooting an adult child. "I suppose I am too suspicious of everyone," he concluded. "But being suspicious has saved my bacon more than once." And "Armchair" had not only used Zodiac words ("needling," "trigger," "hunt," "hunting"), but had lived in Riverside at the time of the Bates killing, quoting events and newspaper articles he had read there. I was never able to track him down.

FRIDAY, DECEMBER 18, 1970

ON Arthur Leigh Allen's birthday, a burglar broke into a woman's home. The thief took pains to conceal his identity—adhesive tape on his fingertips, a white handkerchief tied over the lower part of his face. The sleeping owner awakened to find a man standing over her, brandishing a baseball bat. Snatching up a rifle under her bed, she sent a glancing blow to his arm. Ripping the rifle away, he lacerated her forehead with the bat. Her daughter, awakened by the struggle, glimpsed the intruder fleeing down the hall. "He was dressed in a dark nylon ski jacket, dark pants, navy-blue knit cap, and wearing welding goggles," she said, "but before I could get a better look, he switched off the light and vanished." He left a bloody handprint on the wall, but no fingerprints. In the entire time he had been in the house he had not spoken. The Contra Costa County Sheriff's Department issued an all-points bulletin for him; they believed he might be Zodiac.

FRIDAY, FEBRUARY 4, 1972

SEVEN long months had crawled by since Armstrong and Toschi had questioned Leigh Allen that sizzling August morning. As far as they knew he was still attending spring and fall sessions at Sonoma State. Probably a hundred new suspects' names had crossed their desk in that time. Allen's name lay somewhere at the bottom of that pile. And still the tips poured in. "A lot of people would want to cooperate and forward this or that to you," Toschi told me. "All the while you get the feeling down deep that they're trying to pick your brain. The nagging feeling was that the case was a 'round neck.' The round neck means the trash basket in your office, which means it's going to end up in a file as 'Unsolved.'

"We just couldn't handle all the tip calls. The other guys in the office were getting angry at us. 'Hey, guys, we didn't write the letters,' we told them. 'We just answer the phone. If we turn somebody off, hang up on what could be a positive lead—we're not going to make this case and we've got to make this case. Please don't hang up on anybody.' " They followed up the most promising tips, but time was on Zodiac's side. In two weeks, the State Supreme Court would rule capital punishment unconstitutional. Thus Zodiac, if captured, would no longer face the death penalty. Witnesses and surviving victims, fearful of Zodiac, went into hiding or moved away. Physical evidence began to be lost or destroyed. Meanwhile, the detectives could only speculate what the "Cipher Slayer" was doing.

IN SANTA ROSA at 4:00 P.M., Maureen Lee Sterling and Yvonne Weber left the Redwood Ice Skating Rink at Steele Lane. The two twelve-year-olds began to walk home, stopping along the way. Sterling, long brown hair parted in the middle, wore blue jeans, a purple pullover shirt, a red sweatshirt with a hood, and brown suede shoes. Weber dressed similarly—blue jeans, lavender and white tweed pullover shirt, black velvet coat, and brown suede boots. Like her companion, she had blue eyes and parted her long blond hair in the middle. Both girls were known to hitchhike. Along their way, they disappeared.

Leigh Allen quit the oil refinery at 4:00 P.M. each day and left immediately to beat the traffic. His route from Pinole took him west on Highway 37 to San Rafael, where it intersected 101

North. He drove on to Novato, Petaluma, Sonoma, and finally Cotati. A little before five he would have crossed the girls' path.

SATURDAY, MARCH 4, 1972

SIXTEEN days before the vernal equinox, at 5:00 P.M., Kim
Wendy Allen left her job at Natural Foods, a Larkspur health
food store. Twenty minutes later the nineteen-year-old Santa
Rosa Junior College student was seen at the Bell Avenue Freeway entrance. She began hitchhiking north on 101, hefting an orange backpack and clutching a straw carry-bag. A beige
three-quarter-length coat protected her against the chill wind.
Like the little girls from the skating rink, she had blue eyes and
long, light-brown hair parted in the middle. Like them, she vanished. The next day, two men discovered her nude body in a
creek bed three miles from Bennett Valley Road. She had been
strangled with a white hollow-core clothesline. Her body showed
signs of being bound spread-eagled for some time somewhere
else. Superficial cuts were on her chest. The killer had kept her
white embroidered blouse, cut-off blue jeans, green cotton scarf,
and one gold earring. He'd carried away an unusual twenty-four-
inch-long necklace fashioned from driftwood, seaweed, seashells,
seeds, and eucalyptus buttons. She might have been raped. That
definitely did not match Zodiac's M.O. However, she was found
twenty feet from Enterprise Road in a body of water, and Zodiac
had once signed "ENTERPRISE" at the bottom of a letter.

TUESDAY, APRIL 25, 1972

JEANETTE Kamahele, twenty, another Santa Rosa Junior College student, was also hitchhiking north near the Cotati on-ramp
of Highway 101 when she disappeared. Her intended destination
was Santa Rosa, where Leigh Allen had kept a trailer since 1970.

FRIDAY, MAY 5, 1972

ALLEN was in a rage—he had just been fired from the Pinole refinery. Though his questioning by the police had been ten long

months earlier, he considered his termination a direct result of their prying and innuendo. Leigh's dismissal would create additional difficulties for Armstrong and Toschi. Now that the prime suspect was a full-time Sonoma State student, studying science and art, he began living most of each week in his Santa Rosa trailer. In the future any serious search required they choose between Santa Rosa and Vallejo—cities outside their jurisdiction. The situation was made more formidable by the fact that Allen was not their only suspect. A couple of others, at least in the beginning, looked good.

A while back, Larry Friedman, an NYPD cop for two years, rang Toschi. They met at a coffee shop. "I thought you would be interested in this," Friedman said. "A Crocker Bank employee lived a block away when Paul Stine was murdered." Toschi already knew. "We had a couple of guys here in San Francisco," Toschi said, "who were absolutely convinced that the Zodiac was a local bank honcho. All the circumstantial evidence fit perfectly. He originally lived down in Southern California when Bates was murdered. He owned property near Lake Berryessa and went hunting often in Montana, a place where Zodiac said he had been active; where it's easy to buy guns that can't really be traced. Their information was so good that we had to check their suspect out. We eliminated the man completely based on his prints not matching those on Stine's cab." The FBI went a step further, analyzing a blockprinted note passed by a robber to a Crocker teller to see if it matched Zodiac's printing.

Another suspect looked like a bear, but a bear with a shock of red hair and wearing dark glasses. The "Bear Man" was a "kinda scary guy," Toschi told me, "steel-wool hair, loping long arms. He collected guns and ammo—a rifle carbine, but no .22's or 9-mm. He was a theater janitor who lived on Hunter Street." Police theorized Zodiac was not a hunter, but might be named Hunter or might even possess a wild beast's attributes. "We put the 'Bear Man' on the lie detector three weeks after the Stine killing. I asked the suspect, who volunteered that he was ambidextrous, to print for me. The writing didn't match. Though he was generally familiar with Lake Berryessa, he didn't know the side roads and was not intimate with Vallejo. I was unable to find anything locally on the suspect, no wants, nor warrants, nor arrests.

"Zodiac might have been a cabbie like Stine. I checked the Department's cab permit bureau back to 1963. If he ever drove a cab in this city, he had to be fingerprinted and photographed as an applicant—I found no such person as the 'Bear Man.' If he drove a cab it was under another name. I rechecked with DMV in Sacramento and they had no record of such a person with a current or past driver's license. However, they purge after approximately seven years. I sent a Teletype to Las Vegas asking for a copy of his driver's license and his photo—a seven-to-ten-day wait for that. And this was just one suspect—back when the case started."

Like Stine, an earlier Zodiac victim had been shot at close range above the ear. Though police often discounted the Lake Herman Road murders of December 20, 1968, as being Zodiac's, a similar contact wound linked them to Stine. Past the rolling hills, peaceful pastures, and rugged quarries out on Lake Herman Road strange things were seen. Three and a half years before, on that pitch-black and lonely thoroughfare, Zodiac had murdered Betty Lou Jensen and David Faraday, two teenagers on their first date. Good kids: Betty Lou an honor student; David an Eagle Scout, recipient of the "God and Country Award."

The night of the murders, Robert Connley and Frank Gasser (of the Gasser Ranch on Highway #2) were out there hunting raccoons. At 9:00 P.M. they drove their red Ford pickup just beyond Gate #10 leading to the Lake Herman Pumping Station. They parked the pickup twenty-five feet into a field of the Marshall Ranch, near the pump house. The gated entrance itself was one-quarter mile east of Lake Herman Cottage. As the gate swung inward, an unidentified truck began going out. The hunters observed a white four-door 1959–'60 Chevrolet Impala parked alongside its path. Gasser, sixty-nine, wearing a hunting jacket and shining a three-cell flashlight, ambled over to the Impala. Curious, he peered into the front seat, then the back. The car was empty. "Perhaps its owner is out scouting the area," he thought.

An hour later Bingo Wesher, a rancher on the Old Borges Ranch by the Humble Oil Company, began tending sheep just east of Benicia Pumping Station #9. He observed Gasser and Connley's truck, recognizable by its wood sideboards and bright color, and saw the Impala parked by the south fence entrance. He could not tell if it was occupied. A "dark car, lacking in chrome" had been seen in the area, and between 9:30 and 10:00 P.M. a blue Valiant, driven by two men, chased another couple along Lake Herman Road at "a high rate of speed." Another witness saw a "White Chevrolet, Impala sedan 1961–63" in the area.

Two other witnesses passed the pumping station entrance at 10:15 and saw a 1960 four-door station wagon facing toward the gate. The two-tone (dark tan over light tan) Nash Rambler was the victims' car. Fifteen minutes later the witnesses returned. The station wagon now faced the opposite direction. At 11:00 P.M. Connley and Gasser finished hunting and saw the Impala was gone. The Rambler was parked in the same spot, facing southwest and in a different spot than police found it an hour later. A Humble Oil worker driving home from Benicia after his grave-yard shift saw *two* cars parked at the pump house entrance. "The car parked nearest to the road was a 1955 or 1956 station wagon, boxy type, neutral color," he said. "The other was parked to the right and abreast of the station wagon. The cars were about ten feet apart. I could not give a description of the make or color of the other car."

THE RAMBLER'S MOTOR was still lukewarm when Detective Sergeant Les Lundblad of the Solano County Sheriff's office ar-rived at five minutes after midnight. The car's ignition key was on, but the motor was not running. The kids had been using the heater. The front of the four door brown-beige '61 Rambler Sta-tion Wagon in the entranceway now pointed east. The right front door stood wide open, the remaining three doors and tailgate still locked, but the right rear window had been smashed. The girl's white fur coat, along with her purse, lay on the rear seat on the driver's side. Though a deep heel mark was found behind the pumphouse, the gravel surface produced nothing of great signifi-cance in the way of readable footprints and no visible tire tracks were left on the frozen ground.

Coroner Dan Horan, Dr. Byron Sanford, Captain Daniel Pitta, Officers William T. Warner, Waterman, and Butterbach, and a re-porter from the *Fairfield Daily Republic*, Thomas D. Balmer, were already there. Benicia cops Pierre Bidou and Lieutenant George Little, who photographed the two bodies, joined the bustling scene. Zodiac counted on competing police agencies to hamper the investigation.

Warner did a chalk outline around David's body. Horan pro-nounced Betty Lou DOS. and, after Little had taken as many pic-tures from as many angles as possible, ordered her body to the morgue. Sergeant Cunningham had Deputy J. R. Wilson go to Vallejo General Hospital to take pictures of David, but when he

arrived he learned the boy had been DOA. In the meantime Lundblad ascertained that one bullet had been fired into the top of the
Rambler leaving a ricochet mark on the roof. Another had shat-
tered the rear window. An expended .22-caliber casing from the
killer's gun lay on the right floorboard of the Rambler. Nine other
expended casings were on the ground, to the right at distances of
twenty feet, fourteen feet, eight feet two inches, four feet one-
half inch, three feet, two feet three inches, one foot eleven inches,
and one foot one-half inch. They showed how the boy had been
shot as he exited and how the killer pursued the girl on the run.
The fatal bullets that killed Jensen and Faraday were at first
thought to be from a High Standard Model 101. Along the road,
Benicia police recovered a Hi-Standard H-P Military .22 automatic with eradicated serial numbers. It had been previously dis-
assembled by someone and the firing pin altered. They examined
test bullets with six right-hand grooves, as did the questioned
bullets removed from the victims. Different guns had been involved. No one could explain how the killer had fired so accurately in the dark unless he had some sort of light on the barrel.

An irregularly flattened bullet removed from the left frontal
lobe of the boy (he had been shot behind the upper right ear) and
the bullets from the girl were analyzed. All were Western coated
.22 Long Rifle ammo with 6 RH class characteristics. They could
only have been fired from a J. C. Higgins, Model 80, .22 automatic pistol. Betty Lou had been shot five times in the back in a
"remarkably close pattern." Three of the bullets had emerged
from her front. Betty Lou's dress had no smoke or gunpowder
residue in one hole in the center front. Nor was there any tattoo-
ing in the five punctures in the upper right side of her back. However, in the topmost hole in back, a single grain of gunpowder
was discovered. That meant that of all the slugs that struck her,
only one was fired at a closer range. All the others were fired
from at least several feet. Two of the ten bullets fired were never
accounted for, lost in the nearby field.

Lundblad began timing the events of that night. First he drove
to the home of Mrs. Stella Borges, the woman who had discovered the bodies sprawled by the roadside. From her ranch to the
crime scene was two and seven-tenths miles and that took three
minutes. From the crime scene to the Enco Station on East 2nd
Street in Benicia where she had flagged down police was three

and four-tenths miles. It took Lundblad five minutes at the "safe high speed" Borges had driven. "It is two and one-tenths miles from the intersection of Lake Herman Road and Luther Gibson Freeway to crime scene," he wrote, "a three minute trip." Later he also timed the distances between two suspects' homes and the murder site at various speeds. Lundblad learned there had been a prowler around the Jensen home. Upon several occasions the gate leading to the side of the house had been found open.

THE UNSOLVED MURDERS forever tainted the region. On that forsaken road a man in a white Chevy cruised under the full moon. Residents had taken to calling him "The Phantom of Cordelia." A big man was also observed roving the territory on foot, stalking over a gravel path to the old pump house, scouting for game, practicing his shooting, and moving through the quarry and watery areas where he could dive like a ghost. The huge man moved in other remote areas of Vallejo too, tracking the watery outskirts of Vallejo as if seeking something. Three astrological water signs—Scorpio, Pisces, and Cancer—determined the timing of Zodiac's assaults. To prove this, astrologers confidently pointed to his later double shooting at Blue Rock Springs—committed during the sign of Cancer with the moon in Pisces.

Mrs. Stella Borges's ranch sat off Fairgrounds Drive and abutted the Syar Rock Quarry on American Canyon Road. To the east was Borges Summit Reservoir, and to the north a creek that rushed year-round with water. The big man swam in the cold water and stood like an apparition at her gate. Mrs. Borges, an important witness in the Lake Herman murders, saw him there herself. Forty-five minutes before midnight, December 20, 1968, she had set out for Benicia along Lake Herman Road. The lights of her car had illuminated the crumpled bodies of two teenagers at the roadside. Heart pounding, she had raced the rest of the way into Benicia and flagged down a police cruiser. For some reason the stranger reminded her of that traumatic moment.

Her nephew, Albert, had also noticed eerie occurrences a year after the murders. "We grew up on the Borges Ranch," he told me. "My Aunt Stella saw a lot of strange things over the years and so did I. It was her home her entire life. In November 1969, I was in the military and had a weekend pass. My ride dropped me off at the rest area around 10:00 P.M. My brother proceeded down

Lake Herman Road to the rest area with his girlfriend and waited for me. He was familiar with the road and the Zodiac incident the previous Christmas. We all were.

"He was armed with a pistol in his truck on the way back across Lake Herman Road. Not far from the Lake Herman gate someone had lifted a huge log across the road. It was nine or ten feet long. We could not go around. We stopped. I felt uneasy, looked around, and I told my brother to back up and go around the long way to Vallejo. There I called the police and reported it. Later, [to the south] at wooded Dan Foley Park by Lake Chabot, several teenagers on the hill were shooting BB guns. They observed a large man at a distance watching them. He stayed as long as they did, then left. Many people saw this stalker.

"In the early 1970s, we used to go shooting and target-practice by the rock quarry. We had done that for years. My cousins told me about a big guy who used to come up and shoot with a whole armory in his car—military-type weapons, .45 Colts, M-16s, and the like. He wore military fatigues, bloused boots, and all. One day I was up there shooting and this guy was also there. When he saw me he immediately came up to where I was and challenged me. 'What are you doing here?'

"This guy was a gun nut and had burned up one box of ammo after another. He was wearing a black baseball cap and was about six feet one, large and muscular like myself. But I felt at a disadvantage, uneasy because he had strange eyes and he did not take them off me throughout his questioning, even when I told him I was a member of the family. I drove by Lake Herman the next day, and stopped by the gate where my aunt found that first couple of victims, and what a chill I got. It was like the incident had just happened. I thought to myself what if an old Chevy Impala should pull up alongside—then got the hell out of there.

"I came to the conclusion that Zodiac was probably in the Navy or at least worked at the Mare Island shipyard. Vallejo police have fouled up in the past, and I wonder if this fellow was closer to the police than we think. I personally believe that after shooting the couple at Blue Rock Springs, Zodiac did drive down Lake Herman Road and since he was a pretty thorough person, had a police car radio so he could keep tabs on all aspects of information being relayed."

Mrs. Borges's nephew was not the only one who had observed bizarre events on the outskirts of Vallejo. An Oakland man's son had been out at Blue Rock Springs the very evening of Zodiac's Fourth of July, 1969, murder and seen someone quite like Leigh Allen. "They were out riding their motorcycles along Columbus Parkway," the father explained, "when they met a huge man walking along the road. My son was going to offer him a ride, but he was so huge and the motorcycle so small he decided against it. Besides, he said, it was near twilight and the man looked kind of spooky. In any event, he appeared to come from a car parked further down the road. My son described a 1950s black Plymouth, but was vague about the license plate number. It had an 'X' in it, he's sure of that. He was very confident about the make and color of the car. My son was about seventeen at the time, and I am sure he did not repeat his observations to the police, especially when he heard a murder had taken place right after. It probably frightened him in the extreme."

Zodiac was a watcher—no doubt of that. The lonely always are.

SATURDAY, JULY 15, 1972

CAROLYN Nadine Davis, long blond hair parted in the middle, gray-blue eyes, a fifteen-year-old runaway from Shasta County, left her Grandmother Adelian's house in Garberville. In the pocket of her black coat nestled a one-way plane ticket from Redding to San Francisco. At 1:50 P.M. the road stretched ahead. She swung her green-print cloth handbag and eyed passing cars. In the bag was a false I.D. that identified her as "Carolyn Cook." She approached the on-ramp, began hitchhiking on 101 in a southerly direction, and was not seen alive again. The other missing women had been hitchhiking north. If Allen were responsible, the change from a northerly direction to a southerly one was accounted for. He was no longer working in Pinole and traveling north homeward each evening.

8

ARTHUR LEIGH ALLEN

THURSDAY, SEPTEMBER 7, 1972

"THERE was a second meeting with investigators," Panzarella told me. "Leigh was then living in a house trailer somewhere on the coast and I had been there. The most bizarre thing is that hanging on the wall was a picture of him buffed out, a senior in high school, winning the CIA Diving Championship, and this guy's totally healthy looking. Only seven, eight years later, he's a three hundred pound blob."

Bill Armstrong contacted Don Cheney in Torrance again. A year had now snaked by since he and Toschi had questioned Leigh Allen. So many homicides, so many suspects, so many legal hurdles to clear. "Inspector, I was going to call you," Cheney said. "I don't know if it's important, but I thought of something else Arthur Leigh Allen and I discussed in our conversation on New Year's Day, 1969. When Leigh was discussing his plan, I can recall that he asked me how you could disguise your handwriting. I remember my response. I told him, 'I guess you could go to a library and get books on writing examination to find out how writing is identified.' "

Armstrong absorbed this, then asked Cheney again if he was certain about his memory of his conversation with Allen.

"I am positive," he said.

Things were moving again.

Toschi scanned a photocopy of the first letter signed Zodiac— the dread it inspired two years ago still fresh in his mind. "This is the Zodiac speaking," it began. Zodiac had firmly handprinted these three pages twenty months after Allen's conversation with Cheney. After studying the originals and discovering no indented or secret writing, the FBI returned them to Sacramento on August 18, 1969. Thus, Toschi had only a copy for reference. A phrase had stuck in Toschi's mind, and so he leafed through the August 4, 1969, photostat, rereading it, misspellings and all.

"Last Christmass—In that epasode the police were wondering as to how I could shoot & hit my victims in the dark. They did not openly state this, but implied this by saying it was a well lit night & I could see silowets on the horizon.

"Bullshit that area is srounded by high hills & trees. What I did was *tape a small pencel flash light to the barrel of my gun.* If you notice, in the center of the beam of light if you aim it at a wall or ceilling you will see a black or darck spot in the center of the circle of the light about 3 to 6 in. across.

"When taped to a gun barrel the bullet will strike exactly in the center of the black dot in the light. All I had to do was spray them . . ." Here Toschi came to the remainder of this last sentence, one he and Armstrong had ordered the press not to print. It read: "as if it was a water hose; there was no need to use the gunsights. I was not happy to see that I did not get front page cover-age." [Signed with Zodiac's crossed circle and "no address."]

An *electric gun sight*—exactly as Allen had suggested to Cheney. "Leigh actually constructed such a device," Cheney told me much later. "He put a penlight on an H&R revolver with tape." Zodiac, enraptured by his science fiction invention, referred to it again in his November 9, 1969, letter: "To prove that I am the Zodiac, Ask the Vallejo cop about *my electric gun sight* which I used to start my collecting of slaves." Vallejo cop? What Vallejo cop? thought Toschi. Had Zodiac, like Leigh Allen, been questioned by an as yet unknown Vallejo policeman at some point before November 9, 1969?

"The next time we saw Allen was up in Santa Rosa," Toschi explained. "That's when we felt we might have something. Leigh's name was just thrown at us again in a phone call late one morning." Toschi never did determine the exact date of that call. He recalled only that it was summer (it was still light out at eight o'clock that night) and that enough time had passed for witnesses to grow dispirited about the progress Vallejo police were making.

"I would really like to talk to you about a case you and your partner are working on," began the caller circumspectly.

"Are we talking about Zodiac?" Toschi asked.

"Yes, absolutely. You're reading my mind. I'm the brother. I believe you know what I'm talking about."

There was caution and concern in his voice. "I do," Toschi said, recalling the visit he and Armstrong and Mulanax had paid to Ron and Karen Allen's house one August night.

"I feel, and my wife feels, a larger police department with more resources could do a little bit more than what the Vallejo Police Department has been doing. I can only speculate what they are doing at the present time, Inspector."

"Have you given all your information to the Vallejo Police Department?" Toschi asked.

"Yes, but we don't think they have done enough," Ron said.

"When Ron Allen called," Toschi told me later, "he was a very concerned person and really was asking San Francisco to talk to him. He says, 'I need to talk to you fellows and I've already spoken to Sergeant Mulanax and some other officers.' It was like he wasn't getting the same officer all the time, that he wanted to pass information on. And right away my brain is thinking ahead like, 'Oh, God, here we go again because I've got to talk to Jack Mulanax. We can't drop the ball—I mean, it's his jurisdiction.' "

"Where are you?" Toschi asked.

"I'm in the city," Ron Allen said, and told him where—between Market and Mission on First Street.

"Can you get away this afternoon for fifteen or twenty minutes so we can talk to you and just see what you have?"

"Yes, I can take a break. How soon?"

"Can you spare some time so we can come down immediately?"

They agreed to meet in the lobby of the PG&E Building in downtown San Francisco in about thirty minutes. "What are you going to be wearing?" asked Toschi. "The two of us will be there."

"And that's how it all started," Toschi told me. "We naturally went in and ran it by our boss, Charlie Ellis, real quick. I told the lieutenant what we got and he says, 'Another one, another tip.' I said, 'Charlie, this is a brother of the man that he believes is our killer and he lives in Vallejo. This sounds awfully good. He really wants to talk to us,' I explained. 'We can't turn it down.' He said, 'OK, get on it.' Then we ran it by the chief of inspectors, Charles Barca. 'You usually get your best information from a member of the family,' he said. I had a smile on my face.

"Ron was so sincere on the phone, within thirty or forty min-

utes we're talking to him in the lobby of his workplace. As soon
as he came out of the elevator, we looked at him. He was very
slender, wearing a suit, and balding a bit. The strain had obviously worn on him. I could see a bit of relief that San Francisco
was involved and I realized he recognized us. 'Thank you, Inspectors, for coming down so quickly,' he said. 'I've just got to
talk to you.' And we sat down and took some notes. Soon as we
spoke to him I could detect the truth coming out of his mouth.

"Initially, what we did was listen. If you want to learn something, you listen. We asked him if we could speak with his wife.
He said, 'Of course. I'd like you to speak with my wife because
she feels like I do.' And we felt this sounds pretty good, the best
that we ever had of any suspect, with a brother coming forward
and not being satisfied with what the other sheriffs' and police
departments had been doing.

"We told him we'd like to come to his home that evening and
take in-depth statements with his wife and get some proof and
corroboration. 'I hope you don't have a problem with that,' I said.
'No,' he said, 'My wife feels the same way. We're both frightened. I'd like you to talk to my wife.'

"We called Jack Mulanax to set it up. 'I talked to the guy,' Mulanax said. 'We've checked Allen out pretty well.' 'I know,' I told
him, believing him to a degree, 'but Ron's giving us some more
information and we just have to tell you we're coming into your
territory. It's police courtesy. The brother called us. We can't put
it away.'" The behavior of the Vallejo P.D. had always puzzled
Toschi. It was as if a second mystery underlay the watery town of
Vallejo, invisibly affecting the investigation at every turn. "For
some reason Lynch and Lundblad didn't want to come to some of
our early conferences in Sacramento. And here Bill and I are
driving ninety miles up there.

"We arrived at the Allen home at 7:30 P.M. It was still light out.
Karen had expected us, but rambled for twenty minutes not really
saying anything. It was corroborated later that evening how serious they took us. 'I know there are a lot of leads coming in and
clues,' she said. They had consulted an uncle before calling, to be
certain they were doing the right thing.

"Everything was coming out slow, but every time she would
say something of substance, Ron would shake his head, and say,
'Yes, that's true.' They were both in sync with each other out of
their fear and concern that he was still out there.

" 'We're very frustrated,' Karen told me. 'We just don't know how serious Vallejo took us. I know there are a lot of leads coming in. We just decided to call you because we were seeing your name and Inspector Armstrong's name in the papers.' 'Because of the letters to the *Chronicle* and the media coverage,' I told them, 'we're getting it all. We sure would like to spread it around a little more.' That got a little chuckle from both Ron and Karen. 'When we get a call, we take it seriously,' I told them. 'We just decided, you took the time to call, we'll take the information now and notify the detective from that jurisdiction, see what he knows and maybe it will ring a bell.'

"I noticed that Ron was speaking with even more emotion than earlier. It was as if a little frustration had entered Ron and his wife since they saw nothing more was coming from the Vallejo investigation. Ron and Karen told us that Leigh had spent time in Southern California and was familiar with the area, but they weren't too sure exactly what he was doing because he was on his own a lot.

"As we progressed we learned about the school in Sonoma and that he had a trailer up there. 'Leigh has a couple of old junkers, old beat-up cars,' Ron told us. 'He's what you would call a professional student.' Allen's sister-in-law told us that the suspect was now residing alone in a house trailer in Santa Rosa part of the week [Tuesdays, Fridays, and Saturdays]. Apparently this is where he kept all his personal property. We just didn't have enough at the time to move up there. You can't just go running in ten different directions. We were very careful to see the chief of inspectors when we came back, to keep him apprised of every move we made. 'Keep working on it,' Barca said.

"Next morning, I went in to see Walter Giubbini. We knew we needed more, but we had to fill in the number-two man in the D.A.'s office. All the fingerprinting had been negative and the handprinting of Arthur Leigh Allen had, according to Mulanax and Lundblad, been negative, but the chief assistant sat straight up as we told him what the Allens had related. 'We're pretty excited about it,' I said.

" 'I wonder why Vallejo didn't call you guys,' said Giubbini, 'and tell you everything about this Arthur Leigh Allen.'

" 'We're giving them everything we've got, Walter, so we can get closure on this. Do we have enough for a search warrant?'

" 'Frankly, you don't. Unless you get more physical evidence, all you have is theories and speculations by the brother of Leigh Allen.'

"'We're making some enemies with the other jurisdictions, these other detectives,' said Toschi.

"'That's natural,' said Giubbini. 'D.A.s are like that too. They want to hold on and hog the case. But this is too good for you to just drop off with Jack Mulanax. You work it. They called for you. It sounds good, but work it up a little bit more.'

"We just kept moving along on Allen," continued Toschi, "kinda focusing on him, but not ruling anyone else out. You can't do that if you want to be a good detective. Because if all you're thinking about is 'John Doe,' when 'Charlie Smith' is actually your suspect, you're in real trouble. We weren't getting tunnel vision on Allen and excluding other suspects. Still, he was the best we had had up to that time. Most of what Ron and Karen told us had already been discussed with Mulanax and Lundblad, only with more feeling with us. We were satisfied with Mulanax and his investigation. He did what he could. But I kept in contact with Mulanax, Lundblad, and Nicolai and Narlow.

"In Vallejo there was resentment, which bothered me all the time, especially when we went over to their headquarters. You could sense uniformed guys kind of turning their backs and staring at us. Here I am walking in with my large black folder, which I had with me constantly. We were goading the other guys, saying, 'Stay with him. He's too good to let go even if you've spoken to him ten times each. We are very impressed with this suspect.' We were getting a lot of misinformation from Vallejo, Solano. This is why there is such a long delay before we got a warrant."

Each time Toschi descended from Homicide, he passed Giubbini's office in the west corner of the third floor, and Giubbini would call out, "Catch Zodiac yet?" Then he would laugh. But as the two investigators continued to gather evidence for a search warrant, he slowly became a believer. "Keep trying," Giubbini said.

"Finally, when we felt we had built up enough information," said Toschi, "that's when we went to our lieutenant again. 'I think maybe we could get a search warrant,' I said. We had a lot going, but we just pursued the case much more than the other detectives working on Arthur Leigh Allen. It just sounded so right. That's how we ended up finally getting a warrant."

It was the information about Leigh's trailer that impelled Arm-

strong and Toschi to seek a search warrant specifically for Santa
Rosa. They began laying the groundwork—a time-consuming and
tedious business. The D.A.'s office, specifically Fred Whissman,
in one county, San Francisco, had to be convinced. A judge, James
Jones, Jr., in another county, Sonoma, had to grant a warrant. If
they wanted to search Allen's basement in Vallejo or his locker at
the refinery in Pinole, that required warrants from Solano County
and Contra Costa County. And negotiations with two other judges
and district attorneys.

"And all the time more information was pouring in to Armstrong and to me from Allen's brother. I just kept gathering it up
and putting it all into a large homicide case folder. Then more
physical evidence, until we reached a point where we went
again to Giubbini and this time he listened. 'Type up a search
warrant for Allen in Sonoma County,' he said, and we did."

THURSDAY, SEPTEMBER 14, 1972

"WE compiled enough to complete an affidavit through our district attorney and search whatever property Leigh had in Santa
Rosa," Toschi said. At noon, Bill Armstrong filed an affidavit for
a search warrant to the City of Santa Rosa Municipal Court,
Sonoma County. Specifically, he and Toschi wanted a close look
inside Leigh's Universal trailer parked at the Sunset Trailer Park.
He requested the warrant include the shed Allen kept adjoining
the conventional trailer. Armstrong described to Judge James E.
Jones, Jr., the property they sought: two 9-millimeter guns, ammunition for them, and any expended 9-millimeter casings; a .22-
caliber semiautomatic pistol, ammunition for it, and any
expended cartridges from that weapon. They were especially interested in any pistol with a flashlight attached to its barrel.

The detective listed other evidence, items that fell under the
province of stolen property: identification taken from the body of
Paul Stine, keys to his yellow taxi, and the missing portion of the
cabbie's bloodstained shirt. Until recently Zodiac had been including bloodstained squares of the fabric inside his letters. All
communications from Zodiac had abruptly ceased eighteen
months ago. Toschi suspected they would never receive another
scrap of that gray-and-white-striped sport shirt. From the Lake
Berryessa attack Armstrong designated the square-topped, black

executioner's hood with a white circle and a cross emblazoned on it; black Wing Walker boots, size 10^1/2 R; a blue bloodstained windbreaker jacket; a large foot-long knife, one inch wide with a wooden handle with two brass rivets and tape around the handle. Armstrong did not list the wooden brass-riveted scabbard for the knife. He spoke to the judge in chambers and went over some of the more confidential information with him. A stenographer took down his words.

"I remember the judge reading our affidavit and saying he actually felt we had him. 'Good hunting, Detectives,' he said. 'I believe you finally have your man.' And the D.A. here in San Francisco said, 'I think you've got him.' Even though other detectives had talked with the brother, we couldn't drop the case. Our district attorney felt the same way. We just had to be sure. As usual we shared everything we did with Vallejo. We even told them we were going to Santa Rosa with a search warrant in case they wanted to come along. And they said, 'No.' Bill Armstrong and I didn't even know if Vallejo was being up front with us in 1969–70 and '71. They almost resented us because of everything flowing into San Francisco because of the *Chronicle*. I told Giubbini, 'Bill and I aren't out to badmouth the other detectives. We have a job to do.' "

Toschi picked up aspirin at the little cigar shop in the Hall of Justice. He grabbed some animal crackers from the corner store. "I'd usually bring in two or three boxes when we'd start to go on call on Monday morning," he said. "I got so I liked them. So little time and I had to eat something. My head was almost coming off from stress. I chewed more than my share of aspirin every day, and especially the day we went to Santa Rosa."

Toschi and Armstrong, accompanied by Bob Dagitz, an SFPD fingerprint examiner who had worked the Stine murder, and two local deputy sheriffs, arrived at 2963 Santa Rosa Avenue. Santa Rosa was a busy road not too far from the rush of traffic. Some of the trailers had gravel lawns spotted with foliage more suitable for the desert. They began hunting for the trailer.

"When we make an arrest, our work in Homicide begins," said Toschi. "Is it a strong case for the grand jury? Is it a weak case? How can I build it up? What didn't I do properly? Unlike my television counterparts, much of my time is spent in dealing with the families of the deceased and the families of the suspect. I must sympathize with one and be extremely sensitive with the other. I'm an average guy and I'm an honest policeman. Anyone who is allowed legally to carry a loaded gun, and the right to shoot it, has power, but it calls for a lot of common sense. When I first put on my first gun I felt like a cowboy. I have only used it twice." Under his corduroy jacket, on his left side, Toschi wore his upside-down triple-draw lightning rig. A spring in the holster held his .38-caliber Colt Cobra in place. They might be going up against a dangerous and powerful man. A refill of six bullets and handcuffs on his right side balanced the weight.

"As I said, I've drawn my gun twice. I was fired upon on September 22, 1956. Afterwards, they said I'd saved the life of a man who had been shot a few seconds before I got there. I threw him to the ground as I saw they had a shotgun. I couldn't I.D. either one because it happened too fast. I saw the gun at the window, actually kicked in the door—it was not bolted too well, and caught one guy. Got the shotgun. The other guy got caught in the backyard. About an hour later I wondered, 'Why was I playing such a cowboy?' That's the closest I came to being killed."

Ron and Karen Allen had provided them with precise directions on the trailer's location. Sadly, they had never visited the trailer. Toschi, to be certain, had Mrs. Reese, the trailer court manager, show them specifically which stall the professional student used. They walked unsteadily along the tar, concrete, and gravel sections that made up the stalls. At each, an aquamarine pole sported a miniature white streetlight. A few trees were struggling to grow. The sky was so crystal blue it made their eyes ache. "That's it." Reese gestured. "A-7." The trailer's license, AP 6354, jibed with their information. "But he just drove off before you arrived," she said.

Leigh had been in such a hurry that he had left his trailer door standing open. Had he somehow known they were coming and fled with incriminating evidence? His immediate flight was suspicious, but there was nothing they could do about it. The suspect, a police groupie, was friendly with many officers and might have been warned. "You get friendly with cops and you hear things," said Toschi. Perhaps his relatives had had a last-minute change of heart. The detectives just didn't know. All they knew for certain was that they were dealing with a highly intelligent and cunning man.

Toschi and Armstrong spent the time poking around the exterior. Allen had made some alterations to the trailer, an earth-colored affair streaked with rust in places. "It was a standard trailer," said Toschi. Tapered concrete blocks supported the off-wheels trailer. A locked shed adjoined it. What the detectives didn't know was that Allen had recently repaneled the interior of one of his trailers, possibly this one, maybe the one in Bodega. Was something hidden within those walls? "We kind of moseyed around because we had a search warrant," said Toschi. The investigators invited themselves in and made a cursory inspection of the trailer. It had an acrid smell like the refinery. Toschi indicated a map of Lake Berryessa taped to the wall. Zodiac had attacked a couple there.

Bob Dagitz had been excited about Allen as a suspect as soon as he heard Allen was familiar with Berryessa and the outskirts of Vallejo. He knew Leigh was ambidextrous, good with a bow and arrow, and proficient with various weapons. Toschi thought that Allen fulfilled everything he thought Zodiac should be. He moved Allen's bed away from the wall and discovered the largest jar of Vaseline he had ever seen. Several large, uncleaned dildos rolled out at his feet. Sadomasochistic pornography was stacked in a box, and male blow-up dolls were in the trailer. Books on chemistry and biology were everywhere, many stamped with Allen's name. Some bloodstained clothing littered a table. But they knew Allen was a hunter. Toschi pushed the bed back into place and entered the small unkempt kitchen. He pried open the freezer. Little animal hearts, livers, and mutilated rodent bodies were inside.

Though no real sex was involved in Zodiac's assaults, technically he was a sexual psychopath or, more accurately, a sexual sadist. Stanford's Dr. Donald T. Lunde told me that sexual sadists commonly acted out sadistic impulses in their early teens—torturing and killing cats, dogs, and other small animals. "He tortures and kills substitute victims, small animals," he said. "There certainly is the need to kill . . . something at certain intervals." Lunde believed that in adulthood, such an individual, if it were made very difficult for him to kill humans, might revert to killing animals. "It would be better than nothing," he said.

"The sociopathic murderer usually has a physically cruel, rejecting father and perhaps a hysterical, seductive mother," Dr. Manfred Guttmacher reported in *The Mind of the Murderer*. "The effects of cruelty on the small child are more than simple neglect. In retaliation, the sociopath inflicts cruelty on others and feels no guilt in doing so. The earliest objects of his cruelty are often animals."

Though Allen was working toward a degree in biology, he hadn't yet requested permission from the state to dissect and experiment on small animals. He would file an application for a scientific collecting permit with the Resources Agency of the California Department of Fish and Game. "I intend to collect the following species," Allen would write, "chipmunks—number indefinite. I expect to collect in the following localities: Marin County, Sonoma County and Mendocino County, (Possibly Solano, Napa & Lassen). I desire to collect by the following methods: Live traps (Havahart & home-made)." He was under the sponsorship of Dr. John D. Hopkirk, an associate professor of biology of Sonoma State College, where Allen majored in biological sciences and minored in chemistry.

Forty-five minutes after racing off, Allen returned. They heard his old clunker approaching, and were outside to meet him as he parked. A cloud of dust arose. "It was nice seeing Allen drive up and really introducing ourselves," Toschi said later. "Both of us said, 'Leigh, how are you—we're San Francisco police inspectors.' His car was dirty. Through the dirty rear window, we could see clothes, papers, and books in the backseat. He was frightened when he showed up because he had never had two detectives actually talking to him with a warrant in hand and we took him by surprise—the first time he had met two cops who meant business, face to face, inches away, and he didn't know if we were going to arrest him." Because Leigh was into a lot of other stuff, he wasn't sure, at first, what had brought the police to his trailer.

The huge chemist crawled out of his car.

"What's all this about?" he said coolly.

Allen didn't recall Toschi and Armstrong from their visit to the refinery a year ago. He should have remembered, or might have been shamming.

"We want to talk to you, Leigh," said Armstrong. "We have a search warrant for your trailer and for your person. We have information that you are a very good suspect in the Zodiac murders."

Allen explained he thought Zodiac had been arrested. "Besides, I live in Vallejo," he added, "and I've already talked to Vallejo P.D."

"We know," Toschi said. "Here's your copy of the warrant."

"Well, help yourself," conceded Allen with a shrug.

Now the investigators began a more exhaustive scrutiny, dragging furniture away from the dingy windows and drawing back the sheets. Toschi tugged the bed away from the wall as if for the first time. Again dildos rolled out.

"I just sort of fool around," Leigh said matter-of-factly.

He did not seem at all embarrassed by that, or the sadistic pornography the detectives ferreted out. In the close quarters of the off-wheels trailer they were aware of how physically powerful their suspect was. "Allen was an awesome and frightening man, a beast," said Toschi. "He was so upset and angry at our being on his turf at Santa Rosa. Over the next hour, we tore apart his place pretty good. I remember for some reason he took an immediate dislike to me personally. And I was always the good guy. The D.A.s would use me to disarm these guys. I remember some of the guys saying, 'With Dave it just comes natural. People believe him.' I would just get them to talk to me, and I mean this without being pompous. But Armstrong told me afterward, 'I don't understand it. He doesn't like you. Everybody likes you.' Even Bob Dagitz, who was with us to take his prints, said, 'That's the first time, Dave, I ever saw a suspect not like you.' "

As they questioned Allen, Toschi did most of the talking, still playing good cop. Allen had an "I've seen through your sweet-talking act" look on his face. Toschi continued to probe. He noticed Allen was wearing a ring with a "Z" on it and the Zodiac watch, a gift for Christmas, 1968. He was practically shouting that he was Zodiac. "We have to take your prints," Toschi told the student. Obviously annoyed, Allen fought against that. Finally, Dagitz got good fingerprints. He went to a lamp in the corner, and began making comparisons to the prints found on Stine's cab. They believed Zodiac had left behind eight points on each of two fingerprints on the taxi. Partial fingerprints usually contain twelve characteristic points. All fingerprints have a delta, which serves as a starting point to tally the number of friction ridges separating it from the core of the pattern: radial loops, ulnar loops, arches, tented arches, and whorls. From the symbol numbers assigned to the components, the final classification is evolved. Toschi knew that less than twelve points of similarity would be subject to an expert's "opinion" and that fragmentary prints, such as they had, most often could not be positively matched. He also knew that Dagitz was one of the best print men.

Dagitz worked quietly by the lamp in a corner of the trailer. He wrote down: "0 9 R 001 13/ 4 18 U 101 13." Then they went about getting samples of Allen's handprinting. Toschi had two sheets of paper with typed sentences supplied by Sherwood Morrill. He had been carrying them around for three years. "Sherwood had given us forms when we had the opportunity, as he put it, 'to have a strong suspect' print for us," recalled Toschi, "and I had them ready. On the original letters, the ink was quite dark, as if Zodiac had pressed very, very hard. He was very deliberate in what he was saying. The printing was small, most of it lower case. Once you saw one, you would pretty much immediately recognize another as from him." The detective told Leigh he had to reprint the sentences on the first page. "We want you to print right- and left-handed and in upper case and lower case," he said. "We want you to print this list of sentences."

"You'll notice," Toschi told me later, "that in the exemplar that Leigh printed for us we had him use a black felt-tipped pen. We thought since we were going this far, we might as well do it right. There are only a few companies putting out such inks as he uses. Sherwood had always said that Zodiac was probably printing right-handed in his letters. I asked another expert [Postal Inspector John Shimoda] later and he felt the same way—'the printing was of a right-hand type.' But Allen was known to be ambidextrous, and I remember him telling us that he 'usually did things left-handed, but could use both hands in certain activities.' All his family and friends told us positively that Leigh could write, shoot, and shoot bow and arrow with either hand."

Toschi showed Allen the phrase "up until now I have killed five." "We want you to just print the way you normally print," he said. "I understand you have some ability with your left hand," Toschi added. "I don't do it left-handed," said Allen. "Who told you that?"

"We know what you can do and what you can't."

Allen had been born left-handed and forced to be right-handed in elementary school. Everyone there knew that. He cooperated with the investigation and wrote handwriting exemplars with both his right and left hands. Allen appeared to have some difficulty writing left-handed. "I can't," he said.

"He is ambidextrous," thought Toschi. "Do the best you can. Print capital letters, small letters. Print what we tell you," said

Toschi. Allen didn't like that at all. "We had him go from 'A' to 'Z' and from '1 to 10.'"

"Why can't I print what I want?" he snarled.

Toschi, impatience showing in his voice for the first time, told him, "Because this is what we want you to print." "The suspect's right handprinting and his left handprinting were almost identical," Toschi told me, "but right-handed his printing was a bit larger. When you see Leigh again you might pay attention to what hand he uses to write with. Allen appeared to be disturbed as he printed. It was not as neat as samples of his earlier writing."

Then Toschi asked Allen to print, "This is the Zodiac speaking."

"What are you making me say? That I'm Zodiac?"

Toschi told him no, and promised if the printing did not match Zodiac's, they would walk away. "We will rule you out completely. But we have to be sure."

Right-handed, Allen wrote the phrase in large letters. He was obviously altering his printing. But Allen's printing had that spacey quality found in the Zodiac letters. Toschi noted, "His printing varied from small, neat, sloppy, then larger in the Santa Rosa trailer. He printed a bit larger. Zodiac's lettering was quite small." Toschi laid down Morrill's second page of quotes. "Print, 'In answer to your answer for more details about the good times I had in Vallejo, I shall be very happy to supply even more material.'" he said. Allen copied it faithfully, repeating the word "more."

Then Allen was ordered to print a phrase from a letter in which Zodiac quoted from memory and paraphrased Gilbert and Sullivan's *The Mikado*. "All people who are shaking hands shake hands like that." The last lines Allen wrote tilted toward the bottom right side of the page, as was common in Zodiac letters. He also copied, "I am no longer in control of myself." On December 20, 1969, Zodiac had written: "I am afraid I will loose control again and take my nineth & possibly tenth victom."

But time was running out and the policemen had found no smoking gun inside the trailer connecting Allen to the Zodiac. "Allen seemed to know what to say," said Toschi. "Not a dumb man. A very wily man. I'll never forget being in his presence. He mentioned Berryessa. He shook our hands. We left our cards.

"And I could feel the hatred as we were leaving. He must have been relieved, thinking that 'I'm not going to get busted,' but also thinking, 'Are they going to come back?' As I left I said, 'I'll be seeing you again, Leigh,' Anything he was planning went on hold. Allen wasn't cool when we left. There was a lot of frustration when we left the trailer court."

The detectives adjourned to the Holiday Inn Coffee Shop at 3345 Santa Rosa Avenue, about six blocks away, to have lunch and discuss the exploration. It was hot. Toschi could tell Dagitz was pretty depressed. The fingerprint expert put down his cup and said, "The prints on Stine's cab, if they were those of Zodiac, do not match Allen's. It's a positive no."

"But," said Armstrong, "there were so many fingerprints in this public cab, that it is unknown that if, in fact, we have Zodiac's fingerprints at the crime scene or not. In some of the letters Zodiac wrote us, he bragged that he put airplane glue on fingers to obliterate any fingerprints."

"So they have a latent print," Mulanax later told me. "It's my own personal opinion there's a lot of doubt this could be a Zodiac print. You dust a cab and you're going to lift some latents off it. Doesn't necessarily mean it's the guy who did the job. On the same thing, up in Napa, they have a partial palm print, but how many people use a public phone booth?"

"When we drove back from Santa Rosa," said Toschi, "even though we were told we had to have a little bit more, we then went up to see Sherwood Morrill. The refinery where Leigh had worked was not too far from Vallejo. Every time I pass it going up to Sacramento, I'd see the darn thing and it would bring back memories. I would think, 'I wish we could close this case.' This is what was on my mind constantly. Constantly. And I felt we did."

In Sacramento a heavyset, scholarly man in a three-piece pinstripe suit greeted them. Morrill took the two pages Allen had printed. He studied them through his thick glasses. That night he would put them under his twin microscope. "Morrill, to be honest, shot us down," Toschi recalled, "He phoned and said, 'Sorry, Dave. There's just no match. I'm sure you have the right suspect and I'm sure you're on the right track.' Sherwood indicated that the handprinting was *similar,* but not the Zodiac killer's."

"The thing that impressed me about the handwriting," Detective Lynch recalled, "every time I'd take a handwriting sample to Morrill, he'd just sit at his desk and I'd hand it to him and 'No good.' He did that I don't know how many times. All I know is that when Zodiac was writing these letters, he was either drinking, smoking pot, or taking some kind of narcotics because it just seemed to me that as he wrote his handwriting would just deteriorate."

Terry Pascoe, a Department of Justice Document Examiner, reported to Armstrong. "If the writing had been a product of a mental state," he said, "the writing of a subject can be different when in a different mental state, or it could be a case of an intentional deception. With the talents that [Allen] has, writing with both hands, this could be done." He later told Detective George Bawart that "a person of high intelligence could study the methods used to examine handwriting and fool a documents examiner." Afterward Bawart reported, "Our handwriting expert, Cunningham, confirms that if Allen had the ability to write with his left hand, this could explain the inability to match the handprinting to Arthur Leigh Allen."

Armstrong listened intently to Pascoe. "Do not eliminate this subject because of handwriting," he warned. But Morrill, who had examined all the known writings of Zodiac, told Toschi and Armstrong that he did not feel a mental state would change a person's handwriting. He was a rival of the younger Pascoe and the two often differed on opinions. Armstrong was never able to reconcile this problem. It was not unprecedented. Peter Kurten, the Dusseldorf Ripper, wrote letters reproduced in the same newspaper his wife read each morning. She never recognized the writing as her husband's. Kurten's altered mental state while composing the notes made him a completely different person with a different handwriting. I wondered if Leigh had other personalities. "By the way, Robert," Morrill confided to me later (November 17, 1980), "I do now note that the printing that Allen is doing is contrived and not natural to his own."

Toschi had thought they were really going to find something. "As soon as we started getting information from the sister-in-law and the brother," he said, "I felt Allen was the one. It all sounded just perfect, but we just couldn't find a way to prove that Leigh Allen was the Zodiac killer. We had done everything but stand Arthur Leigh Allen on his head. We found no physical evidence inside the trailer linking Allen to the Zodiac case. Everything he had, according to his brother and sister-in-law, was in that trailer. We checked the Department of Motor Vehicles. He might have some other trailers and vehicles not registered. A very shrewd, very wily individual."

The mistake lay in failing to obtain search warrants for Vallejo (in spite of Allen's ailing elderly mother) *and* Santa Rosa. The detectives might have had the misfortune to search the wrong place. From the inception of the murders, Zodiac had used the multiple-county strategy, striking in unincorporated sections of Vallejo or areas of confused jurisdiction between sheriffs' and police departments. Benicia police actually secured the Lake Herman Road crime scene until Vallejo sheriff's men could be brought in. And of course the VPD wanted part of the action. And so did the Oakland P.D.

If Arthur Leigh Allen was Zodiac, then after the trailer search, he had only to speed to his Vallejo basement and destroy all physical evidence connecting him with the crimes. And what of Allen's other trailers? He might have caches in every county Zodiac killed in. "We were always wondering," said Toschi, "is there another vehicle nearby? We were just wondering if we could find the right one. The right piece of evidence that says, 'That's him. Gotcha.'"

"When Armstrong met with Cheney and I in another meeting," said Panzarella, "that's where I learned about the trailer search. Armstrong's telling us about dead animals, all the vibrators Leigh had for having sex with himself, dildos and all that stuff. But they still couldn't get anything on him. The more I think, over the course of a lifetime, when I think of the most interesting people I've met in my life, Leigh certainly was one of them. And the more we know about him, the more we know he was certainly capable of doing something like that. You've got a smart guy who decides his contribution to the culture is he's going to murder people in unincorporated areas mostly manned by small police departments. You know it's pretty easy to get away with that if you're smart. It's all circumstantial, but who else could it be but Leigh Allen. It frightens me, I'll tell you that."

And thus the best Zodiac suspect of all had passed every one of the detectives' tests and they went on to other suspects. So far Zodiac had sent three pieces of the gray-and-white-striped sports shirt he had torn from Stine after shooting him. Toschi estimated, "That leaves about 120 square inches of the shirt still unaccounted for." At the *San Francisco Chronicle,* we all awaited the next scrap of bloodied fabric and the horrifying message wrapped around it.

9
POLICEMAN AND
SAILOR

BUT that blood-soaked letter did not arrive. Zodiac had apparently disappeared. But on the Southern California front, Zodiac's shadow was not only present, but looming larger. After sleuthing hundreds of hours, the Santa Barbara County Sheriff's Department believed they had finally linked Zodiac to the deaths of Domingos and Edwards.

In July 1971, when Detective Baker of the Major Crimes Unit sent out a statewide Teletype, he'd asked for similars. "Both Bill Armstrong and Mel Nicolai gave me a call," he told me, "and expressed their suspicions that our case may be linked to Zodiac. Just on the basis of the description I offered them there was a good possibility Zodiac was responsible. I ended up traveling and talking to most of the investigators in most of the jurisdictions where the crimes were attributable to Zodiac. And just reviewing their cases and talking with them and they in turn reviewing what I had.

"Mel Nicolai, who I judged to be one of the single most knowledgeable people on all of the cases, told me he felt our case may well be the work of Zodiac. If it isn't, it amazes me how someone could commit murders like those of Linda and Robert and not be heard from before or since. I've worked on other serial-killing cases and the psychopathology involved in our case is no different. When the Lake Berryessa circumstances were described to me, the hair on the back of my neck stood up. I'm sure you can discern the striking similarities."

Just as in the vicious Berryessa attack, the victims were students, a young couple reclining on a blanket by an isolated shore. A sexual sadist tends to target members of his own race, often chooses victims with specific occupations or similar characteristics. His apparently random victims are chosen because they meet some psychological or symbolic need within the murderer's system of delusions. A sadistic sociopathic killer like Zodiac, say FBI profiles, "selects his victims for the purpose of venting certain deeply rooted sexual and sadistic urges, such as the need to mutilate parts of the victim's body to achieve sexual satisfaction." Once he is captured, the killer's detailed and grisly confession itself is a brutal assault thrown in the face of the police.

What if Zodiac was choosing victims who were students like himself? Robert and Linda were targeted because their car on the road above had attracted a roving killer who followed their path down to the water. In both the Napa and Santa Barbara slayings the attacker brought along a knife, a gun, and precut lengths of clothesline. And why tie victims he intended to kill? So he could torture? A serial killer's pleasure springs from his ability to intimidate, command, and exert power over his captive. Terror and the power it brings are a sexual sadist's trademarks because he feels terror and is powerless. Such a man as Zodiac kills those, young couples, who share an intimacy he is incapable of sharing. Gratified by the sight of a cowering, whimpering hostage, he is allowed by the rope to prolong the killing as long as he wishes.

"Both victims were hit in the back (relatively close grouping considering they were running away when hit)," said Baker. That linked Baker's case to Zodiac's Lake Herman Road shootings, also accomplished with accuracy and tight grouping. Zodiac had shot a fleeing woman with deadly accuracy while racing behind. He had done it in the pitch blackness of a country road.

"On the floor of the shack were two empty fifty-round boxes for Winchester Western Super-X .22 long-rifle cartridges," said Baker. "Spent casings had been found along Robert and Linda's flight path. They had six lands and grooves with a right-hand twist." Zodiac had used Super X copper-coated .22 long-rifle ammo in the Lake Herman murders. The double murders had been committed on December 20, 1968, two days after Allen's thirty-fifth birthday. The recovered slugs, in good condition, also had a right-hand (clockwise) twist with six lands and six grooves—a "six and six."

"Stock numbers on the boxes found in the shack could be traced," Baker explained. "The ammunition lot number was TL 21 or TL 22. Our W-W ammo was probably purchased at Vandenberg Air Force Base Exchange based on the fact that it was the nearest source for that lot number. The only store anywhere within a hundred miles that sold it was VAFB. It was determined to a degree of probability to have been purchased there. However, it could be that the same ammo lot number (metallurgical-common origin/batch) was available at other bases as well. The usual clerk at the base exchange at the time was a man named Summers or Sumner. The SAC unit base near Lompoc is less than an hour's drive from the crime scene. That was just one more thing that told us that there might be a connection to Zodiac—I was also considering March AFB or Travis AFB.

"It's not so much hard evidence that links Zodiac with the double murder here, but the pattern of the slaying. We don't have any corroborating fingerprints, bullet or casing marks, or eyewitness observations. If there had been any shoe prints, anything identifiable, I would have jumped on that just for the possibility because I was aware of the Lake Berryessa case." The shoes Zodiac wore at Lake Berryessa in September 1969 were sold through base exchanges only. "Military shoe prints would have been significant. And if there had been anything, I certainly would have remembered that. Whether or not the Riverside case was a Zodiac killing, our case preceded the others by at least three years, far earlier than would be expected. There appears to be a high degree of probability that this subject is responsible for the double murder in our county. Several significant similarities between our case and the others, as well as other evidence, all tend to connect Zodiac with this crime.

"When I last talked to Bill Armstrong at a CHIA conference in San Francisco, he told me he'd never think of the Zodiac murders without including our case as one of them. I never had contact with Dave Toschi after our initial meeting at their office in 1972. I've felt very strongly about it ever since. It's not something that goes away over time. It's the kind of thing that sticks with you." Baker was the kind of cop who would never give up. Outside of Jack the Ripper, there had never been a greater uncaught or more elusive monster than Zodiac.

"The very real possibility of a connection of our case to the core Zodiac case," said Baker, "is the impetus that has brought me to believe that my decades-old suspicion of our case being the work of Zodiac was not misguided. Not to overstate the role of the Domingos/Edwards case in the realm of ultimately solving the Zodiac mystery, I will emphasize again that I firmly believe, within the context of what is probably his first murderous rampage, that within our case lies the solution."

Zodiac himself had provided the link between himself and Baker's case, and had done it in such a devious manner that I only recently tumbled to it. It took an understanding of Zodiac's mind-set of mirror images and transparencies to unravel his visual clue. In his letter of June 26, 1970, Zodiac had circled double-peaked Mount Diablo on a cut section of a Phillips 66 road map. Apparently, Mount Diablo was important to him—its elevation of 3849 feet calling to mind that Stine died in front of 3898 Washington, an address Zodiac himself chose. The map, coupled with a two-line code at the bottom, supposedly told where his bomb was set. On July 24, he dropped another clue. "PS.," he wrote. "The Mt. Diablo Code concerns Radians [a mathematical term representing an angle of measure] &#inches along the radians." Mt. Diablo is a bench mark used by the U.S. Geographical Survey to separate north, south, east, and west— the towns connected by a 57-degree radian. The map also mentioned something a pilot might use—"magnetic north." An "F"-shaped symbol coupled with a backward "7" appeared twice on his threatening Halloween card to Avery. "F" stood for wind speed and direction—north at fifteen to twenty miles an hour. The complete symbol was also an exact copy of a cattle brand used on Fred Harmon's Pagosa Springs, Colorado, ranch. Harmon's comic strip cowboy hero, Red Ryder, was a highly recognizable salesman for air rifles during the 1940s and '50s.

"Zodiac's Mt. Diablo code is a binary spacing code," an expert told me. "The top line is the alpha line, the bottom line is the beta line. This code uses Greek letters, which are to be used as numbers. Example: Alpha=1, and Beta=2. Delta=4. The code operates by the key code letter, and upside-down Greek Gamma, Gamma=3. Therefore, to start this code, you 'ask' the code key questions, like: Who are you, what is your message?" But the map said something entirely different, something visual.

First, I knew that Leigh loved *Mad* magazine and that the Zodiac code of April 20, 1970 ("My name is—") could read "ALFRED E NEUMAN" when deciphered. "By the way have you cracked the last cipher I sent you?" he asked in the same letter. *Cracked* magazine was *Mad*'s chief competitor. Since May 1964, *Mad* had featured a visual puzzle on its inside back cover, a "Fold-In." The instructions read: "Fold this section over left, then fold back so 'A' meets 'B.' " I folded the map so that the ruled corners met at the right edge. Then held the map up to the light so that the back shone through. The crossed circle with an arrow at the twelve o'clock position pointed to the *exact* site of the Domingos/ Edwards murders.

BELOW MOUNT DIABLO, Leigh began to sail again, losing himself in a seemingly endless thousand-mile maze, the Delta. The huge tideland marsh, fed by the Sacramento and San Joaquin Rivers, was diked with countless levees for flood control. Yet Allen never really lost himself in those twisting channels. A point of reference, Mount Diablo, constantly towered in the distance— the amount of acreage visible from its peak second only to that seen from Mount Kilimanjaro. With his flat feet, Allen felt most at home on the water or in the air.

"Big" Dan Blocker, 350-pound star of the *Bonanza* television western, had died suddenly during the previous summer. Allen ceased wearing his enormous white cowboy hat. He could no longer be "Hoss."

TUESDAY, NOVEMBER 21, 1972

AN anniversary of sorts—three years earlier, David Odell Martin came to the FBI's attention when he slashed his wife and eleven-year-old daughter with a broken bottle and knife. Just before police fatally shot him, Martin shouted, "I'm the Zodiac killer!" Armstrong immediately informed the FBI: "Martin is definitely *not* identical with UNSUB in this matter." Toschi told me, "In the first four years of the Zodiac case, I would say about fifteen men have told cops throughout the country that they are Zodiac. Some of them were drunk at the time, some had obvious mental problems, the rest were being booked on other charges and were seeking publicity." When cranks weren't confessing, rumors took the place of new leads in the investigation. One such attributed an undertaker's murder and theft of his embalming fluids to Zodiac.

In Santa Rosa, thirteen-year-old Lori Lee Kursa went shopping at the U-Save Market with her mother. Blue-eyed, long blond hair parted in the middle, she was distinctively dressed in polished-denim bell-bottoms, a brown leather jacket, and brown suede cowboy boots. Around 5:30 P.M. she apparently wandered off. Half an hour later, Lori was observed briefly by a family friend, Barbara, in the same market, but after that nothing more was seen of her. Immediately, her mother reported her missing. The search dragged on through November and into the first week of December, but police unearthed no leads. "You know what was strange about our victims?" Santa Rosa Sergeant Steve Brown later told me. "The first one he threw in the ditch was found by bike riders the next day, so he decided, 'I better hide them a little bit better.' Then he ended up throwing them out by Franz Valley and it's pretty remote. You would need to know that area. You don't just drive there. I recently re-drove it. Of course if the killer lived here and drove around a lot he would know. I'm thinking about a guy who's living in Lake County or Napa County who traveled that road back and forth and who worked over here. If you are going out of Santa Rosa, the dumps are all on the left side of the roadway. You wouldn't pull your car over to the left side, facing the wrong way, to dump a body. He's not going to park on the right side, drag the person across the road and throw them. It doesn't make sense. I was thinking, just like you, he goes out, there's a shed, trailer or barn that he uses. And after they're dead, when he comes back, he's now on the right side of the roadway. That's when he stops and dumps them and then goes back into Santa Rosa."

On December 12, a hiker, Lex Moore, stumbled across Kursa's body in a ravine, about fifty-five feet from Calistoga Road. She had been dumped at the scene completely nude and her body had frozen from the extreme cold. Police estimated she had been dead only a week, though she had been missing for three full weeks. She had been kept alive "somewhere," but they had no suspects.

Someone had broken her neck, dislocating her first and second cervical vertebra. "Strangulation," Stanford's Dr. Lunde explained to me, "is not like shooting someone with a gun. It involves a kind of muscular tension . . . the sensations that come from that play a part in the sexual aspect of these people for which sex and aggression seem to be intertwined. It is also a way of proving to the person their power over the victim. Assertion of raw power, and since that is a big part of the enjoyment for these people, it is prolonged by strangulation. . . . I know one such person who very consciously, more than one, at least two, have volunteered they would take twenty, thirty minutes to strangle victims to prolong the pleasure so to speak."

Kursa's unusual clothes were missing. She had not been sexually assaulted. Unsuspected by the police, the solution to another mystery lay only one hundred yards away. There, a shallow grave in a ravine near the roadway concealed Jeanette Kamahele's corpse—her hands and ankles bound to her neck and white clothesline wrapped around her neck four times. But because the area was deeply wooded, police failed to find her and would not for many years—not until July 6, 1979.

THURSDAY, DECEMBER 28, 1972

AT four in the afternoon, twenty days after a freakish snow dusted Twin Peaks and Golden Gate Park, two men discovered the bones of Maureen Lee Sterling and Yvonne Weber. They were off a rural road 2.2 miles north of Porter Creek Road in the Franz Valley Road area. A powerful murderer, to avoid leaving tracks, had bodily lifted the corpses over shrubs and a ditch, then hurled them down a sixty-six-foot embankment. Apparently, he considered his victims as rubbish to be dumped.

Cause of death and any sexual assault were impossible to determine, but patterns linked the homicides to the others. The killer had murdered them elsewhere and kept their clothes. And the killer tied knots like a seaman. How would those knots match up with those in the Santa Barbara murders—granny knots and marline hitches? The victims had been abducted in this rotating order: on Friday, Saturday, Tuesday, Friday, Saturday, and Tuesday. All vanished around 5:00 P.M. in a period of growing darkness. All had been found in the rural, semi-isolated eastern section of Sonoma County near lakes, rivers, ditches, and streams. The Santa Rosa crimes were water-related by name: Mark *Springs,* Calistoga (Water), *Creek* Valley. The furthest point between discovery sites was sixteen miles. Sterling, Weber, and Carolyn Davis, with a seven-month gap, were found in the exact same spot—2.2 miles north of Porter Creek Road on Franz Valley Road. However, Kim Allen may have been sexually assaulted and that did not fit Zodiac's pattern.

"As far as the murders go," continued Baker. "I was almost thinking a postman or PG&E guy just because of the places that they go. The last girl that was found was in a very remote creek. It's not a place where you can dump them off the side of the road and they land there. The three on Franz Valley Road were found in the same location along the side of the road. You don't have to throw far to get where they landed. The last one we had in the creek, I don't know how the hell he got her in there."

Several months earlier, officers on the way to the Santa Rosa area that a killer had used as a dumping ground for murdered Santa Rosa coeds had stopped in their tracks. Walking down the road toward them and from the secluded murder area was Arthur Leigh Allen. "I travel this road to go skin-diving," he said. In the same direction Allen visited two friends at Clear Lake. "Leigh always picked up hitchhikers especially while attending Santa Rosa JC and Sonoma State University," a source told me. "This always bothered my mother. He picked hikers up on the highways. I remember the two girls disappearing from the skating rink and the other murders. Those bodies discovered on Franz Valley Road and in Calistoga weren't far from my parents' home."

FRIDAY, DECEMBER 29, 1972

SINCE August 4, 1971, when police questioned Leigh for what they erroneously believed was the first time, Zodiac had sent no letters. But we hardly needed more clues from the killer. We already knew a lot about Zodiac. He could be caught if we put our minds to it. All the early suspects were singled out because their handprinting was like Zodiac's or they resembled the composite sketch. Few were as tall or heavy as the killer actually was; some were slender as a boy.

Zodiac had three qualities, had to have these qualities—he was strong and he was smart and he possessed specialized technical proficiency in code, chemistry, firearms, engineering, electronics, and bomb-making. More telling, Zodiac knew forensics, leaving behind false clues and wearing glue on his fingertips. In fact his marksmanship skills, knowledge of police I.D. techniques, and use of Highway Patrol cutoff maneuvers to box in his victims pointed to Zodiac being a policeman. Two victims had been reaching for their licenses when he blinded them with a flashlight and unleashed a fusillade of bullets.

And yet Zodiac was compelled to deride police in his letters, the thrill of baiting them becoming a powerful motive in his game of outdoor chess. He taunted authority as if striking out against a controlling figure in his daily life—a boss, a father, or a policeman. Serial sadists, enraptured with the various tools of police work and with policemen themselves, were frequently police groupies. Some sexual sociopaths dressed in uniform when trapping and torturing their victims, often applied for police work, or expressed a desire to work in some law enforcement capacity. Invariably they would offer aid in the hunt for themselves. The known serial killers were remarkably alike.

FBI agent John Douglas's psychological profile of the Atlanta child murderer spoke volumes. He said the killer "would live in the area, sometimes pose as a police officer, show extreme interest in media coverage of the case, and have difficulty relating to members of the opposite sex. In fact, children who lived near [the suspect Wayne] Williams thought he was a policeman because he drove cars that looked like police cars, showed them a badge, and ordered them around." Williams monitored police-band radio, just as California multiple murderer Ed Kemper did. Kemper frequented a local bar to become pals with off-duty policemen. "He showed me his gun and his handcuffs right here in the bar," recalled the bartender. "He handcuffed a friend and shoved him up against the wall. . . . You see, Kemper always wanted to be a policeman. All his friends were cops. He used to talk about it all the time . . . said he had been hired as a security guard somewhere in the Bay Area—but he was only a big guy who sometimes worked as a gas station attendant." After slaying his mother, the Santa Cruz giant left a note behind, ridiculing his former friends on the force.

Ted Bundy used a gold badge and handcuffs to masquerade as "Officer Roseland" at a Salt Lake City shopping center. One of the "Hillside Stranglers," Kenneth Bianchi, had wanted to be an L.A. policeman, even taken a police science course at a Rochester community college. When cops apprehended Bianchi in Bellingham, Washington, he was enrolled as a deputy in the sheriff's reserve training program. His white, late-model auto with silver spotlights mounted on both sides resembled a police car. Inside his black attaché case he carried a highway patrolman's badge and cuffs.

John Wayne Gacy, as a youth, dressed in the policelike uniform of his local civil defense squad. Fascinated by the trappings of law enforcement, he obsessively fixed upon James Hanley, a detective with the hit-and-run unit. Gacy became "Jack" Hanley, a brutal, muscular homicide cop who existed only in his mind. Jack, "a devoted hater of homosexuals," was the savage, sadistic cop that Gacy both admired and feared. When Gacy was drunk or stoned, his alter ego assumed control and committed the acts a sober Gacy never could.[2] Because Jack had been in charge, Gacy suppressed the details of his crimes. He forgot the acts he had committed on the boys he buried in the walls of his house. Fantasy Detective Jack made nightly forays into the seamy sections of town, cruising slowly in an old black Oldsmobile, radio scanner squawking, spotlight and red lights rotating. Dressed in a leather jacket, trousers, and highway patrolman's shoes, Gacy picked up boys and handcuffed them. Some psychiatrists analyzed Zodiac as being at least "a latent homosexual to whom bullets and knives afforded perverse satisfaction."

Dr. Lunde warned to look for a suspect who had a collection of guns and early interest in guns, knives, and various instruments of torture. "As an adult," Lunde wrote in *Murder and Madness,* "a collection of such instruments, proficiency in their use, and an emotional attraction to weapons may be seen which goes far beyond that of any ordinary collector." Serial killers will become incredibly skillful in their use. Whenever Zodiac's lair was uncovered and a search made, I was certain huge numbers of weapons would be present—guns, bombs, or the "Death Machine" Zodiac bragged about. Had Arthur Leigh Allen—like Williams, Bianchi, Kemper, Bundy, and Gacy—once wanted to be a policeman?

He had.

On May 2, 1952, Allen, then nineteen, sought employment with the Vallejo Police Department. They turned him down. "He applied right out of high school to be a Vallejo cop," a source explained, "and they said no. Therefore he had a very good reason

---

[2]Another Gacy personality was a party entertainer, Pogo the Clown. Gacy painted an oil of Zodiac in costume and auctioned it off one spring. Actor Johnny Depp owned a Gacy painting. "They told me when I got it that the proceeds went to a charity or to the victims' families. . . ." Depp said. "But I found out that wasn't the case. So I got rid of it. Fascinating from a psychological point of view, but really dark stuff."

for hating the Vallejo Police Department—rejection." Allen offered his heart to the law again much later. On June 11, 1964, he was a non-certified personnel applicant at the Watsonville Police Department. Watsonville spurned him too. Sometimes it seemed everyone did. "Well, there you go," said Toschi. "A guy who is a 'wannabe' cop and cannot make it, hates all cops. It's been proven. They hate any authority figure after that because they couldn't pass whatever tests were necessary."

Chicago clairvoyant Joe DeLouise, who felt tuned into Zodiac's mind, agreed. "The person who created Zodiac was somebody very familiar with law enforcement," he said. "I think he was an ex-cop. In his letters to the police he knew everything that was going on with the police. He knew his victims. I feel he will kill until he is caught." Had Leigh, like Kemper, gotten close to the police and learned about the impending search of his trailer? California Highway Patrolman Lynn Lafferty had been Leigh's childhood friend, and possibly Allen may have wanted to emulate him. Lafferty had been anxiously searching for Zodiac on his own.

Leigh had been an occasional teacher at Travis AFB, where Wing Walker shoes were sold at the base exchange. He qualified for exchange privileges on several counts—as a dependent of a Navy commander, an employee, and as a former Navy man. Naval enlistments ran from four to six years (with thirty days leave each year), but Leigh served only from 1956 to 1958. I was told why. "Allen was in the military—in the Navy," the daughter of a woman Leigh once dated platonically told me. "What led to his being discharged was his arrest by the Vallejo Police Department for disturbing the peace [on June 15, 1958]. He had gotten into a fight with a friend [Ralph Spinelli]. He went into the Navy in 1956, was in there two years, and less-than-honorably discharged—a cheap way to get rid of someone you don't want. I think Leigh Allen was trying to become a frogman in the Navy. For either psychological or physical reasons they would not accept him into the program for deep diving or being on the submarines for long lengths of time. My mother remembers this as a very, very large disappointment for him. I believe he did have an intense dislike for his father because of his militaristic attitude. I believe that when my mother was ever at his house, he had to address his father as 'sir.' Perhaps his father's influence had something to do with this also. My mother felt this period of time had a great influence on his life."

Though civil charges were dismissed on July 8, 1958, Allen received a "less than honorable discharge" from the Navy late that year. One of the ancillary reasons for his expulsion was that he had again left weapons in plain sight in his car. From 1959 on he listed his draft status as "Non-finished active duty and reserve time, USN." Because of the police, Allen's greatest ambitions would never be realized. He would never become a Navy Seal or submarine commander or cop. By the end of 1972 Allen had at least five reasons for hating the police—his rejections by Vallejo and Watsonville P.D., VPD's arrest of him and resulting Navy discharge, his firing from the refinery, and the humiliating search of his trailer. If he were Zodiac, he had a sixth reason to despise cops—SFPD had nearly captured him.

In the Navy Allen had worked on a refrigerator ship, mostly scraping and painting hulls in the bright California light. "Leigh was also an excellent marksman in the Navy," my Vallejo source verified, "one of the best in his group. Additionally, he often wrote to my mother and used the signals used by the flags at the bottom of the letters [Zodiac symbols in the letter codes could be matched to various semaphore flags]. Yet she burned the letters after her knowledge of Leigh later being sent to Atascadero."

He had even taken training in code. Zodiac had a masterful knowledge of code. "He did know code, and not only sewed well but was a sail maker," said a source. The neat stitching on the hood worn by Zodiac at Berryessa suggested a man who could sew. It was doubtful Zodiac could ask anyone else to sew him an executioner's hood. Leigh not only learned aquatic scuba diving during his Navy stint, but briefly worked as a wire operator, third-class radioman. Napa Captain Narlow was convinced that whoever Zodiac was, he also had technical knowledge of a #15 Teletype transmitter—he had duplicated its circuitry on one of his bomb plans and an early note attributed to him had been on Teletype paper.

"The plans for Zodiac's bomb came from [the schematic of a] UP 15 teleprinter," an expert told me. "I also noticed that in his schematic diagrams, he properly draws 'jumpers' over two intersecting lines. I think these are the best clues for finding the Zodiac and that there is more than a fifty percent probability that he was an amateur radio operator (also known as 'hams'). First, operators who used RTTY (Radio Teletype) used these surplus machines. . . . Secondly, the simple fact that he uses 'jumpers' on his schematic diagram tells me he has more than just a passing knowledge of electronics, which hams must master . . . other possible alternatives are Navy and Coast Guard personnel such as electronic techs and radiomen."

The relationship between heavy Leigh Allen and his slender father was complex. The strongest Navy influence came from the father. Ethan Warren Allen, a well-known, highly decorated Naval commander and pilot, was born April 6, 1903, in Meade, Kansas, the son of George M. Allen and Cora Woodard, both of Kansas. Leigh's father, a twenty-five-year Vallejo resident, put in twenty-four years of service in Hawaii and on Treasure Island in San Francisco Bay. In his retirement, Ethan became a draftsman for the City of Vallejo. When he married Bernice Hanson of California, they had two sons, Arthur Leigh and Ronald Gene. Ethan passed on a love of hunting, flying, and sailing to both, but his elder son, Leigh, took it most to heart.

It was no coincidence that Leigh hunted, had a pilot's license, and sailed. But after his plane crash, Ethan, no longer the vibrant and confident officer he had once been, could not curb's Leigh's outbursts and abuse of Bernice. The death of his stern father set Allen free, but the earlier jet crack-up had given him license to pursue his desires. In this home, dominated by a strong-willed woman, the father, Ethan, became a shadow in the years before his death. Ethan died of carcinoma of the prostate with metastases on March 17, 1971.

January 4, 1971, two months before Allen's father died, an anonymous letter came to the paper:

"If you are game print the following letter. An open letter to The Zodiac. You need no explosives for your big **blast**, just go to the nearest Police station and tell the truth about the man who has made a killer out of you, your father who has been getting away with famous American crimes since 1947 and is now an expert at giving killing lessons. Once you asked 'What will they do to me?' You will be placed in a mental institution which is better than a session with a double edge sword or a shot in the back because after the conviction of the scapegoats for your father's murders with your help, he will have to take care of you since you have been placing a dent into his good reputation by duplicating his murders." The typed letter went on to talk about an older brother. "Think about the big noses you could rub so many big booboos, it is fantastic. . . . You could also clear up a little mystery. If two people with only their hands tied do not run out to seek help, is it not because they are already in the process of being killed by two men. . . ."

Father and son killing alongside one another? An odd theory and an even odder fantasy.

Something certainly had happened in Zodiac's life during the month of March 1971. After a six-month gap, Zodiac had penned two letters—March 13 to the *Times* and another on March 22 to the *Chronicle*. The first used the phrase "don't bury me . . ." and the second depicted a man digging with a shovel.

Ethan lingered in the Oakland Naval Hospital for seventeen days. As Allen's dad was dying, he was hospitalized in the 94566 postal district, the same ZIP code from which Zodiac mailed his letter to the *L.A. Times*. The two threatening March letters might have been Zodiac's panicky stab at anonymous immortality. I recalled how old-fashioned Zodiac's clothes had been—pleated pants pointed to an older man, or someone wearing an older man's clothing. The Zodiac costume was really only Navy dress, his appearance only that of a sailor: close-cut hair, shined shoes, bell-bottoms, dark navy-blue jacket. Had Allen, out of hatred or love, dressed in his father's clothes to do his killing as Zodiac? But Ethan, unlike his son, had been a slender man and Leigh, because of his size, could never have worn his father's Naval costume.

Sergeants Lynch and Lundblad had interviewed Allen from the first, Lynch more than once. Each time Allen pointed to his scuba gear or smiled his watery smile. His alibi was that he had gone diving alone or with people whose names he did not know at "Fort Point" or "Bodega Bay." On the outskirts of Vallejo the quarries and creeks, ponds and lakes ran still, cold, and deep, holding who knows what secrets and mementos. The weapons police sought might even lie beneath the frigid clear waters of Lake Berryessa.

Sources speculated that Zodiac had financial resources because he "purchased any number of guns, attended theater, saw numerous films, read multiple newspapers, overposted his letters, and had the luxury of free time in the summer and many cars and residences." Others speculated that Zodiac was either rich or received money from relatives or a trust fund. Leigh Allen's family had some money; police had known that from the first.

10

THE DEVIL

THOUGH eight months had dragged by since Toschi and Armstrong ransacked his trailer, Allen knew he was still under scrutiny. He owned a police scanner and listened in on Vallejo police staking out his basement from a block away. But for large stretches of time he was unobserved. The Zodiac case was simply too immense, the pool of suspects too enormous, and manpower stretched too far for unbroken surveillance to be feasible. And there were hundreds of other suspects. One of Zodiac's chief hunters, Dave Toschi, was often sidetracked by illness or suddenly diverted from his pursuit by other tasks.

"We were not only working on Zodiac when it came our week to go on call," Toschi told me, "but catching other cases. That particular week we had four. The night before we had a fireman stabbed to death out in the Haight. I was so exhausted because we had to go into the office on Saturday and I had nothing to eat but animal crackers and cold coffee. Then I dropped into bed about 8:30 P.M. An hour later the phone rang. I was barely able to get out of bed—punchy—a headache, but I had to get up. We had another one."

Mayor Joe Alioto also handpicked Toschi as a special investigator for the San Francisco Criminal Grand Jury on March 6, 1973, the first such assignment since a 1936 scandal. Alioto wanted Toschi to probe two riots and two fires at the San Bruno main county jail. Chief Don Scott and Chief of Inspectors Charlie Barca called Toschi in. "The mayor wants you to take statements at the county jail." "This really stinks," said Toschi. "I don't want to get involved, Chief." "You've been ordered. You're on loan, Toschi, as of tomorrow morning. And keep quiet about your findings."

"And I did," Toschi told me. "I worked alone to investigate the recent uprising at the county jail. The department was in terrible, terrible shape." Toschi's assistance was invaluable. James Rodman, Grand Jury foreman, wrote Chief Scott that the SFPD was "indeed fortunate to have persons of Inspector Toschi's calibre as a member of its staff. It would have been impossible to carry out our assigned duties were it not for his assistance." Leigh Allen put his experience as a Union Oil chemist to use. His new job with Union Richfield in the East Bay allowed him time to settle down evenings in front of his trailer. He was a likable man when he chose to be (his staunch and unshakeable Fresno Street defenders, the children who thought he was a cowboy star, his drinking buddies, all were proof of that). These days, though, he carried a grim set to his mouth. He still had not forgiven the ransacking of his trailer or the oil refinery visit that got him fired. He stood in an arid patch of gravel, drinking a Coors, leaning back against the still-hot metal of his trailer, and watching autos rushing by on Santa Rosa Avenue. Droning like insects, the cars spun away, turning the bend toward remote Franz Valley Road. Crickets chirped. A warm westerly shrouded the court. He faced west, rocking on his heels, and peered beyond two pink flamingos listing drunkenly in the gravel. Between their metal legs echoed the tumultuous roar of traffic on 101, which ran parallel to Santa Rosa Avenue.

Leigh shuffled inside, where he had unlimited time to brood and to hate the SFPD. When he wasn't working, diving, or hunting, he sought diversions. Each year he attended the Scottish Games with his mother. But he missed the family dinners. "My mother longed for a happy family life," said a friend of Leigh's. "I think she enjoyed going to Leigh Allen's house because it appeared to be such a 'nice family.' Everyone had nice table manners, and I think Leigh's mother decorated the house very well—that type of thing. It only goes to show you you can't go by what's on the surface." Leigh continued to attend Sonoma State College, majoring in biological sciences and working toward a master's in mammalogy/biology. He had minored in chemistry, and had already earned a degree in botany and elementary education on the G.I. Bill in 1971. Learning came easy to him. Life did not.

TUESDAY, JULY 31, 1973

JUST around that bend from Allen's trailer and down the country road, 2.2 miles north of Porter Creek on Franz Vallejo Road and down a familiar wooded slope, bodies continued to be found. Caroline Davis was discovered in the *exact* spot as Sterling and Weber. It could not be determined if Davis had been sexually molested. Zodiac had threatened to experiment with different ways to kill people, and it appeared he or someone else was doing just that.

Her body exhibited signs of tetanus, such as rigid muscles, indicating strychnine poisoning. Death from strychnine is similar to that from lockjaw, but more rapid—about fifteen minutes. Because of the irritating action of the poison on the spinal cord, muscular twitchings lead to generalized convulsions that become so intense the spine arches. The body's entire weight is borne on the heels and back. Finally, the skin darkens to gray-blue and respiration ceases. Sergeant Brown wasn't so sure Davis had been poisoned. "It's kinda like when we get lab results on our autopsies of a guy who has a lethal dose of amphetamines in him," he said much later. "If the guy is a chronic crank user a lethal dose to him and me are going to be totally different. As for strychnine poisoning, the state lab told me there's a hallucinogenic mushroom that creates strychnine or a derivative of strychnine when it's in your body. Basically, it's like when a junkie uses heroin it becomes morphine in his body. It doesn't necessarily mean this girl was poisoned; it means that she had probably taken these mushrooms. It doesn't mean that poison killed her, but it might have been a contributing factor. She also had a good ligature mark on her neck."

WEDNESDAY, OCTOBER 24, 1973

ZODIAC'S symbols were always open to diverse interpretations. His crosshair symbol, used in targeting nuclear bombs, led police to quiz a nuclear weapons expert stationed at Travis AFB. His other signs represented weather symbols to a pilot, silver hallmarks to a jeweler, and something else entirely to a postman at the North Station Post Office in White Plains. "I spotted a Zodiac cryptogram in the *New York News*," he explained to me. "After showing the three lines to several other postal employees, they all agreed that the symbols in the cryptogram were the same twenty-five symbols used in the Civil Service Post Office examination." Zodiac's symbol could also represent the astrological Southern Cross inscribed in an ellipse.

Chemistry formulas and symbols danced through Zodiac's letters. That the bombs he diagrammed were chemical bombs had not been lost on Toschi. Leigh Allen was an East Bay chemist. The previous April, the entire region had been jolted when a chemical plant there exploded. Physicist John Dalton's icons for types of elements and their atomic weights resembled Zodiac code symbols—hydrogen: a circle with a dot at its center and sulfur: a crossed circle—the killer's personal signet. The aroma of sulfur and brimstone persistently clung to Zodiac. One could almost hear the clatter of cloven hooves.

At the stroke of midnight the Devil made his appearance in the Zodiac case. A San Francisco man, attending a nude rock dance of the Venus Psychedelic Church on Third Avenue, arrived dressed as Satan. As he approached a group of four nude men, one was leading a discussion about Zodiac. "Zodiac must be some sort of devil or fiend," interjected the costumed devil. The man discoursing about "Mr. Zodiac" wheeled suddenly and pointed a finger at him. "YOU ARE THE ZODIAC!" he shouted. The red devil smiled, blushed beneath the red dye staining his face, and replied, "I am Satan incarnate." He moved on. However, the man followed and drew Satan aside. "I am the Zodiac, you fool," he hissed, "and I made a point of outfoxing the police and newspapers. I have killed many more than have ever been identified as Zodiac killings."

"Is this because Zodiac has already killed twelve of the astrological Zodiac signs?" said Satan uneasily.

"I have killed more than thirty-seven," said the burly but good-looking stranger. He now seemed, the devil recalled, "cool, calm, collected . . . an OK, normal, 100 percent All-American Guy, sound as he could be." "Most of my victims are unknown," he continued, "and never even linked to Zodiac. It's just a game like Monopoly, chess or checkers or bridge. I enjoy killing people as a game between myself and the police. Killing to me means no more than flicking ashes." The man rushed away with a pale, thin-lipped woman. The reveler never saw either again. Oddly enough, a future letter from Zodiac on January 30, 1974 (the last time he gave a specific figure) claimed almost the same number of victims—thirty-seven.

"We continued to get tips on Satan worshippers and astrology freaks throughout the investigation," Toschi said. Zodiac's arcane symbols drew wild theories, even threats against those involved in the occult. Satanist Anton Szandor La Vey, master of the Church of Satan, publisher of *The Cloven Hoof* and *The Satanic Bible,* received a death threat from someone who thought he might be Zodiac. Because of the astrology angle, witchcraft symbols, and satanic black robes (the "Code Killer's" grisly executioner's costume had obvious ties to the Black Mass), La Vey himself had once been a suspect. Immediately, he sent the letter over to Avery at the *Chronicle.*

"Dear Satan . . . Now women lay in the streets in your Devil control. But of course all things come to ends . . . forces are working against you. My fight against you has been going on for many generations with little success. This really bothers me, Satan, to no end! You can choose your choice of weapons, but I prefer knives. . . . I wish more than anything to have your blood on my sword."

"He prefers knives," thought the journalist. He rang fellow reporter Dave Peterson for his opinion on the threat. "And knives are used in rituals," Peterson told Avery, "which brings me to black magician Aleister Crowley's ceremonial hooded robe. Crowley's robe, used in arcane rituals, was emblazoned with the Rose and Cross of the Secret Order of the Golden Dawn—a crossed circle." If Zodiac was part of a satanic cult sacrificing victims in accordance with the phases of the moon and religious holidays, that might explain everything. How else could Zodiac drive so many different cars, kill over a sizable geographical area, come in so many shapes and sizes, and write letters in different handwriting styles? The hand of Satan had to figure somewhere in the mystery.

"Satanism—possibly," said Zodiac buff David Rice. "Satanism is a more fruitful area." Zodiac used inverted words, the number thirteen, Sartor Crosses, and Black Mass phrases. He employed astrology and numerology and drew evil eyes and bloody crosses. His triangles (representing the Holy Trinity) were turned upside down. I had heard tales of the Blue Rock Springs victim's interest in the occult—"a candle and skull in her

San Francisco apartment," said her sister, "witchcraft in the Virgin Islands where she had gone skin diving on her honeymoon," and "a Vallejo satanic cult."

Later on October 24, Dr. Gilbert Holloway, an ESP expert, was interviewed by Jack Carney on KSFO Radio. "I have a possible leaning that the killer's name is something like Cullen, Collin, or Callen," Holloway said. He spelled the names out. "I see a detective with an Italian name—something like Banducci or Sanducci, tackling the Zodiac. But he has poison on his body like Herman Goering and does not expect to be taken alive. . . . Zodiac has some acquaintance with the First Church of Satan in San Francisco. He is under largely Satanic influence."

Satan caught the interest of the California Department of Justice too. Their 1971 report from Napa read:

> "Because of Zodiac's letter talking about the afterlife and 'slaves in paradice,' the Department of Justice focused on people in groups who had these weird beliefs and they were able to eliminate everybody including all male members of the Manson family."

"[Zodiac] has an evil deity with him who advises him," an acknowledged mystic explained. "I saw it when I was in that card shop on Market Street." To give weight to his comments, the seer included copies of his psychic resume and a letter from the Premonitions Registry in New York. Peter Hurkos, consulting psychic on the Boston Strangler and Sharon Tate murders, received threats from Zodiac while he was in Palm Springs. He offered his services to the SFPD to help catch Zodiac (in exchange for a plane ticket to San Francisco), but they turned him down.

"Did Leigh ever discuss an afterlife?" I asked Cheney much later. "What were his feelings?"

"Victims to be slaves in the afterlife," replied Cheney tersely.

MONDAY, DECEMBER 13, 1973

A broad-shouldered man continued to stalk the marshes, quarries, and lagoons along Lake Herman Road. Winds from the west stirred fields of brittle grass. As evening fell, he stood motionless—indistinguishable from surrounding rocks. The same setting sun that colored the boulders gold enlivened his impassive face. Meanwhile, in San Francisco the wait was maddening. Thirty-four months had passed since Zodiac's last letter. Why? Zodiac was all we talked about, all we thought about.

Over on Bryant Street, Toschi fished out a Zodiac letter received that morning. "I assume the writer wants me to think he is Zodiac," he said with a sigh. "He uses an Oakland address as a return, but the Oakland police building has a zip code of 94607. However, the writer has the San Francisco Hall of Justice code correct, 94103. The word 'HOMICIDE' on the envelope is written by a clerk in our mail room." He held it to the light and squinted. "Notice the obvious crossed *t*'s and the dots over the *i*'s. Notice the paper size is 8½ by 11, and a legal-size envelope, different from the odd size of the Zodiac letters. This size envelope and size of paper is consistent with the stationery given inmates in the county jail or in prison. It is different from the Zodiac letters and has a different watermark. Another hoax! As far as phony Zodiac writers, the number would be more like, what, Bill? Fifty so far?"

Something about Zodiac led to imitation: first hoax letters, then attempted murder, and finally homicide. For ten days in May 1973, a Richmond teacher had been bombarded by menacing calls from a sobbing man identifying himself as Zodiac. "I'm going to kill the lady in the blue house," he told the teacher. "I went to a Martinez school in search of victims, but left because the police were there." Afterward, the teacher discovered his back door had been pried open by a prowler. Shaken, he went to the refrigerator. Absentmindedly, he took a swig from an open bottle of cola. A metallic taste filled his mouth and he quickly spat the drink out. Someone had added a lethal dose of arsenic.

Another Zodiac copycat nearly severed noted lamp designer Robert Salem's head with a long, thin-bladed knife. Homicide Inspectors Gus Coreris and John Fotinos, called to his posh workshop behind the San Franciscan Hotel, discovered his mutilated body on a bloody mat. In the victim's own blood, the killer printed on his body and the wall, "Satan Saves—ZODIAC." Salem's murder was solved in a horrible way. South of Big Sur, a Highway Patrolman pulled over two young Wyoming men driving the car of a young social worker found floating in the

Yellowstone River. His heart, head, and limbs had been severed as if in ritual sacrifice. "I have a problem," one of the men told the officer. "I am a cannibal." Both were carrying well-gnawed human finger bones in their pockets.

Like Zodiac, Paul Avery typed on a manual typewriter, had intimate knowledge of the *Chronicle* and police techniques, and wore Wing Walker shoes. Like Leigh Allen, Avery had been born in the thirties in Honolulu and raised in a military family as the son of a career Naval officer. He had his own theories about Zodiac. "He might be some sort of merchant seaman," Avery told me, "because for long intervals we don't hear from him. For some reason Zodiac's grown cautious. Whether or not 'Zode's' in prison or has simply stopped killing, I still have to contend with this—" He snatched up a particularly vicious copycat letter:

"Paul Avery: I killed Erakat [Zuheir Erakat, a victim of the Zebra killers, a case Toschi had been assigned]. The Blind Lady is next, then you. The Grand Finale will be suicide, with TV coverage, from the Golden Gate Bridge. Soon My mission in life is done. Aloha." *Two* Zodiac symbols served as a signature to the letter.

"Scoop. Paul Avery and the Fuzzy S.F. Pigs: a .45 automatic and a plastic bag with a draw-string over his head got his cooperation, but he was yellow and whined. That deal was extra and commissioned by someone now dead. My California activities are unaffected—just on ice presently—you are still there, so say your prayers—the Zodiac cannot be trifled with. Zodiac Claims 17 . . . Paul Avery—Hah!"

The thirty-nine-year-old former war correspondent found himself buried beneath tips. "This is the half-brother of the Zodiac speaking," one fretted. "I'm concerned that Zodiac might be using my High Standard .22-caliber semiautomatic pistol." But of them all, Willy's[3] story was especially tragic. Willy's family, convinced their son was Zodiac, sent stacks of handwriting exemplars, along with their own handwriting expert's opinion, to Avery:

---

[3]This name has been altered.

"After lengthy study and consideration of specimens of handwriting done by 'Zodiac' and comparison with letters written by him, it is my belief that all of these handwritings were done by the same person."

"They don't seem to be nuts," *Chronicle* reporter George Murphy advised Avery, "just a pleasant couple who believe they are acting as good citizens. My first reaction is to go to Oakland and ask their suspect, who's now out on bail, if he's the Zodiac. I'll be around for further interrogation this afternoon, but it doesn't seem like Zodiac." Willy had been jailed soon after Zodiac's letter to Belli, but Avery scanned a few passages anyway.

"I am sorry for all the people that I have killed and maimed," wrote Willy. "But understand something if you can, every person that I ever killed actually deserved it. . . . I never wanted to become what I was, it was an accident when I killed that first man in San Francisco, and from then on I had to do what they wanted. Do you know what it's like to look someone in the face and then pull a trigger. You never get used to it. And I'm not crazy, just always scared."

Avery realized "Willie" thought he was a mob hit man. With a shudder, he forwarded Willy's letters to Sherwood Morrill, who said, "They're *not* Zodiac's handwriting." The reporter was burning out. Lines etched his face; against the bright blue shirts and red neckerchiefs he often wore, his complexion stood sallow.

SATURDAY, DECEMBER 22, 1973

TOSCHI and Armstrong worked to exhaustion, grabbed a bite at Original Joe's, then rushed back to their office to begin the daily cycle all over again. The Zodiac case was like the tide—hopes lifted, only to be dashed against the rocks. And yet beneath the surface they felt tremendous currents—another unsolvable mystery, a hint of deeper crimes as they waded through sluggish water. To the north in Santa Rosa, outside their jurisdiction, bad things continued to happen. At the winter solstice, a day that held significance to Zodiac, Theresa Diane Walsh was hitchhiking on

101 from the area of Malibu Beach to her home in Garberville. A silver handmade cross swung from her neck, a fire-opal ring and a copper-band ring flashed on her fingers. Ten dollars of colored beads she used for making bracelets rattled in her backpack. Somewhere along the way, she too disappeared. Her strangled body, hog-tied with one-quarter-inch nylon rope, was discovered next to Kim Allen's in a creek six days later. Zodiac had tied his victims at Lake Berryessa with clothesline, but Walsh, like Kim Allen, may have been sexually assaulted and this was unlike Zodiac, whose pleasure was pain.

MONDAY, JANUARY 28, 1974

ALL month long the world's oceans had been uncommonly wild, whipping the West Coast with fury. Hurricanes, high tides, and thunderstorms relentlessly beat the shores. A major coincidence of cosmic cycles had occurred. Earth, moon, and sun had aligned in a nearly straight line—a configuration called syzygy. During the new and full phases of the moon, positive ions charged the atmosphere and freaky, motiveless murders occurred as far away as Miami.

Zodiac hunched over a light table, the glow highlighting his intent face. In the past, his desire for notoriety had compelled him to boast. Now a more commanding power, a celestial power, drove him to break his three-year silence. Because of the timing of his killings, experts had long believed Zodiac was "moon mad"—sensitive to the gravitational influences, enhanced luminosity, and electromagnetic field changes of full and new moon phases, changes that affect the human nervous system and increase the brain's nervous activity.

"If one considers the human organism as a microcosm," psychiatrist Arnold L. Lieber wrote, "comprising essentially the same elements as, and in similar proportion to, those of the earth's surface—approximately eighty percent water and twenty percent organic and inorganic minerals—one could speculate that the gravitational forces of the moon might exert a similar influence upon the water mass of the human being." Studies on nuclear magnetic resonance demonstrated that biological tissues respond to the interaction between moon and Earth. These biological tides might be sufficient to trigger emotional, psychological, and physiological outbursts in certain predisposed individuals.

"Ironically, on dark, moonless nights," Toschi told me, "all my years in Sex Crimes, Aggravated Assault, and Homicide, my home phone was relatively quiet—even when on call. When it was a clear, bright moonlit night, nights of full and new moons, violent crime increased. Inevitably the Toschi home phone would ring—Operations Center reporting marital fights, shootings, stabbings—all night long. Contrary to popular belief, dark spooky nights would be a normal tranquil night for a policeman." At Stanford, Dr. Lunde suggested another possibility for the timing of Zodiac's assaults. "Were Zodiac's nighttime murders always at a time when there was fairly good moonlight?" he asked me. "Always a full or new moon," I replied. "So he would be able to see at night," said Lunde. Coincidentally, a *Sacramento Bee* Sunday article on Morrill had appeared prominently the day before, January 27. So the new letter might in part have been an ego thing, a competition with Morrill for publicity.

Zodiac bent to his labor. A film had been terrifying San Francisco, much as he used to, receiving as much publicity as he once had. Lines of thrill-seekers stretched around the block, sixty thousand since Christmas, waiting to enter the Northpoint Theater and see *The Exorcist*. Once inside, after a two-hour wait, a few immediately exited and were sick on the sidewalk. Zodiac had seen them himself—"Disgusting!" his letter commented on this phenomenon and the sickness of the public at large. He had revved his car and rushed away. The postmark, 940, wouldn't be much help to the police. It only indicated the letter had been mailed from an adjacent county south of San Francisco and picked up before noon on Tuesday.

WEDNESDAY, JANUARY 30, 1974

FOR over a month the two-man Zodiac Squad had not seen any real action. Zodiac had mailed his last letter just under three years ago. The number of tip letters dwindled, falling from fifty a week to ten to practically none. Toschi, working ill and out of sorts, had taken to glaring at the sealed five-foot-tall steel-gray filing cabinet crammed with Zodiac artifacts. "One drawer is marked 'Concerned Citizens,'" he said. "The second drawer is for suspects only." (Ultimately there would be eight drawers.) "Do I think we'll ever catch the guy? Of course I do. I have to feel that way, or I'd have given up long ago. To me it's a major challenge, a major case. Bill and I are the Zodiac Squad of the country."

Recently they had been busy tracking down the infamous Zebra killers who slaughtered fifteen and wounded eight random victims over a 179-day period. Though all of the victims were white and all of their assailants black, that was not why the religiously motivated cult murders came to be known as the "Zebra" killings. "The special unit we put together worked mostly at night," Toschi explained, "because that's when the killings were occurring. They used a radio channel that was seldom used to keep it available for anyone who called in who might have seen some suspects. They put it on 'Channel Z,' which was never used at all. It was 'Z' for 'Zebra' and the press picked up on it and our killers became the Zebra killers." Members of this fanatical cult had to pass an initiation that consisted of shooting or hacking to death men, women, and children in order to reach the rank of "Death Angel." Two nights ago, between 8:00 and 10:00 P.M., another Zebra murder had set off a round-the-clock manhunt. Dog-tired and aching, Toschi had stayed in bed this one morning. He glanced at the clock, studied the sky outside. Everything was out of kilter. As a fuel-saving device, Daylight Savings Time had arrived three months early this year. Toschi, unaware the killer's unexplained silence was about to be broken, buried his face in the pillow. Over at the *Chronicle* Carol Fisher slit open a letter, froze, and read the following:

> "I saw and think 'The Exorcist' was the best saterical comidy that I have ever seen. Signed, yours truley: He plunged him self into the billowy wave and an echo arose from the suicides grave titwillo titwillo titwillo PS. if I do not see this note in your paper. I will do something nasty, which you know I'm capable of doing"

This wasn't the first time Zodiac had quoted Gilbert and Sullivan. Carol recognized the "titwillo" lines from the second act of *The Mikado,* specifically the aria of Ko-Ko, the fainthearted Lord High Executioner. Three and a half years ago the killer had also paraphrased *Mikado* lyrics ("a little list he had of all those who would never be missed"). He had quoted them at great length from memory. Divergencies from the original text, primarily Acts I and

II, proved that. "And that singular anomaly, the lady novelist" had been changed to "and the singurly abnormily the girl who never kissed." Various alternatives to lady novelist—lady dramatist, lady motorist, lady bicyclist, etc., were usually suggested by the actor portraying Ko-Ko. I believed that Zodiac's little list was a roll call of real people he knew and whom he fancied had wronged him— "banjo seranader," "piano orginast" and "all children . . . up in dates [students]." Police had always believed Zodiac had essayed the role of Ko-Ko professionally. I suggested a college production.

The night Zodiac hailed cabdriver Paul Lee Stine, the Lamplighters had been rehearsing *The Mikado* nearby on a stage smaller than a Pacific Heights living room at Presentation Theatre, 2350 Turk Street. During their entire run, from October 18 to November 7, 1969, no Zodiac letter was received. Scrawls at the bottom of the new letter even resembled the rounded ersatz Japanese calligraphy on Ko-Ko's paper fan. On January 30, 1974, music director Gilbert Russak was still putting Ko-Ko, Nanki-Poo, Pooh-Bah, Pish-Tush, and Yum-Yum through their paces. Carol thought Zodiac might be a member of that cast.

In the letter's lower right-hand corner, Zodiac had printed "Me-37 S.F.P.D.-0." Fisher called Homicide and they rang Toschi at home. The detective, burning with fever, forced himself up. The last time he had felt this bad was on the front lines in Korea. Drafted after leaving Galileo High, he had faced seven months of hard combat with the 24th Infantry Division. Within half an hour, Toschi had parked under the *Chronicle* tower, ridden to the third floor, and was reading Zodiac's score. "Thirty-seven!" he muttered, praying the killer was lying. "Another Gilbert and Sullivan swipe and another shot at SFPD," said Toschi. "Jeez, why does he single us out every time. What is this grudge? And why Gilbert and Sullivan?"

Dr. Murray S. Miron of the Syracuse Research Institute reached some conclusions on the new letter. In a confidential FBI psycholinguistics report, he suggested "suicides grave" might indicate Zodiac was contemplating suicide. Miron referred to Zodiac's letter to Attorney Mel Belli in particular. It contained hints of a depression that "frequently overtakes him. . . . It is not entirely unlikely that in one of these virulent depressions, such individuals could commit suicide." Possibly, the suicide Zodiac

references is "the symbolic death of Zodiac . . . the sociopathic
personality eventually 'burns out' . . . as he ages."

"I would agree," wrote FBI profiler Douglas, "that the Zodiac
might eventually commit suicide, but I also believe that, even in a
depressed state, the Zodiac wrote letters with the goal of manipu-
lating, dominating, and controlling their recipients and the larger
audience he knew they would reach."

Once a paranoid schizophrenic is into his mid-thirties (if he
does not kill himself), the rage may burn itself out or go into re-
mission. If Zodiac had symbolically died, then the killer might
lead the rest of his life uneventfully. He might not recall he had
once been Zodiac. Miron believed the killer to be a Caucasian,
unmarried male . . . "isolated, withdrawn and unrelated in his
habits, quiet and prepossessing in disposition." He thought Zodiac had "good uncorrected eyesight because of the use of
minute distinguishers for the differing code symbols."

Police had once studied surveillance photos of the Bates burial. Many killers were unable to stay away from their victim's funeral. For that same reason the *Chronicle* snapped pictures of the
extended lines curling around the Northpoint Theater and stretching up Powell between Bay and Francisco Streets. Photos were
taken each night on the chance Zodiac would see *The Exorcist*
again. Perhaps he would wave to the camera.

The *Exorcist* letter carried only a single eight-cent Eisenhower
stamp. Zodiac usually doubled, tripled, even quadrupled postage.
A similar sociopath, the Unabomber, who came after Zodiac,
stockpiled large quantities of symbolic stamps long before he began posting his heavy mail bombs. For the bomber, Eugene
O'Neil stamps signified a hidden message. Maybe O'Neil's plays
were a grim comment on the Unabomber's troubled family life.
Other stamps indicated the strength of the infernal device or target selected—specific or non-specific. Only the bomber knew
what each symbolized.

Zodiac's paired stamps of presidents—Lincoln, Eisenhower,
and FDR—might be equally symbolic—all had served as
wartime presidents. Lincoln stamps might indicate someone
named Green (Lincoln Green), Ford (Ford's Theatre), or Booth
(the assassin Booth or any actor for that matter). FDR stamps
might stand for Delano, a county abutting Deer Lodge, Montana,
a spot linked to Zodiac by his own words during a conversation

with a surviving victim. This time Zodiac had decorated the lower right-hand corner of his envelope with gummed labels. Running vertically were these instructions:

> "Stamps in this book have been gummed with a matte finish adhesive which permits the elimination of the separation tissues. This book contains 25—8 cent stamps—four on this pane and seven each on three additional panes. Selling price $2.00." In the upper right corner were the gummed stamps "MAIL EARLY IN THE DAY" [showing clock hands] and "Use ZIP code."

Did zip *code* somehow match up with one of Zodiac's numerical codes as a key? The *Exorcist* letter re-energized the case. "Since the latest Zodiac letter was published," Toschi said, "I've had fifty people in my office! Each claims he knows Zodiac personally. Bill and I have probably followed up a thousand leads in this case and heard a lot of weird stories. People tell us they're sure it's their neighbor because he looks like the drawing and walks around with a knife in a scabbard. . . . There are times when you're listening to this and it's hard to keep a straight face. But I feel I've got to listen to everyone, no matter how outlandish their story is."

THURSDAY, JANUARY 31, 1974

"ARE you aware of a rumor going around concerning a possible link between Zodiac and the San Francisco choral group the 'Lamplighters'?" a woman informed Avery on Thursday morning. "A girl I heard talking about it used to belong to the group and thought one of the men in the group fit the description of Zodiac. She was reluctant to go to the police much as we tried to persuade her. Then it was dropped and I'm not sure what became of her. In any case, did the police check out that group? Zodiac (who's probably Mr. Ordinary Guy Leading Typical Life who also happens to be a psychopath)—obviously listens to Gilbert and Sullivan. I would have written this directly to the police but what with giving parking tickets and busting pot rings, I know they are too busy to fight crime. All us ordinary citizen taxpayers are imprisoned within the walls of our homes because murderers, rapists and burglars who are free to roam can't seem to get caught until they call in from a phone booth with their exact longitude and latitude."

THURSDAY, FEBRUARY 14, 1974

CAROL opened the morning mail and got a second shock—the floodgates had truly been opened:

"Dear Mr. Editor: Did you know that the initials SLA [Symbionese Liberation Army] spell 'SLA' an old Norse word meaning 'kill.' [signed] a friend."

Though the hand-lettered postcard was of doubtful authenticity, she alerted the FBI. They included it in their inventory of valid Zodiac letters. Almost three months passed. The next communication would be real—Zodiac was growing bolder again—restless, the old passions rising to the surface.

MONDAY, APRIL 15, 1974

LEIGH had been let go from Union Richfield. Adrift again he ceased attending Sonoma State University and began work at the Sonoma Auto Parts Store at 248 West Napa in Sonoma. Financially, his next job was a step down, but he knew and liked engines. He had gained expertise at Wogan's Service Station before being fired. On a brighter note, Leigh was working with Jim, a friend he could confide in. "I'm almost through with all my academic requirements at Sonoma State," he told Jim, although he would not receive his degree for another eight years. He told Jim other things too, unsettling hints about a secret life. Perhaps, now that Leigh's professional student days were ending, good things would begin to happen for him. At age forty-one, he was about to go out into the world. The fires were cooling. Zodiac was, for all purposes, dead and Leigh Allen had a friend to confide in.

WEDNESDAY, MAY 8, 1974

EVERY homicide Bill Armstrong investigated impacted him as hard as his first. The cold, dreadful finality of the deed always brought him up short. "Probably a .38," said Armstrong at a crime scene. "Looks like the slug stopped here, behind the forehead." He pointed to a swollen bulge just above the victim's eye, then stood, shaking his head. "We're really just information gatherers," he said. "We put each case together the best we can and lay it on the table for the courts to decide."

Meanwhile, Zodiac was writing yet again. As with *The Exorcist,* he had returned to being a defender of public morals:

> "Sirs—I would like to express my consternation concerning your poor taste & lack of sympathy for the public, as evidenced by your running of ads for the movie 'Badlands' featuring the blurb 'In 1959 most people were killing time. Kit & Holly were killing people.' In light of recent events, this kind of murder-glorification can only be deplorable at best (not that glorification of violence was *ever* justifiable) why don't you show some concern for the public sensibilities & cut the ad? [signed] A citizen."

Constantly suspicious, Zodiac drove to Alameda County to mail his latest letter. But as days passed, he scanned the front pages and grew furious. He had warned them before how much he hated to be ignored and what he would do if they showed him no respect.

MONDAY, JULY 8, 1974

FUMING after a full month's rejection, Zodiac puzzled why his tongue-in-cheek *Badlands* letter had not been printed. Over the years the publicity-mad killer had tried to sneak letters into print under pseudonyms, mailing them from everywhere except where he really lived. All because the police had gotten too close to him; it was dangerous to mail any letter signed "Zodiac." Because the *Chronicle* might be testing him, he prepared a second letter, a swipe at a *Chronicle* columnist, and signed it, "A citizen." He raced to San Rafael, deposited it in the first post box he reached, then rushed home to worry.

WEDNESDAY, JULY 10, 1974

ZODIAC had no way of knowing his first letter hadn't reached the *Chronicle* until June 4 and they *really* were testing him. Although he had not signed it "Zodiac," Carol recognized his handprinting. "He's not fooling anybody—no matter what his game is," said Toschi as he scanned the postcard. "There's no doubt in my mind about either one . . . he's trying to slip letters and cards into the *Chronicle* without being detected." They also recognized a letter mailed two days ago as a Zodiac communication. The killer wrote about *Chronicle* columnist Count Marco this time. The former hairdresser was "The man women love to hate," or as *Time* put it, "The voice from the sewer."

> "Editor—Put Marco back in the hell-hole from whence it came—he has a serious psychological disorder—always needs to feel superior. I suggest you refer him to a shrink. Meanwhile, cancel the column. Since the Count can write anonymously, so can I. The Red Phantom (red with rage)."

Why had Zodiac singled out the Count, an anti-feminist, nationally syndicated radio commentator whose real name was Marco Spinelli? Did another Spinelli somehow figure in his past and was this threat, in Zodiac's maddening indirect way, actually meant for him? The Count was almost as colorful as Mel Belli.

Count Marco's business cards carried a royal crest. He lived in a fourteen-room apartment at the Stanford Court and wore a watch with sixty diamonds surrounding its face. He owned three Rolls-Royces, each with a chauffeur and footman. One Rolls was painted with twenty coats of silver to match Marco's hair. He reserved the second for hauling his considerable luggage. The third belonged to his dachshund, and she was driven about attired in a diamond and emerald tail ring, crocheted hat, dark glasses, and a white mink stole. Her fur was dyed to match the Rolls.

More than three years previously, the Count had received another anonymous letter. "Dear Morning Star," the January 11, 1971 letter read. "Don't you worry, Don't you fear, Tea-time comes but once a year. . . . To lift thy spirits columnist Three bags of Tea within to twist Those drops of lemon (aromist), Also

enclosed a few biscuits, Approved and used by 12 fair fists—
Faithful Savant. Have a nice day!" Count Marco had joined the
Chronicle in 1959, the same time as Avery, but had had enough of
such unsigned love letters. He left to divide his time a bit more
securely between Hawaii and Palm Springs.

FRIDAY, SEPTEMBER 27, 1974

SPORTING his Zodiac watch and ring, Allen, now weighing 240
pounds, spent the morning in his trailer, puttering about. An
hour later, his world collapsed. The crunch of boots on the
gravel had already alerted him, so he didn't jump when there
came a furious thumping on his trailer door. "Open up!"

"Who's there?"

"Sonoma County Sheriff's Department!"

Deputy Haas's arrival was not totally unexpected. Events had
been set in motion on September 23 when a complaint was
lodged against Allen. Yesterday the Sheriff's Department had
filed against him in Central Municipal Court. "You're under arrest," Haas said. "The charge is PC 288, 288a—child molesting
and exciting the lust of a minor under fourteen years old." Between July 11 and July 25, Allen had enticed two boys into his
trailer bedroom. Afterward, he had pressed money, two quarters,
into their hands.

"I know you don't like it," Allen told the deputy, "but I'm just
a nasty man."

"It was one of the oddest remarks I had ever heard under the
circumstances," recalled the officer.

As soon as he was arrested, Leigh wanted a pencil and piece of
paper so he could work out his thoughts on paper. He was trying
to decide if he should plead guilty or not. He drew a line down
the middle of the paper. On one side he wrote "guilty" and on the
other "public defender," then listed the pros and cons of each. He
began to sob.

The next day, Allen was released on $5,000 bail for each count
of felony child molesting. However, back in Vallejo, he told
friends he had been arrested because he "was the Zodiac."

"In 1974 Leigh Allen molested a nine-year-old boy from the
Fremont Elementary School in his trailer." A Santa Rosa police

sergeant elaborated. "Another eight-year-old was there too. Leigh had lured them inside to see some chipmunks and committed lewd acts involving oral copulation upon the two children. The file says he worked part-time at Yaeger and Kirk's Lumber Yard. And we have his traffic ticket here. He has a 'D file.' On the file is a notation that I've never seen before: 'RS-6,' [a CI&I high priority code] and this notation is marked 'yes.'" The daughter of a woman Allen had known for years related, "As I understand his incarceration at Atascadero, it was for molesting the son of a female friend of his. The boy was maybe anywhere from eight to thirteen years old. The version he told my mother was the woman was just jealous of his relationship with her son. I believe he was dating the woman. He said that was why she had turned him in—jealousy." This turned out not to be true. Their relationship had never been anything but platonic, as had all of Leigh's relationships with women.

"Sexual sadists like Zodiac are limited or incapable of forming normal adult sexual relationships," Dr. Lunde told me. "And so what are the alternatives? One is sex with dead bodies or killing for sexual satisfaction. Another is sex with children." CI&I, alerted by the arrest, requested Allen's Valley Springs School file and began probing for earlier signs of improper relationships with children. Police also contacted every school where he had taught. As authorities tried to build a bigger case, Allen remained free on bail. He took to harassing a deputy testifying against him. At night, he stood menacingly outside the man's house. Finally, the cop rushed out and chased him away. Just before Leigh's trial, someone mailed an anonymous typewritten letter to a local judge. The judge brought it into the Calistoga P.D.

"Did you miss me?" it read. "Was busy doing some nefarious destardly work, for which I am well suited. . . . Ah yes! Justice shall be done. I had to laugh. [San Francisco *Chronicle* columnist] Herb Caen mentioned that Toschi was the only man looking for the Zodiac. Zodiac gave me a car to pick up the evidence. He knew my *Plymouth* was sabotaged."

A disabled Plymouth had been spotted by a teenage boy at Blue Rock Springs the night of the Fourth of July murder.

THURSDAY, JANUARY 23, 1975

POLICE drove to Allen's home in Vallejo and rearrested him. His mother let the deputies in and they descended to find Leigh shrieking in the center of the basement. Live chipmunks were crawling all over him—the pets and victims he let share his subterranean room. "Squirrel shit was dripping from his shoulders," recalled one cop. "He remained in our custody from that date on. When he was at the Sonoma County Jail, cell block #2B2, he came to the attention of three Mexican guys who tried to 'punk' him. He let them screw him. Later, in court, the other little boy testified against Allen."

THURSDAY, MARCH 13, 1975

SERGEANT Mulanax had not given up on Allen, and wrote the FBI:

"SYNOPSIS: Subject fits the general description of Zodiac. He was born in Honolulu, Hawaii. He attended school in Riverside, California. He is employed in Oakland Calif. He is a convicted sex offender of children. TYPE OF EXAMINATION: Evaluation of fingerprints and palm prints. Evaluation of handwriting exemplars submitted, with evidence on file. MATERIAL SUBMITTED: 1. Two yellow pages of yellow material (partial text of Zodiac messages.) 2. Red diary written by subject over period of one year. 3. Palm prints of subject of left and right hands. 4. One white sheet containing Zodiac text, written with ink pen by subject. 5. Solano County jail arrest record."

Later that day Allen was sentenced to Atascadero State Hospital for the Criminally Insane.

"As for the little animals Leigh always had," a friend of Allen's told me, "he definitely had lots of chipmunks, and even a skunk at one time. When he was sent to Atascadero he gave the animals to the Elnoka Nursery off Highway 12. He had an abundance of the little creatures. I remember hating to see them caged all the time and now Leigh was going to be caged as well."

A sharp-eyed officer, Sergeant John Burke, noticed he was wearing a Zodiac wristwatch and entered the fact in his file.

FRIDAY, MARCH 14, 1975

LEIGH arrived at Atascadero and began serving his sentence. Back in 1969 he had shown his sister-in-law several pages of handprinted legal terminology and cryptograms. "They pertain to a person who had been committed to Atascadero State Hospital for molesting a child," he had said. "This is the work of an insane person." Leigh had been prescient, for he was now in that very situation. Meanwhile, all Zodiac-type attacks, sightings, and letters ceased. That inactivity from Zodiac was extraordinarily telling. Only the investigation continued, grinding slowly, but exceedingly fine. The old clock in the Homicide room in San Francisco ticked on as if measuring off three years as slowly as it could.

Meanwhile, Allen's friend, Jim, was troubled. "Leigh called me at work one night," he told me later, "I felt sorry for him so I would listen. That's why he thought I was his buddy. 'I have to go to jail,' he said. 'I need to come down and talk to you. I have some unfinished business, something I want to get off my chest. I want you to be by yourself, and I want you to wait for me after work.' I thought, 'Good grief, this is weird. All these stories are flying around. I don't know if I really want to meet him after work alone.' But I told him I'd wait for him. After work and a couple of beers, he'd go through his two-hour dissertation. Another kid was working with me, Paul Blakesly. So I told Paul, 'You know, old Leigh wants to come down and see me by myself, and I don't really trust him. I don't know what he's got up his sleeve, so would you hang around and break a beer with me and we'll wait for him.' So we laid a couple of club-like things around the store just in case. Old Leigh comes down and, of course, he looked like hell. His eyes were all red, and he had a little stubble all over his face. He had been crying his guts out. He wanted to spill the beans—that he was being investigated for the Zodiac thing when they'd picked him up again.

"He's going on with this big story all about Zodiac. Leigh claimed he was being checked because a bunch of girls had disappeared up the Russian River area, and they were all on his days off or time off. The police had come down and checked his time-card records behind closed doors. A lot of coincidences pointed to him, he said, but they were circumstantial. It seemed so beyond comprehension that I was afraid if I start repeating all these stories—Christ! They could hang him on a story and I don't want to tell them the wrong thing. This went on to probably nine o'clock at night. Nothing happened and we all parted ways.

"Leigh once told me he was at a Fosters Freeze in Vallejo. He was out of school and a couple of kids were teasing him about his new pair of tennis shoes. Before it was through they ended up in some kind of scuffle. Coincidentally police held it against him because the kid reported it and later on it turned out this was the kid killed up at Berryessa. He told me it was stuff like that that was getting him in trouble. Leigh was a pretty good-sized guy. He started one of those, 'You know how you get a guy down when you throw a punch at him?' 'Not really, Leigh.' 'Pretend like you're going to hit me.' 'Leigh, I don't want to hit you.' 'No. Just pretend. Just stick your arm out.' 'OK, get it over with, whatever you're going to show me.' I went to put my arm out and within a blink of an eye, I'm on my back and he's got his knee in my chest. I didn't think a big fat guy could move that quick. I had no idea how capable he was. It was shocking, because of his stature, other than being big and strong, he wasn't an athlete. To perform a move like that, to make it so rapid and smooth—there was no sensation of being thrown down. He just did like you were a feather.

"Old Leigh came into work one day after college. 'This morning on the way back,' he said, 'I stopped by a place and checked it out. I was wandering around this house they were building and in this window sill was this unusual old gray J.C. Penny radio from the fifties.' Boy that really opened my eyes! That was my radio I had when I was a little kid and we had it in the window of the house. I realized that he had been out to the house my wife and I were building just off the front kitchen window of our family home. My mom was home constantly in the kitchen. We also had a dog, a collie, that was pretty vocal. He didn't miss anything and somehow Leigh had come out there and made this visit and my mom didn't see him and the dog never barked."

11

ATASCADERO

ALLEN had been to Atascadero before, but in the capacity of a therapist. Now he returned as a prisoner. If police had comprehended how repugnant the mental institution was to him, how terrified he was of being confined there, they might have employed a useful tool. Allen's fear might have been used as a pry bar to extract information about Zodiac. But Allen coped, began working in the print shop, and soon had mastered new techniques. In the print shop he devised a plan to get the police off his back.

Back home the *Times-Herald* reported that:

> "Zodiac is still considered a possible suspect in a series of Sonoma County killings. . . . Zodiac threatened in one rambling letter to torture his victims, and Sonoma County has some murder victims who were tortured to death through slow strangulation and by administering strychnine. . . . Sonoma County's seven young female victims [between 1972 and 1974] all were dumped in rural areas. A Sonoma County man recently was considered a Zodiac suspect but was ruled out, according to Sonoma Sheriff's Captain Jim Caulfield. He was a molester of young boys, however, and has been committed to Atascadero State Hospital."

"While Leigh was in Atascadero," a Vallejo source told me, "I think that's when my mother first became aware he may be the Zodiac. He wrote to her that they suspected him of the crimes. At one point, I think my mother called him there and spoke to him. She asked him directly if he was the murderer. I believe he was somewhat jovial about it, but never admitted to the crimes. She verified that he was the suspect through the Santa Rosa District Attorney, John Hawkes."

Leigh, signing himself "Drawer A," wrote Jim in Sonoma. "If Zodiac writes one letter while I'm in here," he wrote earnestly, "then that will clear me of being the Zodiac." The remark was puzzling. Everyone knew Leigh was imprisoned for child molesting, not for being Zodiac. He repeated the same remark to women he knew. In his long outdoor chess game with authorities, Allen seemed always one step ahead. For the second stage of his plan, he hoarded his daily medication and got a job in the dispensary. Like Zodiac, Leigh knew explosives. For his third step, he and a companion began building a bomb to blast their way out of the prison.

MONDAY, NOVEMBER 3, 1975

IN order to pass various psychiatric tests during his incarceration, Allen boned up on the proper responses to make. He took all his tests in this fashion: "He would not smile or show emotion and would speak in a low monotone." He took tests as a man drugged. During TAT (Thematic Apperception Test) evaluations, Allen was asked to make up stories based on simple line drawings portraying people in ambiguous situations. ("Explain what is going on in this picture.") Indirectly, his answers revealed aspects of his subconscious feelings and personality—"he has a violent fantasy life . . . a hyperthymic (highly emotional) individual unable to establish normal social contact."

Finally police decided to give him a lie-detector test. "A polygraph machine is only a stress detector and anxiety detector," Toschi told me. Lie detectors, a favorite investigative tool, are fallible and register false positives about fifteen percent of the time. Polygraphs measure changes in pulse, blood pressure, and breathing, but can be tricked by really good liars.[4] Even the term "lie detector" is a misnomer. Erle Stanley Gardner wrote in his *Court of Last Resort*, "Lie detection is impossible. What is possi-

---

[4]When FBI Director Louis Freeh ordered stepped-up polygraph testing of agents to bolster the bureau's internal security system, the agency's nine thousand agents were troubled.

ble is the detection of stress (and in a few cases the covering up of stress). A polygraph or Psychological Stress Evaluation test should never be used as the sole judge of a person's innocence. As with all scientific evidence, these tests need to be evaluated. The lie test is not permitted as evidence in court except by stipulation because it is undependable and subject to the interpretation of the operator. As late as 1998 the Supreme Court would rule lie detectors unreliable. Leonarde Keeler, though not the inventor of the lie detector, had done the most to refine the machine. The lie detector is in use today much as he developed it. Briefly, the polygraph records changes in the body's physiological responses to questions."

Details for the test were ironed out, and Leigh agreed. "What happened," Detective Bawart told me later, "was a guy from the Department of Justice who was working under Fred Shirisago went down to Atascadero and they put Allen on a polygraph. That was Sam Lister—the head polygraph guy at DOJ." Allen entered a plain soundproofed and air-conditioned room. Lister had him sit in the examining chair. Carefully, he hooked him up to three devices, a procedure alone that usually causes stress in a subject. First a blood pressure-pulse unit—a sphygmograph—an instrument similar to that used to take blood-pressure readings—was connected to graphically record the movements of his pulse. After the blood pressure sleeve was wrapped around his biceps, a flexible corrugated tube, a pneumograph, was strapped around Leigh's chest to measure changes in his respiration. Finally, an electrodermal unit, usually metal tubes clenched in both hands or electrodes on the hand (a monitor pinched on a fingertip), measured galvanic changes or responses in his skin. As the prisoner's reactions to each question were recorded on a moving strip chart, he was observed through a two-way mirror.

Were he to lie, his heart would beat faster, his breath come more quickly, and changes would take place in his skin moisture. Pens on a moving strip of graph paper recorded reactions. Leigh had already been put at ease in a cordial pre-interview. Leigh kept to a monotone and did not smile, later claiming the test lasted ten hours. "A polygraph will take maybe an hour—max," Toschi told me. "Allen's lying about that." There are usually ten to twelve questions, and those are brief, basic, and easy to understand. Leigh was asked his first name, his last name. After each question there was a pause of fifteen to twenty seconds. Then he was asked if he knew who had killed Darlene Ferrin, the Blue Rock Springs victim.

"No," he said.

"Do you live in California?" asked Lister.

"Yes."

"Did you yourself kill Paul Lee Stine on October 11, 1969?"

"No."

"Were you a resident of Vallejo?"

"Yes."

"Did you have anything whatsoever to do with this homicide?"

"No."

"Are you forty-two years of age?"

"Yes."

"Are you deliberately concealing or withholding any guilty knowledge of the homicide at Washington and Cherry Streets?"

"No."

"Is today Friday?"

"Yes."

"Have you deliberately lied at any time during this entire interview?"

"No."

"Let's do the test once more completely," said Lister. It was common practice to talk over results and learn the reasons for responses. "People overreact, underreact, have guilt complexes, are frightened, are angry," said polygraph expert Chris Gugas. "The examiner has to take into account variables such as intelligence, emotional stability, reaction to shock. The process is never cut-and-dried." Thus the expert can start again with a revised set of questions, or repeat the same questions so responses could be compared. Lister indicated that Allen had passed his polygraph examination both times. "He is not the Zodiac Killer," he said. Allen called afterward to tell his family and friends that he had passed and was not Zodiac.

"And they ran Allen at Atascadero and he came up clean," Bawart lamented. "That bothered us. Well, we had two other experts read his charts, and they say, 'He was on drugs during this time.' Our polygraph examiner, Johnson, examined the charts and said, 'It's my opinion that Allen was on some type of drugs while he was taking the test.' It was also his opinion that Allen did not pass the polygraph exam and that it was inconclusive. And then we served a search warrant at Atascadero and I had a bunch of shit about that, but anyway, he was on Thorazine. Atascadero is a mental hospital and many of the inmates are on different types of tranquilizers. These other guys who read the charts said, 'Hey, old Lister here didn't give him any control questions about whether he was on any drugs. We're looking at this thing—this guy's loaded. You could've asked him if he had a mother and father and he would have said no."

Polygraph tests can be neutralized by a subject through drugs or pain, but the subject's responses would be noticeably high and flat. Allen had reportedly stockpiled his daily medication of Valium tranquilizers and pilfered Thorazine, a drug prescribed for extreme paranoia, from the dispensary where he briefly worked. "Thorazine was for the really psychotic patients," said Bawart. "It wouldn't be the common drug they would hand out, but he had access to the dispensary. They were giving Valium to him. All he had to do was save it up. This is only guessing. You know you're going to take a polygraph test—you've got your buddies down there. In fact he had a strong buddy—he was going to build a bomb and blow his way out of Atascadero and they caught him. That infernal device was close to lethal quality."

Dr. J. Paul De River, in *Crime and the Sexual Psychopath,* wrote that "disregard for civil or moral law, and the cunning and stealth are also part of the make up of the 'non sexual' psychopath. Like his sex-motivated counterpart, he is only 'mad' sporadically, and for the rest of the time he might lock the details of his acts out of his consciousness."

"Allen had a letter," Bawart continued, "that he phonied up that was signed by—the guy's name was [Jim] Silver, an investigator. And Silver had done some correspondence with him [requesting a polygraph examination]. Allen got Silver's signature from the correspondence. Allen worked in a print shop there at Atascadero Hospital, and he made up a letter that he duped on this guy Silver's signature with a phony Department of Justice heading on it. He had used a mechanical means to lift the signature of the investigator from a document, placed it on prewritten letters, and printed them up. It was a letter to any law enforcement agency and, as I recall, said: 'To Whom It May Concern: This man is not a suspect in the Zodiac case and has been completely cleared. He has passed a polygraph examination and law enforcement should no longer consider him a suspect in the Zodiac killings.' Just a bullshit thing so he could show people. Of course Silver would never write such a letter." Though he had passed the lie test, Allen had lied about the letter clearing him.

MONDAY, DECEMBER 1, 1975

ALLEN wrote a Santa Rosa Superior Court judge, telling him of the lie test results and including "a copy of a letter received from the State Department of Justice" exonerating him.

"After five years of being the subject of investigation, interrogation, search and other forms of harassment," he explained, "I was finally subjected to ten hours of polygraph examination, administered by the Justice Department, here at the hospital. I signed away my rights and cooperated fully, in order to finally resolve the issue, and have subsequently been removed from the Department's suspect list for the crimes specified in the enclosed letter.

"Since . . . I doubt the Department will take the trouble to distribute their findings to other concerned agencies, and since I do contemplate returning to the Santa Rosa area to live, I am taking it upon myself to impart this information to you, in the hope that it will find its way to its resting place in the proper file. I am hoping that, in the future, I will be able to go in peace, and not get sweaty palms at the mention of another unsolved homicide.

"The above has been quite a weight on my shoulders for the last five years. Now that I am cleared, I do heartily wish to forget the whole miserable affair. . . . Thank you for your time and consideration, and have a pleasant Holiday vacation. Sincerely, Arthur Leigh Allen, Case #74-0109-68."

Though Allen claimed to have been the subject of five years of investigation, he had not become a real suspect until 1971. In his mind he must have dated the beginning of his troubles from Sgt. Lynch's brief questioning at Cave School.

All through the rest of 1975, Leigh's mother faithfully wrote to him in prison, one of the few still corresponding with him. But in counseling, Leigh revealed how cold he felt her letters were and how much he hated her. Leigh felt an even stronger hatred for Atascadero. He feared staying there more than he dreaded the police. At night he could hear strange cries echoing down the highly polished floors. A big man could be afraid too.

While Allen was locked away, brooding and planning, the Vallejo Sheriff's Department doggedly pursued their Zodiac investigation. "Zodiac was a certain man," Les Lundblad told his son, Les, Jr., who had just returned from a golf match. "The only time I played golf," Les, Jr., recalled, "I played in a foursome with this man. I produced a Polaroid of the foursome to my dad and he pointed the 'beady-eyed' man out." Detective Sergeant Lundblad thought this beady-eyed suspect was protected by a powerful official. Later an ex-Highway patrolman interviewed Les, Jr., and told him that this official had ordered Sergeant Lundblad to back off. The son didn't think his father would have obeyed that order, but was at a loss to explain why more wasn't done with the 'beady-eyed' man. However, the late Sergeant Lundblad's interest in this early suspect predated the police interview with Leigh Allen in 1971 and his subsequent visit to Atascadero to see Allen who had by then become the chief suspect.

Sergeant Ralph Wilson told me that when Lundblad returned from Atascadero, he said, "That's him!" His remark carried conviction. Three years later, I was in the main sheriff's office just above the jail—Fairfield, California, Criminal Division. Captain Vince Murphy had arranged for me to look at some evidence. The switchboard operator, a slim, dynamic woman, paused between calls and recalled the late Les Lundblad with admiration. "I was there when he came back from Atascadero," she said. "He was furious. 'That's him!' he said, 'That's Zodiac. That's the son of a bitch and we can't do anything about it!' and he believed this right to the day of his death."

The operator was troubled, concerned that she once had spoken to Zodiac when he called the sheriff's office. Zodiac had told her his real name, but she couldn't remember it. She'd lost the name in all the excitement. "I worked closer with Lundblad than with Lynch," Narlow told me. "I always got the feeling that Lundblad knew who Zodiac was. That story [about Cheney and Allen talking about hunting humans] is so bizarre you don't know whether to believe it or not. Sometimes people concoct things like this for whatever reason. But that story about him talking about those things is so pat, that if in fact he did say it, then he has to be the Zodiac." And so Toschi, Armstrong, and Mulanax probably had the right man, but somehow were being outfoxed. No one could get around the handprinting, the partial print on the cab, and now the lie test. Those obstacles were the big three. The *Sacramento Bee* and *Santa Rosa Press Democrat*'s secret witness programs established a $20,000 reward for Zodiac's capture, adding to Yellow Cab's existing reward. So many Zodiac tips trickled into Vallejo P.D. that Detective Bawart was assigned to help track new leads.

12
WITCHES

SONOMA County Sheriff's Detective Sergeant "Butch" Carlstedt blinked, then looked again. He perceived links between twelve Jack the Ripper–style murders and the long-sought Zodiac. Zodiac might be arranging his crimes in a broad "Z" extending over the Bay Area. He might be tracing out an even larger "Z," encompassing the entire West. Sonoma County Sheriff Don Striepeke agreed, pointing to Rodeo; Vancouver, Washington; Seattle; Salt Lake City; Santa Fe; and Aspen-Vail as locations where girls were slain. He surmised this psychopathic killer might practice witchcraft, killing slaves for his afterlife just as Zodiac had boasted. Ultimately, though, the assailant turned out to be Ted Bundy, not Zodiac.

But Striepeke was not deterred. From the beginning, Zodiac's occult bent had fascinated him. The sheriff examined diagrams—a series of arranged sticks discovered at a murder site along semi-remote Franz Valley Road. Was this a witchcraft symbol? The sticks formed a square and a rectangle joined together to indicate a human figure. Inside the rectangle were two stones, and outside, two more pebbles. Four sticks ran around the outer edges. Striepeke thought the design might represent the black magic "Seal of Vassago." Vassago is a mighty prince who declares things past, present, and future and discovers what has been hidden. A local teenager claimed it was a design he made to show his girlfriend the shape of his new trailer, but it still might be a witch sign. Zodiac also used other esoteric symbols in his codes—dots such as those used in astrological horoscopes. The nearly invisible Zodiac scarcely needed witchcraft—the Santa Rosa murderer was powerful enough to heft bodies over a ditch and hurl them considerable distances down a hillside. Witches mail bloody swatches of cloth to their enemies. So did Zodiac.

Berkeley Chief of Police Wes Pomeroy was interested in the occult angle too. He had written to the Department of Justice, OCCIB, on February 14: "Enclosed are five photographs of various signs photographed in a rural (Vallejo) area. Please determine if the enclosed photographs represent signs in witchcraft. If so, please determine what each individual sign's significance is in mutual cases of interest."

"It's highly doubtful that witchcraft might be involved with Zodiac," David Rice assured me, "as the *Wiccan Rede* prohibits harm to anyone, including animals."

I DROVE TO Vallejo to ask Sergeant Lynch about Zodiac again, hoping he might recall something new. I recalled how, after the Lake Berryessa stabbings, Lynch had issued a public appeal to Zodiac to surrender. "We will see that he gets help and that all his rights are protected," promised Lynch. "[Zodiac] is obviously an intelligent individual. He knows that eventually he will be taken into custody. So it would be best that he give himself up before tragedy is written in blood." I sat down in his darkened dining room. "I think there were five of us in the investigation bureau," he began softly. "I think what really happened was we were spending so much time and going so many places that I guess they got dissatisfied with the way it was being handled . . . when we first started on this case there was this guy George—he used to go down to the coffee shop [where Darlene Ferrin waitressed]. He was trying to date her, but for some reason Dee [Darlene's nickname] didn't want to have anything to do with him. Constantly bothering her and following her. Dee was deathly afraid of him. The whole investigation originally seemed to focus on this guy." George hadn't visited his familiar watering hole, Jack's Hangout, since the July Fourth shootings. Next their search led Lynch and his partner to the Kat Pad on Sacramento Street, Kaiser Steel in Napa, then to the Pastime bar in Benicia. "Me and Ed Rust," said Lynch, "we found out he quit the Pastime, and went up to Yountville. I got a description of him from his landlady, Mrs. Violet Peeler. He was five foot seven, with a stocky build and a dark complexion. Kind of plump with dark straight hair. Unfortunately, while George had a water-related last name, he had an airtight alibi too." A December 3, 1964, Solano County

Fairfield police report, 242, PC Battery, gave George's weight then as a mere 127 pounds.

"In Vallejo, we checked everybody out," Lynch concluded. "Once I got a call from someone who said Zodiac lived on Arkansas Street. I drove over there and found a man whose only connection was that he'd painted stars on his ceiling, including the Little Dipper. Everyone was a suspect and no one was safe." Even in the dimness, I saw the toll the case had taken on Lynch.

SATURDAY, JULY 24, 1976

"I watched Herman die in my sleep for eight weeks," Inspector Armstrong told the press, recalling Police Officer Herman George. George had been gunned down in the street in November of 1969. "He died a very slow and painful death. . . . When I leave the office at night I forget the job completely. I never discuss my work at home . . . well, I can't really. I find other ways to unwind." Armstrong became a man who could never sit still, a man constantly in motion. Finally, he burned out on Homicide. The next day, Armstrong transferred to the Bunco Division, leaving Toschi as the last remaining San Francisco policeman working the Zodiac case.

"At least a year before he left Homicide, Bill just didn't want to do it anymore," Toschi said. "Now that I'm the only one working on it, I never let a day go by without remembering Zodiac. It's gotten to be more personal. Every day I wonder what became of him."

Six cab drivers had been murdered since Stine's killing in 1969 and six suspects had been arrested and tried. Five were convicted of first degree murder, one of second degree. Just ten days after Stine's senseless murder, Toschi and Armstrong had investigated another Yellow Cab driver slaying only blocks away . . . "driver shot in the head . . . wallet stolen, cab lights left blazing . . . engine running. A row of brightly colored shirts littering the sidewalk." Toschi and Armstrong quickly nabbed a Tenderloin busboy in bed with his girlfriend. She had nagged him about money, so he flagged down a cabbie, held him up, and shot him during a struggle. "I took twenty-seven dollars off him," the chain-smoking youth said, "then threw my .22 revolver down a storm drain. I knew I'd get caught. I left my fingerprints all over the cab. I've got a record so I knew it was only a matter of time before you picked me up. Sure, I feel bad about it . . . especially for his wife and little girl. Whatever I get, I got coming. You don't kill someone and not pay for it. You see, I never wanted to see the inside of a jail again." Only Stine's killer still remained at large. It began to look as if Zodiac might win his lethal chess match with the police simply through attrition.

"My mom and I," a Southern California resident later told me, "visited Mr. Allen in Atascadero State Hospital almost every Saturday, and when he was released he even stayed at our house just north of Atascadero and west of San Luis Obispo. . . . I remember when he stayed at our house, he stayed in my mom's room with her. She always said that nothing happened, and I tend to believe her, since I remember him as not a very sexual person. Mr. Allen was very good to all of us kids. He spent a lot of time with my brothers and us girls. He taught us basic values, he was an avid nondrinker and non-smoker. He had a lot of small pets. He especially liked kangaroo rats, and had a permit to keep them and do research. He taught my brother how to drive, shoot, fix cars, and do all of those other guy things. He used to go to his various trailers, and they used to go target shooting in the mountains and river bottoms of Northern California. Mr. Allen was an expert marksman."

While Allen was incarcerated, Zodiac refused to die, living on in speculation, in every dark shadow along a lake and in all our hearts. If Zodiac had simply faded away, good men like Toschi, Armstrong, Mulanax, Lynch, Narlow, and Avery had been beaten.

TUESDAY, AUGUST 24, 1976

THE 1965 blue Volkswagen van bus had been in and out of the garage on A Street several times. On June 23, 1976, its owner had the motor overhauled for $520.74. In July, Wilfred Roenik, manager of the German Car Center east of Merced, noticed the van back again. A fix-it ticket said the rear lights weren't working. "The vehicle has ground problems," Roenik explained, but its owner did not ask to check the headlamps. The owner reappeared on August 2, saying he needed a voltage regulator and battery. Those were installed for $39.05. On Tuesday, August 24, he returned the battery. "It cost too much," he complained, and that afternoon installed his own new battery.

Around 8:00 P.M. the van's owner, a forty-one-year-old Santa Rosa Junior College teacher, climbed behind the wheel. He was tall, six feet three inches, 190 pounds, with brown hair and hazel eyes. An ex-soldier, he had served at Fort Hamilton, New York. In 1959, he'd received an early release from the Army as an overseas returnee. Six years later, he became an English teacher and part-time art instructor.

It was a clear night, the road ahead was dry. He was not under the influence of barbiturates or alcohol. He had just eaten. Going only fifty, five miles under the speed limit, he took his van eastbound onto an expressway with no streetlights. Highway 12 began as two lanes separated by a forty-foot-wide divider strip, really only dirt with grass and weeds, then abruptly became a four-lane divided expressway. At 8:30 P.M., just where the highway curved west of Wright Road, the van's headlights blinked out. At the start of the divided section, the VW eased onto the center divider and drove along there for a distance. The van ignored the curve, kept going straight, and flew across the dirt divider into the westbound lane.

A man en route to a friend's home in Sebastopol entered the point where the two westbound lanes merged to one. He could clearly see the headlights of other vehicles in the eastbound lanes. "Oh, my God!" he cried when he saw the van cross straight into oncoming traffic. There was no braking action, only light skid marks about two feet long just before impact. The van collided head-on into a 1972 Toyota traveling west in the #1 lane. Both vehicles bounced nine feet into the #2 lane and came to rest on the north asphalt shoulder less than three thousand feet east of Merced Avenue. Both drivers were pinned in their cars. At 8:50, the fire department extricated them. The woman driver in the Toyota would be OK.

At 9:00 P.M. they wheeled the teacher into the Santa Rosa Memorial Hospital Emergency Room and doctors began working on him. Deputy Durham spoke with Dr. Larson. The wounds were severe: a tear of the pericardial sac of the heart and left pulmonary vein . . . abrasion of the zygomatic arch, multiple fractures of the right lower extremity, a fracture of the left hip and right arm, multiple fractures of the ankle, laceration left lower leg, radial and ulna on right. They couldn't keep his blood pressure above 60. At 1:25 A.M. the teacher died on the operating table. Sheriff and Coroner Don Striepeke ruled the cause of death to be: "Shock due to multiple traumatic lesions."

Durham retained the teacher's wallet and personal property. The only address they had on him was a P.O. box in Santa Rosa. The deputy ran a 1028 registration check, and learned that the victim lived in a trailer home in Sebastopol. At 9:30 A.M., Durham spoke with the teacher's ex-wife and discovered he had been having some epileptic seizures controlled by medication. At 3:00 P.M. Investigator Siebe, interested in items inside the trailer, sealed it. It wasn't until November 8 that police returned the property, noting for their records: "Landlord and Ex-wife are going to itemize things in his room and store them at landlord's place to free the room." Why did police keep the teacher's possessions so long? Were they connected with the Santa Rosa murders? A decade would pass before I found out.

FRIDAY, AUGUST 27, 1976

AT midnight, San Francisco Supervisor Dianne Feinstein, working late at City Hall, opened the last of her mail. "Did you miss me?" a note read. "Was busy doing some nefarious dastardly work, for which I am very well suited." She rang the police, they called Toschi, and at 5:00 A.M., unshaven and bleary-eyed, he hustled upstairs to study the letter. "This isn't from Zodiac," he explained. "It's 'Old Tom' playing games again. I've got an entire file on Old Tom's bogus letters. Oddly enough, he isn't drunk when he writes his Zodiac letters. The typing is far too elaborate for a guy who is sauced. And a guy who keeps doing a thing like that when he's sober has gotta have something wrong with his head. He's killing himself with alcohol." The detective arranged for the McCauley Clinic to treat Tom for malnutrition; tried to get him into Napa under a section of the Welfare and Institution Code about being a danger to himself. However, Tom, an old pro, got himself a writ, and eight days later a judge dropped him back into the Tenderloin. I visited Old Tom in his flea-bitten hotel room, found him curled up on a urine-stained mattress. He was totally obsessed with the case. If that made him crazy, then we all were.

Toschi still had seven years left until his minimum retirement date. "I'm watching the mailbox," he said, "to see if I get a seventh-anniversary card from Zodiac." An ad had run in that morning's *Chronicle*: "ZODIAC Your partner is in DEEP REAL ESTATE. You're next. The Imperial Wizard can save you. Surrender to him or I'll terminate your case. R.A."

13
THE VOICE
OF ZODIAC

TOSCHI bumped into Karl Malden ("Lieutenant Mike Stone" on *The Streets of San Francisco*). The actor was on location at the police identification bureau, shooting a scene with costar Michael Douglas. Malden recalled Toschi from a meeting the previous year and hailed him. "You had that unusual upside-down holster and gun," he said. "I had never seen anything like it." They spoke of the job like two cops. "I'll get Zodiac some-day," Toschi vowed to Malden. "And I'll bring him to justice. That's my motivation—justice. I'm not a vengeful type, but when a life is taken, there must be justice. He has taken six lives; who knows how many more? I work with death, sorrow, and tragedy. Yet I like my job because it's a useful one. I bring in killers for society's judgment. Ringing bells and knocking on doors, good old-fashioned police work. That's what does it. I've even gotten religious-type letters where they tell me to pray, to talk to God, and then I'll catch Zodiac, they say. These people don't know they're talking to the biggest believer around." It was a speech he not only gave often, but believed in his heart.

"The Zodiac case is like the unsolved Black Dahlia murder in Los Angeles," Toschi told me later. "The chief detective in that case always said he would know the killer if he questioned him by means of one secret question he never revealed—I've held a couple of things back from the press too. . . . I remember meeting Clint Eastwood while he was making *Dirty Harry,* an almost shy person . . . faded jeans, a T-shirt, white tennis shoes, and he was a star. And Stu Rosenberg, the director of *The Laughing Police-man.* Walter Matthau was wonderful, Bruce Dern terrific in that film. Stu took a cab and met us at a murder scene. 'I don't know how you do this,' he said. 'My God!' "

Two months later, the House Select Committee sought out the nation's top investigators and invited Toschi to participate in a second look into the assassinations of John Kennedy and Martin Luther King, Jr. He declined. The assignment would have taken him away from Zodiac for two years. As Christmas approached, Toschi's mood lightened. One of the crime lab people snapped a candid shot of him grinning on the phone and wearing fellow Inspector Rotea Gilford's Zebra-patterned hat.

FOR YEARS, AMATEUR sleuths had groped for any clue that might unmask Zodiac. His use of English was a valuable lead. A U.C. Berkeley linguistics professor, examining Zodiac's use of vernacular, concluded he was of English or Welsh extraction. English cartoonist Jim Unger, who drew the syndicated strip *Herman,* was once a British policeman. "The letters from Zodiac show he is a man from the north of Great Britain," Unger said. "Of course, we know he speaks with no accent, but he may have lived there." A British police car currently in service was called the "Zodiac," its hood insignia a crossed circle. Author Nancy Ashbaugh told me: " 'Tit Willow' is a song sung by English mothers instead of 'Rock-a-bye-Baby.' Zodiac mentions peppermint and 'phompfit.' Zodiac means pomfits, a term for candies. 'Give the child a pomfit [violet squares and lavender squares].' There are pomfits in *Alice in Wonderland.*" A mind reader stated, "Zodiac is definitely of German-Irish ancestry."

Writing in future tense—"I will . . . I shall," Zodiac also used purposeful misspellings. Was there a man in the case who, in his daily life, habitually misspelled words in a mocking, taunting, or jocular manner? Spelling mistakes in the three-part cryptogram might not be encrypting mistakes, but a hidden message. Zodiac had used extra letters such as the *r* in "forrest" and *e* in "expeerence" and omitted letters such as the *s* in "dangerous." Using these divergences, Zodiac buff J. B. Dahlgren was able to spell "Science is mysterious Isis," but admitted that skilled anagramists might find better combinations.

Along with oddly spelled words, *X*'s ran through Zodiac's letters: "X'mas" and "Super X." The circled 8 in the letter might be a Taurus or Cancer symbol. Toschi, himself a Cancer, had gotten in the habit of regularly picking up astrology magazines hoping one might provide an overlooked clue. An astrologer, using the dates when Zodiac had struck or mailed letters, tried unsuccessfully casting his horoscope backwards. "That way I can ascertain his birth date." Another was sure Zodiac was a Capricorn. "Saturn is the ruling planet of Capricorn and Zodiac's activities are tied to certain events in Saturn," he said.

"Look in the *Chronicle*," John H. Grove advised, "and see what the horoscope recommended on days he killed. After all, Hitler wouldn't move without his astrologer's okay. . . . Cappies are usually good spellers, and his errors could be a ruse to throw everyone off the track. Zodiac appears to be strongly affected by the dice naturals 7 and 11, the latter especially. Apart from gambling and the occult his assumed name may be interrelated with his love of eleven. The word Zodiac is derived from the ancient Greek *Zodiakos*. The Hellenes had no separate numbering system, each alphabetical letter having a numerical value. I was amazed when I computed the numerical value for *Zodiakos* and found it to be 1111. Is Zodiac aware of this? He probably is. He may be crazy or a doper or both, but he is neither stupid nor illiterate."

If the number eleven was important to the killer, what did twelve mean to him? There were twelve signs to the Zodiac. Zodiac's nature (and that of most serial killers) was to clip and collect stories about himself. Since buying three papers a day might attract undue attention, he might have home subscriptions to them all. The *Examiner* had not only buried Zodiac on page 4, but begged him to surrender to them (an unwise suggestion to a madman who enjoyed being in control). Zodiac never wrote them again. Police might look for a man who had many subscriptions, but canceled the *Examiner*.

WEDNESDAY, MARCH 30, 1977

ALLEN had now served thirty months—two years and fifteen days at Atascadero. He was returned to the Sonoma County Jail to prepare for a May 13, 1977 probation hearing. He waived that right.

TUESDAY, AUGUST 30, 1977

LEIGH had spent a total of 150 days in the Sonoma County Jail. Between there and Atascadero he had been behind bars for two years, four months, and twenty-five days. During all that time not one offense attributable to Zodiac had been committed. The attacks in Santa Rosa had ceased; no new bodies were discarded below Franz Valley Road; no genuine letters from Zodiac had been received. Even as late as this nine hundredth day of Leigh's captivity, a note—a sentence—a single word post-marked from outside Atascadero would have removed Allen from the suspect list. But Zodiac's last letter had been received three full years before—July 8, 1974.

In the afternoon, a Sonoma County Sheriff's Department deputy ushered Leigh downstairs. Their heels echoed in the long impersonal hallways. The deputy arranged white plastic numerals, #4-7-9-3-2, below Leigh's face for an I.D. mug shot. He was garbed in prison clothes, his mustache and goatee now showing gray. His expression was scowling, though the next day he was to be a free man. A friend of mine saw a different expression in the same photo. "I think he looks sad," she said.

California law enforcement authorities, under Section 290 of the State Penal Code, relied on convicted sex offenders to keep tabs on themselves by notifying police when they moved. Since the state had no enforcement program, it was no surprise that only a handful of the multitude of discharged offenders were currently registered. Atascadero officials notified the prison registry and the registry notified Vallejo authorities that Allen was on the streets again. The next step was up to him. He returned to his cubicle, his steps echoing down the halls, his image reflected full length in the highly polished floor bigger than ever.

WEDNESDAY, AUGUST 31, 1977

LIBERATED from Atascadero, Leigh Allen went to stay with friends in Paso Robles. The following day Toschi received a typed letter from him, the first mention of Zodiac within recent memory. "Killers invariably try to inject themselves into the investigation," I said to Toschi. "Have any of the suspects ever offered to help you catch Zodiac? With his disdain of the police, Zodiac would be irresistibly drawn to offer to catch himself."

"Only one," he said.

"And I bet it was typed."

"Yes, it was. It just arrived." He searched his desk. A bright shaft of light cut through the grimy window. Traffic crawled sluggishly along Bryant Street. The old sign flashed its red neon in bright sunlight, "OK BAIL BONDS—OPEN 24 HOURS—WE SPECIALIZE IN TRAFFIC." Toschi found the letter and read aloud: "If I can ever be of any help to you just let me know. I'm sorry I wasn't your man, but I'm out now and I've paid my debt to society. [signed] Leigh Allen."

"Sorry I wasn't your man!' " said Toschi in wonderment. A note like this, with its mocking tone, was exactly the kind of letter Zodiac would write. "He's the one," I said.

Back at the *Chronicle,* a sick, unpostmarked letter signed with a Zodiac symbol arrived that afternoon. Even crank letters like Old Tom's were treated seriously. Actually, any Zodiac letter, no matter how obvious a hoax, always created a stir. No possibility could be dismissed. Police lavished attention on each because Zodiac's handprinting may have changed over the years.

"ILL DO IT BECAUSE I DONE IT 21 TIMES I CANT STOP BECAUSE EACH THAT I KILL MAKES IT WORSE AND I MUST KILL MORE MAN IS THE MOST PRIZED GAME ILL NERVER GIVE MY NAME. . . ."

What perversity drove anyone to copy Zodiac? Future copycats had darker motives and bloodier hands. They went further than imitating writing—they acted on the Zodiac crimes themselves.

TUESDAY, JANUARY 3, 1978

ALLEN returned to Vallejo. Water Town had changed little—lying clean, sprawling, and mysterious as always. Robert Louis Stevenson once said, "Vallejo's typical of many small California towns—a blunder." First thing, Leigh applied as a fleet mechanic to Benicia Import Auto Service. He was honest about his past. "I served two years and a half at Atascadero," he admitted. After they hired him at $6.15 an hour, he roved the hills trying out his

wings. He was seemingly unaware the search for Zodiac had not
abated in his absence. The same hounds were still howling and
leaping all about him and across the waters in San Francisco. But
on a national level, the FBI focused on new Zodiac suspects:

"At Buffalo, New York. Will question an informant regarding
his knowledge of and basis of his allegation of Zodiac's activities, and why he considers him a suspect in the ZODIAC case,"
read a bulletin. "At Jacksonville, at Tavares, Florida. Will advise Lake County as a possible ZODIAC suspect. Will obtain
photos of subject and furnish to Sacramento, and also to Buffalo. ARMED AND DANGEROUS."

The gray straits appeared icy in the morning. Leigh parked
where a causeway across the Napa River and the straits joined
Vallejo at the west to an island. He gazed toward Mare Island. In
Water Town's early days, a barge transporting a herd of livestock
had overturned. General Mariano Guadalupe Vallejo, an early California land baron, had rescued a white mare swimming for the island and christened the cay Isla de la Yegua—"Island of the Mare."
    Across the water, battleships moored alongside three-tiered
warehouses with brick smokestacks. The Naval Shipyard was
Vallejo's principal industry, served by third-, even fourth-
generation workers. During World War II it returned a thousand
repaired ships to duty and manufactured three hundred submarines, destroyer escorts, sub tenders, and landing craft. The
West's oldest Naval installation assembled battleships like the
California, cruisers like the *Chicago.* It was the first Pacific yard
to build atomic-powered subs. The shipyard, completely self-
contained, manufactured everything it needed from bricks to rivets. Allen was equally self-sufficient. He gazed longingly toward
the sea, drove into work, and got bad news. Import Auto Service
was laying him off. "So soon?" said Leigh. "Business has just
been too slow," said the manager. Allen clenched and unclenched
his fists at the hopelessness of it all.

FRIDAY, APRIL 28, 1978

ON Monday, someone had dropped a letter with too much
postage and signed "Zodiac" into a mailbox. Its postmark desig-

nated a Santa Clara or San Mateo County origin. On Friday, April 28, the *Chronicle* received its first Zodiac letter since 1974. If it was not a hoax, the killer had been elsewhere for almost four years. The letter met all the usual requirements of a genuine Zodiac communication. But it had a forced look about it, and quite quickly cries of "Hoax!" went up. Sherwood Morrill in Sacramento ruled it authentic. For a while so did John Shimoda, Director of the Postal Crime Laboratory, Western Regional Office, San Bruno. Eventually Shimoda reversed his position and sided with expert Terry Pascoe, claiming it to be a clever hoax. I wanted it to be authentic, but as time went by, my doubts about the letter increased. The cunning forgery would cause agony for everyone.

"He's lurking somewhere," Toschi told the press, "and it scares the hell out of people, including my wife. The case has put considerable strain upon my family. My three little girls were not big enough in 1969 to appreciate the magnitude of the case, but they were old enough to hear stories from their schoolmates that their daddy was working on a case about a dangerous murderer. They would come and tell me they were afraid that something horrible would happen to me. They lived with this fear. Of all the cases I have handled, this one is really a personal case. . . . He's playing the ego game, trying to taunt us. . . . I try not to let this bother me, but it's frustrating. We have not given up. The case is worked upon anytime something is forwarded to us and we act upon it. The surrender box is still open."

MONDAY, MAY 15, 1978

"**I** wasn't surprised a popular film like *The Exorcist* drew Zodiac out back in '74," Toschi told me. "This guy is a real nut on movies." I showed him an anonymous letter sent to me—exactly the kind the egotistical, publicity-mad killer might write: "To Editor, or who ever is in charge of the Zodiac," it said. "Have you ever considered making a short film about the Zodiac?

"Like some of those Hitchcocks, you know where you have to come to your own conclusion for an ending as to who is the killer? If a muvie could be made, it can be shown in one of those small theaters where mostly sex muvies are shown so that it will look like some unknown thought of the idea just to make money on something that sells. . . . As I look at it, since the Zodiac takes so much pride in himself for his work, He'll probably love the thought of a muvie about himself, and since he feels shure knowbody knows him, there is no reason for him not to go and admire himself. . . . Thank you—no name . . . sorry for the mess, but I'm kind of in a hurry, I have work to do."

TUESDAY, MAY 16, 1978

BECAUSE of furor over the April hoax letter, cries for Zodiac's capture intensified. San Francisco residents put Police Chief Charles Gain under terrific pressure to solve the case. He asked FBI Director William H. Webster to analyze six Zodiac cryptograms mailed to local papers in 1969. Gain wrote:

"Three of these were subsequently broken but the others remain unsolved. We request that a new attempt be made to break these ciphers—ENCLOSED: 1. Photo copy of 'Zodiac' letter with 13 characters. 'My name is——.' 2. Photo copy of 'Zodiac' letter with 31 characters. 3. Photo copy of cryptogram excerpt from letter. 4. Copy of three broken cryptograms."

FBI attempts to decrypt, using the old key as part of a combination cryptosystem, failed, as did linear and route transposition. Experts examined the first and last halves for a cyclic use of variants, did hand anagramming with the message as written or backwards or written columnarly. They read it as first line forward and second line backward. They ran a sliding word through the messages. They tried concentrated anagramming—"took, look, book, cook, shook, hook . . ." All endeavors were non-productive. Toschi was not too surprised. Like many policemen, he had no great faith in the elitist bureau.

FRIDAY, MAY 19, 1978

IN the meantime, Gain obtained FBI lab results on his petitioned comparison of the Zodiac letters. The Questioned Documents examiner considered sixteen manila folders containing the letters between October 13, 1969, and April 24, 1978. The expert renumbered them Q 85 through Q 99. (The Riverside letters, including the desktop, were studied separately in photographic form and labeled Qc100.) The report, in longhand, read:

> "The handprinting on the Q 85–Qc100 letters show a wide range of variation and various writing speeds. Additionally, portions of the material, particularly the three Riverside letters, may have been disguised or deliberately distorted. For the above reasons, the handprinting examination of these letters was inconclusive. However, consistent handprinting characteristics were noted in the Q 85–Qc100 letters which indicate that one person may have prepared all of the letters including the Riverside letters and the message found on the desk top in the Riverside case."

A month later Gain requested the Behavioral Science Unit at Quantico review the letters' contents and develop a psychological profile of Zodiac. Later I called to see if Cheney ever wrote any letters to Leigh Allen. "I couldn't help but notice that your printing resembles Zodiac printing," I said. "Could Zodiac be copying your handprinting?" "Maybe!" said Cheney. "Before changing to permit microfilm, upper and lowercase lettering was standard drafting practice." Cheney, an engineer, referred me to *Technical Drawing* (Geisacke, Spencer, and Mitchell, Macmillan, 4th edition). "Though I never got a letter from him with double postage," he said, "Leigh typed his letters and recipes, misspelling certain words on purpose."

Allen began meeting with his parole officer, Bruce R. Pelle, Deputy Probation Officer, County of Solano. Pelle noticed that Allen consistently wore old-fashioned pleated pants to their conferences. Their first monthly meeting was troubling to Pelle and uncomfortable for Allen. The parole officer attempted to see just what would set him off, threatening him with a return to jail if he did not cooperate more fully. This brought a lowering of his head and a refrain of "I wouldn't like that at all." Allen's improper relationships with children had not concluded either. When Pelle first visited Allen's home with his partner, Lloyd, the parolee had all the neighborhood children out front riding bicycles. Leigh had them circle their car waving red flags to direct the officers into the driveway. He also maintained a friendship with a nine-year-old that would only cease when she reached sixteen.

One evening, Pelle gazed out his apartment window at the Bodega complex where he lived. Two stories below, the smell of chlorine and suntan oil drifted upward. Next to the intermittently sparkling pool Leigh was holding hands with a little girl—a direct parole violation. Pelle realized that Leigh had followed him home after their session. For some reason the ex-convict was trying to intimidate him or taunt him by his close proximity to a child. Why? Pelle made some calls, learned the girl was Leigh's cousin, and ultimately let the matter pass. Shortly afterward, he learned that Allen was a serious Zodiac suspect.

"In fact the day I found out," he told me, "I was home looking at copies of the Zodiac letters. All evening I kept getting these calls where someone would just breathe. I kept telling my girlfriend, 'I think that Allen knows that I know and that he knows that I know he knows.' I told him:

" 'Arthur, you're suspected of being the Zodiac.'

" 'I know,' he said.

" 'What do you think about that?'

" 'I think that was a real misnomer to do that to me. I think it was unfair.'

" 'It was?'

" 'Yeah.'

" 'Have you read the reports?'

" 'Yeah, I know what they're talking about and that's all a pack of lies.'

" 'Wouldn't the person who was the Zodiac feel that it was a pack of lies?'

" 'Probably. Who in hell is going to admit to being the damn Zodiac.' "

He told Pelle that on the day of the Hartnell and Shepard stabbings, he was supposed to be at Lake Berryessa catching ground squirrels to dissect. "Amazing coincidence," Pelle remarked. He was also disturbed by Leigh's mental evaluation. "Basically, Arthur is an extremely dangerous person," he told me later. "He is sociopathic and possesses an incredibly high I.Q. Allen is repressing very deep hatred and is incapable of functioning with women in a normal way." Apparently, after his 1971 oil refinery questioning, Leigh, at the urging of his family, had been evaluated by psychiatrists at U.C. Berkeley and Langley Porter. They had worked up mental reports on the prime suspect from May 1973 until September 26, 1974, when he had been first considered "capable of murder, dangerous." Doctors had looked for indications of self-mutilation drives and a disregard for the sanctity of human life. They noted his impulsiveness.

I asked Pelle if he had seen a light table or enlarger at Leigh's house on any of his visits. I suspected Zodiac had projected grids through an enlarger onto his blocks of cipher to align them so perfectly. "Yes," Pelle said. "I recall seeing an enlarger in his home." But of course there had to be one. Whoever Zodiac was, he had to have access to a light table, grids to position his symbols, a T-square and triangle and other drafting tools. Ethan W. Allen had been a draftsman for the city of Vallejo. Such items were the tools of his trade. As a professional artist, I knew that the Zodiac letters, the 340-symbol code in particular, would tax the most experienced craftsman.

"Leigh's got a new motorcycle now," Pelle told me, "applegreen [a color close to Cheri Jo Bates's lime-green VW]. It's not registered in his name, but a friend's. And he's got a new job too. Leigh told me how much he hates working for a living. Told me forcefully. But when he chooses he can project a calm and reasonable front. He's working part-time at the California Human Development Corporation [1004 Marin Street] as a senior-citizen aide. 'For $4.00 per hour,' Leigh explained, 'I take seniors to and from hospitals, inspect and install security devices in their homes.' Security devices—that's mighty interesting. As for Leigh's brother, Ron, he's now a city planner. He's still worried about his brother, but rarely has any more contact with the police."

One evening sometime later, I drove out to the first Vallejo crime scene—Lake Herman Road. Other visits had been at midnight, the time of the murders. Tonight the wind trembled the trees along the road. The landscape, lost and found in every curve, was finally swallowed up in white fog. After Allen's release from prison, gossip again mentioned a big man roving near the water pumps and lake. He scouted, practiced his shooting, and climbed through quarries where he could dive. All of Zodiac's murders had been water-oriented—Blue Rock *Springs* (eerily reminiscent of Allen's old school, Valley Springs), *Riverside, Lake* Berryessa, *Lake* Street (his requested first destination in Paul Stine's cab), and *Lake* Herman Road. Though I found the Lake Herman double murder site virtually unchanged, one alteration had been made. The little gravel lane just past the chain-link fence leading to Pump House #10 now had a name. A brisk wind rose, ruffling the standing water as I made my way to the gate to read "Water Lane." That told me that a decade ago Zodiac had been extraordinarily familiar with Vallejo. He had selected an unmarked path that fit his mania for water-named sites. He knew all the secrets of Water Town.

TUESDAY, JUNE 27, 1978

AND still we received tips portraying "what sort of guy Zodiac might be . . ." "I feel that he might have a bike or motorcycle," a San Francisco art director suggested. ". . . is bordering on genius . . . untapped and untrained perhaps, but mentally superior to the ways in which he has been able to make a living . . . that he is hardly an accepted individual at all, but considered curious, temperamental, and a socially limited personality. His split personality is fed daily by insults and fringe knowledge . . . of which he is a miserable spectator, not participant. He is, in my imagination, 35 to 40 years old. He is deathly afraid of women or impotent. He is, if the man is guilty of the wasteful, senseless crimes you've had to report, in dire need of love. He also needs help. Unfortunately, he also needs to be caught."

Assistant FBI director Thomas Kelleher, Jr., advised Chief Gain on Tuesday that they had been analyzing the unsolved Zodiac ciphers since their acquisition, particularly the 340-symbol cipher. "The Laboratory will continue analysis of these ciphers as time permits. You will be notified immediately of any positive results." Cryptographers searched for hidden ciphers and messages. "Initial letters of words, first, second, third last letters of words; line beginnings, line endings," they reported, "did not spell anything." There were no extraneous markings, no indentations, no invisible writing. As for Zodiac, he was invisible too.

MONDAY, JULY 17, 1978

AFTER controversy over the April Zodiac letter, Inspector Toschi was reassigned to Robbery Detail. An unfounded allegation that he had written the letter caused his transfer. "Police officials emphatically denied reports that Inspector Dave Toschi, who has investigated the Zodiac case for nine years, ever was suspected of forging the latest letter attributed to the murderer," reported the Associated Press.

"Now Mr. Toschi will know what it feels like!" Allen told Pelle through clenched teeth after he read of the transfer. Leigh still remembered his dismissal from the refinery bitterly. As for Toschi, a great weight was lifted from his shoulders.

WEDNESDAY, JULY 19, 1978

AVERY was among the missing too. "Paul Avery and Kate Coleman who wrote the sizzling expose of Black Panther violence in the July 10 *New Times,* have gone 'out of the area' after receiving the predictable threats," wrote Herb Caen. The bogus letter reopened old wounds, driving the populace to seek closure on the long-unsolved case. Zodiac tips quadrupled. "The Zodiac was shot to death by San Francisco police in March of 1976," a reader informed Caen, "about four months after he set the Gartland Hotel fire that killed thirteen people." Next day, an anonymous typewritten letter from Los Angeles also arrived at the *Chronicle*:

"I am the ZODIAC and I am in control of all things," it read. "I am going to tell you a secret. I like friction tape. I like to have it around in case I need to truss someone up in a hurry. . . . I have my real name on a small metallic tape. You see, while you have it in your possession, I want you to know it belongs to me and you think I may have left it accidently. I am athletic. It could be swim fins, or a piece of scuba gear. But maybe you play chess with me. I have several cheap sets in closets all over. I have my name on the bottom of the lid with the scotch tape. . . . My tape is waiting for me all over California. Do you know me? I am the ZODIAC and I am in control."

MONDAY, JULY 30, 1978

ALLEN, while driving with a suspended license on July 30, was involved in an accident in Mendocino involving a car licensed ZEB

577. The State Farm insurance underwriter who insured Allen's car knew him personally. Several days later, a woman approached the agent's desk at the Rohnert Park regional office, stood silently for a moment, then asked about obtaining accident file #91505505086. That was Leigh Allen's file. "Why?" the agent asked. "Because they're watching any activity going on about this man," she said. "Be careful not to get yourself involved with information about him. They'll want to know what you're up to. Two fourteen-year-old girls have disappeared in the Vallejo area, but I seriously doubt Leigh's up to anything since he's being watched so closely."

WEDNESDAY AUGUST 23, 1978

A few days earlier, Toschi had slipped and fractured his ankle on an oily spot in the police garage. He chafed at anything that took him from work. Anxiously, he consulted a bone specialist. "Toschi," the doctor joked, "every cop I know wants to extend his disability time a bit more and here you want to get right back to work." Toschi only smiled and returned to the job with his special jelly-shoe soft walking cast on. By week's end, he was limping along on his bandaged foot as briskly as he normally walked.

Utilizing the content of authentic Zodiac letters, the Behavioral Science Unit (BSU), headquartered at Quantico, Virginia, within the FBI National Academy, attempted to develop a better psychological profile of the killer. "Results will be forwarded to your division for transmittal to requesting agency when completed," BSU notified the San Francisco FBI Headquarters. This Training Division of the Justice Department had been established in the early 1970s. "But how many serial killer cases has the FBI solved—if any?" said one agent publicly.

Just as Avery and Toschi were putting Zodiac behind them, Captain Ken Narlow of the Napa Sheriff's Office was becoming increasingly obsessed. "Many of the leads we were originally blessed with," he told me in our interviews of August 25, 1978 and August 12, 1980, "have become old and deteriorated to the point where they don't have much value anymore. I still think Zodiac is out there someplace. I sometimes look out the window and wonder how close we've come to him at times. We rattled so many cages and kicked so many bushes along the way, we must have been near him at least once."

These days Narlow thought about one particular man. "I've always been high on him," he told me. "We never had enough evidence to bring him in and roll his prints. The more we started leaning on him, the more naturally defensive he got. The first couple of times we talked to him he was very open; then it got to the point where it was 'Either do something or leave me alone!' He came down to complain and saw Avery at the *Chronicle*. The first time we went over to his place by the water, we were there several hours. Very intelligent person, very interesting person. He didn't mind talking about his past." The cops sat down and passed him copies of photos of Zodiac's victims. The suspect realized they were not only gauging his reactions, but trying to get his prints. So he picked up the pictures, looked them over, began to hand them back, then said, "Oh, I'm sorry, I got fingerprints all over them. Let me wipe that off for you." And he wiped them off.

From beneath a light brown, reddish-tinted Buster Brown haircut, the animated face of Oliver Hardy peered out at the cops. The eyes darting behind dark-rimmed glasses were pop-eyed as a neon sign, but highly astute. During the prolonged questioning the suspect, though occasionally falling silent on sensitive subjects, dominated the conversation. "He just talked a mile a minute," Narlow told me. "He had me so confused I couldn't even write a report when it was over. This guy takes over when you're around him and talks." The suspect spoke of his two loves—engineering and show business. He had done bit parts in movies in Southern California and, like Zodiac, could quote Gilbert and Sullivan by rote: "I spent two seasons singing grand opera and I'm a voracious reader. I am one of those singular people blessed with almost total recall. I can remember the exact address and telephone number of the house I lived in in Texas in 1939. I can remember all the old *King Kong* and *Dracula* pictures and where I saw them."

"He has a [Model 15 Teleprinter] Teletype machine in his little basement theater," Narlow told me. "That's a sample of printing from his [Royal portable] typewriter. . . . He did have three months of code school and has got an alias that I think is actually his real name. I don't think we were able to establish this through a State Division of Public Safety check. A friend of mine I went to the FBI Academy with did some background investigation. He was supposedly born in Lubbock County, Texas. . . ."

"Where the term 'fiddle and fart around' is used," I said. "And he can sew. He has designed and sewn costumes in Hollywood." The subject had lost his mother at age five and from then on "was on the outs" with his father, "a wealthy oil man."

"There is also a certificate on file for his alias," said Narlow. "Back in Texas a doctor just filed a birth certificate and that was it, not like today's date and age. So as we speak, there's still some question as to whether or not these two are one and the same individual. A delayed certificate was filed in Probate Court showing that he was born in 1928 *and* 1926.

"A local guy is so convinced that this man is the Zodiac that he started his own book and then went to the television people and hired an attorney. He was going to blow the whistle on this guy Andrews as a responsible.[5] I told him you better be sure—there ain't no way in hell that I can prove it! You're just going to leave yourself wide open for a libel suit. And finally the television people backed off too because I haven't heard any more about it from them. Besides, we weren't able to establish that Andrews had any sort of proficiency with guns." Nervous, temperamental, the suspect once said, "What I have is better than sex!" He told a Sambo's Restaurant waitress he was "going to come back and blow her legs off."

"Avery determined that this man was a student at Riverside City College," continued Narlow, "but I was never able to confirm that. There's his apartment in San Francisco, the one that was supposedly underwater. [On April 20, 1970, Zodiac wrote that the bus bomb he kept stored in his basement had been a dud. "I was swamped out by the rain we had a while back," he explained.] He worked at the San Francisco Airport—as a matter of fact he would have been working there about the time of Cheri Jo Bates's murder in October 1966. Well, I'll tell you, if he is not the Zodiac, I'll take one just like him."

Two months before the first Zodiac murders, the subject had colorfully remarked, "I felt the smartest thing I could do would be to pull an Anton La Vey. He couldn't make it as a bar organist, so he looked at himself in the mirror one day and said, 'I am a character.' Then he hired a press agent and became Satan. I am a

---

[5]This name has been changed.

character too, right off the old screen, but I can't afford a press agent. I am also humble—because I see how absurd this game is!" Zodiac had written, "I am insane, but the game must go on."

My friend, Fay Nelson, spoke with Andrews in San Francisco. "His car at the time of the Blue Rock Springs murders was a white Renault Caravelle, a car similar to the Corvair in appearance." We learned Zodiac was not this man, but there was a link of sorts—he had a vintage movie theater. Police thought so too. They compiled a list of everyone who ever worked there. I discovered the following: *The Most Dangerous Game*, a film that inspired Zodiac, had played there in May 1969. After January 1, 1969, the theater had gone to Friday night showings and Zodiac had begun attacking on Saturdays. Darlene Ferrin, the Blue Rock Springs victim, had written two names in her notebook—"Leigh" and "Vaughn." Robert Vaughn was the name of the silent-movie organist at the Avenue Theatre. Both he and Avery's suspect had worked there since March 1968. Was this a theater Zodiac frequented regularly? I decided to pay another visit there and find out.

FRIDAY, SEPTEMBER 1, 1978

CLASSIC cars parked on the rain-slick street made the silent-movie palace at 2650 San Bruno Avenue hard to miss. The theater's large domed ceiling had once been decorated in a Spanish motif. Now, around a chandelier right out of *The Phantom of the Opera,* an artist had painted all the symbols of the Zodiac.

Narlow's suspect managed the theater, existing in genteel squalor to finance his passion for flickering silents and early talkies. He defrayed costs by exhibiting unique contemporary films. The previous week he had shown a 3-D thriller, *Man in the Dark*. On Fridays "Photoplays and Concerts with full Wurlitzer accompaniment" were featured. Fans flocked to these early Pathe Freres Films, D. W. Griffith one-reel Biographs. They adored stars like Mary Pickford, Lionel Barrymore, Doug Fairbanks, and Buster Keaton.

Waddling like Charlie Chaplin, round-backed, roly-poly, and bandy-legged, the suspect roamed the aisles bellowing "Road to Mandalay." At any second his two-hundred-pound, five-feet-eight-inch frame threatened to burst from a tux three sizes too small. He recited Shakespeare in a booming voice. The surviving victim at Lake Berryessa had characterized Zodiac's voice as "like that of a student . . . with some kind of drawl, but not a Southern drawl." Andrews admitted that though his own voice was moderate in sound, "that is, not high- or low-pitched, I have something of a gift of mimicry—I can imitate W. C. Fields and have done both male and female voices on the radio—and I just enjoy what a pompous ass I am. . . . I may look OK on the outside, but inside . . ."

While Vaughn, the organist, pumped on a mighty Wurlitzer pipe organ (Zodiac had mentioned the "piano-oginast" on his "little list" of potential victims), Narlow and Avery's interesting find became the projectionist. After the double feature they ripped down a handprinted felt-tip-pen poster advertising "The Big Parade with John Gilbert and Renee Adoree." Someone at the theater drew them for the constantly changing bills. I retrieved another from the gutter and took it to Morrill in Sacramento. He studied the handprinting. "With the exception of the three-stroke K it's a good match," he said, beaming. "That's the closest Zodiac lettering I've seen!" Not only might the theater's discarded posters have provided Zodiac with his alphabet of printed letters, but the Academy Standard leader on each strip of film was fittingly a crossed circle.

WEDNESDAY, OCTOBER 17, 1978

I drove over the Golden Gate Bridge toward Santa Rosa in a steady downpour. I stopped along the way and parked amongst the gray warehouses where the theater manager had once kept his warren of connected apartments. The building had been redone and repainted, the old line of mailboxes in the courtyard taken down, and his gadget-cluttered rooms (movie equipment, theater seats, rows of 35-mm monochrome film-processing machines) emptied. Time was marching on and Zodiac was no closer to being caught than a decade ago.

Leigh was nowhere around his trailer when I got there. Eighteen days earlier he had ceased installing home security devices and quit his job as a senior-citizen aide in Vallejo. "Could Narlow and Avery's suspect and Leigh Allen be working together?" a policeman suggested to me. "Check out the possibility, however remote, that there is a connection between the two." The thought of some sort of Zodiac confederate was never far from my mind. I had noticed the odd spacing in the Zodiac letters: "He plung ed him self . . . wand ering." It reminded me not only of sign painters who did one letter at a time, but someone taking dictation, writing each syllable as they came, stringing them together like a cars on a train and with no regard to sense.

THURSDAY, OCTOBER 18, 1978

BILL Armstrong retired from the SFPD. "I could feel the fire had gone away," Toschi said of his partner. "I remember, when he left Homicide in late '75, he told me, 'Toschi, I've stood over my last body.' However, the fire was still burning inside me." The same day Allen begrudgingly began seeing a mental health professional.

As a condition of his release from Atascadero, Leigh had been required to see Dr. Thomas Rykoff, a Santa Rosa psychiatrist.[6] Prior to their first meeting, Leigh, as he had in prison, probably combed the library. In the 1960s he asked Cheney, "Are there books on how to disguise your handprinting and change your appearance?" Cheney said, "I'm sure they exist." It made sense he would now bone up on proper responses to psychiatric tests. Under present law, a fragmented man such as Zodiac could not be considered legally insane. Dividing "sane" from "insane" becomes difficult with "murderers who seem rational, coherent, and controlled," wrote Dr. Joseph Satten, "and yet whose homicidal acts have a bizarre, apparently senseless quality."

Unlike schizophrenics, a sexual sadist such as Zodiac "does not exhibit obvious aberrations, but takes considerable pains to appear normal and avoid capture. Of all murderers, he is most likely to repeat his crime." After the first killing, these intelligent killers become amazingly proficient at concealing themselves. They take great pains to appear normal, but often perversely throw suspicion upon themselves. The cat-and-mouse game with the police eventually becomes the principal motive for the

---

[6]This name has been changed.

crimes. Behind a smiling, secretive facade, he feels vastly inferior, hostile, anxious, and persecuted. Yet that perverse urge to call attention to himself as Zodiac is an itch almost impossible not to scratch. Or was Leigh's secret that he only *thought* he was Zodiac?

No one knows what creates a compulsive killer—a missing sex chromosome?—an event during the first six months of life? Whatever the cause, the condition is incurable. Cruel, rejecting parents and peers create pressures expressed in childhood by bed-wetting, shoplifting, and animal torture. With the awakening of puberty, the anger manifests itself in ever-increasing and cleverly concealed acts of sadism. Sheriff Striepeke's privately commissioned psychological profile stated Zodiac was a white, unmarried man under thirty-five years old "who tortured animals, had a passive father and dominant mother, and may have spent time in a mental institution." Meanwhile, Leigh Allen continued to daydream in his trailer and basement. Dwelling in an escapist world of science fiction and the occult, arrogantly intolerant of people, he tended to set his own rules. "I've been able to personally study several of these [serial killers] very closely," Dr. Lunde told me. "Bianchi's responses on psychological tests are almost verbatim like Kemper's. The whole sort of thing of seeing animals torn apart and blood and animal hearts."

A psychologist working under conditions of Allen's parole evaluated Rykoff's tests and findings. When he gave the suspect a projective test, a Rorschach (ink blot) test, Rykoff was warned to look for answers that contained the letter *z*. "The odds of more than one answer beginning with *z* are very remote," the analyst told detectives before the Rorschach test. "I don't expect any." The first two mirror images Leigh was shown reminded him of "a zygomatic arch." The analyst was shaken by this. He went on. "What do you see in this?" At the end of the tests, he found that Allen had given five *z* responses, far outside the norm. Cabdriver Paul Stine had been wounded in the zygomatic arch by Zodiac.

A doctor's report on Leigh had said, "He's potentially violent, he is dangerous," and "he is capable of killing." The same analyst thought Allen had "five separate personalities." Split personalities would explain how he passed a lie-detector test; why his handprinting did not match Zodiac's. The psychiatrists' conclu-

sions were mounting: Leigh "is extremely dangerous and is a sociopath . . . is highly intelligent and incapable of functioning
with women in a normal way . . . has a potential for danger." In
their private sessions, Dr. Rykoff discovered the violent side of
his new patient's nature. Any kind of accusation set him off. The
subject of his mother or prison enraged him. Leigh became defensive, shaking with anger until he regained control, then became sarcastic. His remarks, icy, though witty, were packed with
puns and double meanings. Immature, self-centered, with a
strong ego, he had a taunting way of speaking, but was capable of
great personal charm. When Allen spoke of Zodiac, he felt persecuted. Worst of all, he cried—long heartrending moans. Between
sobs, Dr. Rykoff felt Allen was "repressing very deep hatred."
But on another level Leigh aced every perception test from
blocks to puzzles. "This guy can look at something, figure it out
in a matter of minutes, and do it with the least amount of energy
and effort," one expert had said. "And he laughed at other people
for stumbling through the same task." Allen took his psychiatric
tests under duress and always in the same manner: "He would not
smile or show emotion and would speak in a low, measured monotone." Allen's parole officer, Bruce Pelle, came to know this
menacing, focused monotone well.

Rykoff's sessions with Allen were conducted as a favor to
Lieutenant Jim Husted of the Vallejo P.D. and Pelle. Rykoff was
in the middle of studying Leigh when a new patient was signed
on—a young woman. She desired to be hypnotized as part of a
training program for a social rehabilitation group she was organ-
izing in Santa Rosa. Rykoff welcomed her, unaware that she was
Leigh Allen's sister-in-law, Karen. Whether or not the police suggested Karen see the same therapist as her brother-in-law is open
to speculation. But Husted, head of the Intelligence Unit, was
wily. Through his manipulation or not, somehow Karen ended up
with Rykoff. During their sessions she remarked about a chemist
brother-in-law and his dark side. Rykoff saw the man constantly
preyed on her mind. As Karen expounded more of her impressions and suspicions, Rykoff began to realize the character she
was sketching seemed familiar.

"He spoke of man as true game," she said. "Once he and his
brother got in an argument over dinner. He leaped on him and began choking him."

"What's this?" thought Rykoff. "That sounds just like Arthur Leigh Allen. The potential for danger is just the same."

THURSDAY, NOVEMBER 15, 1978.

DR. Rykoff had Karen back in. He placed her under a deep hypnosis conducted by Husted and Lieutenant Larry Haynes of the Concord P.D. Haynes, trained by the LAPD's Law Enforcement Hypnotic Institute, had hypnotized one of victim Darlene Ferrin's baby-sitters back on June 16, 1977. "Does it matter how much time has passed since the incident?" asked Rykoff.

"No," replied Husted, who gently uncovered a number of large crystals he kept swathed in soft black fabric. Each glittering gem hung from a slender chain. Haynes induced a hypnotic trance by swinging or spinning a crystal. This time, when Karen recalled the choking incident over dinner, she saw something new.

"There was a second figure," she said.

"A second figure?" said Husted. The big blond officer leaned forward. Rykoff put down his pen.

"He was on top of Ron as well," she said. "I could see a second ghostly figure of Leigh on top of my husband, another identity. It was as if he were a second Leigh Allen. When Leigh stood up, he seemed to change into yet another personality, like Jekyll and Hyde." A source told me, "Leigh was a twin whose brother died at birth." Then Karen recalled the paper she had seen in Leigh's hand in November of 1969. This was the note she had mentioned to Toschi and Armstrong years before. Husted and Haynes were certain she was deeply under and not fabricating the vision. Hypnotists have to be careful not to give subtle, unwitting suggestions to a person under hypnosis and create what they want to find. "Sometimes it's difficult to distinguish what is in a person's mind from what you are putting there," said Haynes.

"It was covered with strange lines of symbols," she said. " 'What's that?' I asked him. 'This is the work of an insane person,' he replied. 'I'll show it to you later.' He never did, and replaced it in a gray metal box he kept in his room."

Haynes, Rykoff, and Husted were desperate to see what had been on that paper. But how? It had been destroyed long ago.

They decided to see if Karen could redraw these arcane symbols under hypnosis. In automatic writing, she slowly drew four lines of symbols. Automatic writing was normally sprawling and un-controlled, but Karen's was straight, gridlike—like Zodiac's codes. The symbols closely resembled the third line of the Zo-diac 340-character cipher mailed to the *Chronicle* on November 8, 1969. As the mesmeric session progressed, she spoke more and more about Leigh. Karen began to shake and tremble. Her knuckles whitened. Husted had Haynes bring her out of the trance. Afterward, in his office, he showed me the writing. Though I wasn't allowed to photocopy possible evidence, I was allowed to copy it down as exactly as I could. Reproduced for the first time here are the symbols Karen wrote:

Hypnosis was popular at this time, but by the 1980s state law enforcement agencies would rarely use it as an investigative tool. In 1982 the Supreme Court would curtail the scope of testimony from witnesses who had been hypnotized, deeming such ac-counts inherently unreliable. Later, California law would be shaped to the court's decision—hypnosis could be used only to clarify information given before a person was hypnotized. Testi-mony obtained under hypnosis could only be used in court after a judge has ruled that the evidence could not be acquired by any other means.

"Potential for danger," Rykoff had thought. Increasingly, the doctor became more apprehensive of his patient and his "dark sense of humor." At the beginning of the month, he had asked his brother, a San Francisco policeman, to look into the matter. The officer asked Toschi and the reply was anything but reassuring. "I remember Dr. Rykoff's brother coming up to me," said Toschi, "a really sweetheart of a guy, really straight up front. No games. He wanted some information for his brother and so I told him, 'We felt strongly then [August 1971] and now that Allen was our best suspect. We cut him loose in 1972 because we weren't able to find any physical evidence connecting him to the crimes. We did everything we could with the guy. Personally, my gut feeling is that he is the man. Tell Dr. Rykoff that when he talks to Leigh, do it in a place that he can get out of in a hurry . . . and above all—don't make him angry." The officer reported back to his brother. "I've found out he's the prime suspect, in the Zodiac case," he said. Rykoff blockprinted the word "sociopath" by Allen's name in their next to last session. The term meant he was "selfish, impulsive, and unable to learn from experience. He felt he was above moral codes and laws and was the most likely type of murderer to repeat his crimes."

More unsettling, Leigh had caught me watching him more than once. Later, on March 12, 1980, I was waiting in a darkened car on Tennessee Street as he drove by. He slowed alongside. I turned and looked directly into his eyes.

FRIDAY, NOVEMBER 17, 1978

LEIGH, as a member of the Pacific Multi-hull Racing Association, sailed only one of the boats his mother had bought him. He stored the second, an adapted boat that "ran on unknown fuel," elsewhere.[7] His tan station wagon, #XAM 469, sat by the curb unused. On December 31, 1975, he had registered a special construction trailer to be "used as a camper." Where he kept it no one knew. Rumor had it, it was stored in a friend's woods. One of Allen's 1971 checks, made out to Talltree Trailer Storage, suggested he was renting spaces for trailers somewhere else.

"You know, [Phil] Tucker was questioned by our department," said George Bawart, "He was always a pretty straight shooter. When he left GVRD, I wasn't too much younger than he was. I

---

[7]#CF 9127 FD License, Sticker # H107782.

knew him. I knew his family. If I were to say, just to guess, I wouldn't think he had anything to do with Zodiac." When Allen worked at GVRD, next to the police department, he could have had access to reports, police techniques, and day-to-day gossip. Once a police groupie, always a police groupie.

14

SUSPECTS

THOUGH juggling caseloads of robberies, Inspector Toschi still felt an allegiance to the Zodiac case. Between November 20 and November 24, he received a typical number of phone tips on his former case. "The first call was from an unemployed freelance writer who seemed in too much a hurry to get to meet me," Toschi said. "I thought about not going on my own time to meet him, but I called the guy back and decided he was sincere about giving me information. He was an ex-NYPD man himself, and he said he could see how the Zodiac case after ten years had really gotten to be an ego thing when you're so involved as I was.

" 'If anyone in the country deserves to make the arrest on Zodiac,' he said, 'it's got to be Dave Toschi.' I thanked him, but since I was officially off the case, referred him to Jack Jordan. Next, a lady named Katrina called. She had gotten short shrift at SFPD. To set her mind at ease, she sought me out. She had a suspect in mind, an ex-boyfriend who had accidentally died in 1973. Fortunately, I didn't have to refer to the files. I had the information in my head and answered her queries in about three minutes. Finally, at week's end, a D.A.'s investigator stopped me in the elevator. 'I've got some info on an old case of yours,' he whispered. 'I want to talk only to you on it.' I listened and committed the tip to memory. So, I can never get away from the Zodiac case and I do not think I ever will. It's become part of my life—on and off duty."

On the morning of November 24, up at Lake Berryessa, Cindy, a waitress working at Moskowite Corners General Store, watched a strange man enter. He sat down in the rear and stared at her so long he made her nervous. Finally, she approached him. "Can I get you anything?" she asked. "Do you know you're a very good-looking woman," he replied. She went back to the counter. After a time he left. Only then did she recall that nine years earlier, on the terrible day two PUC students were attacked, a similar-looking man had been drinking a Coke at the same table.

Police originally attributed the 1971 murder of Lynda Kanes, another PUC coed, to Zodiac's hand. "I have always been haunted by this maniac Zodiac," a PUC graduate told me, "because I was attending PUC in Angwin during the time Bryan Hartnell and Cecelia Shepard were stabbed. This was a very traumatic thing to happen to anyone . . . but especially when it took place so close to home. I attended her funeral at the PUC sanctuary, which had a massive turnout, and wondered if the killer could be there secretly delighting in the pain of all who were grieving for Cecelia. The police [and FBI] thought so too and took extensive photos of the crowd at Cecelia's funeral.

"I also remember very well the Lynda Kanes incident. I remember the day her car was found—radio still on—but no Lynda. I remember the light snowfall the next morning, the barricades, the horseback posses, the bloodhounds, and police asking for volunteers from PUC and others in the vicinity to help search the rugged area by foot. It sent chills through my soul as I remembered the countless times I have traveled windy, lonely Old Howell Mountain Road . . . not to mention the countless times I have driven up to Lake Berryessa alone and spent the day wrapped up in a book while baking in the hot sun. At the time most of the locals believed the killer was 'Willy the Woodcutter' who lived at the base of Old Howell Mountain Road where it meets Silverado Trail. Willy got his name because he could be seen most of the time at his house chopping firewood. Lynda used to stop and chat with him on her way back to campus from town via Old Howell Mountain Road." Zodiac, much to our relief, had not been involved. In 1971, in Napa Superior Court, Walter "Willie the Woodcutter" Williams was convicted of Kanes's murder. Her bloodstained clothing had been found in his home.

THURSDAY, DECEMBER 7, 1978

ALLEN had been driving on a suspended license. In the morning his new driver's permit (#BO 67-2352) became effective just as Homicide Inspector James Deasy received the keys to that tough little number called Zodiac. Deasy, formally of the SFPD Gang Task Force, hunkered down to take on the job of fielding Zodiac tips. Gathering leads on an unsolvable case was character-building, but futile. An informant rang Deasy from Canada, claiming that a now-deceased Albion, California, public safety officer, retired Fire Chief Ralph Perry, had been Zodiac. He alleged Perry had owned a Zodiac-style hood. The tip became more intriguing when Deasy attempted to check Perry's prints.

MONDAY, DECEMBER 18, 1978

"THE funny thing about it is," Deasy said, "we tried to check this guy's fingerprints through his agency's print files and found out that they had no prints on record for him. Neither did the State Department of Justice. Neither did the FBI. We came up totally blank on this guy's prints. Spooky." Deasy and Captain Narlow knew they had to convince a D.A. to issue a court order to exhume Perry's body and take prints. He wondered how long fingertip ridges survived underground. "Can you successfully lift prints from a corpse?" Deasy inquired of their print man.

Without enough information to obtain a search warrant, they conducted two explorations of the home with Perry's widow's permission. During the first exploration, they turned up an illegal silencer for a .22-caliber pistol. "The widow said that her husband, right out of the blue, once asked her an odd question," said Deasy. " 'Aren't you afraid, going to bed every night with the Zodiac?' " Deasy paused to sigh, then added, "We thought we were getting pretty close at that point. Sometimes you get a feeling in the pit of your stomach and you say to yourself, 'You just can't eliminate a suspect who looks good in every other respect just because he's too old.' I told her on our second trip that we had only a few more questions that we wanted to check up on, just to satisfy our minds. She wasn't too happy about it, but she let us do it. I told her that if we didn't find what we were looking for, we wouldn't be back, and we haven't. It just wasn't there." In Vallejo, Leigh Allen celebrated his second birthday since leaving prison.

WEDNESDAY, JUNE 13, 1979

"**PERSONNEL** Order: Captain's Order #21 Effective 0800 hrs., Inspector David Toschi, #1807, presently assigned to Pawnshop Section, Property Crimes Division, is assigned to the Robbery Section. Captain Charles A. Schuler, Commanding Officer, Personal Crimes Division."

15
ARTHUR LEIGH ALLEN

THOUGH Leigh accumulated no more boats, his list of trailers continued to grow. The universal house trailer Toschi and Armstrong had searched was only one of many. Another special-construction camper, #GS8803, was kept in an unknown location. While Leigh lived in his trailers, sailed, and flew his plane, I spoke again with his P.O.

"Basically, Arthur is that interesting in that he has access not only to the vehicles he owns, but to those of his friends. Almost any vehicle he wants. His mother has a Mercedes. He's got a white '62 VW Karmann Ghia now—just like Hartnell's. I wonder if owning a car exactly like the Lake Berryessa victim's is a subconscious call for attention." Leigh had registered the car's license, #DXW 186, only eight days ago. An identical auto had attracted Zodiac at the virtually deserted lake, signifying to him that potential victims were picnicking on a narrow peninsula.

During the summer, Leigh's childhood friend Harold Huffman had driven his VW Dasher by Vallejo to introduce his eight-year-old son, Rob, to Allen. Harold had married Leigh's friend, Kay. "I had seen Harold play football and swim," Kay told me. "I knew who he was, but I didn't know him. At the end of my first year at junior college, a mutual friend introduced us. He had come back to see the coaches. He offered me a lift home and I took it. I offered him coffee and he accepted. I didn't know how to make coffee and he didn't drink coffee. He drank it anyway. That was the beginning of the love story."

"Leigh was like a grandpa figure," Rob recalled, "a tall, heavy-set, balding man who lived in the basement of an old house." Rob played with his chipmunks while Leigh loaded wire traps into the trunk of their car. Leigh left the cages at various rest stops on their way to Lake County. "I hope I don't get caught," he re-marked slyly, "I no longer have a valid trapper's license." Rob took a quick liking to him. "He was quite funny," he recalled. "Leigh told great stories at night when the three of us stared at the stars and treetops cocooned in our sleeping bags. By day, he would entertain me . . . by doing somersaults off an old diving board into the shimmering melted snow below which sprayed in every direction upon his impact. He limped on earth, but was an acrobat in the air and water. Like a fish, he used to sneak up on me underwater in the kiddie section of the lake and grab my sub-merged legs—he could hold his breath for an eternity, so I never knew where he was."

The trio picked up the still-empty cages as they hurtled north to Blue Lake. At the cheap motel where they stayed, Leigh showed off by diving into the motel pool and swimming the perimeter of the pool underwater for nearly two minutes. Toward the end of their stay Leigh slammed the car door on Rob's toe. The boy be-gan to weep. "You're tough and brave," Leigh told him. "Most boys your age would have cried. You aren't a sissy." After that they were real friends. Rob visited him at Ace Hardware and ate with him and his father at the corner IHOP.

THURSDAY, OCTOBER 11, 1979

A major coin shop robbery had occurred on Irving Street and Toschi had been searching for witnesses. He realized it was the tenth anniversary of his most daunting case. At 6:26 P.M., instead of going home, he stopped to relive old memories on the corner of Washington and Cherry. He heard the evening news blaring from a nearby home as file footage of the Stine murder unrolled. As he drove away, Toschi could not escape the sense that he had not been alone on that dark corner among the solemn mansions.

WEDNESDAY, OCTOBER 31, 1979

ON Halloween, Leigh registered *another* special-construction trailer, #ME86336. Why so many in so many places and what did he keep in them? Certainly, he feared a second search, and knew such an inquisition must come eventually. However, he feared something more than any intensive inspection of his dreary basement. Any parole violation might remand him to Atascadero, which he dreaded above all. Recently, I heard, on old Lake Herman Road where the Northern California Zodiac had begun back in 1968, a boy was found shot between the eyes and a girl strangled.

MONDAY, JANUARY 28, 1980

LEIGH, already wrestling with weight and blood pressure problems, now battled a growing alcohol and vision problem. Haltingly, he strolled the short distance from his Fresno Street home to 1131 Tennessee Street—his new job at Ace Hardware. He later claimed March 19 as his first day, but actually began January 28. Steve Harshman was his new boss; Dean Drexler his supervisor. Drexler immediately put Leigh in charge of selling electrical supplies. Eventually, Harshman would make Allen a buyer for the garden and tool department. Highly educated, the former convict knew he was worth more than the $5.35 an hour they were paying him. Quite quickly, he became dissatisfied in another area. Working every day but Sunday gave him no time for other things.

A letter delivered to the *Chronicle* that morning read: "This is the Zodiac speaking, I have moved to higher country for my next victem good luck Zodiac." The return address on the envelope was "guess?" But the postage was not excessive and the ink red, not blue—another copycat. In Sacramento, I visited Sherwood Morrill, CI&I's handwriting expert. Morrill had been born and bred to the investigative bureau. His father, Berkeley Police Sergeant Clarence S. Morrill, opened CI&I in 1918. "My father was a little fellow," Morrill said. "He was five feet eight inches, weighed about 140 pounds dripping wet. When they lobbied the bill to open the state bureau, they set it up with a board of managers. An independent agency—they had a sheriff, a chief of police, and a district attorney who were appointed by the governor for staggered terms. In theory, no one person or board could get control of the office. My dad wasn't going to take the civil service exam but his boss, Chief August Vollmer, one of the most progressive officers at the time, insisted. Dad came up here, opened the agency (January 1, 1918). He died in 1940 and he'd been at CI&I all that time."

It was Chief Vollmer who encouraged San Francisco writer Dashiell Hammett to speculate whether or not it was possible to transfer fingerprints from one place to the other. Hammett decided prints could be forged successfully by laminating a set of prints onto fingertips, as he had a blackmailer do in his story "Slippery Fingers." Zodiac had written that he used glue on his fingertips. Was this the secret of the unmatchable prints on Stine's cab, the phony clues Zodiac claimed he left behind for police to find?

Morrill had wanted to be a ballplayer, but instead learned handwriting analysis under Charles H. Stone, the state's first documents expert. "He'd been chief of police of Bakersfield before that," Morrill said. "My dad hired him to be assistant chief, but put him in charge of Questioned Documents. He took me aside when I graduated from high school and told me, 'There are no documents schools. California will grow and with growth comes litigation and with litigation comes the need for documents examiners.' I studied psychology and science, and after working for seven years took to the courtroom. In 1933, I went to work for Questioned Documents and they put me under Stone."

"Because Zodiac wrote in manuscript instead of cursive," Morrill said, "that presents some idea of his actual age." Teaching that style of writing had been confined to a few selected schools in the U.S. (such as Pleasant Valley Grammar School in Camarillo, California). In 1969, those students would have just turned thirty-five. Sherwood was studying a vicious piece of hoax mail addressed to Herb Caen. A huge staring eye, deliberate misspellings—"We have suche fun on the way here. We kill manie hitchhikers so slow to danse"—and comments about hot irons echoed earlier Zodiac letters. "This is the second similar note we've received," science reporter Dave Perlman had written in a *Chronicle* memo. "It seems unusually ugly so I thought maybe the FBI folk would want to be aware of it."

"What I look for when making an analysis varies," Morrill explained. "If a person has a peculiar style of writing, maybe one or two characteristics will tip you off. I just did one yesterday. There were several similarities, but there were several big discrepancies, which rules it out. Now this is the same way you make an identification in fingerprints. If you have enough points, a partial print often contains twelve characteristic points and no significant difference, you have an identification. The average print has about fifty ridge characteristics. The same thing happens if you find enough individ-

ual handwriting characteristics in a person's handwriting and no significant difference, you have an identification. But any one significant difference would throw it out. You'd have to discard it. You may
feel that it's still the same guy, but he made a goof. Now a significant
difference is one that can't be reasonably explained."

Zodiac might have memorized a series of just such "goofs"
and used them consistently in his letters. The significant difference from his true writing might be explained if he had trained
himself to make these goofs.

"What's so unusual about the *k* Zodiac makes?" I asked.

"That was one of the things at first we thought was consistent,"
said Morrill, "but Zodiac got away from it. He made it in three
parts, but since then he's made them like you or I might make
them." If that *k* had been window dressing, then it was another indication that Zodiac's writing—that checkmarklike *r*, that cursive
d always on the verge of falling over, and that three-stroke *k*—
could be a purposeful fabrication. At times I suspected Zodiac had
a confederate who wrote the actual letters.

A handwriting expert analyzed Zodiac's writing:

> "See those looped 'd's? That means he's arrogant and proud
> and also doesn't feel secure about himself. Misspelling words
> like 'nose' is an effort at disguise, an effort to make the letter
> seem anonymous . . . when you combine his very rushed writ-
> ing, indistinct letters, variability in the spacing, variability in
> the letter size, that would be an indication of a manic-
> depressive. In addition to that the writing slants downward at
> the end. Even if he starts up by the end of the line most of the
> letters have fallen down, which be indicative of a depressed
> state. . . . Zodiac tends to dot his 'i's very close to the stem . . .
> where the writing is beginning to fall over the 'i' dots are still
> fairly carefully dotted. . . . He is also a very lonely person and
> is very sensitive to criticism which means he might get upset
> if you called him crazy instead of clever."

TUESDAY, JANUARY 29, 1980

"**WHAT** is it about San Francisco?" lamented Herb Caen. "What is
it that seems to attract the dreamers and deviants, kooks and cra-
zies. San Francisco seems to be the last sanctuary for the rootless

in its tolerance for every form of lifestyle." The area had been inflicted with a blight of serial killers, kidnappings, urban guerrillas, religious cults, and political assassinations. Charlie Manson recruited his family from Haight-Ashbury's drug culture and flower children. The region attracted Juan Corona (murderer of twenty-five transient laborers), John Linley Frazier (who killed five to halt pollution), and Herbert Mullin (who slew thirteen in a deadly four-month orgy to prevent a state-destroying earthquake). In the Bay Area the SLA kidnapped Patricia Hearst and used cyanide bullets to slay Oakland School Superintendent Marcus Foster. The New World Liberation Front, the Zebra Killers, Jim Jones's People's Temple, Dan White, and Zodiac all called the environs home.

AVERY AND TOSCHI tried to forget Zodiac. So did I, especially at the beginning of a new decade. We knew a little more now. In the 1970s serial killers were still a relatively new phenomenon. In the 1980s efforts to understand and profile violent repeat offenders began in earnest. On July 11, 1984, the Justice Department would propose a special unit at Quantico, Virginia, to be called the Violent Criminal Apprehension Program—VICAP. FBI agents—psychologists, psychiatrists, and regular investigators—pooled their resources, their jobs to make psychological portraits of serial rapists, child molesters, arsonists, and killers. Interviews with mass murderers and sexual deviants might explain what motivated them to commit their atrocities. Ultimately VICAP, to uncover uncaught repeat murderers like Zodiac, developed verbal and mental pictures of serial killers. First, they listed traits they held in common. Zodiac, a combination of hedonistic and control-oriented types, was technically an "organized nonsocial offender."

"Organized killers are called nonsocial because they elect to be socially isolated," wrote expert Greg Fallis. "Although they are often glib and charming they may feel nobody is quite good enough for them. They . . . are often quite clever. More self-assured than the disorganized asocial offender, these killers are willing to travel far to find their victims."

MONDAY, MARCH 3, 1980

"**ALLEN** has a friend I haven't told you about before," Lieutenant Husted of the VPD explained, "and he seems to have confided in him that he is the Zodiac killer and told him details of some of the murders. I'd like to put that friend, Jim, under hypnosis. This is the same man Allen met at the Sonoma Auto Parts Store and wrote from Atascadero. Remember? Leigh was hoping that Zodiac would kill again and clear him. While Leigh and Jim were drinking one evening, Allen allegedly confessed he was Zodiac. He offered to testify, but got cold feet. He's afraid of Allen and his wife has begged him not to speak with us. Eventually, Allen did as much as fess up to a second man at the store."

But neither witness was ever hypnotized, and like so many leads, this one was pursued no further. Leigh continued hunting in the hills—carving out the hearts and livers of captured squirrels and storing them in his freezer. Could the "death machine" in Zodiac's basement have been a reference to a freezer compartment that held the bodies of dissected chipmunks? This dismembering of birds, squirrels, and mice by the ambidextrous chemist fit the pattern of serial killers who tortured and killed animals. He had given it a new twist—masking his dissections with an assortment of scientific permits.

MONDAY, APRIL 21, 1980

LEIGH'S list of vehicles grew. He registered a 1965 Buick sedan, a blue Skylark, #MLZ 057. And he still had the Karmann Ghia, gray Corvair, three special-construction trailer campers, and two sailboats. He had reportedly owned a brown Corvair in 1965 similar to the car Zodiac used during the Fourth of July murder. However, though Leigh once owned a 1957 Ford, he may only have been glimpsed in Phil Tucker's 1958 Ford sedan, which Tucker had given him permission to drive. I often circled by the Fresno Street home and saw his tan station wagon parked in front, unused. Most of the time Leigh worked within walking distance at Ace Hardware, though I knew he hated walking because of his limp and fallen arches.

16

ARTHUR LEIGH ALLEN

IN front of Ace Hardware, five wheelbarrows were lined up beneath a poster of a smiling Suzanne Somers. She was dressed incongruously in a Santa outfit. Inside, Leigh was no longer secluded in the rear. He manned the front register, conversing with customers in a loud voice. The name "LEE" was sewn neatly over the left breast pocket of his orange work coat. His boss, Steve Harshman, initially ordered the correct spelling ("LEIGH"), but the shorter version was cheaper. I needed more samples of Allen's handwriting, but it was becoming difficult to trick him into printing anything. Allen was piling boxes of fire extinguishers as a friend of mine approached.

"Could you help me find these items?" Fay asked. He stacked three more boxes without looking up. "If I help you, will you help me?" he said deliberately. He picked up a small basket, filled it with her supplies, and tossed her list on top. "Couldn't you write an itemized receipt for me?" she said. "One of those people at the front registers will help you," he replied. "I'm not authorized to do that. Have a nice day."

I spoke again to Allen's parole officer. A sensitive young man, Pelle had been disturbed by various mental evaluations of his parolee. Allen's tests matched the profile a Napa State psychiatrist, Dr. Leonti Thompson, had drawn up. "[Zodiac's particular type of psychosis] creates a deepening helplessness," Thompson commented, "from which the victim occasionally rouses himself by a terrific output of psychological energy . . . and if to that private world of the schizophrenic is added the paranoid's delusion of persecution or grandeur, then sometimes that distorted world becomes a place where murder is born."

"He is an extremely dangerous person," Leigh's analysis read. "He is sociopathic and possesses an incredibly high I.Q. . . . Subject is repressing very deep hatred and is incapable of functioning with women in a normal way." He is "a loner, inept at establishing any sexual relationships beyond those of children."

"I talked with Arthur about his mother," Allen's parole officer told me, "and that's one of the major things in his therapy and the way he relates to life. I approach this from the aspect of a parole officer and contrary to the image of me, I'm pretty much into how people are and what changes motivate them. Basically, Arthur is that interesting."

"Do you think he hates his mother?" I asked, recalling Leigh's comments at Atascadero.

"Oh, yeah. He absolutely hates her," said Pelle with feeling. "She's in her sixties and would say to Leigh about the father, 'He never takes care of his familial responsibilities. All men are all assholes. . . . You're just like all other men. You're this, you're the other.' Years of that completely demolished Leigh's ability to have regular heterosexual relations with an adult female. One of the things he does frequently is when his mother says, 'Why are you the way you are?' he says, 'The reason I'm all fucked up is because of you. You made me the way I am!' And she feels really guilty and the guilt comes out and she refuses to do anything to stop whatever behavior he's involved in, at least whatever behavior that she knows about."

The NYPD's top psychologist, Harvey Schlossberg, profiled Son of Sam and reached findings that applied to Zodiac. "The inspiration for all his hate and revenge is much more likely to be a woman—a mother, sister, or girlfriend who rejected him. Historically such maniacs do disappear. Jack the Ripper was never captured, nor was the more recent San Francisco Zodiac killer." Zodiac would have a seductive, dominant mother who gives affection and rejection erratically. Serial murderer Ed Kemper, a six-foot nine-inch-tall, 280-pound murderer of women, also fantasized about killing his mother. Seven female victims in Santa Cruz were surrogates. He saved her for last. Her scolding tongue no longer would disapprove of him.

Sexual sadists, because of their confused sexual identity, possess a great underlying hatred of women. Zodiac's emotions were as tangled as a strand of DNA—violence to him was love; love was violence. He was unquenchable in his blood lust, and the only successful relationship Zodiac could ever have with a woman was murder.

"The sister-in-law knew the psychiatrist," continued Pelle, "knew that she was revealing things the family wanted to keep secret, but as a good citizen felt obligated to come forward. Allen had always considered her an interloper." Pelle, to keep from fixating on Allen, considered other Zodiac suspects. "There was this girl, Julie," he told me, "who had run away from her home in Oregon and fallen in with a Hell's Angels gang member. One day she tells me that there won't be any more Zodiac killings or letters. 'There was this guy who hung around with us. He wasn't a member of the Angels, just a hanger-on,' she said. 'This guy says he's the Zodiac and I believe him. I know he's the Zodiac, but he O.D.'d last year on heroin—right here in Vallejo.' The girl had divorced (her husband was from Vallejo), and gone back to live in Oregon with her child. She said only that the guy wore glasses and plaid shirts. She didn't remember his name." The Hell's Angels connection rang a bell. Initially, Sergeant Lynch suspected two Hell's Angels had committed the Lake Herman Road murders. On three different occasions, he and his partner had thrown them in jail for gas station robberies. "They shot people," Lynch said matter-of-factly, "but are in prison now."

The next evening, Sunday, I parked across from Ace Hardware. Framed in the light of the window, Allen stood out as an orange blotch in the twilight. I watched as he stocked a peg board with electrical cords. Was this Zodiac, under glass and in plain sight for all to see? When Leigh quit the store at 6:15, he was wearing a dark navy windbreaker such as Zodiac wore during the Stine murder. I asked Leigh's boss, Steve Harshman, for samples of Leigh's printing. He angrily refused, but I left behind my business card with my new unlisted phone number where Allen could see it. From that point on, I received hang-up calls at midnight every Saturday night. They were unsettling, even frightening, but I did not change the number. I did not want to lose even that tenuous contact with the suspect.

FRIDAY, AUGUST 8, 1980

"**I** agree the killer is keeping his own file and mementos geographically quite a distance from where he lives and works," one reader suggested. "Zodiac didn't stop killing during some years. Perhaps he changed employment and that caused him to kill elsewhere occasionally. In the workplace he is mild, discounted and comes across as slightly distracted. I bet his payoff is not in murdering specifically, as much as in his knowledge that he is finally powerful enough to have some momentous impact on others' lives. He can confound the police and the best minds in his area, therefore he is smarter than anybody. He can kill, therefore he exists."

Allen, dissatisfied with his job at Ace, applied for an adult-education class after work. The class schedule still gave him Friday evenings off—the time Zodiac had done some of his killings. But as months passed, he became more disenchanted.

FRIDAY, NOVEMBER 14, 1980

"**I** don't see any possibility of advancement," Leigh explained to Steve Harshman. "I work every weekend and only get one day off a week." Thus, Allen resigned his job at Ace Hardware, never realizing what a staunch defender he had in Harshman.

SATURDAY, NOVEMBER 15, 1980

LEIGH'S new job as a warehouse supervisor in Benicia at Spectro Chrome Graphics paid $5 an hour, less money than he had been making, and the job was farther away. Under his new boss, Harriet Hurba, he coordinated supply, receipt, delivery, and distribution in and out of the plant. Leigh wrote Pelle about the new job. The letter carried too much postage and the handprinting on the envelope slanted downward like Zodiac's. "It was almost as if he wanted me to think he was guilty of being Zodiac," said Pelle. "All I could get out of this guy was a typed letter. And very neat. By the way, our chemist's into foot-powered planes now." Pelle laughed. "He's actually trying to build one that flies, even with his weight and blood pressure problems. But Leigh's highly suggestible. His interest in man-powered flight probably came from a namesake, Bryan Allen. Last year he began telling friends he was considering building a foot-powered plane." On June 12, 1979, Bryan Allen, a Visalia resident, successfully crossed the English Channel in a bicyclelike aircraft, the "Gossamer Albatross."

"And of course," continued Pelle, "when that young girl was abducted last year we thought of Allen right away. Not only was he driving a white van like the one seen, but he told me he was in that area and had engine trouble. It really had me going for a while, but the police found the guy who did it.

"Leigh's incredibly strong. When he worked at the [Sonoma] auto parts store he was always getting hassled by the guys there and he dared a guy to come at him. Allen picked up the guy and hurled him across the room into a stack of empty cardboard boxes."

"A few times when Leigh and I would be coming back from someplace," Kay Huffman recalled, "we'd see a gang squaring off in a fight and he would say, 'Oops! Gotta hurry up and take you home so I can change my clothes and get back for the fight! I keep chains in my trunk for such events.' And so that's what he'd do." "One time Leigh took on a whole gang that had earlier harassed him," Harold Huffman recalled. He had witnessed many of Leigh's furious, youthful outbursts. "He ground out the leader's eye with a thumb, sending the other members fleeing." Sandy Panzarella later told me, "Remember the story of Leigh kicking the shit out of the five marines on a San Francisco street? Well, he had enormous physical strength. That was a true story."

In San Francisco a personal ad appeared in the *Chronicle*: "BIG 'Z' Welcomes Big 'A'. Permission granted." And in San Francisco Zodiac continued to prey on Toschi's mind. He recalled the days when Ron Allen would call to express his fears. "He just couldn't figure out why Vallejo P.D. had ceased looking into his brother," Toschi told me. "What had happened? I never knew and it bothered me."

"By 1980," John Douglas wrote, "I'd been at Quantico a few years and had some research under my belt when I learned the FBI wanted to take another look at the body of Zodiac literature. I remember getting a file of letters to look at, and I had several conversations with Murray Miron over the finer points of our analytical approaches. Before we could get too deeply involved, however, the letters were pulled. I never did find out what prompted the renewed interest at the Bureau, or what caused our involvement to be canceled."

New adventures occasionally took Toschi's mind off Zodiac. His encounter with San Francisco's "Human Fly Bandit" was one. "He's six foot one, 205 pounds," he told me. "Now that's one big fly. With all his robbing gear—ski mask, surgical gloves, hooded jacket, and sawed-off shotgun, he was eerily reminiscent of Zodiac in costume. And this big fly is quite acrobatic. We called him and his partner the Human Flies because of their daring mobility on top of elevators and their cunning in maneuvering hotel elevators as they wished. I never saw such an ingenious method of robbery before. With an obvious knowledge of elevator electrical circuitry, they first disconnected the elevator alarm bell and emergency phone. They rode atop the elevators, then trapped their victims between floors. Sometimes there can be as many as twenty-five people squeezed into these elevators and if these Human Flies strike, then they will get a big score. I've got to admit it takes guts to ride 'shotgun' on top of an elevator on the twenty-fifth floor. Flinging open the escape trap in the elevator roof, the Flies covered their victims with a shotgun, lowered a mail sack, ordered the guests to fill it with valuables and credit cards, then drew the sack up. They struck at the luxury Holiday Inn and a week later at the Hyatt Hotel. I was kidded by every cop I saw. 'Hey, Dave, catch any flies today?'"

Toschi kept tabs on any use of the stolen credit cards. "At one point," he told me, "I was just two days behind the Flies when I heard from Portland that they had a suspect with one of the stolen cards—the Flies were finally getting sloppy. Then the Alameda County cops picked up two others trying to use stolen cards. It broke the case for me. I notified the East Bay cops that I had another suspect in custody in Portland and suggested they tell the main suspect, in the Santa Rita Jail in Alameda County, that San Francisco was going to book his brother for robbery. The plan worked. The kid broke and protected his older brother. So now they're saying at the Hall of Justice, 'There're no flies on Dave.'"

MONDAY JANUARY 12, 1981

"I understand Les Lundblad had a guy he liked a lot," I mentioned to Sergeant Mulanax at his Vallejo home. A cheery fire crackled in the fireplace. Deer heads stared back at us with glassy eyes. "Lundblad had gone to a mental institution at Atascadero in 1975 and come back and said, 'That's the guy. That's Zodiac and we can't do a thing about it.' "

"Well, I worked pretty closely with Les," Mulanax told me. "He was inclined to get real high on a suspect where I wasn't."

"Was this Leigh?" I asked Mulanax.

"That was the only suspect I ever developed that I had any strong feelings about," said Mulanax. "His father was a retired commander or lieutenant commander in the Navy, a much-decorated serviceman. In fact, he worked for the city for a while. Old-time family, respected. He was an assistant engineer or some damn thing for the city. I didn't know him. Allen was down on the first Zodiac murder. Down at Riverside at that college. But this was a long time ago and what was this, 1966? And this is off the top of my head."

"He was working at an Ace Hardware store in Vallejo."

"I don't think there's anything to prove now, but at the time I was real high on him. I think Armstrong and Toschi were too. Also Nicolai."

"Did you ever have anyone besides Allen?"

"The only one that ever turned me on was Allen."

"Do you think Zodiac is still alive?"

"We had numerous meetings and it's the consensus of the group that the guy is either dead or in a mental institution or penal institution."

"Of course that's where Allen was from 1975 until 1977."

"I wasn't aware of that."

"And what I thought was interesting is that after Toschi and Armstrong questioned him in his trailer, we stopped getting letters at the *Chronicle*."

"In Vallejo," he said, "we wrote detailed reports and Dave and Bill, they didn't. They'd scratch it on a piece of paper."

"How did you personally get onto Allen?"

"Some people who knew him . . ."

"Oh! The two guys he told he was going to become Zodiac."

"Yes."

"What gets me about that is that it's such damaging testimony. I understand one of the men might have had a motive to lie in that Allen supposedly had made improper remarks to his daughter. That made me doubt it a bit."

WEDNESDAY, JANUARY 14, 1981

ALLEN remained the best suspect. Outside of his admission that he had been in Riverside, police had ferreted out no concrete evidence of his presence in Southern California where Zodiac claimed to have killed others. "Leigh's family had told us something about Leigh being around the Riverside area in the middle or late sixties," said Toschi. "I was surprised that [Vallejo Lieutenant Jim] Husted said, 'Forget about Riverside because we can't place Leigh Allen in the area.' Of course, yes, he was there. Allen's own family had told us that he had spent time in the Riverside area and was familiar with Southern California, but they weren't too sure exactly what he was doing because he was on his own a lot."

"Leigh stayed with families down south before and after Atascadero," I told Toschi. "He worked in the area, often drove to Riverside on weekends for car races, and later he flew a plane there. On Monday, Mulanax confirmed Allen was at Riverside City College in 1966 when the murder occurred."

Toschi sighed. "We were the first ones to apprise Mulanax of Leigh, very, very briefly, when the family first came to us," he said. "They had already scanned Leigh very briefly. Mulanax's eyes really popped. He actually thought we had him. To this day we still may. Mulanax liked Allen very, very much. Jack was so high on Allen in those days we were working with him. He said he had never come across a better-looking suspect. That's the way I felt also. We left Allen's file in our metal file cabinet, two manilla four-inch envelopes of material on Allen, and we just put it away with much regret. We just didn't know where to go. Jack says he has an inch-and-a-half file at his house. Could it be he has information that never got into the file at Vallejo? It's a bit frustrating to realize that we had to put his folder back in our files." Allen's indelible presence tracked all over the south—in Pomona, Hemet, Torrance, San Bernardino, Paso Robles, Riverside, and San Luis Obispo. Police had no substantial evidence that he was left-handed.

17
ZODIAC SUSPECTS

OTHER policemen besides Toschi and Narlow had cherished suspects. Highway Patrolman Lyndon Lafferty pegged Zodiac as a resident of Fairfield, a town east of Vallejo. Since December of 1969, a Fairfield copycat had been dispatching typed letters to the *Chronicle*:

> "This is the Zodiac speaking I just need help I will kill again so expect it any time now the [next] will be a cop . . ."

Two days later he wrote again, enclosing a drawing of a knife titled "The Bleeding knife of Zodiac," Page fifty-nine of an astrology book, *Day-by-Day Forecast for Cancer* and a horoscope forecast for Leo. "I just need help I will kill again . . . I just want to tell you this state is in trouble . . ." he wrote.

Harvey Hines, a former Escalon, California, police officer, believed he had found Zodiac. In November 1973, while taking night-school criminology in Sonora, he stumbled across reports of a flirtatious man who approached two South Lake Tahoe women in 1971. A year earlier, possible Zodiac victim Donna Lass had disappeared from there. Intrigued, Hines inquired at the hotel where she worked as nurse and came up with a suspect who had studied basic codes at radio school. He had been arrested multiple times since 1946, and in 1969 lived near where Paul Stine had picked up Zodiac. Hines later told *Hard Copy*, "My suspect is the Zodiac. Every fiber, every part of my being tells me he is the Zodiac Killer." A televised clip showed a pair of slipper-clad feet—the suspect retrieving his morning paper. "Hines's been chasing this guy through Vegas casinos with a video camera," a cop told me, "screaming, 'He's the Zodiac!' " But Zodiac was six feet tall, 240-plus pounds, and about thirty-five. Hines's suspect was three inches shorter, ninety pounds lighter, and twelve years older.

Was there a connection between Lass and someone from Riverside? The theory was that Zodiac had been a former kidney dialysis patient of Donna's when she worked at Riverside's Cottage Hospital. Her roommate, Jo Anne Goettsche (Get-She), had also been a dialysis nurse since 1975. "Donna had never told me about any such person," she told me. "Her family, though, asked me the same question. We worked on the same surgical ward at Letterman General Hospital in the Presidio [where Zodiac had been last seen] and several corpsmen there were giving flying lessons over in Hayward. We used to go flying with two men from Riverside in 1970."

"Where was this?"

"Oh, right here in San Francisco."

"San Francisco?" Mulanax had told me that Darlene Ferrin had also gone flying with two men, but he'd never checked them out. Leigh Allen flew. "I don't know if I can remember their names," Jo Anne said. "Donna was here in San Francisco from February to June of 1970. She moved to Lake Tahoe to work and three months later vanished. Donna was kind of naive, and not very experienced with men. She was easily drawn away. She was hooked on gambling. That's why she went up there. She liked to ski and liked to gamble, so she took the job in the casino hotel [the Sahara Hotel, Stateline, Nevada] as a first-aid emergency nurse. I went up alone to meet her over the weekend, having talked to her earlier in the week. She had moved to a new apartment, so that's why we were meeting at the hotel on Saturday night. That was the first day she had the apartment and I didn't have the phone number. I was supposed to meet her when she was getting off work, and she would show me where she lived. She was nowhere to be found so I stayed in a motel overnight and then looked some more. I didn't know what to do. It wasn't like her to just not show up. When I came back to the city Sunday night without finding out anything, I don't know why I didn't call the police. I was young, I guess."

Donna's older sister, Mary, told me, "Donna was always people's favorite nurse. She used her credit card on Saturday [September 5, 1970] and went to work that night. She worked from six at night to two in the morning. She was writing the log of the day at 1:45 A.M. (the last people she saw were the Bentleys from San Francisco). As it ended 'complains of,' [c/o], her pen just trails down the page, dragged from the last word she wrote to the bottom of the page as if she had been interrupted. It was not signed." Donna's car was later found parked near her new apartment.

An unidentified male caller rang Donna's landlord and employer and said that she would not be returning because of illness in the family. "They had received a phone call that she had an emergency at home," said Jo Anne, "and when her boss called home to her mom, she said, 'There's no illness in the family. That call is a lie.' That's when we knew. And we went there that night." The family flew out from Sioux Falls, South Dakota. "We went to San Francisco and Jo Anne met us at the airport and drove us to Tahoe," said Mary. "And she had been up there to see Donna. I had been on vacation with Mom and my four little kids and we were there just two weeks before Labor Day. Then Jo Anne went up there to see her for Labor Day, and so we went up Sunday night. We couldn't get a word out of anyone at the casino—where she was or what was going on. As for the police, they wouldn't even put it out as a missing person until forty-eight hours had passed. The police had been in the apartment and searched it. We went back up on the third of October and came back on Monday the fifth. There was someone Jo Anne and Donna were dating from Sacramento. There was a phone call South Lake police had received from Sacramento, but he never called back." Jo Anne said, "Her sister had a private detective pursuing the investigation for years, but they never found her—ever! It was very strange."

"What was really strange," Lynch told me, "is some guy came up to Vallejo P.D. one night and he was drunk. He said he had been trying to report Donna Lass's disappearance to SFPD, but apparently the guy was a heavy drinker and when he had gone there they'd thrown him out. He knew there had been a previous murder in Vallejo by the Zodiac so he came up here to report. I talked to him for a long time, but I can't think of that guy's name. Or the name of the musician he thought was involved, but that orchestra was in Tahoe at the time this girl disappeared. They never found her did they? No."

There was a tenuous Tahoe connection with Leigh Allen. A friend of Leigh's had bought a hotel there, and Leigh might have been visiting him the night Lass vanished. And I found a connection to the 1963 murders of Robert Domingos and Linda Edwards near Santa Barbara. "Donna left Sioux City, went to Minneapolis," said Mary, "then went to Santa Barbara and worked. They took this doctor east to this big convention, and when she came back she went to San Francisco to Letterman General. The pay was good, but she got awfully tired of the hours—weekends, nights. Her friends from Santa Barbara had moved up there to Lake Tahoe. 'Oh, we have the perfect job for you. Come on up and join us and live with us.' And so that's what she did for the summer."

Under "Personals" in the *Chronicle* I spotted this ad:

> "ZODIAC, We offer a National and interested forum to hear your story as you wish it told. Would like to interview you with complete anonymity. Contact THE AQUARIAN AGE magazine 270 World Trade Center, SF 94111."

They gave a local number and stationed a worker by the phone in case Zodiac should call. The worker might still be waiting.

MONDAY, JANUARY 19, 1981

As Mulanax and I drove to Blue Rock Springs, I watched storm clouds sweeping in from the San Pablo Bay. "Most of them I'd get a specimen of their handwriting," said Mulanax, explaining how he processed Zodiac suspects, "and have Morrill check it out. Either that or the physical description was so far off in age or some such thing where it couldn't logically be the suspect."

"You mentioned this Tommy 'Lee' Southard?" I said.

Mulanax laughed. "That Southard," he replied, "was one of the early suspects. A serviceman at Mare Island, as I recall. I didn't investigate him. Lynch and Rust conducted the investigation on him. Six weeks or a couple of months after this [Blue Rock Springs] shooting happened they came up with him. He looked pretty good for a while."

"Southard lived at home with his mom," Lynch added, "and wore thick-lensed glasses. He also lived downtown in an apartment. We had a burglary case on the guy and I tackled him at a restaurant. He was a real oddball. He cut his wrists when I arrested him, and was later killed downtown in a bar shooting on Virginia Street."

Zodiac raced down to Napa after the stabbings at Lake Berryessa and rang up the police from a pay phone only four-and-one-half blocks from the police station. Narlow found the location intriguing. "A guy here in Napa is very proficient at making bombs," he told me, "and happens to trade at the barbershop directly across the street from the booth where the call was made." Police technician Hal Snook, rushed in his dusting of a wet palm print on the receiver (he was needed at Lake Berryessa), feared botching the job. He used a combination of a hot light and blow-drying to accelerate the process, got some prints from the phone booth[8] and sent them to the FBI. Tommy Lee Southard was the first they tried to match. The FBI Identification Division replied on October 23, 1969:

> "Seven latent fingerprints, three latent palm prints and one latent impression which is either a fingerprint or a partial palm print appear in the submitted photographs and are of value for identification purposes. We compared those prints to Thomas Leonard Southard—no identification was effected. We could not rule him out conclusively since we do not have his palm prints."

Latent prints recovered from the Lake Berryessa victim's Karmann Ghia were compared with the comparable areas of the latent prints. Again no identification with Southard was effected. The FBI tested the Napa phone booth's prints against Zodiac's first letter to the Vallejo *Times-Herald* because someone's prints were recovered from that letter. The prints did not match the car, cab, or booth fingerprints. Or Southard's.

FRIDAY, MAY 15, 1981

CI&I in Sacramento became the clearinghouse for all future Zodiac investigations. A decade earlier Paul Avery, in a confidential memo to his editor, Abe Mellinkoff, had suggested just such a centralization. Toschi at the time had already been concerned

---

[8]Located at the Napa Car Wash, 1200 Main Street, twenty-seven miles from Lake Berryessa.

about Avery. "I think he wants to become more than an investigative reporter," he told me. "I think he eventually wants to run this investigation." Toschi was right:

> "I met with Attorney General [Evelle J.] Younger for 45 minutes," Avery wrote confidentially, "outlined the Zodiac case in some detail and proposed to him that the State DOJ take over and coordinate the investigation of the case by forming a special Zodiac Squad made up of detectives from the various cities and counties which have actual or highly possible Z murders." Three days later Avery sent Younger a resume of the case, writing that "I am eager to begin assisting in the formation of your 'Zodiac Squad' and to plan its direction."

Since a multitude of jurisdictions, counties, and departments were involved, their records had to be gathered and reorganized. Many files were missing, scattered over the state, hidden in basements and attics or taken away as mementos. Inspector Deasy personally drove the SFPD's files to Sacramento. On May 15, at 7:11 A.M., police and FBI agents arrested David Carpenter as the Trailside Killer at his San Francisco home. This wilderness murderer shot and stabbed hikers on Mount Tamalpais above the Golden Gate, at Point Reyes Seashore, and in the Santa Cruz forests. Interestingly, Carpenter had hinted to accomplices that he was Zodiac—an intriguing possibility. Photos of Carpenter from 1969 with glasses and crew cut bore a striking resemblance to Zodiac's wanted poster. Carpenter had been in prison when some Zodiac letters were mailed. But during the Trailside attacks police had ruled Carpenter out as a suspect because state computers listed him as being in jail. In reality, he was living in a halfway house and walking the streets of downtown San Francisco.

Another riddle—the inoffensive ex-convict stuttered badly, while the Trailside Killer did not. However, at his San Diego trial, Carpenter explained, "When I sing [and he sang], I don't stutter. When I whisper [and he whispered], I don't stutter. When I get really angry! [he roared] I don't stutter!" The jury drew back in terror. Carpenter the Trailside Killer was a different person than Carpenter under control. Perhaps Zodiac was someone else too when he wrote his letters—an inoffensive person who, from day to day, no one suspected.

"Another suspect, Mike, a six-foot-tall, eyeglass-wearing ex-Navyman, had moved the day of the Blue Rock Springs murder," Mulanax told me. "He owned a 9-mm and a .45-caliber gun and, like Allen, worked at Union Oil. When he got too excited he would put his thumbs against his nose and scream. Early on, we had been looking for a Taurus and Mike was a Taurus. His neighbor verified he was familiar with Lake Berryessa. But that went nowhere. He did look good for awhile."

THURSDAY, OCTOBER 8, 1981

FEW outside the FBI guessed the Unabomber existed. At the end of a sixteen-month period of inactivity, the nation's first domestic terrorist struck. He placed a bomb inside a large paper-wrapped parcel at Utah's Bennion Hall, where it was safely defused. On an April morning fifteen years hence, when Ted Kaczynski was captured in a remote, snowbound Montana cabin, the Unabomber would become an important Zodiac suspect. It was not hard to see why.

"I was the first one to do that story," Rita Williams, KTVU-TV Channel Two reporter, told me. "I did it like a week after he was arrested. I got the fingerprint guy out in Walnut Creek to look at Kaczynski. These FBI guys I knew were laughing at me—'Oh, there's no way. It can't be.' I said, 'Come on, he really fits as Zodiac. That strange family, mathematical mind . . . chemical bombs . . .'"

The implication was that Zodiac had vanished because he had become the Unabomber. Here are reasons why that might be true. Both were pipe-bomb-makers. Both mailed police taunting letters with too much postage, boasted of their intelligence, and promised dire consequences if their words were not published. The Unabomber wrote the *Times,* threatening to bring down a California jetliner with a bomb, then admitted it was "a joke." Zodiac promised to blow up a school bus with an electronic bomb, but rescinded his promise.

Kaczynski had been a professor at UC Berkeley from 1967 to 1969, when Zodiac became active. Ted resigned June 30, 1969, and Zodiac first wrote the *Chronicle* a month later. The Unabomber exploded his first confirmed bomb on May 26, 1978, and a month afterward Zodiac allegedly wrote his last letter. Kaczynski wrote the *San Francisco Examiner* a month later. The two wore military gear—the Unabomber military fatigues, Zodiac a Naval costume. Both used disguises, a hooded sweatshirt, a hood. Inexplicably, there were times when the Unabomber and Zodiac simply stopped writing and killing. Both were asexual beings with dominant mothers and absent fathers. Both understood the complexities of code. Code is nothing more than mathematics and Kaczynski was a brilliant mathematician. At Berryessa the surviving victim reported that Zodiac claimed to be an escaped convict from either Colorado or Deer Lodge, Montana. Deer Lodge lay sixty miles from where Kaczynski eventually built his isolated cabin in Lincoln, Montana.

However, equally compelling reasons convinced me that Kaczynski was *not* Zodiac. In 1978, the Unabomber, in his guise as the "Junkyard Bomber," was using match heads and rubber bands to create his bombs. Nine years earlier Zodiac had mailed the *Chronicle* electronic and chemical bomb diagrams far more sophisticated than the Unabomber's a decade later. Would Zodiac regress and lose the ability to create advanced bombs? More than likely, by 1978, he would be building better bombs. The Unabomber remained unknown for so long because he didn't write the press. The publicity-hungry Zodiac always used his murders to gain publicity immediately afterward. The Unabomber wrote the *Examiner,* disguising himself as "FC." Zodiac, with few exceptions, took pains to identify himself as Zodiac, and verified his identity by providing confidential facts or pieces of bloody evidence.

The Unabomber targeted groups—computer experts and salesmen, behavioral modificationists, geneticists, engineers, and scholars. But his bombs were delivered in such a way that anyone could have opened them. In 1987, he left a bomb in a Salt Lake City parking lot for anyone to find. Zodiac's targets were always specific with rigid requirements. He stalked his victims—young lovers, students by lakes on special days—with a different weapon each time. Kaczynski was obsessed with wood and wood-related names, while Zodiac was obsessed with water and water-related names. Kaczynski loved nature—he apologized to a rabbit for shooting it. Zodiac loved to hunt animals and progressed to people as wild game. In 1967 Kaczynski was in Ann

Arbor at the University of Michigan getting a second doctorate when three Riverside letters were written by Zodiac and postmarked in Riverside. In 1971, Kaczynski moved to Lincoln, Montana, and was living there when Zodiac letters at that time carried Bay Area postmarks. Zodiac's excessive postage was engendered by a rush for publicity, while the Unabomber's stamps served two uses. The value and subject of the stamps were a numerical code indicating the type of bomb inside and a symbolic statement. The second use was to direct the flow of the parcel. Overposting made certain the package would not be returned to the fictional sender; too little postage insured that the bomb would revert to the return address—the actual target, a scientist on the Unabomber's hit list.

The physical appearance of Zodiac and inner workings of his mind present the biggest differences between him and the Unabomber. Zodiac, "lumbering" and "bearlike," differed considerably from Kaczynski's lanky and gaunt frame—143 pounds, five feet nine inches tall. Zodiac, physically powerful, had a paunch, stood close to six feet, and weighed around 240 pounds. Though Kaczynski kept a journal in code (speedily solved by the FBI), it compared in no way with the intricate, unbreakable ciphers of Zodiac nor with his handwriting.

The Unabomber's own words offer the biggest difference. His manifesto's tone is flat, unimaginative. Where are Zodiac's clever turns of phrase and imagery frightening enough to galvanize a city? The professor in Kaczynski lectures us, while Zodiac's colorful expressions and memorable use of popular culture are intended to frighten, bully, and mystify—not instruct. His letters possess an ironic, biting quality that overflows with melancholy, even despair. They chill anyone who reads them. When Zodiac was angry, we felt it.

Zodiac gave his motives for killing as "collecting souls for the afterlife" and the thrill of hunting people. The Unabomber's apparent lack of motive made the search for him difficult. Zodiac obviously hated women. Kaczynski, to the end, dreamed of a wife and children, and envied and detested the brother who turned him in for possessing that domestic bliss. Kaczynski's true hatred was reserved for those in the academic world who had surpassed him. Zodiac was master of all weapons, the Unabomber only of bombs, which he had trouble making lethal. Zodiac had an intimate knowledge of Vallejo. Kaczynski did not. Like a poisoner, Kaczynski imagined the death agonies of his victim from as great a distance as possible. "By gun, by knife, by rope," Zodiac got as close to his victims as he could.

18

ARTHUR LEIGH ALLEN

FRIDAY, MAY 22, 1981

"**I** was terminated from Spectro Chrome Graphics in Benicia (with *no* warnings or conferences) quite by surprise," Leigh said of his May 22 firing. He suspected he could put his finger on the reason. "I believe my problem started three weeks prior when I destroyed a roll-down door with a forklift. The estimate was $2300."

TUESDAY, JUNE 30, 1981

"**I** am intelligent, hardworking, honest, dependable, and punctual," Leigh wrote, applying for other work. "I am looking for a job where I can learn and advance myself in the long term and hope you will consider these points in evaluating my application." He was asked, "Have you ever been convicted of a felony or a misdemeanor?" "Yes," he answered, "I committed one count of PC 288 and was sent to a state hospital for two years. I am now still taking therapy as was required by the courts." His application, received July 1, 1981, was printed neatly—all the *g*'s were straight and all the *d*'s cursive. There was even a three-stroke *k*.

WEDNESDAY, JULY 8, 1981

ALLEN snared a new job on his old stamping grounds—a Benicia industrial park at the end of Lake Herman Road. Leigh's friends told me he often parked at a promontory where Lake Herman Road intersects Highway 21, northeast of the Benicia-Martinez Bridge. He popped open a Coors, drank, and scanned Roe Island, Ryer Island, and a hundred sealed battleships dismally riding their anchors in Suisun Bay below. The gray entombed fleet, mothballed remnants of World War II, probably made him think of his father and his own failed submarine career. He still hated working, but the new position gave him ample time to drink, visit his trailers, and make subtle digs at the police. He continued to wear a Zodiac skin-diving watch and a Zodiac ring. He continued to mention Zodiac to his friends, leaving a trail of hints scattered behind.

He started his car and swung onto the rutted road. At home, a letter had slid down the mail slot into his basement. After a long delay, he was going to receive his bachelor of science degree from Sonoma State. Authorities still had not searched that dank and dreary basement where bombs and a "death machine" might be stored.

Though diabetic, Arthur Leigh Allen began drinking beer from a quart jar. He rode his green motorcycle, laid out remodeling plans for his home, and bought more books on electronic gear, maps, and the occult. He studied birdhouses, and continued building a plane. Dr. Rykoff reported regularly on Leigh's progress and rehabilitation. Apprehensive of his patient, the doctor played taped excerpts of their sessions for a Santa Rosa cop. He was shaken too. Eventually, Rykoff fled to a wilderness hospital. Everyone who came in touch with Zodiac was hurt in some way. George Bawart told me the bizarre story.

"The doctor had come to believe that Zodiac was his patient," said Bawart, "and made hours of tapes which he wanted to publish. He had tapes that Allen had made claiming to be Zodiac. Allen had talked to his doctor about putting bamboo stakes in pits around his house. The sharpened ends, covered in manure, would both wound and infect, even kill. I went up and interviewed Rykoff at some sanitarium. He was in a wild area and kept looking frantically in each corner. 'Look out for the snakes,' he cried, dancing about. 'The snakes—everywhere.' I laughed, then jumped. I looked, and there really was a rattlesnake. The biggest rattlesnake I'd ever seen—right by my boot—rattlesnakes all over the joint. God, for a psychiatrist, he was goofier than a bedbug." Or just frightened?

In early 1970, long before Leigh began seeing Dr. Rykoff, a rumor circulated in San Francisco that Zodiac had lost a letter addressed to a psychiatrist he was then seeing. Allegedly, it contained a death threat to the doctor's family. A passerby found the letter and turned it over to the police, who interviewed the doctor. Because of professional confidentiality he refused to name his patient, a Bay Area resident. Within this doctor's files, some believed, lay the real name of Zodiac.

"We went down and saw Pete Noyes," Bawart continued. "He was one of the producers of *Johnny Carson* or *Jeopardy*. Somehow this guy got involved with Rykoff, Santa Rosa cops, and all this goofy stuff. It was absolutely bizarre the stuff they were doing. They were gonna protect this Dr. Rykoff because Arthur Leigh Allen was gonna come kill him. They thought one of the lieutenants on the Santa Rosa Police Department was in cahoots with Leigh Allen. After I finished this I wondered, 'Are these guys pranksters? Are they just that paranoid?' Crazy stuff. It was to the point when I developed all this—this guy in Santa Rosa didn't want to talk to me. I was very straightforward. 'I'm retired. I'm working this as a private contractor for the Vallejo Police Department Homicide Investigation Division and I want to talk to you.' Well, he wouldn't talk to me in Santa Rosa. He insisted on meeting me in Petaluma, and he met me with his partner, a young fellow. This guy, this cop, was real kind of superior-acting, as if I were a dummy. That's fine. To get what I want, I'll take that tack. And so we sat there and we chatted."

"The main guy in this thing is somebody just too big. He'll get you and he'll kill you," he told Bawart.

"Well, tell me who it is," Bawart said.

"I won't," he said.

"Wait a minute, pal," Bawart said. "You're a working cop and you're telling me you won't tell me something that's germane to my investigation."

"I won't."

"Well, let me tell you what's going to happen. I'm going to go back and speak to Captain Conway and Captain Conway is going to our chief of police and say, 'There's a Santa Rosa cop that won't cooperate with an investigation.' Our chief of police is going to call your chief of police and I can bet you dollars to doughnuts, fella, you'll find yourself sitting in an office and telling me what I want to know. So make it easy on yourself and tell me now."

"No."

"Well, you'll hear from me."

"Next day, sure as shit, that's what happened," Bawart told

me. "This guy was ordered in the office. We all sat down. He finally told us who this really bad guy was—who turned out to be
[a superior officer]. The reason he was a really bad guy is because his backyard backed up to Ron Allen's. That's no big deal.
Ron Allen was a North Bay city planner. We interviewed the officer and Ron Allen and there was nothing to it. I got some handwriting out of some guy out of Santa Rosa—not related to the
psychologist, that was sent to me by this guy's girlfriend. I
looked at it. It's a dead ringer. The way he made his [check
mark] *r*'s and everything. But I take it to the handwriting people
and this was a letter that says, 'Hey, honey, I want to get back
with you.' It wasn't a threatening letter. He was a kind of half-
assed stalker and wouldn't let her go. Anyway I took it to the
handwriting guy and he says, 'Definitely not.' They must know
what they're doing, but I've seen things in Allen's handwriting
that look good to me."

WEDNESDAY, FEBRUARY 17, 1982

TOSCHI had been having a little discomfort from recent surgery.
The month before, an ulcer had brought on massive internal
bleeding. He had been rushed by ambulance to Children's Hospital, but was now recuperating at home—reading, resting, listening
to Big Band records on the stereo, and doing a lot of walking and
thinking about the unsolved case. For a man who excelled in baseball and basketball, any inaction was painful. "There is no police
work being done on Zodiac at all," he complained. "I know this
for a fact." I spoke to Fred Shirisago at DOJ. "Like I say, I have
gotten so many damn calls on this Leigh Allen," Shirisago said. "I
spend my time trying to do background. I don't want to be left
holding the bag, the last person on the case. . . . Look, Allen
might be the guy. I'm not saying he's not. He goes to libraries and
does a lot of research on crimes against women. Every investigator I've talked with thinks it's him. I read everything I can about
the guy."

An Oregon man suggested police could catch Zodiac by creat-
ing a fictional story that the killer was already in custody. "Duped
by the fictional arrest," he said, "we could trap him like a blind
dog in a meat house."

THURSDAY, MAY, 20, 1982

IN November 1981, evidence in the sixteen-year-old Cheri Jo Bates murder investigation had "come to light." Riverside police assigned four investigators full-time and, believing themselves close to a solution, dispatched an outline to the D.A.'s office. "She had a couple of boyfriends and there's one guy in particular. We're convinced the killer might be him," they argued. Since November 1968, they had been convinced one of Cheri Jo's former boyfriends or rejected suitors was her killer. Allegedly he'd had scratches on his face (Cheri Jo had clawed her assailant's face) and had bragged about committing the crime. Not only was there not enough evidence to charge him, but friends alibied him. "The D.A.'s office tore [the outline] apart from their point of view," said Chief Victor Jones, adding, "The person we believe responsible for the slaying of Cheri Jo Bates is *not* the individual other law enforcement authorities believe responsible for the so-called 'Zodiac' killings." Jones believed Zodiac had been in the area, but taken credit for a killing he had not committed. Captain Irv Cross, indicating the seven-month delay in letters, also suggested Zodiac had been trying to capitalize on the publicity.

TUESDAY, MAY 25, 1982

"I called [Detective] Bud Kelly in Riverside this morning," Toschi told me. He had called in response to Chief Jones's press conference. "He couldn't give me their suspect's name, but they feel they know who killed the Bates girl. Some new information developed in the last three months and the suspect does not check out as Zodiac. This suspect was looked at back when the murder occurred. I asked Kelly if their guy was ever in the Bay Area even for a short time. Answer: 'NO.' Their suspect has lived in Riverside all the time.

"Seems the Riverside P.D. has only a circumstantial case against their local man," said Toschi. "No physical evidence can tie him to the case. Kelly says the Riverside County District Attorney does not like the case and is very hesitant about issuing a murder complaint. Kelly says the case will probably never go to trial."

Riverside P.D. still had a single strand of hair caught in the watchband of the paint-spattered men's Timex Cheri Jo had torn from her attacker. Police stored the hair in a refrigerated evidence locker. One day a conclusive test might be developed to either clear or incriminate their suspect. The local man had had frequent brushes with the law. A secret psychological evaluation of Bates's murderer had been completed eleven years earlier for the Riverside D.A. The chief psychologist of Patton State Hospital described Bates's killer as:

"[So] hypersensitive . . . that virtually any little misperceived act could be blown up out of all proportion to the facts. He is obsessed and pathologically preoccupied with intense hatred against female figures—all the more so if he sees the young woman as attractive. Because of his own unconscious feelings of inadequacy, he is not likely to act out his feelings sexually, but in fantasy. . . . I would like to emphasize that there is a real possibility that he can become homicidal again."

Sherwood Morrill showed me a confidential handwriting analysis he had prepared November 24, 1970, for Chief of the Bureau A. L. Coffey and Riverside Police Chief L. T. Kinkead. He had studied examples of the Riverside suspect's writing.

"An examination of enclosures [case # 36-F-586] A through E [three envelopes and letters, photograph of a note signed 'rh' on desk, photographs of five names beginning with H, two letters addressed to an acquaintance of the suspect, seven pages exemplar writing and material of the prime Riverside suspect] resulted in the following conclusions:
"1. It was first determined that the handprinting on the envelopes and letters of enclosure A was by the same person who prepared the handprinting appearing on the desk, a photograph of which is enclosure B of this report.
"2. A comparison of this material with the Zodiac letters revealed many characteristics which resulted in the conclusion that enclosures A and B were in fact prepared by the same person responsible for the Zodiac letters.
"3. The five names beginning with H could not be identified with any of the other material submitted.
"4. The letter postmarked in February of 1968 appears to have been drawn by a lettering set and does not conform with

any of the material submitted. The handprinted letter post-marked January 17, 1968 addressed to the suspect's friend is still in a different person's handprinting but does not conform with any of the other material submitted. It does, however, contain numerous divergencies from the handprinting of the Riverside Suspect and *definitely was not prepared by him.*"

One thing was certain—the RPD's prime suspect's handprint-ing did not match the Riverside letters. Morrill ruled that Zodiac *did* write those letters.

WEDNESDAY, JUNE 2, 1982

AT Sonoma State University, Leigh Allen officially received his bachelor of arts degree in biology with a minor in chemistry.

WEDNESDAY, JUNE 9, 1982

AT his Montgomery Street law office, Belli dropped a tape into his machine. "A pleasant evening to you, Melvin M. Belli . . . (ha, ha, ha, ha, ha)," an anonymous voice cackled. "OK, number one . . . I had thought possibly we might get together and meet and talk. I am at the point in this activity that I have gotten into somehow. How, I don't know. Why, I have no idea. Now what you should do is pull up a chair and sit down with your coffee or tea . . . and relax because I am about to tell you the God-damnedest story you have ever heard. Number one, our common interest is the interest of the Zodiac killer.

"Now this case has been going on for over twelve years. Dur-ing that time—(the reason my voice is going down is I'm turning this radio down. With this hillbilly music you can't hear yourself think). Anyhow, at one point in these photostatic copies that I have of the Zodiac killer there's reference . . . they're talking of the cop. . . . 'Over the years the five thousand people he has inter-viewed, the three thousand tips, the two thousand possible sus-pects . . . ' Anyhow, we're talking there of almost over ten thousand items alone. Now I know where the Zodiac is. I know who the Zodiac is. I know how to identify the Zodiac.

"For over a twenty-year period I have had a sincere interest in symbols, symbols of all kinds. . . . One week I went to a flea market and saw this ring, which I paid sixty dollars for. The ring has no identification marks of any country. The ring presented a challenge, and so I said, 'I'm going to find out everything there is to know about this ring and the symbols on it.' Over a period of four to five months I was laid off and started researching the ring for many hours in the library. I have my own library, about a thousand books.

"Each symbol on top of the ring corresponded to seven different symbols—a total of thirty-seven symbols that related to chemistry and astrology. The underside of the ring had more symbols. The guy who wore this must have really been something. It had been the ring of a blind Norse god. The things that have happened because of this ring are unbelievable. I'm laying this stuff on ya because I know of your sincere interest the last time the Zodiac was active . . . you're the very best of attorneys in the U.S. today. Now the reason that this cop could not catch Zodiac or even relate to him is because he has such a spiritual background, such a reasonable amount of intelligence. He is the most intelligent man in the United States today.

"He comes from fire, he returns to fire. How are we going to identify this guy? He has a ring on his finger decorated with a sign of the Zodiac. That sign, the sign of the Zodiac, is the sign of the ox. Now remember well, my slim friend (heh, heh, heh), his full power consists in the power of words and the jumbling of words. His method of attack on these innocent young people was not of a frontal assault. His attack was first with the knife, then with the gun, the rope, then reverting back to the knife for the blood ritual itself. The Zodiac's ring is a blood stone, a darkish-green stone with sprinkles of red, and is governed by Mars. The blood stone and the ox are connected. Darlene Ferrin had seen Zodiac kill someone [a fact not widely known until four years later]."

The speaker knew of a Zodiac ring such as Allen had worn since the murders began, a ring compelling Zodiac to do horrible things. The unknown voice might not be Zodiac, but his remarks about a Zodiac ring were truly unsettling.

THURSDAY, OCTOBER 11, 1984

"I really didn't think this fifteenth anniversary of the San Francisco Zodiac killing would stir up this much interest," Toschi said.

Herb Caen wrote:

"THURSDAY, OCT. 11, is a special annvy. for Police Inspector Dave Toschi. On that day in 1969, 15 yrs. ago, Toschi, then assigned to homicide, was summoned to Washington and Cherry, where a Yellow Cabbie had just been murdered. Four days later, a bloody swatch of the victim's shirt and a letter from The Zodiac arrived at the Chronicle—and thus began the string of still unsolved Zodiac killings, most of them accompanied by taunting letters. The last one to Toschi said simply 'ME-37 (killings). S.F.P.D.-0.' After slaying the Yellow driver, The Zodiac presumably faded away into the nearby Presidio forest. He could be walking down Market St. this very minute. . . ."

WEDNESDAY, JULY 3, 1985

AFTER thirty-two years on the force, twenty-five of those as a police inspector, Dave Toschi, now fifty-two, quietly retired. He had already realized his life's dream when he joined the force in 1953, spending seven years as a patrol officer in the Richmond District. "My dad always said that if I was a cop, I'd always have a paycheck to bring home. He said I'd never get rich, though. He was right." As a homicide inspector, Toschi won gold, silver, and bronze medals of valor. "I still consider the Zodiac case the most frustrating of all my cases. I really believe it gave me bleeding ulcers." But he was proud of contributing to the solution of another case that had a "Z" in it—the Zebra murders that claimed the lives of twelve San Franciscans between 1973 and 1974. "I'm gratified that I was part of a team that brought that terrible case to a successful conclusion."

Toschi spent five years in Robbery Detail, receiving police commission honors as a "Heroic Officer" on February 22, 1984. Then he transferred to the Sex Crimes Detail where he spent a year. Now, after working every crime against persons there was, including Aggravated Assaults, he was retiring to become head of security at the Watergate apartment complex across the Bay in Emeryville near Berkeley. Within a year he would also be a li-

Commissioned Zodiac composite by Sonoma County Sheriff Don Striepeke done in 1975.
Collection of the author

Arthur Leigh Allen, 1967 driver's license photo.
Collection of the author

Arthur Leigh Allen, 1990 driver's license photo.
Collection of the author

Arthur Leigh television interview Thursday, July 25, 1991.
Courtesy KTVU-TV

October 11, 1969. The Stine killing. Inspector Dave Toschi (at right in gray).
The dead cabbie is sprawled across the front seat,
head resting on the cab's floorboard. Stine's left arm, watch left by killer,
dangles from passenger side of his Yellow Cab. *Collection of the author; police photo*

Napa police technician studies Zodiac prints leading to Bryan Hartnell's
car at Lake Barryessa.
Collection of the author; police photo

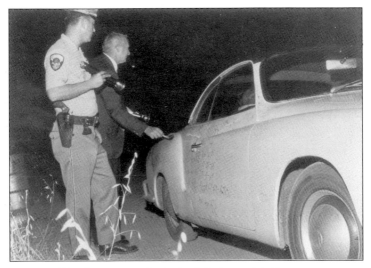

Napa detectives standing by the victims' car at Lake Berryessa,
Zodiac writing scrawled on car door.
Collection of the author; police photo

Police aerial view of the Napa murder site at the end of the peninsula.
Collection of the author; police photo

Inspectors Toschi and Armstrong at the morgue. They were able to match a
bloody swatch mailed by Zodiac to the *Chronicle* to the remnants of
Paul Stine's gray and white shirt.
Collection of the author; police photo

Captain Ken Narlow
Courtesy of Ken Narlow

Dr. Donald T. Lunde of Stanford
Collection of the author

Postal Inspector John Shimoda.
Photo provided by law enforcement
to the author.
Collection of the author

Captain Roy Conway
Collection of the author

Lt. James Husted, Vallejo P.D.
Collection of the author

Sergeant Jack Mulanax
Collection of the author

Detective George Bawart
Collection of the author

Melvin Belli, defense attorney
Collection of the author

On December 27, 1969, attorney Melvin Belli
reads Zodiac letter of December 20.
Collection of the author

Sherwood Morrill,
CI&I's Chief of Questioned Documents
Collection of the author

San Francisco Chronicle
reporter Paul Avery.
He is wearing Wing Walker
shoes and is at Hamilton AFB.
Collection of the author

Inspector Dave Toschi
wearing his famous gun
(worn by Steve McQueen
in the movie *Bullitt*).
Collection of the author;
police photo

April 3, 1974.
S.F.P.D. Homicide Inspectors
Dave Toschi and Bill Armstrong.
Collection of the author; police photo

Detective William A. Baker
in 2001.
Collection of the author

NOTE TO THE READER: The following letters and envelopes, along with those previously reproduced in *Zodiac*, constitute all of the killer's exceedingly rare communications. Many of these letters have been lost by the police over the years. *Zodiac Unmasked* is the only place the reader can find these historical and chilling letters reproduced.

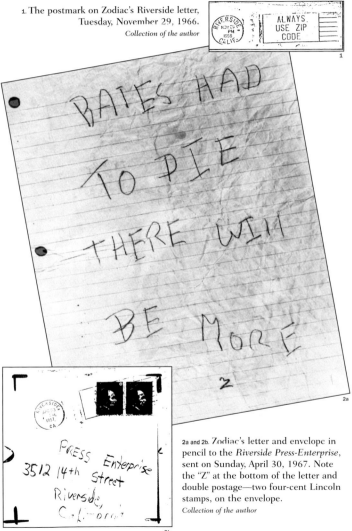

1. The postmark on Zodiac's Riverside letter, Tuesday, November 29, 1966.
Collection of the author

2a and 2b. Zodiac's letter and envelope in pencil to the *Riverside Press-Enterprise*, sent on Sunday, April 30, 1967. Note the "Z" at the bottom of the letter and double postage—two four-cent Lincoln stamps, on the envelope.
Collection of the author

3a and 3b

3c

3a, 3b, and 3c. Front and back of envelope to the *Vallejo Times-Herald*, mailed July 31, 1969. Inside contained one-third of a Zodiac cipher.
Collection of the author

4

4. Zodiac letter of July 31, 1969, to the *Vallejo Times-Herald*. The following day, police fumed the letter with Ninhydrin, a chemical that develops prints. That caused the hand-printing to blur.
Collection of the author

Q2 D-69028059 LL
LABORATORY
L.C. A-7042

tapes. I did not leave the scene
of the killing with squealling
tires + racing engine as described
in the Vollejo paper. I drove away
quite slowly so as not to draw
attention to my car.
The man who told the police
that my car was brown was a
negro about 40-45 rather shabbly
dressed. I was at this phone
booth having some fun with the
Vollejo cop when he was walking
by. When I hung the phone up
the damn X ⊙ thing began to
ring & that drew his attention
to me + my car.
Last Christmass
In that episode the police were
wondering as to how I could
shoot & hit my victoms in the
dark. They did not openly state
this, but implied this by saying
it was a well lit night. + I could
see the silowets on the horizon.
Bull Shit that area is suronded.

5

Here is part of a cipher the
other 2 parts of this cipher are
being mailed to the editors of
the Vallejo times + S F Exam
iner.

I want you to print this cipher
on the frunt page of you
paper. In this cipher is my
identity.

If you do not print this cipher
by the afternoon of Fry. 1st of
Aug 69, I will go on a kill rampage Fry. night. I will crase
around all weekend killing lone
people in the night then moere
out to kill again, untill I end
up with a dozen people over
the weekend.

6a, 6b, and 6c. The envelope, letter, and one-third of a three-part cipher that Zodiac sent to the *San Francisco Chronicle* on July 31, 1969. Letters mailed to the *Examiner* and *Times-Herald* measured different sizes and indicated the killer was using remaindered paper. *Collection of the author*

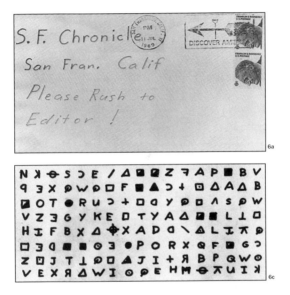

6a

6c

7a, 7b, and 7c. Salinas schoolteacher Donald Gene Harden's original worksheets for decoding the first part of Zodiac's three-part cipher sent to Bay Area papers on July 31, 1969. This remarkable deciphering was an important break in the Zodiac investigation. Note: The first third appeared in the *Times-Herald*, the second in the *Chronicle* and the third in the *Examiner*. *Collection of the author*

YES/MET#E/H◇③ ⊖ W/O I A ◎LM◻
○ フ K Q ᴃ/Iᒷ ⊖ W/O I A ◎LM◻ ⑭/T H R I ㅗ

BPDR+τ πe◇N ◇BE/U H I T/
LING(EX PE R ENGE/T IS/

Z D ○ O N W I E ◇+ ⊥/L ⊙ ⊐ I R ◇H
EVEN/BETTER/THAN GET

⊐ A P R ◻ T X Q͐ d e/≠ ◻ X フ ◎ A
F I NG/Y O U R/R O C K S/O F W

R ◻ M △/R u ⊥ /├ /⊖-N/V E K H A G
I T #/A G I R L/T H E/B E S T/P A

Q π 工 ᵒ フ フ T フ △/L M ⅃ M ◇ Z ◎ P
R T/○ F/T フ I T H A White N I L

Φ u q A △ ᴃ V W/R e B o R N E
D I e/T W I L L I B E

Λ/π S Я J 工 Ϥ ⊙ △/◻ Ꝕ ◎ ◻ △ Φ G ◻ E M
W/P A R A D I R e/N N D/A L/T H

⑤∼
(M)∼

Sonnea

8. Front and back of the envelope of Zodiac's letter to the *San Francisco Chronicle*, October 13, 1969.
Collection of the author

9. Front and back of the envelope to Zodiac's letter to the *San Francisco Chronicle*, November 8, 1969.
Collection of the author

10. Front and back of the envelope to Zodiac's letter to the *San Francisco Chronicle*, November 9, 1969.
Collection of the author

in my killings I wear transparent finger-tip guards. All it
is ii 2 coats of air plane coment
coated on my finger-tips - quite
unnoticible + very efective.
3 my killing tools have been bought
en through the mail order out-
fits before the bon went into
efect. except one ◉ it was
bought out of the state.
So as you see the police don't
have much to work on. If you
wonder why I was wipe ing the
cab down I was leaving fake clews
for the police to run all over town
with, as one might say, I ♯gave
the cops som bussy work to do so
keep them happy. I enjoy needlling
the blue pigs. Hey blue pig I
was in the park —you were useing
fire trucks to mask the sound
of your cruzeing prowl cars. The
dogs never come with in 2
blocks of me + they were to
the west + there was only 2

11a-11e. Pages 2–7 of Zodiac's letter to the *San Francisco Chronicle*,
November 9, 1969. (Page one of the letter was reproduced in *Zodiac*.)
Collection of the author

groups of parking about 10 min
apart then the motor cicles
went by about 150 ft away
going from south to north west.
ps. 2 cops pulled a goof abot 3
min after I left the cab. I was
walking down the hill to the
pork when this cop car pulled up
+ one of them called me over
+ asked if I saw any one
acting sapicious or strange
in the lost 5 to 10 min + I said
yes there was this man who
was runniy by waveing a gun
+ the cops pealed rubber +
went around the corner as
I directed them + I dissap —
eared into the pork about +
a half away never to be seen
again.

Hey pig doesnt it rile you up
to have you noze rubed in your
booboos ?
If you cops think Im going to take
on a bos the way I stated I was,
you deserve to have holes in your
heads.

11b

Take one bag of ammonium nit-ate
fertilizer + 1 gal of stove oil +
damp a few bags of gravel on
top + then set the shit off
+ will positivily ve-talate any
thing that should be in the way
of the Blast.

The death machione is allready
made. I would have sent you
pictures but you would be nasty
enough to trace them back to
developer + then to me, so I
shall describe my mastorpiece
to you. The nice part of it is
all the parts can be bought on
the open market with no quest
ions asked.

1 bat. pow clock – will run for
    aprox 1 year
1 photo electric switch
2 copper leaf springs
2 6V ca- bat
1 flash light bulb + reflector
1 mirror
2 18" # cardboard tubes black with
    shoe polich in side + oats

the system checks out from
one end to the other— in my
tests. What you do not know
is whether the death machiene
is at the sight or whether—
it is being stored in my
base ment for futare use.
I think you do not have the
man power to stop this one
by continually searching the
road sides looking for this
thing. + it wont do to re roat
& re schedule the busses bec
ause the bomb can be adapted
to new conditions.
Have fun !! By the way
it could be rather messy
if you try to bluff me.

PS. Be shure to
print the part I
marked out on
page 3 or I shall
do my thing ✆

11d

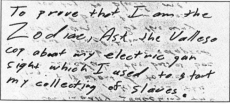

To prove that I am the
Zodiac, Ask the Vallejo
cop about my electric gun
sight which I used to start
my collecting of slaves.

11e

12. Front and back of the envelope to Zodiac's letter to the *San Francisco Chronicle*, April 20, 1970. *Collection of the author*

Editor
San Fran. Chronicle
San Francisco, Calif.

Editor

12

Editor
San Fran. Chronicle
San Fran. Calif.

13

13. Front of the overposted envelope to Zodiac's letter to the *Chronicle*, April 28, 1970. *Collection of the author*

S. F. Chronicle
San Fran.
Calif.

14

14. Single-stamped envelope to Zodiac's letter to the *San Francisco Chronicle*, June 26, 1970. *Collection of the author*

This is the Zodiac speaking

I have become very upset with the people of San Fran Bay Area. They have **not** complied with my wishes for them to wear some nice ⊕ buttons. I promiced to punish them if they did not comply, by anilating a full School Buss. But now school is out for the summer, so I punished them in an another way.

I shot a man sitting in a parked car with a .38.

⊕-12   SFPD-0

The Map coupled with this code will tell you who-e the bomb is set. You have until next Fall to dig it up. ⊕

C △ J I ■ ⊙ K λ A M ꓤ ▲ Ω O R T G
X ⊙ F D V ⳩ ◧ H C E L ⊕ P W △ .

15. Front of envelope and Zodiac's letter to the *San Francisco Chronicle*, sent on June 26, 1970, which contained the threat "to punish them if they did not comply by anilating a full school buss."

Collection of the author

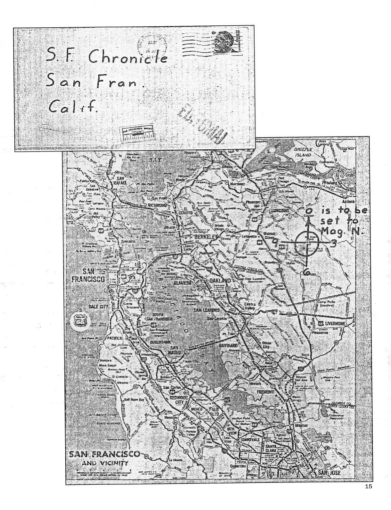

S.F. Chronicle
San Fran.
Calif.

O is to be
set to
Mag. N.
3

SAN FRANCISCO
AND VICINITY

15

This is the **Zodiac** speaking

I am rather unhappy because
you people will not wear some
nice ✠ buttons. So I now
have a little list, starting with
the Woeman + her baby that I
gave a rather intersting ride
fo- a coupple howers one
evening a few months back that
ended in my burning her
car where I found them.

San Francisco Chronicle 1970

16a. Zodiac letter to the *San Francisco Chronicle*, July 24, 1970.
Mailed in the afternoon. *Collection of the author*

S.F. Chronicle
San Fran. Calif

16b. Envelope to Zodiac's letter to the *San Francisco Chronicle*, July 24, 1970. *Collection of the author*

This is the Zodiac speaking

Being that you will not wear
some nice ♁ buttons, how about
wearing some nasty ♁ buttons.
Or any type of ♁ buttons that
you can think up. If you do
not wear any type of ♁
buttons I shall (on top of every
thing else) torture all 13
of my slaves that I have
wateing for me in Paradice.
Some I shall tie over ant hills
and watch them scream + twich
and sqwirm. Others shall have
pine splinters driven under their
nails + then burned. Others shall
be placed in cages + fed salt
beef untill they are gorged then
I shall listen to their pleass
for water and I shall laugh at
them. Others will hang by
their thumbs + barn in the
sun then I will rub them down
with deep heat to warm

17a

17a–17e. The rarest of all Zodiac letters—never before seen outside police headquar-
ters. I was fortunate to see the five-page letter when it arrived at the *Chronicle* on
July 26, 1970. Zodiac paraphrased Gilbert and Sullivan's *The Mikado* in the letter.
Only Zodiac's lengthy letter of November 9, 1969, contained more clues.

Collection of the author

them up. Others I shall
stin them alive + let them
run around screaming. And
all billiard players I shall
have them play in a dark
ened dangeon all with crooked
cues + Twisted Shoes.
Yes I shall have great
fun inflicting the most
deliceious of pain to my
Slaves

= 13

SFPD = 0

As some day it may hapen
that a victom must be found.
I've got a little list. I've
got a little list, of society
offenders who might well be
underground who would never
be missed who would never be
missed. There is the pest-
ulential nucences who whrite
for autographs, all people who
have flabby hands and irritating laughs. All children who
are up in dates and implore
you with im platt. All people
who are shakeing hands shake
hands like that. And all third
persons who with unspoiling,
take thoes who insist. They'd
none of them be missed. They'd
none of them be missed. There's
the banjo seranader and
the others of his race and
the piano orginast I got him
on the list. All people oho
eat pepermint and phomphit

in your face, they would
never be missed They would
never be missed And the
Idiout who phrases with in-
thusastic tone of centuries
but this and every country but
his own. And the lady from
the provences who dress like
a guy who doesn't cry and
the singurly abnomily the
girl who never kissed. I dont
think she would be missed
Im shure she wouldn't be
missed. And that nice impriest
that is rather rife the judic-
ial hammerest I've got him on
the list All funny fellows, com-
mic men and clowns of private
life. They'd none of them be
missed. They'd none of them be
missed. And uncompromising
kind such as wachamacallit,
thingmebob; and likewise; well
—nevermind; and tut tut tut tut,
and whatshisname, and you know

17d

who, but the task of filling up the blanks I rather leave up to you. But it really doesnt matter whom you place upon the list, for none of them be missed, none of them be missed.

PS. The Mt. Diablo Code concerns Radians + # inches along the radians

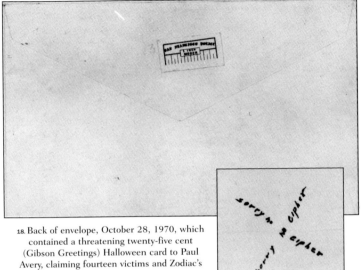

18. Back of envelope, October 28, 1970, which contained a threatening twenty-five cent (Gibson Greetings) Halloween card to Paul Avery, claiming fourteen victims and Zodiac's handwritten message "sorry no cypher."

Collection of the author

18

19. Zodiac's March 23, 1971, postcard to Paul Avery was done with brush lettering. He misspells his name here as "Averly," a common Zodiac touch.

Collection of the author

Editor —
Put Marco back in the Hell-hole from whence it came — he has a serious psychological disorder — always needs to feel superior. I suggest you refer him to a shrink. Meanwhile, cancel the Count Marco column. Since the Count can write anonymously, so can I —

the Red Phantom
(red with rage)

20a and 20b. Zodiac's letter to "Count Marco" Spinelli, July 8, 1974. *Collection of the author*

San Fran. Chronicle

Please Rush To Editor

20c. Envelope to Zodiac's *Exorcist* letter of January 29, 1974. *Collection of the author*

censed private detective. What he did not know was that the Zodiac case was *only half over*.

SUNDAY, JANUARY 19, 1986

"SOME of the Vallejo police agree with author Robert Graysmith, some do not," wrote reporter Gene Silverman on my just released book *Zodiac*: "Vallejo Police Department Detective Sergeant Jack Mulanax—who had inherited the Ferrin case from Sergeant John Lynch, differs from his predecessor on the inclusion of one of the killings. Mulanax believes the Lake Herman, Blue Rock Springs Park, Lake Berryessa and San Francisco taxicab attacks were all done by the same man, that the man was Zodiac, and this is the man [Leigh Allen] to whom Graysmith gave the name 'Starr.'"

"I don't think there is any doubt on those," said Mulanax. "Although I base my conclusions, at least in part, on a large amount of circumstantial evidence. We might find out when more people read this book. Graysmith did a good job and I agree with him. The book actually provided me with information. I didn't know what Napa police had. I wasn't contacted but two times by [Detective Sergeant Narlow].

"Graysmith mentioned the lack of information-trading among police departments as a problem," reported Silverman. "He said in his book, 'I thought to myself that Lynch had cleared Allen because he did not match Lynch's visual impression of the killer.' Lynch says this was true. 'From time to time your mind changes,' he says, 'but certain things stick, such as descriptions of the killer given by victims who either survived or survived long enough to talk.' Lynch also believed there was more than one killer.

"I believe that Zodiac is probably still alive," said Officer Richard Hoffman. "If he'd died there would be evidence found in a place where he lived. The coroner would have come into it. So I think he's still alive."

"Why, in that case, have the Zodiac-type crimes seemed to have stopped?" asked Silverman.

"I don't know he's not killing," Hoffman said. "One of his last correspondences said he wasn't going to talk about it anymore, take the credit for it anymore. This is Graysmith's opinion too."

Pam, Darlene Ferrin's sister, subject of threatening calls every

year on the anniversary of her sister's death, said, "Zodiac is definitely alive. I don't think he's doing any more killings. I think
when he saw the police getting closer, he stopped. I have read
Graysmith's book four times. This book has really jogged my
memory—so much. I'd read two pages and think and think."

WEDNESDAY, FEBRUARY 12, 1986

A twenty-year employee of the Sonoma Sheriff's Department,
retired now and staying at her mother's Vallejo home, wrote me.
"On your TV interview," she said, "you tied in the seven girls
who were found murdered in the Santa Rosa Area in 1972–73 to
the Zodiac killings. I found this interesting because the Sheriff's
Department in Sonoma County never did. I also agreed with you
that the different police agencies did not cooperate with one another or share any information that they might have that would tie
in with what another county might have had."

On August 25, 1976, while working in the coroner's office,
Sonoma County, she learned of a routine traffic accident fatality,
a head-on collision on Highway 12 between Santa Rosa and Sebastopol. The deceased was a forty-one-year-old heavyset male
school teacher. He had taught not only at Santa Rosa Junior College, which many of the victims attended, but Napa Junior College and other surrounding counties including San Quentin.

"I believe he had previously taught in Southern California,"
she elaborated, "but his only relatives lived in the East. Among
the possessions in his van were drawings of some of the seven
victims in the Santa Rosa area, which portrayed them in hog-tied
positions. Included with these drawings were their names and
sexual preferences. There was also a backpack belonging to one
of the victims. Since the sheriff is also the coroner, the deputy
turned over his findings to the Detective Bureau where it was
placed in evidence and the matter quickly dropped. The deputy
said, 'As long as he's dead, for his family's sake, there's no point
in ruining his reputation.' Besides, if they declared him dead and
a new lead came up across country, the detectives wouldn't get to
go on another trip."

She further explained that, as a general rule, the deceased's
belongings are usually itemized and released to the next of kin.

In this case, however, not everything was itemized, only what was in his pockets were returned to his relatives. "By now," she said, "the evidence has long been destroyed. When I left years ago, they were in the process of micro-filming the coroner files and then destroying the file itself. We always kept the driver's license along with a coroner photograph in the coroner's office. The file that was open to the general public at that time did not contain everything on file in the County Clerk's office. However, the County Clerk also wanted to get rid of Coroner files and about 1979 or '80 we discontinued filing them with the County Clerk. His fingerprints should be on file in Sacramento. . . . I think if he was really the Zodiac that he could also be tied into the Riverside murder because of his employment as a teacher down there."

She gave me his name and case file number. Was this the murderer of the young women who passed near Leigh Allen's trailer in Santa Rosa? Leigh had been a student at Santa Rosa Junior College. Could he have had a confederate all along, writing the letters for him, one that had died in a highway crash while he was in Atascadero and could write no letters exonerating him?

"When the teacher's widow was cataloging his property," a Santa Rosa investigator told me, "she came across drawings of people being whipped. The sketches suggested the husband had been involved in S & M. The instructor had drawn himself as a woman and labeled it with the female version of his own name. Chief Wayne Dunham felt the deceased man might have something to do with Kim Wendy Allen's death." Kim, a Santa Rosa Junior College student, had last been seen March 4, 1972, hitching north on 101.

"I've actually got a photocopy of two of the drawings they found," Sergeant Brown told me years later. "He drew Kim and he drew himself as 'Freda.' He drew this other girl and those two girls had classes with him. And he had this hair in his wallet. They tested it, but it wasn't Kim's. I don't think the teacher did it. Maybe, but I doubt it. I read his letters. One investigator thought that the teacher had this sex/slave thing going, whips and chains and all this weird stuff, and he was obsessed with big-breasted women. He probably taught Kim, and when she shows up dead, he became really obsessed with her. A weird dude."

WEDNESDAY, MAY 14, 1986

PIECES of the puzzle began to fall together for Sergeant John Burke of the Santa Rosa P.D. "We have a ten-man team who have been keeping a two-month surveillance on an individual," he told me. "Dave Legrow [a friend of Sheriff Butch Carlstedt] and Gary Crenshaw and I have been going through his file. He was booked at the jailhouse in 1975 and was wearing a Zodiac watch. He's six feet tall, 240 pounds. Born in Honolulu. I'll give you his name in a moment. . . ."

"You don't have to—he was born in 1933."

"Yes, Leigh Allen. It was the weight that threw us at first, but then last night I noticed that at the time of the killings this man weighed 180 pounds. What is unusual about this guy is that we have his 290 sex registrant file . . . these are broken up into an Alpha file and what we call the five-by-eight section, a list of I.D. characteristics. This is the first man I've ever seen to have both classifications. His registration is attached to his Alpha file. He gave his address here in Santa Rosa at his brother's. We might be able to get him for failing to report a move under the sex registration law. In the murders here in Santa Rosa there is something I think no one else knows. On all the bodies were found fibrous hairs. We found matching hairs in Allen's trunk in his car. You know what they were?"

"What?"

"Chipmunk hairs."

"Amazing."

"I know when I got off work last night—got home a little late at six o'clock—my wife was getting ready to go to work. She can't put on her makeup standing, so she sits on the countertop in the bathroom with her feet in the sink. When she heard what I said about chipmunk hairs, she fell off the counter. I had to catch her. Allen was using chipmunks to entice kids. Well, it's not over till the fat man sings."

THURSDAY, MAY 22, 1986

WITH the publication of what I had learned about Zodiac over a decade, an enthusiastic army of puzzle solvers were attracted to the hunt—my intention from the start. As time passed, police files, spread to the four winds, began to show up in the hands of novice detectives. Zodiac buffs dug them from garages and attics, lifted them from trash cans and closet shelves. Each day brought a final solution closer—that moment when someone, somewhere would recognize Zodiac. But after someone mailed me a bloodstained shirt like Stine's, I discovered I could no longer open a single letter. A *Times* interviewer thought I "appeared uncomfortable dredging up details" of Zodiac. I admitted to him I had not read a single one of the thousand letters I had received for fear of getting sucked into the case again. "I can't deal with it—it's hard to explain," I told him. "I don't want to get physically ill again. I can't do it. Not now."

Warily, I studied boxes of manila envelopes forwarded to me— a dozen or so letters packed inside each. I opened them finally, surprised that, with few exceptions, most were thoughtful, ingenious, even clever. This Thursday afternoon Leigh Allen had a minor auto accident. I had to wonder if he was cracking up because of new interest in unmasking Zodiac.

FRIDAY, AUGUST 8, 1986

TOSCHI, currently manager of nationwide Globe Security, received a State Senate commendation for long meritorious service. His joy was dampened when he learned Paul Stine's blood-blackened shirt had vanished from within the SFPD. Three months later to the day, someone got into the *Vallejo Times-Herald* and stole their entire Zodiac file. I recalled how Avery's Zodiac file had also been stolen from his car. I kept mine in the safekeeping vault at Bank of America.

THURSDAY, APRIL 16, 1987

ZODIAC might be powerful, intelligent, and extraordinarily deadly, but he had always lacked originality. From costume to weapons to motive to code symbols, he drew his persona from outside himself—mostly from films. Movie-mad to the extreme, he had thus far resisted demanding a movie about himself (though perhaps he had, anonymously). Two films had inspired his campaign of terror—the first and most influential movie suggested his entire method of operation. He had seen it at a formative time in his life.

19
ZODIAC'S "DANGEROUS GAME"

ZODIAC: HOODED, SECRETIVE, precise—with a predilection for bizarre handmade weapons and unbreakable ciphers. A scent of demonic possession and brimstone clung to Zodiac. Intelligent, compulsive, yet never original, he plagiarized his modus operandi from a watch face, short story, and film. In his deciphered three-part cryptogram he explained his primary motivation—an obsession with Richard Connell's thrilling adventure story "The Most Dangerous Game."

> "I LIKE KILLING PEOPLE BECAUSE IT IS SO MUCH FUN," Zodiac had written. "IT IS MORE FUN THAN KILLING WILD GAME IN THE FORREST BECAUSE MAN IS THE MOST DANGEROUS ANIMAL OF ALL TO KILL. . . ."

Leigh Allen freely admitted he loved Connell's short tale. "It was the best story I read in high school," he earnestly told detectives in that hot refinery office. Connell's story existed as book and film. Which influenced Zodiac—printed story or movie? Subtle differences indicated which. It was possible to learn when "a terrible thought crept like a snake" into Zodiac's brain. "The Most Dangerous Game," printed in *Variety* and published by Minton Balch & Company in 1924, won the O. Henry Memorial Award for that year. The printed version, included in adventure anthologies and high school texts ever since, goes like this:

Sanger Rainsford, a big-game hunter, falls overboard from his yacht. Stranded, he hears the report of a .22, and thinks the hunter must have nerve to tackle large wild game with so light a gun. He meets General Zaroff, a sadistic Russian expatriate sportsman. Zaroff (a name similar to Zodiac) hunts at night with different weapons to make the hunt more exciting. When

Rainsford says he considers the Cape buffalo the most danger-ous of all big game, Zaroff corrects him, "No. You are wrong, sir . . . here in my preserve on [Ship-Trap Island], I hunt the most dangerous game. . . . My hand was made for the trigger, my father said. . . . My whole life has been one prolonged hunt. . . . I enjoy the problems of the chase [so] I had to invent a new animal to hunt. I bought this island, built this house [an an-cient castle with towers and a gargoyle-shaped door knocker], and here I do my hunting." Surrounding are jungles with mazes of trails, hills, and swamps. "Every day I hunt, and I never grow bored now, for I have a quarry with which I can match my wits."

Zaroff's "most dangerous game" is people. He provides Rains-ford with three hours, head start and "an excellent hunting knife." He "cheerfully acknowledges" himself defeated if he doesn't find him by midnight of the third day. If Rainsford wins, the general's sloop will place him on the mainland. Armed only with a .22-caliber pistol and bow and arrow (Allen's hunting weapons), Zaroff pursues his quarry. On the first night Zaroff allows Rainsford to es-cape. Rainsford realizes he is saving him for another day's sport.

The final battle is played out in the mad hunter's bedroom. "You have won the game!" he says. "I am still a beast at bay." Rainsford cries, "Get ready, General Zaroff," and Zaroff is killed. But the written story lacked the costume and pursuit of a young couple by gun and knife that had inspired Zodiac. Zodiac's pri-mary motivation, that galvanizing flash point, was a film, but which one and in what year?

IN A CONVERSATION with his friend Phil Tucker, Allen spoke of a 1945 film, *A Game of Death*.[9] With its stalking by crossbow and Zodiac-like title, the film was likely an inspiration. General Kreigner's insanity is attributed to a wound from a Cape buffalo rather than a need to dispel boredom. Other adaptations of Con-nell's story followed.[10]

---

[9]RKO, *A Game of Death*, directed by Robert Wise, starring John Loder and Audrey Long. Edgar Barrier played the Zaroff character, General Kreigner.
[10]*Johnny Allegro* in 1946 used elements of the story. In 1956, *Run for the Sun*, starring Richard Widmark, Jane Greer, and Trevor Howard, was set on a jun-gle plantation rather than an island. In 1961 came *Bloodlust*, another varia-tion. Cornel Wilde's *The Naked Prey* showed five years later.

Because Willis O'Brien's animation of his giant ape, King Kong, took too many months to complete, producer Merian C. Cooper and directors Ernest B. Schoedsack and Irving Pichel decided to shoot a second movie employing *Kong*'s existing sets and much of its cast. RKO's sixty-three-minute-long black-and-white adaptation of *The Most Dangerous Game* was shot in 1932, a year after Allen's birth. Screenwriter James Ashmore Creelman, while retaining Connell's dialogue, introduced a sexual pathology to account for the cunning Count Zaroff's mania—hunting inflamed his other passions. The hunt as a precursor for sex had entered the equation. Bob Rainsford (Joel McCrea), an American big-game hunter returning from safari, swims to nearby Ship-Trap Island after fake channel lights lure his yacht onto a reef. Count Zaroff (Leslie Banks), archer, waltz composer, and self-confessed barbarian in evening dress, is the perfect host. Costar Fay Wray (Eve Trowbridge) recalled, ". . . the actor who played Count Zaroff with a jagged scar across his forehead had something wrong with one eye and it gave him a really scary expression." Banks's face presented two dramatically different profiles—the left brutish, the right handsome—the result of a serious wound the actor received during World War I. His Jekyll-Hyde quality depicted the schizophrenic qualities of a cultured man possessed by bestial desires. "God makes some men poets," Zaroff explains. "Some He makes kings, some beggars. Me, He made a hunter. . . .

> "One night as I lay in my tent with this—this head of mine, a terrible thought crept like a snake into my brain . . . hunting was beginning to bore me. When I lost my love of hunting, I lost my love of life, my love of love . . . what I needed was not a new weapon, but a new animal. . . . We barbarians know that it is after the chase and then only that man revels . . . you know the saying of the Ogandi chieftains—'Hunt first the enemy, then the woman.' It is the natural instinct. What is woman? Even such a woman as this until the blood is quickened by the kill . . . one passion builds upon another. Kill, then love. When you have known that, you have known ecstasy."

"Here on my island I hunt the most dangerous game," the count tells Rainsford and Eve. "We are going to play 'outdoor chess.' Your brain against mine—your woodcraft against mine. When I was only stirrup high [my father] gave me my first gun. . . . It would be impossible to tell you how many animals I have killed." Allen's father, a military man, gave his son a rifle and taught him to hunt, and Allen was the only Zodiac suspect who was an archer. The image that opens the film is a castle door knocker of a Dying Centaur, an arrow in his breast. A wall painting above the stairs depicts a similar maddened centaur, armed with a bow and arrow, carrying the body of a woman through the woods. The centaur is the astrological symbol for Sagittarius (November 22–December 21), Allen's own zodiac sign.

Zaroff, his Cossack henchman, Ivan, and a pack of hounds hunt Rainsford and Eve. In the film the hunt takes place in one night, not three, and a couple, not a single man, are hunted just as Zodiac hunted couples. If they elude Zaroff in the island's foggy jungle, they will be set free. With his Satanic black hunting outfit, folds gathered and cinched at wrists and ankles, Zaroff races swiftly through the fog behind a pack of hounds. In a sheath on his left side is a foot-long knife. The scabbard is decorated with rivets. In his right hand is a precision high-powered rifle. Pursued in the watery sections—a swamp, a waterfall, the couple finally reach the ocean's edge. The wounded count dies when he plunges over his balcony and is devoured by his own ravenous hounds as Rainsford and Eve escape by boat.

Because of the weapons (especially the bow and arrow), the costume, which so clearly inspired the outfit Zodiac wore at Lake Berryessa, the nighttime pursuit of a couple near water, the concept of outdoor chess, and the image of the Dying Centaur, I am inclined to think this particular film most influenced Zodiac. And it had played at the Avenue Theatre. "Those animals I hunted," says Rainsford, "now I know how they felt." With the lonely, unloved archer, the elite exile, Zodiac had found a resonance with his true life.

RADIO DRAMA, AT its zenith during Zodiac's youth, adapted Connell's tale. The most famous radio version appeared on CBS's *Suspense*, September 23, 1943. Its fifty-eighth show starred Orson Welles as Zaroff and Keenan Wynn as Rainsford. Jacques A. Finke wrote the script for producer-director William

Spier.[11] Augmented by sound effects, full orchestra, and the power of imagination, radio adaptations could be formidable influences. Allen, ten at the time of the broadcast, would have been lying in the darkness listening that Thursday night, lit only by the glow of the dial. The static of the broadcast filled the room. A formative age, ten.

"I don't remember which day we had discussed 'The Most Dangerous Game,' and hunting people," Cheney told me, "but somebody did a television presentation using that plot and I think that's what we discussed, that and the fact that there was a book. The plot has been used and used."

The inspiration for Zodiac's gun that projected a beam of light came from a television show adapted from a story by William C. Morrison. A 1950s *Alfred Hitchcock Presents* starring Myron McCormick featured a young man with a flashlight taped to his rifle. "Just shoot for the dark spot in the light and you will hit your target," he said—exactly as Zodiac wrote. Hunting small game at night, he chanced upon two lovers—result: accidental murder. A vengeful father says at the conclusion, eyes glittering: "The excitement of a manhunt—the most dangerous game!"

---

[11]Two years later, Finke's script was used again, this time starring J. Carrol Naish and Joseph Cotten. Two years after that, Les Crutchfield adapted the story as a thirty-minute program for producer-director Norman Macdonnell's *Escape*.

20
ARTHUR LEIGH ALLEN

ARTHUR Leigh Allen, in spite of financial problems, lacked the willpower to resist a new purchase. He bought a $2,500 foam, fiberglass ultra-light "aeroplane" with a folding-wing option. Likewise, he was compelled to heap on additional paraphernalia, and draw up blueprints for clever modifications. But his deteriorating vision drastically curtailed his active lifestyle. His flagging physical stamina, due to growing diabetes and kidney problems, anchored him close to Fresno Street.

"Kidney failure is a slow process," a nurse explained. "It's only imminent after years and years. You can have it most of your life, but it's only toward the end of the disease that you end up on dialysis. It depends how bad your hypertension is. Through the years the diabetes destroys the blood vessels, causes them to be less resilient, and so you get high blood pressure. Then the high blood pressure destroys the kidneys and you end up on dialysis. The vision goes.

"Naturally drinking is harmful. Your skin color has changed because your kidneys are not functioning properly. And so you look sallow. Dialysis is not painful, but it is debilitating. You will get very weak afterward, and usually not be good for anything the rest of that day. The treatment's for three hours, three times a week, for as long as you live. Sometimes it's longer for people who drink too much. If they're large individuals the time might be extended."

Against doctor's orders, Leigh guzzled beer from a quart jar, scanning the newspaper where conjectures about Zodiac's fate still raged. They were most plentiful on the anniversaries of the attacks, a day such as today. Explanations as to Zodiac's whereabouts ranged from imprisonment to death to police proximity so close Zodiac dared not act. Ill health had hardly been considered in the equation. Thus far, outside law enforcement, Allen's name had not been linked to Zodiac in print. No fraudulent informant could target Allen if he hadn't heard of him. But the prime suspect still flaunted his connection to the case—saving articles about Zodiac and perversely wearing the Zodiac watch and Z-emblem ring. It give him pleasure. Gradually, the genie emerged from the bottle. The leak came not from the media, but the local police department. A substitute teacher in Santa Rosa junior and senior high schools became concerned.

"My occupation has given me the opportunity to observe how local teenagers have reacted to your book about Zodiac," he informed me. "I've seen copies pulled out at free reading time in classrooms all over town, but I never had much interest in the subject until last spring when, at various times, I overheard students and staff members discussing the book. Apparently one of the students is the son of a local policeman, and word has gotten around that the man you call 'Starr' works at Friedman Brothers Hardware in south Santa Rosa. Some of the kids seem to know the man's real name, or think they do.

"This caused me to worry on two counts. First the man they think is 'Starr' may not be him, and an innocent man's reputation is being ground up in the rumor mill. Second, the man might really be Starr and he might really be the killer. This raises the unpleasant image of little bunches of junior high kids trooping through Friedman Brothers on safari following a dangerous paranoid. I'm sorry this sounds a bit negative. I thought your book was well done and I hope your work leads to the killer's capture."

Born in 1971, Harold Huffman's son hadn't been too familiar with the Zodiac case until his father began telling him about his old friend, Leigh Allen. "After my father spilled the beans," Rob wrote, "I read Robert Graysmith's *Zodiac*. . . . I scared myself to death. I knew exactly who 'Robert Hall "Bob" Starr' really was. After digesting this horrific realization, I would brag to my friends regarding all I had learned from *Zodiac* and my father's (and mother's) tales of Leigh's violent outbursts when they were young. I would make all the connections. I would, in turn, scare my friends to death—then break the ice by telling them how Leigh wanted to make raviolis for my father and I, but instead we went to IHOP. On other occasions my Dad would bring home oranges from Leigh's trees, and I would offer them to my friends.

Once digested, I'd reveal to my pals that they had just eaten Zodiac Killer oranges (and again they would be scared to death)."

"Craig,"[12] a young man, also learned of Allen through the Santa Rosa Police. In the late 1980s, he and his dad visited Allen's house on Fresno Street. Allen claimed he didn't know who had turned him in to the police. Craig told him it was Cheney. "I'm very disturbed at the thought of that," Leigh replied. "Don Cheney is capable of perpetuating these crimes and he even frightens me. Don has a terrible temper."

"He seemed to be speaking for Zodiac," Craig said later. "He claimed that he was the one who created the Zodiac codes, or at least the codes were inspired by him. He showed us his own code, which is the one he apparently showed Ron Allen's wife. He had others that were different from what Ron Allen's wife saw." Craig recognized a lot of the symbols as being Zodiac's. Allen told them that the Zodiac ciphers he had in his possession were the original work of a convicted murderer he had met at Atascadero. "It was while I was working there in the early sixties," he said. That much was true. "Yeah, Zodiac got this from this inmate and it inspired his ciphers."

"What do you mean?" asked Craig. "What do you mean? How do you know that unless you're Zodiac?"

Allen continued to draw suspicion to himself with such sly comments and appearances at crime scenes. And time was running out for the investigators—nineteen years had passed since Zodiac's last confirmed murder, thirteen years since his last letter. Would that unsolicited lead linking Leigh Allen to Zodiac ever come?

TUESDAY, OCTOBER 28, 1987

CLAIRVOYANT Joseph DeLouise claimed he'd been tuned into the hooded executioner's thoughts for nearly twenty years. He had once psychically envisioned a box in the Zodiac's possession and advised him to rid himself of it. I wondered if Leigh still had the mysterious gray box he allowed no one to open. DeLouise thought the killer might be a Scorpio or Aquarian because of the figures 11-2 and 2-11, which he kept receiving. Transmissions

---

[12]This name has been changed.

registered on DeLouise's mind: a white dog and horses, loneliness, and an intense hatred of the police.

The Chicago-based psychic, known as the "Prophet of Specifics" because of his accurate predictions, had recently had a second vision. "Zodiac is living near Berkeley," he said on Monday. "I recently got a call from a Bay Area woman who believed she was dating Zodiac. A few weeks after the woman called, I got an anonymous call. 'I'm back,' it said. The woman promised to call me back but never did. She may be dead. I see danger around her. I don't feel that she was putting me on. He's out there now. He's dating and he's killing, but he isn't taking credit anymore. What he's doing now is personal. He feels rejected by the women he's seeing. I think he'll call me soon. I can feel it." As if in response to the psychic's entreaties, a gloved hand dropped two letters into a San Francisco mailbox on the morning of October 28. Addressed to the *Chronicle* and *Vallejo Times-Herald,* both carried Zodiac's familiar salutation.

WEDNESDAY, OCTOBER 29, 1987

THE *Times-Herald* received its letter and passed it on to Fred Shirisago, who had it dusted for prints. "Our guy has never left a print in the past," he said. But the FBI had once gotten a print *similar* to the cab print on one letter. I asked Shirisago if he believed in the bloody print. "I don't know myself," he said. "There were some witnesses indicating that he wiped it all off." A handwriting expert analyzed the printing on the new letter immediately. The first three sentences read like the April 1978 letter. The text said:

> "Dear Editor This is the Zodiac speaking I am crack proof. Tell herb caen that I am still here. I have always been here. Tell the blue pigs if want me I will be out driving around on Halloween in my death machine looking for some Kiddies to run over Cars make nice weapons. . . . The pigs can catch me if they can find me out there. Just like in the movie: The car. Tell the kiddies watch before they cross the streets on halloween nite. Tell Tochi my new plans Yours truly: [Zodiac symbol] guess VPD-0"

Kim Kraus, a Vallejo mother of three, heard about the new letter. "One of the neighborhood boys actually brought a copy of the article down to our house and showed my children. It frightened them."

Darlene's former husband, Dean, had no comment, but his present wife, Kathie, did. "I'm just hoping this is all a hoax," she said, "but maybe if Zodiac surfaces—hopefully without hurting anyone—he might leave a new track that could lead to him being caught—and seeking help. I can't imagine somebody being quiet and staying back all this time if he were as batty as [Zodiac] was. A guy as cocky and conceited as him would have let it be known he was busy again."

"The only thing that would keep this guy back is the police being close," I told reporter Gene Silverman. "I think the police *are* close and I still believe they are going to solve this. From what I saw, the letter looked like bits and pieces of other Zodiac letters. There's nothing original about it. Zodiac always had a macabre bent to his writing, and I don't see it here. He misspelled Toschi, and I can't imagine him doing that. Zodiac, in his way, has a lot of respect for Toschi. But I understand the desire to see the real Zodiac surface. It would be one more chance for him to slip up. I'll be the first to say so—I think both letters are fakes."

"Until Zodiac is caught, this fear will always be hanging over the Ferrin family—over all of us in fact," said Carmela (Leigh) Keelen, owner of Carmela's Cafe. In 1969 she had owned Caesar's Italian Restaurant and employed Dean as a cook. "Every time I get a crank call, Zodiac crosses my mind." At mid-month, Darlene Ferrin's sister, Pam, had discovered a Zodiac symbol scrawled in blue felt-tip pen on her front door, and now a threat to Halloween trick-or-treaters was painted on the garage.

THURSDAY, OCTOBER 30, 1987

DOJ agreed. Captain Conway, relieved the letters were hoaxes, nonetheless put extra patrols on the streets Halloween Eve. Halloween was an important holiday for Zodiac. Vallejo's "Big Game" was traditionally held that day. Zodiac had mailed a threatening Halloween card, and often mentioned "game." Spirit Week for the Big Game included symbolic "burial" ceremonies of the Dr. James J. Hogan Senior High School's football team. Some of Zodiac's victims had been Hogan High students. Vallejo High students stood watch over a coffin that contained a "body" representing Hogan High.

Murder suspect Shawn Melton, a police groupie, confessed to police he was re-enacting a Zodiac murder when he strangled Jeremy Stoner. Melton's first contact with the police had been when he took the results of his own investigation of a Zodiac Vallejo murder to local detectives.

"Jim Lang, and Captain Conway and I met with Mike Nail," Bawart told me, "who was a D.A. then and is now a judge. There was a kind of infamous case from our county, a kid named Jeremy Stoner, a six-year-old, was abducted and ultimately found dead in the Delta. The responsible on that was a guy named Shawn Melton. Melton's father at one time alluded to the fact that Melton wrote letters to the newspaper [like Zodiac] and his terminology was somewhat similar to the Zodiac. Somebody came out with this hair-brained idea that he was the Zodiac. But he wasn't, I can assure you of that! We were meeting with the D.A. at that time to see if he would refile on Shawn Melton. There had been two trials on him and there had been two hung juries." Melton was eventually convicted. He was the first murderer inspired by Zodiac. To our horror, he would not be the last.

TUESDAY, NOVEMBER 17, 1987

"I found it difficult to believe that such a horrifying murderer as Zodiac has not yet been caught," a reader told me. "Your writings on Starr [my pseudonym for Allen] certainly convinced me he is Zodiac. I believe that if the police had searched Starr's mother's house and especially the basement they would have found all the evidence they could possibly have wanted. By this time, Starr has obviously hidden any evidence. He also figures prominently in my mind because Zodiac is obviously an intelligent man who uses deliberate misspellings to throw off the police. Did Starr have a habit of deliberately misspelling words?" A good idea. I checked. Remarkably, I discovered he did.

Some Zodiac ciphers had never been solved. Buffs had not given up trying to crack them. The eighteen characters at the end of Zodiac's three-part cryptogram attracted the most attention. Ruth Gerstankorn rearranged them to read something other than the anagram "Robert Emmett the Hippie" most had already discovered. She found "Before I meet eternity" and another possibility—"Before I meet them I pity them." Another reader said:

"The thing that chilled my blood was that one of the symbols used was a circle bisected by a cross, used in the plotting of what is known as a polar co-ordinate. My supposition is this, the last eighteen characters [BEORIETEMETHH-PITI] in the August '69 cipher is not a name, but more important a location that pinpoints the murderer's location. The letters are in actuality numbers laid out in algebraic fashion on a graph with the graph being laid out on a north-south to east-west grid on principle streets or landmarks in the San Francisco area, with random letters being inserted as a filler to make the line come out even in respect to characters per line. Done in mathematical fashion, the accuracy of this graph could easily pinpoint the location to a specific location in a specific room in a specific building.

"Another point—all eighteen characters are numbers and that both coordinates are followed by numerals after the decimal point. This type of mathematical plotting is widely used in mechanical engineering and would be used by anyone familiar with science. Since the leading suspects had been sailors at one time, the characters could stand for degrees of latitude and longitude. This can be used after compensating for deviation and variation on a magnetic compass to pinpoint a location to within sixty feet, plus or minus. I would, after translation, use an aircraft map of the area of summer 1969 vintage to plot the isogonic lines properly, inasmuch as the location of the earth's magnetic pole does change slightly from year to year. Latitude and longitude are customarily given as a series of numbers followed by a letter, in degrees minutes and seconds."

However, early on, cryptographer Henry Ephron reported to Sergeant Lynch that the eighteen characters were "symbolic dust tossed into the eyes of any would-be solver" to confuse and delay solution:

"No one recognized that these meaningless characters [nulls] are standard practice in cryptography to fill out empty space and equalize groups in size (in this case to fill out the space necessary with similar symbols in order to make the third part exactly the same size as the first two, a project obviously dear to the heart of Zodiac)." Ephron explained that repetitions of symbols, digraphs, and longer groups are the means by which ciphers are solved: "On the basis of frequency the value L should have had only two symbols, but because of the frequency of Ls in his message, he switched after the enciphering was begun to using the square both half-black and fully black, thus giving himself another symbol for L and for greater variety in the double L's he gave up the alternation regularity. But my first discovery on analysis was the identity of the two squares and B (all the symbols for L). Zodiac's symbol for A appears, seemingly by error, as S and S as A. More dust in the solver's eyes! There is no mistake there. He was trying to confuse the decipherer and he did."

Paul Avery still believed the eighteen characters stood for Robert Emmett.

"Everybody loves a good mystery," he said. "People track me down to talk about Zodiac. I'm deluged with phone calls and weird correspondence." "It's the stuff legends are made of," I replied. "In twenty years this case will be like Jack the Ripper. But sometimes I feel like I've created a monster by writing about it." "No," said Avery. "The real monster is Zodiac himself."

To those around him, Zodiac, a borderline psychotic, might appear as well controlled and calm, even reasonable. "He prefers the passiveness of pictures, TV, and the movies," Dr. Murray Miron wrote. "Zodiac would have spent much of his time in movie houses specializing in sado-masochist and occult eroticism." One particular movie had been set at the unique place where Allen's father worked, where Wing Walker shoes were sold, and where Leigh had spent time visiting and going to the movies. This second influential film inspired his letters. It would tell us more about Zodiac. It told us where he had been.

21
ZODIAC AT TREASURE ISLAND

STREETS NAMED STURGEON, courts named Halibut and Flounder intersected, and an Avenue of Palms buttressed the island's west side. An enclosure of tile and marble had once been the Fountain of Western Waters. It had cascaded before a seventy-foot-high terra-cotta-colored statue of the goddess Pacifica. Then, Treasure Island had been a city of light, floating upon the waves in the very climes where Robert Louis Stevenson once trod. It shimmered briefly at the end of the 1930s as a beacon of peace, flickered, and then went out. But for a while the night had been lit with pastel searchlights illuminating domes and towers; colored lights were reflected in still pools and sparkled in falling cascades.

Treasure Island began as a series of jagged surf-lashed shoals north of Yerba Buena Island. Prevailing summer winds from the Golden Gate forced workers to first construct a ten-story seawall. They massed thousands of tons of boulders to erect a barrier thirteen feet above sea level around a square-mile area. The resulting lagoon, a mile long and two-thirds of a mile wide, was then filled in with twenty million cubic yards of seafloor mud. A ramp soon connected Treasure Island with centrally located Yerba Buena Island and the Bay Bridge. Finally, San Francisco decided to hold its third world's fair on the man-made island.

The Golden Gate International Exposition of 1939–40 opened in February 1939. Under bright blue skies, visitors drove across the bridge or came by steam ferries to enter Aztec-Inca "Elephant Gates." The Exposition's features included Pacifica, her hands raised in benediction; the four-hundred-foot Tower of the Sun; and Benny Goodman's Swing music rocking an amusement zone packed with roller coasters, ferris wheels, and nude dancers. A few months afterward, Hitler invaded Poland, and France had fallen by the time the fair closed in September 1940. San Francisco abandoned all plans of converting Treasure Island into a city airport. After Pearl Harbor, the U.S. Navy transformed it into a Naval base, building upon the detonated fragments of Pacifica, converting the Hall of Western States to a barracks, and turning the riverboat *Delta Queen* into quarters and classrooms. They made the Food and Beverages Building the "world's biggest mess hall," altered the large hangarlike buildings behind the Administration Building, and modified the Exposition's three permanent buildings at the south end of the island.

After the war Naval Commander Ethan Allen was stationed at this first U.S. stop for Navy men returning at the rate of twelve thousand a day. In 1947, a fourteen-year-old Leigh Allen wandered the artificial island while his father worked. The Naval Station housed four commands: the Naval Receiving Station, Naval Schools Command, the Naval Station itself (which administered the island), and Western Sea Frontier Headquarters. Movies changed daily and cost only a quarter to see. "He used to watch movies at Treasure Island all the time," a friend of Leigh's confirmed. "My mom worked as a secretary on Treasure Island and she saw him there often and may have been his 'date' at the movies. *The Exorcist* was another favorite of his."

He saw a film about Treasure Island that became a last blueprint for Zodiac—the 1939 20th Century-Fox film *Charlie Chan at Treasure Island,* starring Sydney Toler. In the 1960s local KRON-TV screened its seventy-two-minute length cut to fifty-nine minutes. "Zodiac?" asks detective Charlie Chan (who is arriving in San Francisco by plane from Honolulu—Allen's birthplace). "Yeah, he's the big shot in the spook racket around here," says another passenger. Dr. Zodiac, a crooked medium dressed in black robes, uses his guise as psychic consultant to blackmail his clients. He answers the phone, "This is Zodiac speaking," carries an odd knife, and shoots a crossbow. One of his victims blockprints: "CAN'T ESCAPE ZODIAC—" Eve Cairo reads the minds of assembled suspects at a party and says, "Dr. Zodiac. I hear the name Dr. Zodiac in his thoughts. . . . I can't go on! I can't! I hear death among us! I'm frightened! There's evil here! Someone here is thinking murder!"

Zodiac, says Chan, is "not ordinary criminal. He is a man of great ego. Criminal egotist find pleasure in laughing at police." Chan uses the *San Francisco Chronicle* and its police reporter, Pete (Douglas Fowley), to try to trap Zodiac. "RHADINI CHAL-

LENGES DR. ZODIAC" appears on the front page. A dapper magician, Fred Rhadini (Cesar Romero), of the Temple of Magic on Treasure Island, joins forces with Chan to expose Zodiac. "I accept your challenge. . . ." Zodiac replies in a note pinned to a wall with a knife. In the end, Rhadini turns out to be Zodiac.

"Favorite pastime of man is fooling himself," Chan observes. "So far no one has collected [on the challenge], not even the great Dr. Zodiac." One bet you could be sure of winning was that Zodiac had seen this film and been inspired by it.

"*Charlie Chan at Treasure Island* was Leigh's favorite movie as a kid," his friend Jim told me, "and his dad worked on Treasure Island."

22
ARTHUR LEIGH ALLEN

ALLEN'S mother, Bernice, died at age eighty-three. "Mrs. Allen was dead by the time I got really involved in the case," Vallejo Detective George Bawart later told me. "For the longest time I was aware of Allen. As you know, the chief investigator on the Zodiac case until he retired was Mulanax. Then, when Mulanax left, they turned it pretty much over to me. During this span of time, even when Mulanax was working on it, different things would come in. I might be sitting at my desk and it would be something about the Zodiac. I'd either make a few calls or do what had to be done on it. Most of them were goofy things. I'd tell Mulanax, 'I took this call for you. I don't think it's anything but here's my report on it. Do what you want with it.' He would file it, but then after he retired I became the receptacle for all those kind of calls. I wasn't actively working the case at all. When your book came out our calls went up ten thousand percent.

"I have copies of [Allen's] handprinting done in the Santa Rosa trailer—where he wrote left-handed. Then I seized a whole bunch of writings he had at his house. Forms, letters to friends— the content of it wasn't anything germane to the case. It was casual handwriting he wouldn't be trying to disguise. It was actually his handwriting. We turned those over to our handwriting guy. He looked at it and said it's not the Zodiac's handwriting. That's our biggest stumbling block in that case. There's a theory that when he went into his Zodiac mode he had a split personality and became a different person."

One expert worried Zodiac might be schizophrenic, his Zodiac persona awakened, controlled, or influenced by the lunar cycles and planetary cycles. "What if he doesn't know he's Zodiac?" the man said. "There were long delays in those murders and letters," I told Bawart. "I always chalked it up to the fact that you got real close and Zodiac backed off."

"That's my theory too. They got real close and he said, 'Oh, oh, I better not do anything.' Also, there was a span of time when he was in Atascadero and there were no letters at all."

"What was important was that after Allen's questioning at the refinery, no letter ever again began, 'This is the Zodiac speaking.' From then on he signed them, 'Me,' 'A Citizen,' or 'The Red Phantom.' After Leigh went into Atascadero, Zodiac never wrote another letter. That's got to mean something."

The next day a woman contacted me. "This is a note that was left for me in a Lyons Restaurant in Antioch by an older man," she said. "He said he wanted to help me out with the Zodiac. The handwriting looks to me much like the Zodiac's. SFPD has it. I gave it to Inspector Deasy, along with a tape he left telling me he is my secret admirer." The message was in excellent Zodiac printing and suggested Zodiac had been a stalker:

"Sexual Sadist '61–'62 white chevorlet Impala Stocky man five-foot, ten-inches, paunch 220 pounds. Watched 2nd victim Vallejo-Darlene Ferrin."

FRIDAY, SEPTEMBER 1, 1989

BAWART retired from the Vallejo P.D., but was retained on a contract-type basis to follow up any new Zodiac leads that trickled in. A well-respected detective, he had been lead investigator on the 1989 Hunter Hill Rest Stop murders. "During the span of my career, I don't think the Zodiac is the most interesting," he told me. "Back in '79 a guy on the most-wanted list came to Vallejo, shot a grandmother in the head, and was going to kill a seven-year-old kid. I tracked him all over the United States. The one I'm thinking of is the Fisher Case. It was involved with a syndicate gang out of Kentucky. It was supposed to be the most corrupt city in the world. I went back there and worked with cops who made a thousand dollars a month and lived in mansions. You knew they were on the take. But they knew their business. It really had a twist in the end and if I were going to write a story, I would write a story about that."

WEDNESDAY, OCTOBER 11, 1989

TOSCHI had worked a variety of security jobs since his retirement—Mount Zion Hospital on Divisadero, St. Luke's Episcopal Hospital on Army. At work on October 11, he opened his morning paper to Herb Caen's column.

> "ANNIVERSARY: Today, retired police inspector Dave Toschi will drive to Washington and Cherry, park and observe a few minutes of silent contemplation. At that very corner on Oct. 11, 1969—20 years ago—the serial killer who called himself The Zodiac committed his last murder, shooting a Yellow Cab driver and disappearing into the Presidio, never to be seen again. . . . The Zodiac's last taunting letters to Toschi always ended with 'Me—37. S.F.P.D.—0.' A blowout."

Meanwhile, amateur detectives, undistracted by the grim procession of other murders that police faced, kept after Zodiac:

> "I hope that you have been curious as to who is writing these stories and lessons in deciphering the Zodiac code," a San Francisco man wrote. "First, I'd like every one to know there is a purpose for my writing in this way. I know that there is a God, and he chooses me to do his work. The Zodiac Crimes are not just another mass murderer gone bezerk, and on rampage, no, everything about his murders suggests someone who has planned every detail carefully, step by step. In every communication, he has displayed a clever, even satirical style of writing. This would seem that someone of extraordinary intelligence is committing the murders."

After twenty years some of that confusion was about to be dispelled.

THURSDAY, NOVEMBER 30, 1989

"I wonder if you ever heard of the name Arthur Leigh Allen?" City Hall reporter Bob Popp asked me.

"Yeah, sure. What happened?"

"Nothing, except there's a woman who called in yesterday. She's the daughter of a woman who started to talk to you several years ago and then got panicked and hung up. Scared. But now the daughter wants you to know that the mother is willing to talk about an Arthur Leigh Allen. And that name kind of rang a bell with me a little bit. She wanted to know how to get in touch with you."

"I wouldn't mind hearing from her," I said.

"Where do I remember that name from? He lived up north, didn't he?"

"Right. A scary guy."

"That's what she said. She sounded lucid."

Karen Harris called. "I've waited I guess years to contact you," she said. "Partly because my mother's so afraid of anyone finding out about it. She's very afraid of this person. My mother knew the district attorney in Santa Rosa, John Hawkes. I grew up with his children. He said, 'Yes, that is the man we're watching.' I can understand your curiosity in wanting to solve it. I'd like to find out as much information as I can to give you without letting my mother know. She never really knew anything about him until he was arrested for molesting a young boy who was the son of a friend of his, a woman.

"Then, while he was in Atascadero, he did write to us and say, 'They suspect me of being the Zodiac killer.' I remembered he looked like Burl Ives to me. Just last weekend, over Thanksgiving, I did drive by his house. I heard he had been working at Ace Hardware but had lost his job. I don't think he's working now. I had been to his house as a child (I was an only child) when I was about seven. I remember him drinking the big bottles of beer. My mother was concerned because he was diabetic.

"He lived with a roommate for a while in Vallejo—an Oriental man. I remember feeling more uneasy about him than Leigh Allen. He was of medium build and busy doing small household chores. Based on some written notes by my mother, I think [the roommate] worked for the phone company. . . . And I'm not sure if we were at [Leigh Allen's] mother's house or some other location. I remember him cooking a large pot of chili and we ate that while we were there. We went sailing with him on a catamaran. He does know how to make sails and all that stuff.

"Your book is at home. Mother has all kinds of notes in it of every instance where she remembers incidents. He had the Wing Walker boots—the whole bit. She knew Leigh throughout the time he was in the Navy. The only writing sample she has is from a yearbook and that's the only sample I could get hold of. He was a teacher at an elementary school.

"My mother called you once and hung up. She got scared and didn't want to give her name. But I want to see him again for some reason. I want to watch him."

"You be very careful," I cautioned. "It's a very hypnotic, obsessive, and all-consuming project. That case just eats at you. It just doesn't let go."

"My mother is terrified of this man. He drives by her house sometimes."

"Recently?"

"Probably around the time he got out of Atascadero. She got an alarm system in the house. He still has the Karmann Ghia and a Skylark over by the house in the back of the driveway. They're watching him again according to the sheriff's department. My parents know someone who works there—he's a deputy. Two fourteen-year-old girls have disappeared and now they're watching him again. If he's the one . . . Oh, why can't they catch him? I wish they could catch him.

"Leigh used to write to my mother with these Navy flag semaphore symbols. And she threw all that stuff away—I'd show you, but if my mother were to find out . . . He looks pretty much how I remember him looking. I went by to try and see him from a distance. But he would recognize me. I'm thirty years old, but when I was a child my face looked the same. I look like my mother. I thought for a moment, 'Oh, no. He sees me!'

"During the holidays, such as last Thanksgiving, my mother was very nervous for fear that Leigh was in the area visiting his brother. He used to drive by my parents' home and stop and stare in the windows from the street. That's when my mother put in an alarm system in their home. . . . She was always extremely protective, especially when she began to hear from Leigh Allen again while he was in Atascadero. She used to get mysterious phone [hangup] calls so she got an unlisted number.

"While I was home over last Thanksgiving, my mother brought out your book with all kinds of papers in it. She pulled out an auto accident report that Leigh had recently gotten into. He hit some woman in her car . . . [in Mendocino] the accident was his fault and he had a suspended license. [He was not fined, but his State Farm premium was substantially increased.] As I said, I drove by his house in Vallejo the day after Thanksgiving. It was daytime, but the house was dark inside. Only in one brief moment did I think I saw a figure move by the window, but it could have been my eyes playing tricks on me.

"There were a couple of times my parents would see Leigh Allen walking long distances down roads in the Bay Area. They would offer him a ride, but he would always refuse. There was one point in time, either when my mother had just gotten married or when she had visited him alone, that he said, 'I'll never forgive you for what you did.' My mother told me, 'I was too afraid to ask him what.' She let it drop and never pursued what it was. She had never threatened to turn him in or anything like that. I believe he's homosexual, so I don't know if it's because she married my father. I don't think so. That's always puzzled my mother. However, I think Leigh always cared for her a great deal."

"It's an 'outdoor chess match' between an intelligent sociopath and the police," I told her. "I always hoped that someone would be reading my book, bells would go off, and we'd get that name. I was at a dinner party with some professors Sunday and I said, 'Someday somebody is going to call with that name—out of 2500 suspects, the name that I'm waiting for will come. And here's that call."

"I've waited ever since your book first came out. I tried to get ahold of you once, but you'd quit the *Chronicle*. The Vallejo Police Department told me they bought fifty copies of your book to use as their case file. They gave all the policemen a copy to bone up on the case. You found a lot of information for them."

"I found it all over the state. I was at the *Chronicle* one day when they were remodeling. They lifted this box up. It was just about to go down one of the chutes out the window. It was full of Zodiac stuff. I've had that kind of luck all the way through. As for Leigh, I think as long as he is being watched by the police you should just keep your distance."

"But when I go by his house, I don't see anybody watching him."

"The important thing is that he thinks he's being watched."

"When the kids at Blue Rock Springs were shot," she asked, "did Allen use diving as an excuse, an alibi?"

"Yes. Allen was the first or second suspect they came up with—a major player right from the very beginning. Lynch took

Allen's alibi at face value: 'Where were you at the time of the murder?' asks Lynch. 'I was scuba diving,' says Allen. 'Can you prove it?' asks Lynch. And Allen goes over to the back of his station wagon and points to the tanks. And Lynch says, 'Fine.' Thereafter, every time Allen's name came up, Lynch would say, 'I cleared him.' Leigh's a formidable guy. He's no dummy."

"Allen's very intelligent. And an excellent marksman."

"How do you know that?"

"My mother knew him all through the Navy. My mother's father worked at Mare Island and she used to go to Allen's house all the time. His mother was very domineering, very formal. But my mother always liked it there, because she grew up in a very poor family and she loved going to his house because everything was so nice. And she used to like Leigh Allen. I don't know what happened. My mother will tell me if I ask questions innocently. I'll try and find out more. This case has fascinated me forever. I guess some of it is curiosity, but I would like to see if he's the one and can be brought to justice. He's never admitted to my mother that he was the Zodiac killer, but kind of closely hinted. God, I wish she had kept the letters he wrote her. But she burned them. She got so scared one day, she said, 'I threw them in the fireplace. . . . ' And where is Zodiac now? Don't serial killers usually want notoriety? That's what puzzles me.

"I don't think of him as dangerous now—heavy and losing his sight. And I recall Leigh was so good with children," she said.

"Don't be fooled. I covered the 'Trailside Murder Case' in San Diego. David Carpenter was such a confidence man—he looked like somebody's grandfather—he stuttered—wore thick glasses—it allowed him to manipulate his victims, to play on their sympathies. That's the way a lot of them work."

"I drive by his house," she concluded. "It's very enticing. I just want to watch him. Next time we speak, I'll tell you how he and my mother met and more about his letters."

23

ARTHUR LEIGH ALLEN

"A friend of mine runs a DNA lab," said a close friend of Cheri Jo Bates. "He says that technology is a year or so away from being able to match a hair sample that has been stored away for over twenty years. I do not know how, and if, the hair that was found was stored, but this could be the key to solve her murder." Bud Goding, another reader, echoed her sentiment. "Your report on the Riverside murder stated that traces of skin and tissue were removed from beneath the victim's fingernails," he told me. "Since that case is still open, that evidence should still be available. If it has not been preserved in formalin, it should be enough to perform DNA replication analysis (PCR) and provide a DNA profile of the Riverside killer." However, in order to provide a DNA profile, the follicle of the hair, the root, must be present.

A decade later, the Riverside suspect returned briefly from out of the country. Police got a DNA sample as he touched down at the airport. "The hair is a long shot," said a spokesman, "because we're not sure whether that was the suspect's hair or not." In December 2000, an astounding thirty-five years after Bates's murder, they got results of a DNA analysis from the Department of Justice DNA Lab in Berkeley. The hair was not their suspect's.

Had Zodiac committed the Bates murder? As at Lake Berryessa and Gaviota Beach, the overkill had been horrendous. But there were perceptible sexual undertones—Bates's clothes had been disarranged. If Zodiac was not the killer and had simply taken responsibility in a "confession" letter, how had he known facts "only the killer could know"? "The big thing in Riverside back in 1966," a source explained, "was drag racing. I used to go drag racing every week and since a lot of cops took part, I found out a lot of details about Bates's murder. Leigh Allen was down that weekend for some sort of auto club. Maybe he was there with his little car and heard some of these same details that I did. Who knows?"

MONDAY, MARCH 5, 1990

LEIGH Allen, doing some writing of his own, sent a letter to the young son of a friend. He dated it military-style "5/mar/1990." He said:

"Dear————: Yer mean ol' dad has been keeping me informed of your progress. congratulations on all the neat things you've accomplished. And I have another accomplishment for you—a gift horse, so to speak. Namely I am *giving* you a foam Fiberglass ultra-light. I am been squeezed into a smaller area, due to having to rent out the upper part of my house, and simply must have the space. So, if you can come up with a U-haul or such, you may haul away a ($2,500 invested) aeroplane for free. I will include a slug of associated paraphernalia.

"I have mentioned this to yer dad and he said he'd pass along the infor. He seemed to approve but sometimes he forgets, hence this letter. So if you can inform *me* as to your interest, I would appreciate it. I'll have to move on it very soon. I have all the paper on the plane, and there is a folding wing option. I also have some ideas on finishing it. You can't live with a project all the time I have without getting a few ideas. Hope to hear from you soon.

"Leigh Allen."

TUESDAY, MARCH 6, 1990

KAREN and I finally spoke again. She was very fearful. First she laid out a little family history—her grandparents had come to Vallejo during the Depression and endured "some tough times." Her grandfather worked as a ship welder on Mare Island, while her grandmother drove a school bus. I recalled Zodiac's vendetta against school buses. Bobbie, Karen's mother, was a diver whose picture often appeared in the Vallejo sports section between 1952 and 1957. Sometimes Allen's picture ran alongside hers. "My mother met Allen when she was about twelve or thirteen," said Karen, "when she had first begun diving. He served as a lifeguard at The Plunge, a Vallejo community swimming center, in 1951–52. I think he was a platform diver and a wrestler. She dove with Leigh and trained daily. She almost made the Olympics in Helsinki, almost a runner-up, but she dove out of order and lost the chance. He dove as well. He had that lumbering walk, very clumsy walk when walking down the diving board. My mother always talked about that. When he was a diver, he looked terrible until he left the board and dove. Then he was very graceful in the air. But when walking he was terribly lumbering because of a funny hip. I'll try and get a picture of Leigh from his diving days in Vallejo.

"She started dating him when she was about twelve. He was always a good friend. He never attempted to kiss her—a kiss-on-the-forehead kind of thing, and never made any sexual advances. I do know that while 'dating' him, it was more of a very deep friendship. [Allen admitted that he had never had a successful relationship with a woman.] Bobbie married Mark, a gymnast for the University of California at Berkeley, in 1957 and her diving trailed off. They met while they were both practicing on a trampoline. Mark studied criminology and wanted to be a policeman, but was just a quarter inch too short. Toward the time she met my father and married him, Leigh Allen was rejected by the Navy, a deep blow to him.

"*Leigh Allen definitely always wore the Wing Walker shoes.* He did wear pleated pants all the time. He was very clean cut. He used to use a bow and arrow for hunting, and was also an excellent marksman in the Navy, one of the best in his group. My mother said he did know code. He not only sewed well, but was a sail maker. He was definitely ambidextrous as I've watched him make fishing flies. He was a good typist too.

"Another time we visited him, he took us sailing on his Hobie Cat in Half Moon Bay. Both times I noticed how overweight he was. I knew he was a diabetic, yet he drank beer heavily out of large bottles. Both times [we visited], my mother was very tense. I was born in 1959 and when we visited Leigh, I think I was around nine or ten. If so, this was during the time he may have been allegedly murdering people.

"My mother visited him alone. It was the first time she did

feel some fear for her life because he asked her, 'Does anyone know you're here?' She answered, 'Yes. My husband, knows I'm here.' She told him my father knew, which he did. And then nothing happened. But after that she never went back. And I don't know why she went to see him in the first place. I just wish I knew why she had such concern about Leigh at the time. Something was going on and she felt she had to see him." She called my father the moment she left his house so that he knew she had gotten out safely and was on her way home.

"As I understand his incarceration at Atascadero, it was for molesting the son of a female friend of his. The boy was maybe anywhere from eight to thirteen years old. He told my mother the woman was just jealous of his relationship with her son. I believe he was dating the woman. He said that was why she had turned him in—jealousy. I think he spent about three years in Atascadero.

"While in Atascadero, I think that's when my mother first became aware he may be the Zodiac. He wrote to her that they suspected him of the crimes. At one point, I think my mother called him there and spoke to him. She asked him directly if he was the the murderer. I believe he was somewhat jovial about it, but never admitted to the crimes. He [Allen] often wrote to my mother and used the signals used by the Navy [semaphore] flags at the bottom of the letters. The notes he wrote her were done in blue-ink-type pens—felt-tip pens. She threw away most of the early letters. I wish she had kept them. She burned the rest after her knowledge of Allen being sent to Atascadero. My mother also told me after reading your book, that it fit that his brother and sister-in-law did try to turn him in. There was a bloody knife in his car and that's what really got them concerned—that's what I was told. Some of Leigh's friends were also aware of what was going on.

"I will continue giving you any information I can get. I want to try and get definite dates or general times of certain situations and find out more details of his relationship with family members and my mother. I wish I could get my mother to come forward to the police, but it's doubtful. But maybe she remembers more about the letters he wrote to her. Something that points to him as the responsible party. He told my mother he always picked up hitchhikers especially while attending Santa Rosa J.C. and Sonoma State University. This always bothered her. He picked them up on the highways. I remember the two girls disappearing from the skating rink and the other murders. Those bodies discovered on Franz Valley Road and in Calistoga weren't far from my parents' home.

"Oh, and another thing. He always did talk about 'The Most Dangerous Game' to my mother. In fact I have read the story as a young girl, never realizing that this was a big part of Leigh's life. As for a possible hiding place of evidence, my mom mentions that Allen put up paneling in his trailer—it must have been the Vallejo one or Santa Rosa one. My mother notes she saw white gloves in his trailer in Vallejo and that he did have *another* trailer in Bodega Bay, an area he knew well."

Toschi and Armstrong had never been told that.

MONDAY, APRIL 2, 1990

Two Bernal Heights gardeners digging at 1114 Powhattan Avenue struck metal about six inches down. They unearthed a rusty metal box and pried it open with their shovels. Inside were two hundred sticks of crystallized dynamite that had been buried for years. The SFPD transported the explosive to an isolated site and safely detonated it. Had Zodiac's stash for his threatened bomb projects been discovered at an address he had once had some connection with? I doubted it. But somewhere, Zodiac still had bombs. One day, he's going to die and the police will go through the basement and find guns and bombs—and the case will be solved. Perhaps one person wrote the Zodiac letters and one person killed—only a slim possibility. Zodiac seemingly acted alone at Berryessa. As far as police could tell, one man, the killer, had written in felt-tip pen on the door of his victim's car and that printing matched Zodiac's.

SUNDAY, APRIL 1, 1990

"**You** wanted to know *who* he was," another Zodiac buff, Daniel L. Kleinfeld, offered. I wanted to know *why* he was.

"Zodiac's mother was very protective . . . affectionate, but extremely moralizing. His father—more passive did not have a

great deal of contact with him. To show affection the mother
fed him copious amounts and the stocky child became fat, tor-
mented by classmates. In adolescence he became suffocated
by his mother, unable to break away. He would continue living with her. Condemned by his mother as evil, he grew to
hate her. His feelings of superiority over his peers intensified.
He is a military fetishist, like those who impersonate police
officers or soldiers. Zodiac was raised with a very clear sense
of justice, of righteousness prevailing. Thus he came to his
'slaves' concept. To him, the way his peers treated him was a
grave injustice, which could only be repaid by them doing
him service in 'Paradice'—an afterlife with slaves is always,
to Zodiac, a paradise. He gained a great deal of weight between the shootings on July 4 and stabbings on September 27.
He ate, then murdered. Then ate more."

ZODIAC'S IMAGINATION WAS a slave to popular culture. All the
pieces of the Zodiac persona had been fitted together on the public stage. One incredible inspiration to him—beginning August
16, 1969 (two weeks *after* the Cipher Slayer christened himself
Zodiac), Dick Tracy began pursuing the "Zodiac Gang" on the
comics page. The Zodiacs, in black hoods emblazoned with
white symbols of the zodiac, had drowned an astrology columnist. Tattooed across the face of their leader, Scorpio, was an astrological symbol of Scorpio. Light-haired and moonfaced, he
not only resembled the prime suspect, but a description of Zodiac
as "very round-faced . . . hair combed up in a pompadour." On
August 20, the Zodiacs raid the police morgue. "Masked torpe-
does came in," says the bludgeoned attendant, "demanded the
corpse's shirt." Later Zodiac would steal a victim's shirt and mail
portions to the police. The gang is told, on September 24, "Scorpio has spoken. He is ready for operation west branch." Three
days later Zodiac stabbed two students at Lake Berryessa while
wearing a black hood with a white symbol. "The 'Zodiacs' have
done it again!" Scorpio crows. The day of Stine's murder, October 11, Scorpio drunkenly toasts his success. "To jolly li'l old
us— T' jolly li'l old Zodiac gang." The story line ended November 4, 1969.

But how could Zodiac have seen Dick Tracy's encounter with
a Zodiac criminal before publication? Chester Gould drew *Tracy*
six weeks in advance to allow time for the *Chicago Tribune* Syn-

dicate to make changes and mail proofs to subscribing papers to size, retouch, engrave in metal, and print. Pre-printed color Sunday sections with the same storyline were delivered weeks before that. If Zodiac worked at the *Chronicle* then he might have had an advance look. He was a long time reader of the strip—"The Purple Cross Gang" in a 1936 sequence wore black hoods with white crosses on them. Like Tracy, Zodiac used the archaic spelling, "clews."

More importantly, *Dick Tracy* provided Zodiac with a way to avoid leaving prints. "Put a coating of this liquid cellophane on your fingers," says a gangster. "It prevents fingerprints and it don't clutter up your sense of touch either." On February 9, 1969 Tracy explained blood type analysis on a toothpick left at a crime scene. "As you know, salivary secretion often is used in place of blood for type determination. Your subject had a blood type AB." Though DNA testing had not been introduced, there was a primative version—ABO-PGM testing. Saliva could speak volumes about Zodiac and he knew that. Even in 1969, Zodiac would no more have licked a stamp than he would have forgotten to wear his gloves.

A comic strip and Zodiac watch had provided his name and symbol. Movies such as *The Most Dangerous Game* and *Charlie Chan at Treasure Island* had inspired and influenced him. One prompted him to hunt humans, the other, set on Treasure Island, provided the black hood and salutation for his letters, even inspired Zodiac's duel by mail with the *Chronicle*. But if Zodiac could be motivated by popular culture, others could be influenced by Zodiac himself. It was the most shocking by-product of the entire case. Someone claiming to be the San Francisco Zodiac Killer was shooting people in New York City. Somehow he knew their birth dates and promised one victim for each of the twelve Zodiac signs. We feared it was the original Zodiac, returned at last with guns blazing.

24
ZODIAC II

BOLD HEADLINES SAID it all in the summer of 1990: "GUN-MAN TERRORIZES NEW YORK—CALLS SELF ZODIAC. SHOT 3 MEN, ONE FATALLY, WOUNDED A FOURTH IN CENTRAL PARK." Zodiac was shooting people in an eight-block section of Brooklyn and in Central Park on Thursdays at twenty-one-day intervals.

"When I was a detective sergeant," Mike Ciravolo told me, "I ran the Zodiac case here. At that time they gave me and my forty-nine detectives the Brooklyn Navy Yard. Let me tell you how the case developed. But before I go into detail—when we were working on our case you know what we did? We went out and bought a case of your book, *Zodiac*. I had all my detectives read it to see if they could cull anything that might be of help in our investigation.

"Let me go into 1990 for you. At that time I was a command-ing officer of the crimes-against-senior-citizens squad in Queens. I had a small unit—eight detectives on the beat. I came in at seven o'clock one morning. A detective [Andy Cardimone] from night watch (which works out of the Queens homicide squad right down the hall from us) came up and says, 'Sarge, we had a shooting of a seventy-eight-year-old man last night and he's ex-pected to live. You gonna take the case?'

" 'Sure, we'll take the case,' I said.

" 'Something funny,' he says. 'I found this note on the step and it had these rocks.' He hands me the fuckin' rocks—three stones. 'This note was next to it.' It was the first Zodiac note we became aware of. It said: 'This is the Zodiac the twelve sign Will die when the belts in the heaven are seen.' It had a round circle with three pie shapes in it and a little scribble. We didn't really know what it meant at the time." The killer had followed the victim, Joseph Proce, a retired ice delivery worker, for ten blocks and into his front yard. He asked the old man for water and if he could go inside. "Why do you want to go inside?" Proce asked. "Because I'm cold," he said, then shot Proce with a homemade zip gun and ran toward Eldert Street.

"So when we get to the scene that morning," continued Ciravolo, "uniform officers and the detectives who worked the midnight-to-eight shift have responded. There were some clothes in a heap on the first stoop—this brown stuff where Joseph Proce was shot in the back, and I told Detective Bill Clark, 'Billy, check those clothes over there.' As he's going through he says, 'Sarge, a round just fell out.' 'Let's get it to the lab,' I said. We canvassed the block. It was a very residential block [87th Road in Woodhaven, Queens], and we came up with a witness who saw a guy in an Army fatigue jacket—the witness believed him to be black— running down the block towards Brooklyn. That street sat right on the Brooklyn-Queens border." In California Zodiac killed on town borders in an effort to create confusion and competition between authorities over jurisdiction. "So the old man was taken to the hospital. He was expected to survive. I kept sending detectives back there every day to interview him."

The New York Zodiac murders occurred at the height of the crack wars in East New York, and the 75th Precinct, where two of the victims were shot, averaged a hundred murders annually. Ciravolo continued. "Zodiac said, 'All shoot in Brooklyn,' in some of his subsequent notes. He also used to write '380' or '9m' [nine-millimeter], 'RNL' [round-nosed lead], 'no grooves on bullet—no grooves on bullet—' By the way, there was never any grooves on the bullet. Zodiac never, ever lied about what he said in any of his letters."

"Was he making his own ammunition?" I asked.

"No, he wasn't, but I feel he may have made his own gun." A zip gun, made of duct tape, wood, and pipes of various sizes for different calibers. Ciravolo laid out this chronology for me: "This attack on Proce happened on May 31. So now what happens—I take a copy of this note and I go to Chief Menkin, Chief of Detectives for Queens. 'Chief,' I say, 'I had a strange shooting last night—one of my senior citizens got shot. I think we're going to be able to interview him when he gets off the respirator.' (But he ultimately died three weeks later from infection from the bullet. But we did interview him.) I said, 'I think we got a nut going around here. I hope we don't have a second Son of Sam.'

" 'Well, keep me posted on this,' the chief said. That was May 31. On June 19, I get a call from the *New York Post* that a reporter [Anne Murray] got a letter sent down there. They faxed me a copy. It's our guy—it's obviously the same handwriting—claiming responsibility for three prior shootings. He says he shot a man with a cane in the street on March 8." At 1:45 A.M., Mario Orosco, forty-nine, an immigrant from Medellin, Colombia, finished work at a midtown cafeteria, and left the J train at Crescent Street. He paused at the corner of Atlantic and Sheridan Avenues and noticed a man in a beret and bandana, dressed all in black, walking behind him. He was holding a homemade nine-millimeter gun. Alarmed, Orosco began hobbling away on his cane, but was shot in the upper back.

"Then," Ciravolo went on, "Zodiac says he shot another man [Jermaine Montenesdro, thirty-four] in his left side in front of his house [at Nichols and Jamaica Avenues in Queens] on March 29 [at 2:57 A.M.]. Then he said he shot an old man with a cane on May 31—which matches my case, the Proce shooting. Then he says, 'All shoot in Brooklyn.' So I said, 'He was wrong about my guy being in Brooklyn. He didn't know the way the map gets a little crazy right on the border. Obviously, when he shot this guy in Queens, he thought it was in Brooklyn, but he was about two hundred yards out of Brooklyn on the Queens side. We started checking all the homicides in Brooklyn. None of them matched up. Then we checked all the first-degree assaults—and boom! We got two guys who were shot and they *survived*. So we looked into these, and the next morning the Chief of Detectives summoned us all down to his office and he decided to give me the case with nine detectives to look into this.

"I'd stayed up all night along with a couple of other detectives and we had come up with a theory. 'Look,' I said, 'he shot March 8, then he shot again March 29. Twenty-one days apart, all on a Thursday, by the way—and all in the early morning hours—between 1:45 and 4;00 A.M. So there was twenty-one days in between the first and second shooting. Then sixty-three days in between my old man getting shot—which is three intervals of twenty-one.' "

The New York Zodiac wrote notes taunting the task force, which ultimately numbered fifty men. He vowed to kill one person born under each of the twelve astrological signs. So far he had shot a Scorpio (Orosco, born October 26, 1940), a Gemini (Montenes-dro, born May 28, 1956), and a Taurus (Proce, born May 20, 1912). "So now here we are," Ciravolo proceeded, "sitting in the Chief of Detectives' office on June 20. I said, 'Chief, I think he's going to shoot again. Tonight, after midnight is Thursday and it's twenty-one days since my old man got shot.' So he gives me thirty detectives and everybody only gets two square blocks—'cause all of the shootings are within half a mile of each other. We got the streets blanketed and then all of a sudden—six o'-clock in the morning, I call off the detail and I'm back at the station house. I'm signing everybody's overtime slips and I get a call. He saw us in the neighborhood and jumped on the train." On the nights of the Zodiac's first three attacks, three star clusters—Orion, Taurus, and Pleiades—were all visible. The three would all be seen again on June 21, 1990. The police waited, dreading the outcome.

THURSDAY, JUNE 21, 1990

ZODIAC struck in Manhattan on the first day of summer. The heat was on in Brooklyn. To dodge the tightening police net, he took the subway to 59th Street and went to Central Park about 7:00 P.M. It would be quiet there. He walked around a few hours until he saw Larry Parham, thirty, a former janitor, now homeless. Zodiac had approached his victim days earlier to ask his astrological sign—Parham, born June 29, 1959, was a Cancer. He slept nights on a park bench behind the Central Park band shell. Zodiac sat down a few benches away and waited until a few people still there left. Parham made a mattress from pieces of cardboard and a pillow from his duffel bag. Five hours after the start of Parham's astrological period, and on the cusp of Gemini and Cancer, Zodiac shot him in the upper chest. He folded a note covered with astrological signs under a rock amidst Parham's meager possessions. "In the letter I left," the killer said later, "I used the phrase I read from the encyclopedia. It was to throw you off the track. . . . I just wanted to increase the fear."

Astrologers found themselves baffled in developing a coherent, star-based theory to predict the shooter's next move. Previ-

ously, they had linked the attacks to the first and second phases of
the moon, but on June 21 the moon had been in its last quarter.
Then came a startling headline: "Expert: Copy Cat Attacker Goes
by West Coast Book." "N.Y.P.D. Combs 'Zodiac' Thriller for
Clues," a second headline read. The New York Zodiac was using
the San Francisco Zodiac as a guide. Psychologist Candice
Skrapec, a professor of criminology at John Jay College of Criminal Justice, theorized that the gunman was *imitating* the California killer:

> "He's following an account in the book *Zodiac* written by
> Robert Graysmith," said Skrapec. "He has seen the book and
> read parts of it. The scope sight, the circle with the cross in-
> side, the drawings, the name Zodiac, the astrological compo-
> nents . . . come from the book. We are looking at an
> individual who is thinking the same thing he read in the
> book. . . . With this kind of behavior it would not be uncom-
> mon for the crimes to escalate, and there will be shorter time
> between incidents."

FRIDAY, JUNE 22, 1990

CHIEF of Detectives Joseph Borrelli ("That's Borrelli. Two *r*'s.
Two *l*'s, boys.") once led the "Son of Sam" probe. "The strange
circumstances seem to fall under the zodiac signs of the dates of
the shootings," he said. "In the beginning when we looked at
that, it was pure happenstance. But when you get four out of
four, you began to look at it more closely." The day after
Parham was shot, the *New York Post* received another note from
Zodiac:

> "This is the Zodiac. I have seen the Post and you say
> The note Sent to the Post not to any of
> The San Francisco Zodiac letters you are
> Wrong the hand writing is different it is
> One of the same Zodiac one Zodiac
> In San Francisco killed a man in the park with a
> gun and killed a woman with a knife and killed
> a man in the taxi cab with a gun"

"It was obvious from looking at the letter," said *Post* reporter Kieran Crowley, "that Zodiac was anxious to convince everyone that he was the same Zodiac who had killed people in California years before." Crowley wrote:

"Below the diatribe was a drawing of a chubby Zodiac in a square-topped executioner's mask, with his symbol emblazoned on his chest. To the right he declared: 'Me in the park; is this similar no; One Zodiac.' This was getting interesting. If the California Zodiac had come to New York, it was an incredible story. In fact, it was too good to be true. . . . He wanted us to think he was a heavy-set, middle-aged white guy from San Francisco. Or did he actually believe that he was the California Zodiac reincarnated? The incidents he described, especially the drawing of Zodiac in his executioner's mask, were directly from the Graysmith *Zodiac* book. Graysmith, when I reached him by phone in California, was appalled that someone was apparently using his book as a blueprint for occult murder. The former political cartoonist for the San Francisco *Chronicle* said his illustration of the original Zodiac in a hood appeared only in his book."

Crowley reached me at home. "Oh, my God, I feel terrible," I told him. "This is a copycat and not the same guy as ours. When I first heard about the shootings in New York, I checked up on a Zodiac suspect here who had never been charged. He is still here."

Another reporter wrote: "Fearful New Yorkers are snapping up copies of *Zodiac*, the 1986 bestseller about a Bay Area serial killer," "Graysmith, who spent ten years researching the book, is horrified that it might have become a how-to manual for terror, a macabre guidebook." "I hope it isn't so," I told him too. "I waited a long time after Zodiac ended his killings before writing this book for just such a reason."

MONDAY, JUNE 25, 1990

JEWELERS saw sales of birthstones plummet as New Yorkers pondered how Zodiac had known his victims' signs. NEWS REPORT:

"Police are telling people not to tell strangers their birthday. Four people have been shot, targeted for their astrological signs. Today one of them [Joseph Proce, his third victim] died. The gunman claims to be the Zodiac Killer of San Francisco fame in the late sixties, but police don't believe it. Meanwhile fifty New York detectives are on the case, the tabloids are going crazy and presumably New Yorkers are even more wary of strangers than usual."

"The computerized system," Police Commissioner Lee Brown reassured the public, "enables us to make sure we capture all the tips, all the information that comes in and gives us a chance to pull it up rapidly. The system employs a light scanner that permits clerks to feed information from incoming calls directly into the computer for handwritten notes."

Zodiac II wrote, "Only Orion [The Hunter] can stop Zodiac and the Seven Sister. No more games, pigs." A map published in the *Daily News* overlaid a diagram of the Orion constellation upon a map of the city. The first three shootings in Brooklyn lay over the part of the constellation known as Orion's belt.

THURSDAY, JUNE 28, 1990

ONE man, his symbols, drawings, and letters identical to Zodiac's, brought New York to its knees. Such deadly imitation was unprecedented. I flew to New York, checked into the Omni, and visited the crime scenes. The press followed me, slipping so many notes under my door, I could barely open it. The city was terrified. Mike McAlary wrote in his column:

"I met with Robert Graysmith, a former San Francisco newspaper guy. Graysmith spent ten years investigating San Francisco's Zodiac serial killer. The original Zodiac was a much more lethal guy, Son of Zodiac. No one knows more about the original Zodiac than Graysmith. Son of Zodiac has obviously read Graysmith's book cover to cover. He is using the tome as a guidebook to murder . . . trying his best to imitate the original Zodiac's penmanship. They write in the same poor black lettering. . . . Beware . . . We live in the age of cheap sequels."

"We have looked at that book," said Borrelli. "The New York Zodiac killer probably has too. Investigators assigned to the Zodiac task force believe the gunman stalking New York City had read and copied parts of Graysmith's book." Warren Hinckle in the *Examiner* said, "Borrelli, who follows Graysmith's bible as religiously as does his quarry, has ruled him a copy of the original Zodiac."

A news anchor, her cameraman, and I headed into Central Park in Manhattan. Taking one twisting turn after another, we neared Literary Walk near 72nd Street on the east side. Nobody would be in Central Park at midnight but the extraordinarily foolish and Zodiac. We discussed the case on the bench where Parham had been shot. New York Hospital doctors still had the former Fort Greene resident on a respirator in their trauma unit. The lights above the band shell cast long shadows across the wooded path, as silent and dark as Lake Herman Road or Blue Rock Springs. I gave the interview looking over my shoulder. "We dug a round out of that park bench," Ciravolo told me. "We found a thumbprint on the bottom right-hand corner of his note. The park victim described a man who looked like [TV weatherman] Al Roker. It was of a guy who had asked for his birthday, not the shooter. When you press detectives for a composite sketch to please the press, mistakes like that happen. The sketch was wrong and we knew it. By then it was a citywide case, not just capsulized on the Brooklyn-Queens Border. So that's when we had forty-one detectives and went at it the whole summer. Every twenty-one days when it would fall on a Thursday we'd go out there with a small army in Manhattan, Queens, and Brooklyn."

As I left to go to the airport, I saw police searching Central Park, the crisp darkness lit by flashing red lights. A female worker and her friends at the airport thanked me for coming to New York to help. That alone made the trip worthwhile.

THURSDAY, JULY 12, 1990

"Zodiac uses the trains. We're sure of that," said the police, formulating plans to shut down the subways and trap him if he struck again. Cops cuffed a subway fare-beater after they found a city map covered with Zodiac symbols in his pocket. Hundreds of officers anxiously waited for Zodiac II to strike on his preordained day. "We had in excess of 150–200 bodies," Ciravolo said, "a million supervisors—the overtime was astronomical. At one point we had a hot line set up. It looked like a Jerry Lewis Telethon. We had ten cops who were on limited duty—you know, broken wrist, broken ankle, just sitting there taking phone calls from the public—in excess of ten thousand telephone tips. Each one was checked out. When each one was checked out we went through the book again. And guess what? Zodiac went under. He wrote a few notes, taunting us—'more games, pigs. I've seen you out on Eldridge Lane looking for me, you are not good. You will not get the Zodiac.'

"He wrote things such as this: 'This is the Zodiac. The first sign is dead. The Zodiac will kill the twelve signs in the belt when the Zodiacal light is seen.' We were looking at this note for months and were asking what the fuck is the 'Zody-acal light'? I called NASA and I said, 'Excuse me, Mr. Scientist. Is there such a thing as the Zody-acal light?' 'No,' he says, 'but there is the Zo-die-ical light.'

" 'What the hell is that?'

" 'Well, it's refracted particles of dust coming off refracted sunlight, but you can't see it in big cities. You can see it down in the Caribbean and on a clear night right at dusk.'

" 'When do you see the Zodiacal light?' I asked.

" 'Twice a year. It comes out early in October and it comes out again in March.'[13]

"So this guy started shooting people in March, then he stopped. We got this October coming up, so it's going to be interesting to see if he comes back. He also said, 'Orion is the one who can stop Zodiac and the seven sister,' which is Pleiades, which is another constellation. Out of the four people he shot, he shot all of them in the torso—never any head shots, and three of the four survived. One guy has a round still in him. It's still too close to his spine to remove."

THURSDAY, AUGUST 16, 1990

I returned to New York, staying at Days Inn on 57th Street and wandering the streets in early morning. A garbage strike was in

---

[13]It is also a diffuse glow seen in the west after twilight and in the east before dawn.

progress. Heaps of refuse, blurry with flies, mounded each corner. Zodiac victim Darlene Ferrin's sister, Pam, stepped daintily over the trash, lifting the low hem of her silky dress. She appeared on the *Sally Jesse Raphael Show* and told how Zodiac had changed her life. A man, she reported, tried to pull her car keys from her ignition in front of an Antioch, California, store. He brandished a knife and threatened to abduct her, but she escaped after a struggle. Local police had been skeptical of her earlier reports of death threats—a note pinned to her front door that read "187" [187 is the California Penal Code section dealing with homicide], a coffin delivered to her door, a cross planted on her lawn, and teddy bears with knives stuck in them left on her steps. Antioch Police Sergeant Bob Lowe denied they had dismissed Pam's previous complaints. "Any and all reports of that nature are always taken seriously," he said. Vernon Hockaby of Antioch was more irate. He wasn't related to Pam, but hundreds of callers had phoned his number during the last year.

After making good on a third of his threats, Zodiac II vanished just as the original had. "We went at it for about nine or ten months," Ciravolo told me, "until Chief of Detectives Borrelli disbanded it." Vallejo Detective Bawart, still on reserve to help the VPD solve complex homicides, said, "Zodiac's success in his killing and the success of most serial killers are that they have no connection with their victims. Psychopaths like this usually outgrow it in their later years and later life." Was this the case with the New York copycat? Had he outgrown his rage, gone underground?

In the interim, I learned Leigh Allen was going blind.

25
ARTHUR LEIGH ALLEN

ALLEN'S deteriorating vision, a side effect from diabetes mellitus and arteriosclerotic heart disease, had seriously impeded his activities. Though his kidneys were failing, Leigh ignored his doctor's advice to curtail excessive fluids and watch his weight. As mental acuity decreased, he experienced occasional muscle cramps, flank pain, and muscle twitching. His skin took on a slightly yellow-brownish discoloration. Inside, healthy as ever, anger still blazed.

Long after Allen's release from Atascadero, a staffer, consumed with worry, contacted me. "Is Arthur Leigh Allen still alive and if so is he still a Zodiac suspect?" he asked. Apparently Leigh had told the Atascadero staff he was a Zodiac suspect. "To your knowledge, have there been subsequent child molestation charges brought against this man? It is recognized in the mental health field that child molesters are notorious recidivists. The molesters I've worked with have been repeat offenders." Nor, with the passing of years, had the suffering of the victims lessened. Psychic trauma had especially been visited on the surviving Blue Rock Springs victim—Mike Mageau [*May-hew*], last seen in a Vallejo hospital on August 19, 1969.

Though his operation had been on July 5, scars on the right side of Mike's neck and left cheek shone lividly, mapping a bullet's wandering path. He was a study in agony—jaw wired shut, left leg encased in a cast to his hip; right arm and hand crippled by bullets—as he stared at a slug, floating in a solution in a glass bottle. That slug had been removed from his left thigh. As soon as he could, he disguised himself and fled Vallejo.

"About one and a half years ago," a male nurse in San Bernardino told me, "I saw Michael Mageau as a patient for multiple medical problems that appeared to be psychosomatic, probably secondary to the psychological scars he received as a result of his encounter with Zodiac. He freely volunteered his association with Zodiac and had scars consistent with the described wounds. As I recall he had a run-in with drugs and was a street person briefly. I met his fiancée, who is a strong woman and seemed to be giving him emotional and physical support. They are probably married now. He told me that [Lake Berryessa victim] Bryan Hartnell was living in the area and that he had some infrequent contact with him. I find it interesting that both Zodiac survivors now live in the area where the Zodiac murders began." Hartnell had described Zodiac as 225–250 pounds. Mageau's first description was similar—the man's build was "beefy, heavyset without being blubbery fat." He appeared to have "a large face" and was not wearing glasses. "He weighed 195–200 pounds and was between twenty-six and thirty-six years old. He was wearing a blue short-sleeved shirt." That sounded a lot like the prime suspect.

On this twenty-first anniversary of Paul Stine's murder, Dave Toschi said, "I retired in 1985 without having the pleasure of reading [Zodiac] his rights. Zodiac was the most baffling murder case in our history." With coast-to-coast Zodiacs at large, it seemed unthinkable that the original Zodiac could let such an opportunity go by without commenting on his New York counterpart. Only the most extreme adversity could prevent this prophet of death from gloating over the proliferation of his obscene word. No letter came. Why?

TUESDAY, DECEMBER 18, 1990

LEIGH Allen mentioned the Zodiac imitator to his friends. But he had other things on his mind. I was in Vallejo when, on the morning of his birthday, he donned a sweater his mother had knitted, buttoned his Navy pea coat, and drove to DMV to apply for a two-year renewal of his Class C driver's license.[14] The new license stipulated "RSTP: Corr Lens," but in his driver's photo Leigh is not wearing glasses. He cruised the water town in his

---

[14]LA 554 121790 43/5005 100 32.

VW, finally parking at a golf course. I saw him turn up his collar against the wind, as he studied Water Town. I knew he was intimate with all its watery sections and salt flats. Lake Chabot Reservoir sprang from a dammed stream a hundred years ago. Then a storage cistern in Wild Horse Valley, twenty-two miles northeast, began pumping water to Fleming Hill reservoir. Today, the Gordon Valley project and Cache Slough Pumping Plant slaked Water Town's endless thirst. His eyes roved across the choppy bay, where the hunt for Zodiac proceeded.

Allen was now undergoing kidney dialysis and suffering from diabetes. He walked with a cane, had a heart condition—possibly a circulation problem, and suffered from severe arthritis. Zodiac's withdrawal had been as mystifying as his arrival. When he had appeared twenty years ago, there really hadn't been anything like Zodiac before. He had captured the public's enduring interest. "Zodiac was one of the early serial killers to acquire publicity," said Park Dietz of UCLA. "The use of a logo and encrypted messages made him both well-marketed and of interest to legions of people who would like to solve the mystery." So did the astrology angle.

Zodiac buff David Rice did a breakdown of Zodiac's significant dates, but saw no astronomical pattern. He suggested to me there might be an *astrological* pattern, though, and on his computer, analyzed his findings with an Astr-5-Ø, Tropical Zodiac program.

"If Zodiac were using astronomical events such as the Winter, Summer, Spring, and Fall Solar Ingresses," he explained, "it would seem likely that he would 'do his thing' on the exact day, and not plus or minus 13 days. Not even if he were using the Sidereal Zodiac, which is considered (with an SVP at 28 Pisces) to have a difference from the Tropical Zodiac of 28 degrees (there's still about two degrees to go before the 'Age of Aquarius' replaces the current 'Age of Pisces'), as it would still be off. There might be an explanation, however. Statistical analysis on athletes, using the Tropical Zodiac, placed Mars at the Ascendant (rising) and the Midheaven (culminating) more often than chance allows, at the oh-five level. Doctors and lawyers have Jupiter in these 'zones' instead. Though an astrologer, I'd prefer an astronomical explanation to an astrological one. The former one can weigh and measure, the latter is allegory and probabilities."

Like the original Zodiac, New York's copycat serial killer had vanished without a trace. I prayed for a resolution to the East Coast mystery. It would dispel half the nightmare. In history only Jack the Ripper had his copycats—and now, Zodiac did too.

26
ZODIAC II RETURNS

THOUGH THE SOLUTION to Zodiac II lay years away, let me tell you how it ended—as it began, in a blaze of bullets. On Tuesday, March 1, 1994, New York City police arrested a young man who "wouldn't hurt a fly," packing a homemade weapon. They automatically fingerprinted anyone with a zip gun because Zodiac II had used one. But the gun didn't work, so cops sealed the young man's file with the prints still inside. He returned to his Pitkin Avenue neighborhood, where he was known as "The Vampire." Obsessed with all things military, "The Vampire" collected martial hardware and acted on occasion as a police drug informant. By day, he closeted himself in the nearly abandoned East New York apartment building he shared with his mother and sister and some squatters. He raged against drug users who trafficked the squalid building. By night, he wandered the streets, his Bible clutched under his arm.

"Your Zodiac, I think, is going to be caught," I said on Ted Koppel's *Nightline*. "I have had that feeling from the very beginning. He has already been seen by more people than ever saw the original Zodiac." Jerry Nachman, on the same program, made an interesting point on behalf of the press. "We don't create these situations. The Zodiac had shot two or three people before story one appeared. Son of Sam had murdered between a third to half the number of people he would ever kill before the first Son of Sam story appeared. So, it is not as if it is a chicken and egg thing. Sometimes these crimes have been unspooling for a while before we ever get notified of them or, indeed, get into them."

On Monday, August 8, 1994, my phone rang. "There's a third Zodiac," Pete Noyes, a Los Angeles television newsman, told me. "A story out of New York is that another person claiming to be the Zodiac Killer has written to the *Post* describing a series of new shootings."

"Another or the old one back again?" I said. "A third Zodiac— a copycat of a copycat? What do they think?"

"They say they don't want to say." He read me the AP report:

" 'This is the Zodiac.' Those words, in a childlike scrawl, became the trademark greeting of a killer who filled the New York summer of 1990 with dread. Now after years of silence, the Zodiac killer may be back. In 1990, the Zodiac vowed to kill one person for each of the twelve astrological signs . . . then abruptly quit. This week [August 1, 1994], the New York *Post* got a similar note from someone claiming to be the Zodiac, and detectives are trying to determine whether the letter writer is the killer or a copycat. The letter writer claims responsibility for five shootings that police said left at least two people dead between August 10, 1992 and June 11 of this year. All of the attacks took place in the general area of the 1990 shooting. . . ."

Kieran Crowley phoned right after Noyes. "It's four o'clock in New York right now and it's happening again," he said, "another Zodiac. He's shot five people. Remember four years ago? This Zodiac claims to be the original guy who killed all four. Obviously there are these points of agreement between the letters and the original Zodiac. . . . Do you think it's possible he's taken on the persona, might think he's the real Zodiac?"

"When this imitator came out for the first time," I said, "my mother suggested I say in the press that this guy is not Zodiac. When I did he stopped. Who knows, maybe he really believed he was the San Francisco Zodiac. Or maybe he didn't mean to kill his victims, only wound them. When Proce died, he ceased killing."

"It's obvious to me that he's read your book. He does a box score. He claims four victims four years ago, five now—a total of nine. The police confirmed that the guy in this shooting—they got one ballistics match—a .22-caliber—which was like Zodiac."

"Zodiac used a .22 in his first Northern California murder."

"Do you think he's using your book as a Bible? As far as I can tell he is."

"I feel awful. My purpose in writing the book was to catch Zodiac or get so close that he was stalemated. I think we succeeded. San Francisco's Zodiac was effectively checkmated. With publication of his story and all the clues, with enhanced police scrutiny, we had no more murders, no more letters."

Few killers had copied a novel, duplicating fictional crimes or M.O. in real life. A few instances of fact following fiction: Agatha Christie's *The Pale Horse* inspired a crime. A mass murderer who escaped from an asylum used her book as a guide to commit aconite poisonings. J. D. Salinger's *Catcher in the Rye* has shown up in the hands of a number of madmen—Hinckley, Bardo (who shot actress Rebecca Shafer). Former Berkeley mathematics professor Ted Kaczynski, the Unabomber, copied the plot and philosophy laid out in Joseph Conrad's *The Secret Agent*, about a professor who is a bomber. I knew of no non-fiction books inspiring real-life crimes. I mentioned an article on the subject, "A Writer's Nightmare," to Crowley.

"And it's a writer's nightmare for you," said Crowley. "That somebody studied your book—that's horrible. For you, this is like twice—what the police don't know is if it's the same guy or not. Which is scarier—that it is the same guy who came back or if it's two different ones?"

"Two people that unbalanced and suggestible?"

"Confidentially," said Crowley, "we believe it still may be the guy from four years ago. The descriptions sort of match—I'll get back to you on that."

Next day, he told me about a new Zodiac cipher in the *Post*. "If you put a hand mirror on the left side of the symbols you can see how he created his new alphabet. They look like normal naval flags, but they're not. I and a former Army cryptographer decoded his message. I'll read it to you . . . let me give you the exact wording. One of the reasons I was able to crack it open—turns out they're mirror image naval signal flags [based on a maritime system of International Flags and Pennants]—almost all of them. We didn't know that. We did the standard codebreaking stuff. The symbols were doubled in the horizontal plane, in something known as a 'looking glass' alphabet code. It was likely created by placing a small mirror on the left side of each naval flag symbol. He says, 'This is the Zodiac Speaking, I am in control through mastery. Be ready for more. Your's truly.' Obviously, there are different points of agreement between the letters of the original Zodiac. . . . The police have confirmed they've got one ballistic match—.22-caliber, which was what Zodiac used. The description is not a black guy but that of a dark-skinned Latino."

"That's very different than the original description," I said. "The new one could still be Zodiac III." Retired NYPD Detectives Al Sheppard and James Tedaldi suspected this was Zodiac III—he did not stalk his victims as he had done in 1990, but chose them at random. The 1990 Zodiac had a pattern of attacking on Thursdays and in increments of twenty-one and when certain star clusters were visible in the sky. The latest Zodiac did not follow any pattern. The old Zodiac aimed for his victims' torsos, the new aimed for the head. But both admitted there were enough similarities that it could be the same man.

"AUGUST THE FIFTH," Mike Ciravolo told me, "I get a call saying, 'Zodiac shot people. He's writing notes. It checks out. He's out there again. What was incredible about 1990 was [Zodiac] has all four victims' astrological signs on paper. To this day it is unknown how that happened. What we did was we developed profiles on the four victims that we had back then. What did they have in common? Did they go to the same drugstore to get their prescriptions filled? Do they go to the same barbershop? Do they have a library card for the same branch? Any common thread that we could develop. And do you know what? No. There was just nothing in common with the four of them. Are they all on welfare? No, they weren't. The only thing they did have in common is that there was something wrong with all of them. The first guy walked with a terrible limp. He had some sort of birth defect. The second guy was drunk—he was unconscious—passed out on the sidewalk in front of his house. The third guy was a seventy-eight-year-old man who used to go wandering around in the middle of the night. He had his days and nights mixed up. He was a little senile. The fourth one was asleep in Central Park on a park bench."

"He picked the helpless to shoot," I said.

"But this guy here in 1994 is hitting women as well as men. This guy's stabbing. Which is a lot more indicative of your guy out there than our guy. That's what gives me the creeps about this. I think the 1990 guy and the 1994 guy is one and the same. Now it's starting to lean that way . . . they called me at seven o'clock in the morning and asked me all these questions on television. I had about fifteen minutes to read about it in three newspapers and go on the air. At that time my gut feeling tells me it's not the same guy I investigated in 1990. But now I've had a little time to see that note and go over it. The handwriting isn't the same, but when you're dealing with someone who's so psychotic—his medication could be changed. He could have just thrown the pen in his other hand. We have two matching thumbprints on those 1990 letters, and you know the New York City police department has the FACES System—a computerized fingerprint matchup system. The latent-print examiners used to have to do it by hand. Now if you've ever been arrested, your print is in the system. If you get a latent print off a letter you can match it. There's one detective assigned to just that—he has the prints from the Zodiac in 1990 and he continuously puts it into the computer. There were over 3600 reports prepared on the case. Everything went onto computer. If your name came up early on in the investigation, and now here it is four months later, another detective is interviewing someone and that name comes up. Boom! It would match and you'd be able to cross-reference and report, 'Hey, this guy looks interesting. An independent person told us two months ago about a certain person in the Bronx. Now someone in Brooklyn is mentioning the same name as a possibility. Some bells would go off.'"

"Exactly what they should have done with Zodiac," I said, thinking of Lynch and Mulanax's individual reports on Leigh Allen. Neither knew of the other's questioning. We still didn't know who had been the original tipster who suspected Allen, the man or woman who directed the police to his door. Once more I flew to New York, wondering if there was something in the original case that might identify Zodiac II. Retired Detective Sergeant Mike Race, Kieran Crowley, and I were on the *Rolanda* show. The mix of the cerebral—cops and authors—and the passionate—victims' mothers and families—never really jells. What can you say after a mother has talked about losing her child? "In his coded message," Crowley said, "Zodiac said, 'I am in control.' I'd like him to prove it by sending another message, before he hurts anyone else, because I think it's time for this to move on to the next phase." Crowley's story headlined "MANIAC GOES BY THE BOOK," appeared in the *Post* August 9. Under a reproduction of the cover was the caption: "How-to manual, the real-life crime story that may have inspired Zodiac II." Crowley wrote:

"The Zodiac killer may be using a 1986 book about the original San Francisco Zodiac killer as his guide. Robert Graysmith wrote the best-seller "Zodiac" about the hooded killer who terrorized the Bay Area for years beginning in 1968. . . . Four years ago, Graysmith went through a similar experience when a New York gunman calling himself Zodiac began his shooting spree."

On August 12, 1994, police concluded that the new communication *was* from Zodiac II. He had demonstrated "intimate knowledge" of the assaults—time, place, ages, and genders of the five victims, location of wounds, and caliber of guns (a .22 in four instances and a .380 in a fifth). Some details matched; not all. One victim had been stabbed, not shot. Patricia Fonte was knifed over a hundred times. "We're puzzled," said Borrelli, "but we're fairly sure it's not a hoax." Psychologist Dr. Joyce Brothers said of Zodiac's return: "This is somebody who is totally powerless and who is finding power through publicity. His fantasy is to master the world because he can't control his own life. He wants to be in control. That is his fantasy. He probably does not have a family or anyone who loves him." A Bellevue Hospital forensic psychiatrist, Michael Welner, said, "There is this sense of being a hunter. He is trying to create intrigue with codes. He wants to be glamorous because he's a loser . . . there is an element of sadism about him. I think he's very interested in getting attention . . . it's very cowardly."

Two years would pass. On Tuesday, June 18, 1996, a few minutes past noon, "The Vampire," distraught his teenage sister was running with a bad crowd, shotgunned her. A 911 call—"a female shot in the leg, Pitkin Avenue"—summoned New York paramedics. Moments later, an ambulance squealed to a stop at the U-shaped front of 2730 Pitkin. Medics piled out, leaving the engine racing. They started for the third-floor apartment. "The shooter is still up there," cautioned a neighbor—a shot whizzed over their heads. "We kissed the concrete just as we heard that first shot," said paramedic Chris DeLuca. Lead ripped jagged holes into the ambulance; other shots ricocheted off the sidewalk. Chunks of brick flew. "Get down! Down flat!" More bullets, punctuated by brilliant muzzle flashes, hammered from the upper window. At P.S. 159 across the street, students cried and ducked for cover. Cops, guns drawn, converged on Pitkin Avenue and cordoned off a nine-block

area. For the next three and one-half hours, their bullets, with machine gun-like rapidity, answered "The Vampire's." Bullets cut
from above in a murderous arc, chipping masonry and pinning
down four officers. Cops in helmets and flak jackets wheeled a
metal shield toward the building as the Emergency Service Unit
vehicle, armored with bullet-proof gear, moved in to rescue the
four men.

Sergeant Joseph Herbert, a fifteen-year police veteran, soft-
spoken and neat, negotiated with the shooter from the street below. "I think I will surrender," the shooter shouted, weary of
prolonged battle. From the roof police lowered a yellow flower
bucket to the apartment. "Turn over any weapons," they ordered.
He filled the bucket three times—thirteen homemade guns, Saturday night specials, dozens of rounds of ammo, seven hunting
and military-type knives, and a machete. The siege ended shortly
after 4:00 P.M. and "The Vampire," Heriberto "Eddie" Seda, was
arrested. Inside Seda's room were two fully constructed pipe
bombs and a third under construction. An unexploded bomb
matched three recently left in a Brooklyn parking lot. His library
was what they had been told to look for.[15] Serial killers often read
about others to avoid the same pitfalls that got them caught.

Seda admitted to shooting his half sister in a written confession. At the bottom of the page he drew an inverted cross
crowned by three sevens. "It just jumped out of the page," Herbert said. "I nearly fell off my chair. It was the handwriting! The
t's the s's the m's, the way he underlined certain letters. That,
coupled with the symbol of the inverted cross, made me realize
this was Zodiac. I immediately recognized it. . . . I had studied it
for two years." The symbols linked Seda with drawings made six
years earlier by Zodiac II, who had left a thumbprint on the lower
right corner of his first letter. Herbert summoned Detective
Ronald Alongis, from the NYPD latent-print unit, and asked him
to bring a set of prints to headquarters for comparison. Alongis
had memorized the ridges and swirls Zodiac left on two notes.

About 8:30 P.M., he scanned the prints through a magnifying

---

[15]A collection of trading cards: *True Crime Series Four: Serial Killers &
Mass Murderers,* clippings of *Daily News* crime stories on Zodiac, and a copy
of Michael Newton's *Serial Slaughter, A History of 800 Serial Killers* including a short entry on the original Zodiac.

glass. His eyes got bright, then excited. At 1:20 A.M., after six hours of interrogation, Seda signed a confession to all nine Zodiac attacks, claiming to have been overcome by "urges" to strike randomly. Only by chance had Zodiac II appeared to know some of his victim's astrological signs. "I just wanted to increase the fear in the city," he said.

Zodiac detectives were surprised. "We thought that he lived alone because if he lived with someone, we figured they would have eventually given him up." Ballistics and saliva tests further linked Seda to the Zodiac shootings. He had licked an envelope flap and "Love" postage stamps. Seda had stopped shooting people after 1994 because he "lost the urge." On Wednesday, June 24, 1998, a jury deliberated less than a day before convicting the thirty-year-old high school dropout of three counts of murder and one count of attempted murder. A month later, the New York Zodiac was sentenced to eighty-three years in prison. "You're going to die in jail," said Judge Robert J. Hanophy. "The Zodiac never lied to us," Ciravolo concluded. "That's the saddest thing." Back in fog-shrouded San Francisco no one suspected a third copycat was yet to come. Zodiac III's murders would be terrifying.

THE HUNT FOR the original Zodiac went on. Besides Belli the attorney, he had mentioned two other people in his letters. One in code, "Robert Emmett the Hippie," the other Count Marco Spinelli. Was Zodiac's letter a hidden message to someone named "Spinelli" and could we find a "Spinelli" who had a connection to Leigh Allen?

27
THE BIG TIP

RALPH Spinelli, lying in a cell on his fiftieth birthday, sweated into the thin mattress. Jim Overstreet, San Jose P.D., had arrested him as a suspect in at least nine armed robberies of restaurants. Spinelli knew he could be prosecuted as a career criminal. He had been arrested in Oregon in 1972 for a series of armed robberies of restaurants and served two years of a ten-year sentence in a prison there. Facing a thirty-year sentence, he suggested to Overstreet that he had something to trade. In jail, cigarettes, sex, and secrets were three prized commodities. "The best kind of informant is a two-time loser forty-five to fifty who knows if he goes up one more time he's gong to die in the can," said a detective. "When he turns to us, he has nowhere else to go—he becomes as zealous as a cop." The cops had a "twist," a hammer, on Spinelli and he was "working his beef."

"I know the real name of Zodiac," Spinelli said finally. It was his ace.

Spinelli began to talk in hushed tones and rapid cadence. But for all he said, it was just enough to get Overstreet on the hook. Overstreet realized Spinelli might be inventing a story—a very good chance of that. However, he could not ignore what might be a valid tip. Zodiac was the biggest case there was. He left a message for retired Detective Bawart and Bawart rang him right back. "Spinelli is currently incarcerated in the Santa Clara County jail," advised Overstreet. "He won't divulge what information he has regarding Zodiac unless some kind of deal is made regarding the present charges against him." Bawart sighed. He had heard such claims about Zodiac before. "I'll get back to you," he replied, and called Conway.

"There was this guy Spinelli living in San Jose," Bawart told me later, "pulled a bunch of stickups and they caught him and he said, 'Get ahold of Vallejo P.D. I'll tell you all about a case they're real interested in.' They called us, and Conway and I went down and interviewed him on his birthday." Vallejo Police Captain Roy Conway already knew Spinelli. His name had been prominent in the Vallejo area during the forties, fifties, and sixties. Connections with organized crime were suspected.

Conway, a Vallejo police officer since 1965, had worked with Mulanax, since retired. He was presently commander of the Investigation Division, but the night Ferrin was murdered and Mageau terribly wounded, he had been a sergeant and he and Richard Hoffman had been the first policemen at the scene. Conway personally verified the authenticity of descriptions Zodiac mailed to the press back in 1969. He believed Zodiac had committed those shootings. An anonymous phone call to the Vallejo P.D. had been made from a phone booth near Arthur Leigh Allen's home and near where Tucker kept his car.

Conway and Bawart drove to the Santa Clara lockup, checked their guns, and went in to see Spinelli. He was being held on $500,000 bail while awaiting trial on the charges. The prisoner was anxious. Spinelli knew how much trouble he was in. Though he could go in for what amounted to life, Spinelli still refused to budge. He would not name the individual he knew as Zodiac without being offered a deal. "I war t all charges against me dropped," he insisted.

"Out of the question," said Bawart.

"We refuse to make any sort of deal like that," said Conway.

"And just how do you know this person is Zodiac?" asked Bawart.

"He threatened me several days before the killing of Paul Stine, the San Francisco cabdriver. He wanted to show me how tough he was. He told me he was going to San Francisco and kill a cabbie for me," said Spinelli. "The next day or so a cabdriver was killed in San Francisco and the Zodiac took credit for it." A police report confirmed Spinelli and Allen had had fights in the past.

After a long discussion, Spinelli agreed to give Zodiac's true name to his lawyer, Craig Kennedy, a deputy public defender of Santa Clara County. Throughout the remainder of the month, several meetings were held between Kennedy and his immediate boss, Bryan Schechmeister. The upshot was that no further information would be divulged without a definite deal given to their client. This Conway and Bawart still refused to do. They could play hardball too. It would be interesting to see who blinked first.

THURSDAY, JANUARY 31, 1991

CONWAY received a call from Kennedy. "I can give you the name that Spinelli has," he said. The other side had caved.

Conway waited silently, although he already thought he knew the answer.

"It's Leigh Allen. Arthur Leigh Allen."

Conway let out a slow breath. He already knew all about Lee Allen. He got Bawart on the phone immediately. "LEE" was in the Zodiac cipher. It was the name Allen had worn on his smock at Ace Hardware. Conway contacted Inspector Armstrong in San Francisco. "Yes," Armstrong said, "one of the primary suspects back in the early 1970s was Arthur Leigh Allen." He also verified that Allen's name had never been published in any media to his knowledge. The only persons knowing his name were law enforcement people and only those involved in the actual Zodiac investigation, or someone Allen might have bragged to such as medical personnel at Atascadero and some coworkers at an auto parts store in Sonoma.

"Arthur Leigh Allen and Spinelli were acquaintances way back when," Bawart told me later, "and he [Allen] approached him and told him he wanted to be an enforcer for him. The guy [Spinelli] owned a topless bar. He admitted he was the Zodiac, said Spinelli, and said, 'To show you, I'm going to go to San Francisco and kill a guy.' That was shortly before the Stine killing. Then he supposedly came back and said, 'I'm responsible for the Stine killing.' I know this guy Spinelli fairly well from his criminal past. I didn't know whether to believe him or not."

Spinelli might have invented his story and been trying to win favor. Even if what he said was true, it was not solid supporting evidence that would hold up in court. It was fruit from a tainted tree. But how had Spinelli known to come up with the name Leigh Allen in the first place?

WEDNESDAY, FEBRUARY 6, 1991

CONWAY and Bawart drove to the State Department of Justice, Sacramento Homicide Unit, to see Agent Fred Shirisago. This branch was currently the repository for all the Zodiac cases in the multitude of jurisdictions where the killer had struck. A constant refrain from amateur sleuths regarding the state DOJ was that some at the top level were not always responsive to their information and theories. "They don't always take my information seriously," one told me. "Further one guy claimed that the Riverside killing invalidated my material and he had proof Zodiac did not kill Cheri Jo Bates. He claimed the information provided by Pam, Darlene's sister, was not valid as it was too old. The handprinting I provided by my expert was that 'it looked similar,' but after a killing in Martinez, they said it was not Zodiac's. Yet he refused to allow the other expert, Mr. Morrill, a chance to examine said handprinting."

This was not Toschi's approach. "Just let people know you appreciate getting their clues on how to catch Zodiac," he told me. "I always acknowledge receipt of a person's letter, especially if it appears to have some substance or is sincere. I never know when I'll get a letter that will make or break the case." Shirisago gave Conway all the reports pertaining to the investigation of Arthur Leigh Allen, records that demonstrated San Francisco detectives, specifically Armstrong and Toschi, had conducted the primary investigation on Allen. They spoke with Armstrong, then Conway contacted Mel Nicolai, now retired. Nicolai agreed with Armstrong that the media had never revealed the name of Lee Allen as a suspect in the Zodiac investigation. Bawart followed the local papers devotedly. He too knew Allen's name had never been linked publicly with Zodiac. Spinelli had to have had personal contact with Lee Allen or with a close friend of his. In no other way could he have come up with the name.

"Were there any reasons for Spinelli to lie about the information?" I asked Bawart. "A grudge? A lighter sentence of some sort?"

"Allen had gotten in a fight with Spinelli," he told me. "Showed up at his house and kicked in the door and beat him up. And yes, he provided the information in exchange for a lighter sentence."

Through Sacramento, Conway requested the FBI Director's aid, Teletyping the following:

"The latent fingerprint section is requested to provide Sacramento with photographs of all latent fingerprints developed during the Zodiac investigation, Latent Case No A-10042. The latent fingerprint section is further requested to search the latent fingerprints developed in the Zodiac case through the Automated Identification System and the Automated Latent Systems Model and National Unidentified Latent File. Sacramento is not aware of the requested search as previously being conducted. The photographs of latent prints on file with the Identification Division are being sought at the request of the Vallejo California Police Department, who intends to run the prints, search through the California Department of Justice Automated Latent Prints System [ALPS]."

Compared against *every* suspect in the Zodiac case, prisoners and military personnel, there was no match. How had Zodiac done it?

THURSDAY, FEBRUARY 7, 1991

BAWART contacted Larry Ankron, a psychologist for VICAP at Quantico. Ankron knew all about Zodiac. Bawart told him all Armstrong, Toschi, and Mulanax had learned back in 1971, then gave him the information that Spinelli had provided—the name of Arthur Leigh Allen. The bureau, as it turned out, already had a file (their largest single file in the Zodiac case) on this individual. In Ankron's estimation, Zodiac got as much pleasure from taunting the police and reliving his murders through souvenirs he kept as from the violent acts themselves. "My studies," he said, "show that persons who commit these types of crimes many times keep souvenirs or trophies from these criminal acts. They will take some type of article from their victims such as identification, pieces of clothing, and so on. This is so they can keep these in a hidden place and relive the incident many times over. They will keep journals and newspaper clippings of the crimes themselves. Those who keep these souvenirs have ingenious hiding places within their residences such as false walls, hidden safes, and so on. Many times these individuals will have a storage place at another location where they keep their souvenirs."

Possibly Zodiac's trophies were underwater at a site such as

Lake Berryessa or in the walls of a trailer. Ankron believed the killings were still going on, or had gone on until recently. After all, Zodiac said he wasn't going to write anymore and would make his killings appear as accidents. "The only reason I can think of that the murders had stopped," he said, "is that the man responsible had moved away [although the Zodiac crimes committed elsewhere would be readily identifiable because of his well-known M.O.]. He might have died. Or the police had come very close to apprehending him." Many who had seen Zodiac or been part of Leigh Allen's alibi had died mysteriously. A caretaker's daughter saw Zodiac speeding away from Blue Rock Springs, and died several years after in a car accident. A landlady who could have provided Allen with an alibi perished from a heart attack. Mr. William White, a neighbor [whose son joined the Vallejo force], had seen Allen return home on the day of the Lake Berryessa murder, and died shortly afterward. Frank Gasser, the raccoon hunter who had peered in the white Impala on Lake Herman Road the night of the murders, perished in a freak accident, dying suddenly two years later when he struck his head on a coffee table.

"You know," Bawart told me, "when you investigate so many cases you get to be jaded to the degree that you have so many coincidences you just don't believe in coincidences after a while. Where there's smoke there's fire." He visited Ace Hardware, where Allen had once worked, and contacted Leigh's coworker George Hieb. An ex-city employee, Hieb had worked at the Corporation Yard for many years. In his retirement he was working at Ace Hardware.

"Do you know Arthur Leigh Allen?" asked Bawart.

"I know him quite well," said Hieb. "I visit his home almost on a weekly basis." Though Leigh's mother had died, he still kept to his basement bedroom, though he could have control of the entire house. Hieb too had seen Allen's guns. "A number of revolvers—I think they're .22-caliber, and at least one semiautomatic pistol, but I don't know the caliber." Because Allen had been arrested by the Sonoma County Sheriff's Department for molesting two small boys, the suspect was a felon. Consequently, he was not allowed by law to own any of the weapons Hieb had seen. But in the decade that Hieb had known Allen, he had never discussed the Zodiac case with him. That was puzzling. Leigh had discussed it with others, even led people to think in that particular direction. Bawart cautioned Hieb not to mention the visit, then re-interviewed a number of people who had information about Allen. As much current information about the suspect as possible had to be gathered before they confronted him.

Near the detached garage on the northeast side of 32 Fresno Street sat a broken-down blue "General Motors-type" auto. According to Hieb's information, Allen owned an older black G.M. vehicle. In the driveway were an older-model white Mercedes-Benz and light-blue Volkswagen Karmann Ghia. Allen possessed a white Buick, and Darlene Ferrin had been followed by an American-made white sedan. A silver or ice-blue '66 Chevy with California plates had been seen at Lake Berryessa the day of the attack.

To get the lay of the land, Bawart drove over to 1545 Broadway, where Allen kept a boat and trailer. The location was a single-story residence on the west side of Broadway. To the north of the building stood a detached double-car garage packed with household goods. There were storage areas—places where Allen might squirrel away items—a large lean-to-type storage shed forty feet long and twenty feet deep, and a second storage area at the rear. George got out. Behind the garage, wind whipped grass in a vacant field. The scent of the Bay was in the air. In the center of the field stretched a twenty-two-foot-long blue and white sailboat on a trailer, partially draped by a blue tarp. Bawart surreptitiously lifted the tarp and saw a California license number, NE3725. The boat had sleeping quarters on board, which would allow a person to stay at sea for many days at a time. Bawart also observed an open sailboat some ten feet long. "It looked more like a rowboat," he said. Bawart jotted down that license number too— 9127F. Both were registered to Leigh. His mother had bought him the boats, spoiling him just as his sister-in-law had said. "Allen's been unemployed and living on general assistance for some time," Conway had told him. "He goes diving and races Hobie Cat sailboats." Bawart decided that in addition to a search warrant for 32 Fresno, the police should at least search the sailboat. But the evidence they sought might be sunken somewhere off the coast, beneath blue lake waters, or under the turgid waters of the Delta.

TUESDAY, FEBRUARY 12, 1991

WHEN Conway filed an affidavit for a search warrant, he was looking for evidence kept at the Fresno Street home that might show that Allen had committed a felony. Possibly, they were already too late to find physical evidence. However, an explanation why the murders had stopped seemed to be revealed. Allen was now legally blind. "He was a very ill man," Conway said, "he was fifty-one or fifty-two. . . . He was extremely ill and he'd had that illness for some time. Even though he could still get around he was not very mobile, and there was a lot of focus on him as a suspect. Being a suspect, being ill, and losing interest—all adds up to the explanation as to why." The *why* in this case was why Zodiac ceased killing and writing.

"We figured he wasn't a danger to anyone," George Bawart told me.

On Attachment IV, Conway listed the items they were searching for. Any .22-caliber semiautomatic pistols or any .22-caliber ammo, live or expended, that may have been cycled through an automatic pistol and could be linked to the death of the Lake Herman Road victims, Betty Lou Jensen and David Faraday. Any personal effects linked to victims Jensen and Farraday, Darlene Ferrin or Michael Mageau, Cecelia Shepard or Brian Hartnell. They were also seeking the black Wing Walker-type boots, size 10½ R, Zodiac wore at Lake Berryessa during the attack there. The upper portion of these shoes was manufactured by the Weinbrenner Shoe Company, the "SUPERWEAR" soles by the Avon Company of Avon, Massachusetts. Both the Air Force and Navy issued them. Authorities were specifically looking for any portions existing of Paul Stine's gray-and-white-striped sports shirt. In all likelihood it would be stained with blood. Stine's wallet and I.D. and Yellow Cab's keys had also been taken by Zodiac on Cherry Street that Columbus Day. Serial killers had a predilection for keeping souvenirs of their crimes so that they might relive the moment.

Conway and Bawart needed any firearm that might show evidence of having had a flashlight attached to it; any 9-mm automatic pistols or 9-mm automatic ammunition, live or expended, that may have been fired from a 9-mm pistol. They would try to link this to the murder of Paul Stine. They listed any knives a foot long with a one-inch blade having rivets in the handle and tape around the handle, and a black executioner's hood which covered Zodiac's head and hung down over his shoulders almost to his waist and was sleeveless. A circle and cross were painted white across the chest. Conway desired any diaries or journals that Allen might have kept that linked him with Zodiac or the investigation to catch him. Any item that had the Zodiac's symbol of a crossed circle on it. He made one last request in his appeal: "Your Affiant asks that after the service of this search warrant that the Search Warrant Affidavit and Return of Service be sealed by the court. The reason this request is made is that the Zodiac case has had national publicity and has been one of the few cases that has so inflamed the public that it would serve no purpose for the news media to get information from this affidavit if no charges are filed. In the other vein, if charges are filed, the publicity from this affidavit would tend to make it difficult to have a fair trial."

Police had come to believe that Zodiac was an unsophisticated killer who contrary to former beliefs did not stalk his victims—just came across them in lovers' lanes. But the killer was very familiar with Vallejo and Berryessa and the surrounding area, and victims had complained of being stalked before their deaths.

I also thought sadly of Allen's lost promise—at one time he could have been an Olympic diver. I recalled his yearbook picture and photos of him from junior high school and the 1950s when he was a lifeguard at The Plunge. A clipping portrayed a very slim young man, 180 pounds, about to leap from a diving board. Leigh had been fit and handsome, looking eerily like the first composite sketch of Zodiac. In the time between the murder of Paul Stine and his first interview with Toschi and Mulanax, Allen had gained so much weight, his face had become so owllike, he was compared to rotund Burl Ives the folksinger—but Allen was still relatively young and Ives had been an old man. As it was, these days Allen was just getting by on his $500-a-month disability checks.

WEDNESDAY, FEBRUARY 13, 1991

MUNICIPAL Judge F. Paul Dacey, Jr., Vallejo-Benicia, granted a search warrant (#1970) for Allen's home at 32 Fresno Street and the boat stored at 1545 Broadway.

THURSDAY, FEBRUARY 14, 1991

CONWAY and his men served the warrant—rapped at the door and stood expectantly in the brisk morning air. The door opened and an army of cops entered. After all these years, at last they would finally see what was in that dank tomb of a basement.

28
THE SEARCH

"I'm a nice guy," said Allen.

"What if I can prove you're a mean guy?" said Conway.

"If you had something on me, you'd charge me," Allen said placidly. He leaned on his cane. His eyes, heavily lidded, shone a lustrous brown beneath a massive brow—squirrel's eyes. Leigh's dog, Sobie, was at his feet. Conway pulled out a chair and conducted the interview upstairs where Leigh's parents, Bernice and Ethan, had lived. Scattered all about him, he saw the dusty antiques and mementos of long-ago gentility. Presently, a young woman was renting this upper floor while Leigh exiled himself to the basement. Leigh, however, kept some of his clothes, including shoes, in the upstairs back bedroom. There was a record player in the upstairs dining room and downstairs bedroom, and many records and accessories. He had a Sharp TV and a Sharp video recorder. He had a second video camera, lenses, a black video convertible recorder and stereo adaptor, and many, many tapes. There was a lot of pet equipment.

As he probed, Conway learned little things—Leigh was a gourmet cook. His sausage-making equipment was kept on a high shelf in his bedroom. A hard-bound sausage book and supplies (spices, casings, etc.) were in the laundry room pantry. The shelves held numerous cookbooks. He often printed out recipes for his friends, and enjoyed purposely misspelling words on these recipe cards. "We confirmed this through his brother and other relatives, that he did these misspellings on purpose," Conway told me later. "It wasn't by accident. He'd write recipes, for example, and he'd spell 'eggs'—instead of 'eggs,' he'd spell it 'aigs.' And that was intentional, just to get a chuckle out of people who would read it. He did that consistently, doing that with all kinds of things."

As they discussed his high intelligence, Allen became flippant. "Oh, no!" he said with a laugh. "I'm not gifted." Later, in a television interview on KTVU-TV, he described himself exactly that way. "I *am* gifted." "I don't booze anymore," he said, and admitted his high degree of mechanical ability. "I go to excess with anything."

Conway and Bawart descended into Allen's dark and dreary basement. "It was almost museum-like," said a detective. If it were a museum, then they might ferret out relics of Zodiac's past. The detective's notes, in longhand, stated: "Very dusty + cluttered. Books stamped w/S's name. Dust everywhere." There was an Amana freezer and refrigerator, Maytag washer and dryer, and camping and fishing gear. Conway's men unearthed four boxes of videotapes, a box of audio reel tapes, and one cassette recorder in the basement. They played a few seconds of each of the tapes, then exchanged stunned looks. They climbed the stairs and sat down and played a tape for Allen. Screams of pain filled the room. After the recorded cries ceased, Conway snapped the machine off. There was a long pause.

"That's me," Leigh said.

"Doing what?"

"Spanking a young boy."

"What?"

"A young boy who was feigning pain. I find it sexually stimulating," he said without embarrassment. "I admit to being a sexual deviant. I do get sexual pleasure, cruel pleasure, from sadistic pornography." He noticed the investigators staring at him. "Well, there's a lot of remorse for ya," he said.

The same kind of screams were on other tapes—the cries of yet unknown victims? It was difficult to tell if all were kids, though that in itself was criminal enough. So infatuated with children was Allen that he seemed unable to stay away from them even though it might mean being sent back to Atascadero.

"If I was Zodiac," he said emotionally, "I'd want to get it off my chest. Zodiac would be judged crazy. . . . Zodiac doesn't like to kill. I'd rather be dead than go to Atascadero. I can't be there. I hated the lack of freedom at Atascadero—the crazy people. They play mind games with you there."

The search for the smoking gun continued. Among the cob-
webbed and yellowed clippings in the basement, police ferreted
out a column by Superior Court Judge Thomas N. Healy that
Leigh had snipped shortly after his release from Atascadero.
Judge Healy's "Insanity Defense," an update of the Criminal Insanity Plea as a defense, had run in the *Vallejo Independent Press*
on January 10, 1979. Healy had cited People v. Drew as a redefi-
nition of the legal concept of madness. The M'Naghten Rule, introduced in England in 1843, imposes a legal distinction for
judging legal insanity—requires either that an offender not know
what he was doing at the time he committed a crime, or not know
it was wrong or was under a delusion. Obviously, such a defense
figured into any strategy Allen would use if ever tried and convicted as Zodiac. New York's Son of Sam, David Berkowitz, sentenced to 315 years at Attica, afterward admitted he had faked his
insanity. The searchers discovered miscellaneous papers and
news clips about Zodiac. Among them were several copies of
1982 editions of the *Times-Herald* and the *San Francisco Chronicle* that contained Zodiac stories. Detectives seized two copies
of the *Vallejo Times-Herald* dated June, 3, 1982, and a *Chronicle*
from June 6 of that same year.

Conway observed that though Leigh did a lot of talking, he really never said anything. "There's so many lies I caught him in,"
said Conway, "his denying things didn't have any relevance anymore. The last letter that's attributed to the Zodiac was a couple
of months after he got out of the Atascadero State Hospital. There
were no letters whatsoever during the time he was in Atascadero
State Hospital."

Leigh denied any involvement in the Zodiac murders, but readily admitted that Sergeant Lynch had questioned him in early October of 1969. "I had planned to go to Berryessa on that date," he
said, "but I changed my mind and went to the ocean instead." He
said nothing more about the neighbor who had witnessed him returning home the day of the stabbings. Nor did he mention the
neighbor's death by "cerebral thrombosis—massive" seventeen
days later. According to Conway, Leigh was "very amiable, calm,
and cooperative throughout the interview." But detectives brought
up a mountain of weapons from the basement. "Get a load of
this," one said as they unearthed a Ruger .22 revolver with six live
rounds. A .22 revolver. A Ruger .44 Blackhawk and five rounds. A
Colt .32 automatic and seven rounds. A Remington .22 short-

caliber rifle, a Stevens model 835 12-gauge double-barrel shot-
gun, and a Winchester Model 50 20-gauge automatic shotgun.
Winchester Super, and miscellaneous ammunition for .32-, .22-,
.44-, and .30-caliber guns. A .22 automatic clip with three rounds.
A Marlin .22 rifle with a scope. An Inland .30-caliber rifle. Since
Allen was an ex-felon, possession of firearms was illegal.

Then came a bigger find—Captain Conway's men discovered
four pipe bombs, a primer cord, and seven impact devices (Railway Torpedo). They ferreted out one can of black powder, partially full, and some Euroarms .44-caliber black powder, #13357
variety. They retrieved the following: two safety fuses (green,
two rolls each, 98 1/2 feet) and two rolls of orange safety fuses,
nine non-electric blasting caps, two one-inch galvanized pipes
with one end cap, five pipe thread compounds, six pipe vises.

Inside a cardboard box they located bottles of potassium nitrate, green safety fuse, two bottles of sulfur, two glass bottles of
black material, and miscellaneous fireworks. Years later, I would
find myself one day on the chilly slopes of Lincoln, Montana, at
the Unabomber's tiny cabin. Shortly after Kaczynski's arrest, police recovered items from the cabin identical with Allen's basement chemicals and firing devices. They even unearthed a box
containing fireworks.

"I never left bombs in my basement," Leigh maintained.

"Well, we found some," said Conway.

"I didn't even know they were there."

"Listen," said Conway. "We have your fingerprints on the pipe
bombs under your house."

"No, you don't," he said with a smile. "An ex-con left them
there nine, ten years ago. He's been dead for years."

Conway was later asked, "Did you in fact find fingerprints?"

"Let me answer that this way," he said. "Allen first denied having any knowledge whatsoever of any bombs existing in his basement, and when we told him of his fingerprints on the
bombs—which there wasn't, by the way, then he had an explanation of how he was cleaning up the basement and moved them
from one spot to another. That's the kind of stuff we went
through with him all the time." Allen said that the bombs had
been stored there ten years ago, which would have been 1981, a
dozen years after Zodiac bragged about a death machine in his
cellar. Investigators rooted out a Zippo lighter with "D. E. Brandon" engraved on it. Brandon apparently was the name of the ex-

convict who had allegedly left the bombs, and he was very much alive. The FBI later spoke with the ex-con. He denied "having left several bombs in a friend's basement years ago."

Next they showed Allen a piece of yellow, lined paper. It contained a menu for making bombs. Who could forget that Zodiac, on November 9, 1969, had claimed the "death machine" waited in his basement:

Take one bag of ammonium nitrate
fertilizer & 1 gal of stove oil &
dump a few bags of gravel on
top & then set the shit off
& will positivly ventalate any
thing that should be in the way
of the blast.
The death machine is all ready
made. I would have sent you
pictures but you would nasty
enough to trace them back to
developer & then to me, so I
shall describe my masterpiece
to you. Tke nice part of it is
all the parts can be bought on
the open market with no quest
ions asked.
1 bat. pow clock—will run for
approx 1 year
1 photoelectric switch
2 copper leaf springs
2 6V car bat
1 flash light bulb and reflector
1 mirror
2 18" cardboard tubes black with
shoe polish inside and oute
the system checks out from one
end to the other in my
tests. What you do not know
is whether the death machine
is at the sight or whether
it is being stored in my
basement for future use.

"I've never seen that piece of paper before," Allen said. "I've never seen these documents before." Conway added the yellow paper to his bounty. During most of the questioning Leigh was evasive, leaning on his cane and smiling. And he was wearing a Zodiac Sea Wolf Watch #26894—another version of the one he had worn at the refinery twenty long years ago. Conway bagged it next and put it with the yellow paper. They took away one cardboard box wrapped in a brown plastic bag with "Mrs. E. W. Allen" printed on a label. Then investigators discovered a letter from the Department of Justice signed by Jim Silver saying that Leigh was not the Zodiac killer.

Bawart and Conway knew Allen had forged this letter. "Jim Silver told me how Allen was working in the print shop at Atascadero, that was one of his jobs," said Bawart. "What a devious mind. We found a letter that indicated it was from Investigator Silver at the DOJ. It said Allen had passed the poly exam and should not be considered as a suspect in the Zodiac case. Allen maintained that the letter was authentic. Subsequently, he admitted that he had printed this letter while working in the print shop at Atascadero. We also found the master for this letter. The forged letter was taken in our search of Allen's home and not returned."

They dug up one Sears electric and one portable *Royal manual typewriter*. In 1966, Zodiac had mailed the weakest of many carbon copies, making a match to a specific machine doubtful. Riverside police knew the make, however—a Royal portable. The letter Morrill believed Zodiac typed in Riverside had been done on just such a typewriter. However, since Conway did not believe Zodiac had been involved in the Bates murder, it held no particular interest for him. They rooted out a small flashlight— Zodiac had said that he taped a penlight to the barrel of his gun to give him an electronic gun sight. They ferreted out a hunting knife with a handmade sheath and rivets—at Lake Berryessa Zodiac had worn a hunting knife in a sheaf studded with rivets.

FRIDAY, FEBRUARY 15, 1991

ON the second day of the search, police spaded up the yard, rooted through an old garden, and searched the garage at the rear. There they found a Hobie Cat catamaran and its trailer, a Therome gas grill, a stainless-steel rotisserie, power tools, spray

equipment, Porta-Power (which Leigh called the jaws of life).
Allen remained cool and collected. If the cat was not out of the
bag before, it certainly was now. Neighbors could hardly over-
look the massive police presence and the reason they were there.
The press could not be far behind. Detectives searched every
book on Leigh's shelves along the cellar wall, shaking the pages
to see what fluttered out. They were mostly boating and aviation
publications and books. The detectives rummaged through his
personal belongings, records, and journals, looking for a secret
diary or photographs.

"An explanation for why someone like Zodiac could be at the
murder site for only a short time and yet have details," Dr. Lunde
told me, "one way is that a person takes photographs and studies
them at their leisure when they get home. In that way they would
be able to give detailed descriptions of clothing and yet get away
from the murder scene fast." At one time a suspect in the Zodiac
case who worked for the police had pilfered photos of some of
the bodies. Kemper, at his trial, prided himself on his meticulous
detail, remembering names, ages, description of clothing, bodies,
and locations, almost as if he had a fixation to recall specifics.
Like Vacher the Ripper, once they apprehended him for one
killing, he confessed to all the others in an effort to dismay the
police, taking loving care in his detailed descriptions.

Bawart got a building inspector, who looked around and was
satisfied there was nothing hidden. Sometime after 1969 when
Cheney visited, Allen had built a kitchenette in the basement that
could have concealed items. If he built that, he could have just as
easily built compartments. Allen was known to hide things in that
house. Unknown to the police, when Ron and Leigh were
younger, they used to make their own home brew and hide it under the house. Cheney explained that there was an area under the
main living area where you could bend down and walk in there
and it provided hiding places.

In the end police found no evidence in the yard, garage, or
basement tying Leigh Allen to Zodiac. They went over to 1545
Broadway and searched the boat on its trailer. Again, they discovered nothing. "I found all the formulas," Bawart said of the
basement search, "exactly the same as the formulas Zodiac said
he was going to mix up . . . fertilizer bombs—formulas for ammonia nitrate and stove-oil bombs—and all that. I expected to

find more, quite frankly, but I didn't. There really wasn't a smoking gun." Conway took the most interesting items into his custody, among them "mail-order catalog pages regarding bombs, booby traps, and guns." Zodiac's November 9, 1969, letter had indicated that his killing tools were bought through mail order. Naturally, Allen wasn't wearing his Zodiac watch as he waved good-bye because Conway had taken it with him. That Swiss watch, manufactured by a company dating back to 1882, was a key to the case. Others thought so too.

A seaman, Kevin Moore, wrote me from Saudi Arabia: "A few months back, I saw an advertisement for Zodiac watches in a local store. This in my mind is too much of a coincidence, especially the fact that their logo is exactly like Zodiac's! I had never heard of the watch until I saw this ad, and that in itself is a clue because I don't think it is that common of a watch." A man following Sandy Betts, a cocktail waitress at the Coronado Inn, where Darlene Ferrin liked to dance, had worn such an unusual watch. "Zodiac," she told me, "got his name from the club near Sacramento called Zodiac and *then* found the watch. Have you seen the case the Zodiac watch comes in? The sign is the [crossed circle] and it's in a red satin case. I found it in a window of some used store in Concord, California, about 1975."

But the police search had not been completely unfruitful. Detectives had learned more about their suspect. They deduced from a clipping that if Allen was ever put on trial as Zodiac, he intended to use an insanity defense. After they left, Leigh wrote to friends that he expected to be arrested any day and returned to Atascadero. Police intended to use Leigh's anxiety about Atascadero to their advantage. Now Conway and Bawart knew Arthur Leigh Allen dreaded prison more than the police.

THURSDAY, FEBRUARY 28, 1991

POLICE prepared with the FBI for a second interview with Allen. The FBI had done an analysis of the Valentine's Day search and questioning. In their next discourse with Leigh one of the detectives would be assigned to push certain buttons. The hammer was to be "Allen's possession of bombs." Mike Nail, District Attorney of Solano County, filed a motion to be certain that information contained within the search affidavit be sealed. He and Deputy District Attorney Harry S. Kinnicut wrote that:

> "The people hereby move pursuant to Evidence Code sections 1040–1041 and *People V Sanchez* (1972) 24 Cal. App. 3rd 664, 678 to seal portions of the affidavit for the search warrant herein. These portions contain official information and disclosure is against the public interest. Evidence Code Sections 1040–1041 provide that the District Attorney may assert a privilege to refuse to disclose the identity of informers and official information in the interest of justice."

Judge Dacey ordered that portions of the affidavit be blacked out and sealed until further notice, though state law called for disclosure to the public of any search warrant within ten days after they are issued. However, they had not reckoned on the doggedness of the press. The name of the primary Zodiac suspect was no longer a closely guarded secret. The neighbors' jaws were moving. Soon, Allen's name and face would appear in the papers and on television.

WEDNESDAY, APRIL 17, 1991

AN FBI memo noted that Vallejo had resurrected the Zodiac homicide investigation: "Advised that they are currently conducting a background on a possible suspect ARTHUR LEIGH ALLEN. Vallejo Police have requested assistance in preparing an interview strategy for ALLEN." An FBI special agent had already met with Conway and Bawart on February 28 and March 20, 1991, "in order to discuss specifics of their investigation, and obtain relevant documents."

TUESDAY, MAY 21, 1991

ALLEN had friends in the south, had known them during the time he was incarcerated at Atascadero near their home. Now he wrote them. "His latest letter," one of them told me later, "states that the police have a new witness and that his place was searched again.

He was expecting the police to pick him up anytime. This was only a month or so ago."

Allen gave his first newspaper interview to the *Times-Herald*'s Jackie Ginley.

"On Valentine's Day," the fifty-eight-year-old suspect said, "Vallejo police knocked on my door with a search warrant in hand. These guys tore the whole damn place apart. I phoned them asking when I was going to get my stuff back, and they phoned two weeks later and said there's some new damning evidence. They said they decided to search my house twenty years after the Santa Rosa search of my trailer.

"It's all because they got a false tip from a man who is facing thirty years in prison on an armed robbery charge. He phoned down from Tahoe and said we had a conversation in 1969, and I'd told him that I'd go down to San Francisco and shoot a cabbie. He's a punk and a hood. I've never talked to him in my life."

"It should be mentioned," said Bawart, "that Ralph Spinelli owned a restaurant in the Lake Tahoe area in the early 1980s. It is apparent that Allen must have kept track of Spinelli as we *never* told him Spinelli had any connection with Lake Tahoe." A probable Zodiac victim had vanished from Lake Tahoe in 1970.

"This crap has haunted me for the last twenty-two years," raged Allen. "The police asked me to take a lie-detector test despite the fact that I passed one in the 1970s. I took a ten-hour lie-detector test and I passed the goddamn thing. So they tell me, 'Well, you're a sociopath, and you can cheat on lie-detector tests.' The Zodiac killer is thought to be a sociopath, someone who has no conscience and takes sexual delight in killing people, especially women. I'm considering getting in touch with Melvin Belli, the San Francisco attorney. I've been thinking about it, but then again, this has always blown over when they don't find anything."

Of all the attorneys in the world, Allen mentioned the one that Zodiac had phoned, written, and offered to surrender to—Melvin Belli. Belli and Zodiac went way back. On October 23, 1969, Belli checked with his answering service. His maid had left a message with them that Zodiac had called the previous night while the attorney had been at the International Film Festival. Belli had gotten in too late to hear of the two calls Zodiac made directly to his housekeeper. The gist was that Zodiac wanted to meet with Belli at his home. "Belli knows where he can meet if it's prearranged," the caller said. While Belli had been away in Africa, he had gotten three calls, two of them long distance. He waited all day in vain for the opportunity to set up a secret meeting. Worst of all, Belli feared Zodiac might be someone who knew him. An invisible man, obsessed with the high-profile and flamboyant attorney, had in a moment of crisis given him a clue of the first order to his true identity. To learn of that we have to step back in time, to October 22, 1969, and turbulent, terrifying days.

29
BELLI

"BEING a celebrity," said Belli, "brought me more than my share of crazy cases (that didn't pay me a dime). Take, for example, the long-distance TV romance between me and the notorious Zodiac killer (who may still be at large or, more likely, on ice in a prison where his psychopathology lies mainly dormant)."

At 2:00 A.M., eleven days after Zodiac shot cabdriver Paul Stine, a man phoned the Oakland P.D. "This is the Zodiac speaking. . . ." he said, demanding that either Belli or F. Lee Bailey appear on Jim Dunbar's KGO-TV talk show, *A.M.* He had tried to call the show a few weeks earlier, when both lawyers had appeared that morning, but couldn't get through. It was telling that both men were criminal defense attorneys. "I'll contact them," the cop said. The San Francisco police rang producer Bill Heral and he called Belli and Dunbar immediately, arranging to start the show a half hour earlier than usual. A KGO news bulletin was drafted: "Alleged 'Zodiac Killer' pleads for help in telephone calls to 'A.M.' Program with Jim Dunbar." At home we all watched, waiting for Zodiac to call, waiting to hear the sound of his voice.

"When I emerged from my penthouse on Telegraph Hill," Belli recalled, "I found the place surrounded by cops, even the garage was full of cops. They escorted me down to KGO. There, I also found police everywhere, even in the high, dark aeries of the TV studio, where I could see the glint of rifles at the ready." Belli carried on thirteen conversations that morning. One did not go over the air, a hesitant, drifting voice on the line at 7:10 that was abruptly disconnected. That first caller was frozen out by another, calling himself Zodiac, who kept the line tied up over the next two hours. Belli, though, requested a less ominous sounding name than Zodiac. "Sam," offered the caller. After exchanging a few words, the boyish sounding Sam, complaining of blackouts and headaches, hung up, then called back. Belli thought this one of "those rare cases where one man is acutely aware of two persons living inside his skin, one of them an outlaw who can't help killing." Sam said he wanted to talk to Belli because he didn't want to be hurt. "My head aches," he cried. "I'm so sick. I'm having one of my headaches." Then he gave a little scream and said, "I'm going to kill them. I'm going to kill all those kids!" He hung up and called back, suggesting they meet at 10:30 A.M. at the top of the Fairmont Hotel. Sam threatened to jump if anyone but Belli showed up. Belli suggested Old St. Mary's in Chinatown. They finally agreed on St. Vincent de Paul's Thrift Shop at 6726 Mission Street in Daly City. A rummage sale was being held there later that morning. Belli set off, crouched on the floor of a police car all the way.

Dunbar recalled the scene at the Thrift Shop. During that frightening experience he saw sharpshooters on the roof and submachine guns hidden under priests' habits. Dunbar admitted he was scared. "I had a young family and car payments to make," he said. He envisioned being caught in a hail of lead. Later, he came to think the entire event may have been a publicity stunt. Meanwhile, the cop who had taken Zodiac's 2:00 A.M. call had been watching the show. He was certain he had spoken to the real Zodiac and that Sam's voice was not the same. Belli waited forty-five minutes, but Zodiac didn't show up. "I don't wonder why," remembered Belli. "An army of police from San Francisco and Daly City was there. The cops had been monitoring Dunbar's line, and certainly weren't going to let this opportunity to catch the Zodiac and vindicate themselves before the public . . . I had already made a deal in advance with the S.F. District Attorney, John Jay Ferdon, not to press for the death penalty if the Zodiac turned himself in. I figured that wouldn't be the end of it, however. The Zodiac, judging from his taunting notes to the police and the press, wanted public attention. I was sure he'd call again. He did."

THURSDAY, DECEMBER 18, 1969

ZODIAC called the attorney's home, but got his housekeeper instead.[16] She explained that the white-maned attorney was in Munich, Germany, for a conference of military trial lawyers. "I can't wait," said the caller, who had identified himself as Zodiac. "Today's my birthday. I've got to kill!" He hung up abruptly.

"On December 18, 1969," Belli recalled, "the Zodiac mailed me a brief note wishing me a happy Christmas. I went off on safari to Africa. But while I was there, the Zodiac, according to my housekeeper, phoned me several [more] times."

SATURDAY, DECEMBER 20, 1969

Two days after the call, exactly a year after the first Northern California murders, Zodiac's letter containing a square of Stine's bloody shirt arrived at Belli's home. Unopened, it was forwarded down to his business office to be opened by his secretary. It was addressed "Mr. Melvin M. Belli 1228 Mtgy San Fran Calif." Neatly folded inside of the four-by-seven-inch white envelope was a portion of Stine's blood-blackened shirt and a message in felt-tip pen. A photocopy of the message was hand-carried by a legal associate to Belli, Room #293, the Bayershoff Hotel. Belli opened it with unsteady fingers and read:

"Dear Melvin This is the Zodiac speaking I wish you a happy Christmass. The one thing I ask of you is this, please help me. I cannot reach out for help because of this thing in me won't let me. I am finding it extreamly dificult to hold it in check I am afraid I will loose control again and take my nineth & posibly tenth victom. Please help me I am drownding. At the moment the children are safe from the bomb because it is so massive to dig in & the triger mech requires much work to get it adjusted just right. But if I hold back too long from no nine I will loose complet all controol of my self & set the bomb up."

---

[16]Conversation quoted in FBI report 9-49911-88, January 14, 1970.

"Please help me I can not remain in control for much longer," Zodiac concluded, paraphrasing William Heirens, the 1940s "Lipstick Killer of Chicago." Heirens, a sexual sadist, in a heartrending cry for help, had scrawled on a mirror in lipstick: "For heavens Sake catch me Before I kill more I cannot control myself."

It appeared Zodiac was being sarcastic in quoting Heirens, but Belli thought otherwise. He considered the letter heartfelt. "I believe he wants to stop killing," he said. "I have carefully studied his letter . . . and I feel it was written at a time when he calmly and rationally was considering the future. He knows eventually he will be apprehended and that unless he gets proper legal representation, he will most probably be sentenced to die in the gas chamber. That is why he is crying out for help. . . . Why has he come to me? He wants to be saved from the gas chamber. . . . I think we can do something for him. . . . We might get this guy and save some lives—including his. Maybe we could convince him he would get some treatment and that he would not be executed." Belli offered to bring along a "priest, a doctor, or a psychiatrist" and meet with Zodiac in "the San Marine area or in Nevada."

Belli fully anticipated Zodiac, who had gotten along famously with his housekeeper on the phone, "to be sitting in the front room with the housekeeper, waiting for him, getting on very well." He went on to Naples to defend a Navy doctor charged with misappropriation of military property. "I'd like to finish this case in Naples," said Belli, "but if I get an urgent call about Zodiac I will go back to California at once. I'll catch the first plane back if that is what he wants. I think we will have another communication from Zodiac soon." After finishing a delicious dinner of green ravioli, Belli phoned Avery in a transatlantic call. "It's mighty cold in Naples," he said. "I have the nagging feeling that Zodiac might be someone who knows me." Belli returned to California, saying, "My maid said she was very agitated to see me. She knows his voice."

Toschi and Armstrong rushed to Belli's to discuss the new letter. Belli, silk handkerchief in his breast pocket, French cuffs, silver watch chain on his vest, beamed expansively. "Belli was expecting us, naturally," Toschi recalled, "and he said, 'I'm going to have company, but don't worry about it. They know I'm assisting the police department.' So we asked him, 'Would you mind stepping away from your guests?' We told the man and woman at the table, 'We'd like to talk with Mr. Belli for about ten or fifteen minutes and he told us it's OK. It's about the Zodiac case.' She says, 'Oh, yes, yes. Melvin's told us all about it.' Not only were his dinner guests rapt with attention, but I could tell Belli was loving every moment. He was always on stage and always the star, even in court. I recalled how the jury and even the judge would turn their heads whenever he entered."

"The police stayed on the case," said Belli. "They felt the Zodiac may indeed have killed more persons than they'd originally believed, including one young woman in Riverside, California, in 1966 and another woman in the San Bernardino area in 1967. And then, in 1971, they had a lead that took them right to Riverside University's law school."

SUNDAY, JUNE 8, 1971

BELLI'S next real-life brush with Zodiac occurred in Riverside, where he attempted to strengthen Zodiac's connection between the Bay Area and Southern California. "Dean Charles Ashman phoned me," said Belli, "to say the cops were coming into the school, undercover, to check out one of his law students, a kid who had once threatened a girl he knew and told her he was the Zodiac."

Belli knew handwriting comparisons had been inconclusive. Under the guise of delivering a lecture, Belli hoped the boy, sitting in the second row, might ask a question. In that way, he could tell if his voice matched Zodiac's. Every person crowded around the student was an undercover cop. After the speech the student leaped up and rushed to shake "The Great One's" hand. "You don't know how much I admire you, Mr. Belli," he said. Belli knew immediately it wasn't the same voice he had heard and decided to settle the matter. "Hey, kid, are you the Zodiac killer?" he snapped.

The kid seemed stunned. "What do you mean, sir?" "Are you the Zodiac killer?" said Belli. "I hear you used to call yourself Zodiac." The cops moved in, anxious to hear the kid's answer. "No," he said. "I didn't kill anybody." "I believed him," Belli said later. "So did the cops." As for Sam, I later found him. He was not Zodiac, simply a troubled young man calling from a mental hospital.

A valuable clue lay in Zodiac's long-distance relationship with Belli. At one point, though, the killer seemed to have soured on him.

"If you don't want me to have this blast," Zodiac wrote April 29, 1970, "you must do two things. 1 Tell every one about the bus bomb with all the details. 2 I would like to see some nice Zodiac butons [sic] wandering about town. Every one else has these buttons like . . . melvin eats blubber, etc. Well it would cheer me up considerbly if I saw a lot of people wearing my buton. Please no nasty ones like melvin's Thank you."

Zodiac seemed irritated at Melvin Belli. But why? Recall that on Thursday, December 18, 1969, Zodiac rang the attorney's housekeeper and remarked that today was his birthday. Two days later, December 20, a letter from Zodiac arrived at Belli's office. The FBI quoted that conversation in report 9-49911-88:

VIA TELETYPE ENCIPHERED JAN 14 1970 2:14 PM UR-GENT "ZODIAC." EXTORTION. RE: SAN FRANCISCO AIRTEL. DECEMBER TWENTY-NINE LAST. ON IN-STANT DATE, INSPECTOR ARMSTRONG HOMICIDE DETAIL . . . CONFIDENTIALLY ADVISED THAT UN-SUB, WHO IDENTIFIED HIMSELF AS "ZODIAC," TELE-PHONICALLY CONTACTED BELLI'S RESIDENCE IN EFFORT TO CONTACT BELLI. UNSUB WAS ADVISED BELLI IN EUROPE AND STATED, "I CAN'T WAIT. TO-DAY'S MY BIRTHDAY." SUTEL. ARMED AND DAN-GEROUS. END NSM FBI WASH DC.

Keep in mind that Allen had been questioned by Lynch two months before this call and been let go. Not until his interroga-tion at the refinery twenty months later would he be a viable suspect. Zodiac had felt comfortable in giving his actual birth-day—December 18.

December 18 was Arthur Leigh Allen's birthday.

WEDNESDAY, MAY 22, 1991

THE *Vallejo Times-Herald* headlined: "Signs Point to Vallejo Man; Investigation into Bizarre Zodiac Murders Goes On."

"VALLEJO—Vallejo police seized pipe bombs, an underwater Zodiac watch and other items earlier this year from the house of a Vallejo man who was a prime suspect in the still-unsolved 1969–70 Zodiac killings. No charges have been filed against Allen for possession of the explosives, which he said belonged to an ex-convict who is now dead. And the police investigation remains a mystery. In 1971 San Francisco police targeted Allen as the prime suspect in at least six unsolved California murders and two attempted killings in the 1960s. The killer was called Zodiac because of the cryptic messages he loaded with astrological symbols and sent to the news media and police investigators during the killing spree.

"A series of cryptic letters from the Zodiac came to a three-year halt after Allen's Santa Rosa trailer was searched, Robert Graysmith notes in his 1986 book 'Zodiac.' Similarly, in 1975, when Allen was committed to an institution on a child molesting conviction, Zodiac's correspondence ceased for two years until his release. The linked murders of hitchhikers around Santa Rosa also came to a halt, Graysmith notes. Vallejo police have refused to confirm or deny any motive for reopening the investigation."

"Do I expect an imminent arrest in regards to Zodiac?" said Vallejo Police Chief Gerald Galvin. "No, I do not. It's an ongoing and sensitive investigation."

"Allen looked very good," Toschi told the press. "We searched

a Santa Rosa trailer where he lived part-time in 1972. But an
analysis of his fingerprints did not match partial prints found on a
Zodiac victim's cab in 1969. We could not find enough evidence
on which to convict Allen. I can't discuss why Allen was dismissed as a suspect."

WEDNESDAY, MAY 29, 1991

"LET me tell you what's happened here," Pete Noyes told me.
"Apparently this suspect [Allen] had a series of meetings with a
psychologist in Vallejo. The psychologist was afraid this guy
might kill him. And relayed this information on to a friend and
that's where it all stands now. The psychologist feared for his life.
He works for some institute up there and he gave all this information. The information is out there right now. These people are
trying to sell me the information down here in L.A."

"Don't pay a penny," I cautioned.

"They've got a series of tapes and all that," he concluded.

"Tapes?"

SATURDAY, JUNE 1, 1991

THE same individuals tried to sell the tapes to *Unsolved Mysteries* and were turned down. But Noyes told me, "The cops are very
interested. The story is there. There was some concern that an analyst should not reveal statements made during private sessions."

"I think that under the law," I said, "if a person is a danger to
society, an analyst can turn session tapes over."

"The psychiatrist's brother is a San Francisco cop and they decided to solve the murder on their own," said Noyes. "They went
and staked out Allen's home about eight or nine months ago. A
woman went in posing as a real-estate agent. He got wise to her
and started screaming and yelling at her and chased her out of the
house. He got the license number of her car. It was registered to
her mother. Two days later, there was a death threat made on her
mother.

"The psychiatrist treated Allen in the late 1970s as a condition
of his release. They have all this information. What they said to me
is that this guy told them more than anyone knows who's not well

versed in the case. The guys who have been staking out his house got all this information from the shrink. I just did a check to see if the informant is not a criminal or anything. He's a fifty-three-year-old man with no criminal record."

I didn't correct him. "What's your next step?" I asked.

"I want to listen to those tapes." So did I, I thought.

"Are you going to pay the guy?" I asked. I never trusted the validity of information that was purchased.

"I'm not going to pay him anything." He called back soon after. "Well, I've got Vallejo P.D. coming in here. They're real excited. They say they're real close to solving the case."

I spoke with Jackie Ginley and the Vallejo P.D. because I had gotten a number of calls from NBC and CBS television about Zodiac concerning "some tapes." "Do you think they do this periodically, call up with a hook on the story and try and sell it?" Jackie asked, referring to the tapes for sale. "I'm getting some calls here from people who knew Mr. Allen back in high school. A lot of people. But you know how it is working on a daily paper, there's not much time to devote to something like that."

TUESDAY, JUNE 11, 1991

BAWART and Conway studied Mulanax's files from 1971, then went and talked to some of the same people he had. "A lot of what the informants were telling Conway and Bawart in the early nineties," a source told me, "they didn't tell Mulanax. Maybe they were afraid back then to come forward, but now in 1991 they're not so afraid anymore and just want to get the guy."

"Captain Conway and I re-interviewed Phil Tucker," Bawart told me. "Tucker worked for GVRD. He wasn't really a friend of Allen's. He was an associate, as many other people were [who were] involved in any kind of athletics in that period of time. This interview was in the infancy of when I was doing background work on Allen."

Bawart's seven-page report, *Circumstances Which Indicate Arthur Leigh Allen Is, In Fact, The Zodiac Killer,* would grow to thirty items.[17] "During our interview Phil Tucker was unable to

---

[17] See Appendix for complete report.

remember that Arthur Leigh Allen had told him that he [had] special [electronic gun] sights for shooting in the dark. He did, however, indicate that Allen told him he was proficient in shooting and proficient in shooting in the dark. Arthur Leigh Allen had told him he had read a book . . . about hunting people with a bow and arrow."

Tucker recalled, "Allen was fascinated with the concept of stalking people rather than game. He indicated a number of times that it would be great sport to hunt people as they had intelligence. We were on our way to the beach to go scuba diving when he started discussing hunting trips and ended up talking about hunting people with bows and arrows. I felt he wanted my reaction to these statements. I told him I would never consider hunting people. He tried to make it seem like this was an idea for a book he was going to write. I got the idea that he was really saying, 'Is this something you'd like to do with me?' I just ignored him. I think he told me the name of the book he had read."

"Was the name of the book *The Most Dangerous Game*?" asked Bawart.

"I don't think so." Possibly Allen had mentioned not a book, but a 1945 film, *A Game of Death,* a remake of *The Most Dangerous Game*. "This conversation took place prior to September of 1966 as that's the month and year I married my first wife. That is why I recall the time easily. I did not see Allen to any great degree, nor go out on hunting and fishing trips with him, after my marriage."

"Do you know Donald Cheney?" asked Bawart. Stalking people at night with a gun had been part of the conversation Cheney said Allen had with him New Year's Day, 1969. Zodiac had also alluded to hunting people in his cryptogram.

"I do not," said Tucker.

"Why didn't you give this information to Toschi and Mulanax in 1971?"

"I only answered their questions. They did not ask me so I didn't tell them. I was not asked about any fantasies Allen may have related to me." Tucker also indicated that during the span of their conversation, he saw Allen had a Zodiac brand watch with a Zodiac symbol. Tucker also repeated that he had seen Allen write with both hands. "He uses both hands equally well when handprinting, but his handprinting is not real good." Tucker also mentioned that Allen had an interest in codes, and repeated that he had seen a handwritten Zodiac-type cryptogram at Allen's house. "This was prior to any cryptograms being published in the newspaper," he said. "Allen was the kind of fellow who loved to try and outsmart the other guy."

Tucker related, as he had for Mulanax and Toschi, that in 1969, he owned an older brown beat-up Corvair. Allen had driven this Corvair, but Tucker could not specifically indicate whether Allen drove this Corvair on July 4, 1969. Mike Mageau had described an older brown vehicle, "similar to a 1963 Corvair, older and bigger, old plates," as being the killer's vehicle.

THURSDAY, JULY 25, 1991

Now Allen became more than a name in the police files—he was the subject of the nightly news. "My first occasion to meet Arthur Leigh Allen was in July of 1991," reporter Rita Williams recalled. "We had gotten wind that Captain Conway and his folks had served a search warrant back on Valentine's Day of that year and it was about to be unsealed. We first talked to the captain."

"Why," Williams asked Conway, "haven't there been any charges brought against Allen when you found pipe bombs in his residence?"

"I'm not going to comment on an ongoing investigation," replied Conway.

"Do you think you are close to getting the case solved . . . any closer than you were twenty years ago?"

"Honestly, I don't think so," he concluded.

"Then," recalled Williams "just on a lark, my cameraman and I went to Allen's to see what we might get. It was late one evening. It was summer and still light outside, but beginning to get dark. My cameraman and I walked up to his door, and Nick sort of hid in the bush while I knocked on Allen's door. Allen was not clothed. He had on his bathrobe and yelled out the window, 'Just a moment.' Finally he came to the door. When I told him what I was doing, he surprised me by saying I could come in."

Williams had interviewed both the "Night Stalker" and the "Trailside Killer." "I was alone in their jail cells," she recalled, "but of all the people I've ever interviewed, none had ever given me chills like Arthur Leigh Allen. That was the thing that got me. He had this demeanor about him. He was just so big and so kind of apelike—just scary. It's hard to describe, but you could see the strength. And that some of the things he was accused of doing, you could see he could, in fact, accomplish. He was the kind of man that, even though he was very sick—at that time he was on kidney dialysis and had high blood pressure, was taking all sorts of medication—he was still a frightening presence.

"When he had agreed to my request for an interview, I paused. I had second thoughts. He had not seen my photographer some distance away, and I was not going into that house alone. Finally, the photographer was allowed to enter too. At first Allen told us we couldn't take any pictures. He just wanted to see what we were doing there. But over the course of the next hour and a half, we sat down and had a discussion with him.

"He had that sort of barrel chest, huge shoulders. He wasn't all that heavy, because he was on dialysis then. Even though he was sick, everything about him was ominous. He had on a housecoat and combat boots—big heavy boots—'clomp, clomp, clomp!' Then later, he changed clothes in the midst of the interview." Allen donned a transparent blue sport shirt, vertically ridged with two filigreed designs and unbuttoned to show his broad chest. His herringbone pants were old-fashioned, pleated and a grayish brown. On his right wrist a Band-Aid covered a needle mark made that morning.

Williams, blond, attractive, and long-legged, was dressed in a short red jacket over a black tailored suit, accented by gold jewelry. They made an odd couple as Allen led her through a tangled, disorderly garden. A chain-link fence reinforced with wood and wire ran along the perimeter. Allen pointed out where the police had retrieved bombs from beneath the house. "Allen talked about how the police had robbed him of stuff," recalled Williams, "harassed him and taken things he had never gotten back—sentimental stuff from his mother. He was quite upset." A hot wind rose against the pearl-gray sky.

They descended into the dusty basement room. It was warmer there. Williams sat with her back to a rugged homemade bookshelf of unfinished wood. She studied the items on the wall. Was that a Boy Scout felt band with every badge they awarded? Was it Allen's? A local child's? Dust covered an audio device—sounding machinery used in diving; a few diving, swimming, and spear-fishing trophies lined a shelf. Various photographic supplies were above her head. A Dustbuster (covered with dust) hung from the wall. On the floor a gallon container with a handle sat next to a small table. On that table, captured in the glow of a swivel lamp, lay a clutter of electronic equipment—a stereo, a reel-to-reel tape recorder, video games, a VCR, audio cassettes, and a black-and-white phone. Near a clock sat an almost empty stein of beer though Allen was not supposed to drink. There was a glass ashtray, though Allen did not smoke. An empty dinner plate had been tucked under one shelf. She returned her focus to Allen. Police had taken away many items; none of the things Williams was most interested in were present—Zodiac watch, guns, bombs, clippings.

As they spoke, Allen sat rigidly upright, hands folded in his lap, like a reprimanded student, and perched on the edge of what Williams took to be a rumpled couch covered with a blue blanket and two white pillows. Only later she realized, "That was where he slept." His bald head was framed by tan curtains painted with a design of bonsai trees and a blue sea stretching beyond. Allen's elderly tan dog lay against his left hip, striking out with his hind leg occasionally.

"I've lived in this house since I was eight," said Allen. "My mother died three years ago and ever since I've lived here—alone—in this room. I began taking kidney dialysis in April of 1991. First two times a week, then three times. I blew up like a blimp. My weight shot up to maybe 280 pounds. Finally, I was taking ten injections of insulin a day. Eventually I returned to my present weight of 220 pounds."

Williams told me later, "Though he was an obviously ill man, Allen was still a powerful, frightening presence. In his prime he would have been terrifying. I had read the book and I knew some things to ask. I started out by acting as if I knew nothing about the case, and getting more specific during the interview, and just let him talk. He said it was all circumstantial evidence, that there was never anything to pin him to be the killer, or, in fact, Captain Conway and the Vallejo police would have arrested him and charged him. He talked about some pipe bombs found under his house."

"I didn't know the bombs were there," Allen explained. "An ex-con friend, now dead, asked me to store some things more than a decade ago. They must be his. They told me my fingerprints were on the bombs. I don't believe that. I wouldn't be sitting here if they were and there's really no way they could get on there. . . . I think there probably is a Zodiac still out there and he's just laughing himself to death."

"Allen lived with his mother," Williams said. "He never married. He was arrested once for molesting a small boy and served time in Atascadero. He broke down and choked up on that. 'I realize now how horrible that was,' he said, 'and what an impact I may have had on that child. I'm not the kind of person to hurt anyone.'

"I asked for a response to the fellow [Cheney] who had gone to authorities about his remarks about hunting people—but first I quoted Zodiac—'I like killing people because it is so much fun. It is more fun than killing wild game in the forest because man is the most dangerous animal of all to kill. . . . '

"Allen tells me that he read that story, 'The Most Dangerous Game,' back when he was in the eleventh grade, and it had such an impact on him that he then was shooting jackrabbits and that was the only thing he could ever kill, and that he indeed had not said that recently. 'Well, he built this into something much, much grander,' said Allen, 'and remembered other conversations that we didn't have and decided, well, I must be the Zodiac. That was something that we talked about back when we were in high school together and he's mistaken. Everybody's trying to get publicity. In fact I had never said that.' Allen never went to high school with Cheney, and did not meet him until 1962.

"Allen has all sorts of explanations for everything," Rita recalled. "Three or four times throughout the interview, he mentioned that he had never read Zodiac, yet he would mention things that are in that book that he would not have known simply from interviews that Captain Conway and others have done with him. And then he would start back and say, 'Wait a minute. No! I've never read that book. I heard that he said that.' And he took great liberties with the truth there and that was not true. [Zodiac is visible under papers on his desk in the filmed interview.]

"And I used the summation that was in the book—about Allen's mother being very domineering and that he was not the favored one in the family, that his brother, who looked more like his mother's side of the family, was the favored son, and that Leigh had been under the dominance of his mother all his life. Very crass—[Allen] said several things about bodily functions of his dog and other things, I think more for shock value and to see how I would respond. But certainly throughout the interview, he denied that he was the Zodiac. He said in fact that he was another victim of the Zodiac because he was a victim of more than twenty years of police harassment for being an innocent man.

" 'They've offered me many opportunities,' he said, 'the most recent last Valentine's Day, to confess because then I'd be at peace with myself. Well, you don't get peace with yourself by confessing a lie. And this is what it would have been. . . . The little kid who lives next door, fifth grade, they're studying the Constitution and she got ticked off. "Haven't they ever heard of innocent until proven guilty?" she told me. Well, bless her . . . They haven't arrested me *because they can't prove a thing*,' concluded Allen, his voice quavering dramatically. 'I'm not the damn Zodiac. Excuse . . . excuse me.' He lowered his head and seemed to weep. 'Twenty-two years of this . . .'

"Having done this for almost twenty-five years of interviewing all sorts of killers, you just kind of get feelings. I can tell you my cameraman, as we got in the car that night, turned to me and said, 'Gosh, I think we just interviewed the Zodiac.' He was so convinced."

Williams's interview ran that night: "For more than two decades," said anchor Dennis Richmond on the *Ten O'clock News*, "police have suspected a Vallejo man of the unsolved Zodiac serial killings. Tonight we'll hear from that man. It's been more than two decades now since the infamous Zodiac shocked the Bay Area and the nation. Police are still working to solve those crimes. On Monday, authorities in Vallejo will unseal the results of one bit of that investigation. The search of the house of a man who's been called the number-one Zodiac suspect. Now for the first time that man has told his side of the story in a television interview. He spoke with us on condition that we not show his face." Allen's face was electronically concealed and shown in silhouette to mask his true features. It had to make viewers even more curious.

"Is this man the notorious killer known as the Zodiac?" asked Rita Williams. "Or is he a victim of more than two decades of police harassment? His name is Arthur Allen. He's fifty-eight now, diabetic, and had just come back from kidney dialysis when we talked with him at his Vallejo home last night. Back in the late 1960s, when Zodiac terrorized California, Allen was in his late thirties, sixty pounds heavier, strong, a biology graduate student.

And in this book, considered the definitive study on the Zodiac [shows the book *Zodiac*], Arthur Allen, known fictionally in the book as Bob Starr, is considered the investigators' number-one suspect. . . .

"One widely quoted letter from Zodiac said he likes killing people because it's much more fun than killing wild game, because man is the most dangerous animal of all. And in the early seventies, a friend of Allen's went to police, telling them Allen had told him virtually the same thing just before the killings began," said Williams. "From then on Allen was a suspect. In 1971, police searched two cars and a trailer he was living in in Santa Rosa. But for some reason they never searched the Vallejo house he shared with his mother until her death three years ago. 'Every time, I thought it was laid to rest, it would come screaming back,' said Allen on camera. 'The last time was St. Valentine's Day. Happy Valentine's Day!'

"Armed with a search warrant, police spent two days in February going through the house and garage. They dug up part of the yard, took Allen's Zodiac diver's watch, which he says his mother gave him, and pulled pipe bombs out from under the house. Allen took a lie-detector test back in the seventies while doing time for molesting a nine-year-old boy. He says he passed it, but authorities told him he was a sociopath and could cheat. Still, he's never been charged with any of the Zodiac crimes and he says he's lost jobs, friends, even medical care now, because police imply he's a killer."

The filmed interview ended with Allen collapsing and sobbing. Rita Williams told me later, "However, he didn't really cry. In looking at the tape, he kind of turned it on and turned it off. When Allen lifted his head his eyes were dry. I definitely felt he was pretending."

ALLEN NEXT SHOWED up on KPIX, Channel 5, the local CBS affiliate.

"I'm not the Zodiac. I've never killed anyone," he said. "They have me questioning myself. I search my memory for blanks—blank spaces—there are none. I was first questioned by police in late 1969. The cop said that someone thought I might be the Zodiac killer and reported me. At the end of the interview he said, 'Well, Zodiac had curly hair and you obviously don't.' So that was it.

"I've been questioned at least five times over the last twenty years. I thought it would stop after a ten-hour lie-detector test I took and passed in 1975. I once got a letter from the Department of Justice certifying that I am not Zodiac. The letter said I was no longer considered by the state to be a suspect in the Zodiac murders. I can't show it to you now. The Vallejo police seized it when they raided my house in their latest attempt to prove I am the Zodiac killer. The only way I can clear myself is for the real Zodiac to confess—if he's still alive. All I can do is suppose on that. The other way I can get peace for myself is when they find me dead and gone. I admit a large number of coincidences point to me."

Allen later told Harold Huffman, "They missed a few things—like the silencer I had hidden in my socks in the dresser."

Examiner reporter Lance Jackson rang me: "I heard about Ralph Spinelli, a career criminal, picked up somewhere around San Jose," he told me. "He got picked up and he's been charged with nine robberies. And so he starts singing—Arthur Allen's the Zodiac. He's looking at a long term, so maybe he was singing to try and get himself out of jail. Of course, the cops said now he's backing off and he's not sure he's going to talk. Did the cops call you? They told me [last week] they were trying to get in touch with you."

"What do they want?"

"The Vallejo cops told me they were going to be getting in touch with you. They brought this guy back who used to be there . . . Barlow? [He meant George Bawart.] He's going to be coming in a few days a week and working with Conway. They want to see you because they're trying to dig into it a little seriously again."

"That's good. If they come up with suspects none of us have ever heard of, that's all right too. It doesn't matter to me as long as they do it."

"Right. Let's get it done."

For Zodiac's favorite paper, the *Chronicle,* Lance Williams interviewed the perennial suspect. "I'm a disabled former schoolteacher," said Allen. "I was a teacher in the San Luis Obispo School District for a total of ten years, and spent seventeen years as a student. I once served three years in a state mental hospital for molesting a child. And I used to wear a 'Zodiac'-brand skin diver's watch. I've passed every evidentiary test the cops have thrown at me. I passed a polygraph. One policeman said, 'You're a sociopath—you can cheat a lie-detector test.' Another said I'm a genius. . . . I feel like I'm being messed over. The Justice Department wrote me a letter absolving me of guilt.

"As for the bombs and guns, they're the property of a friend I met in the mental hospital years ago. This damned thing has been haunting me for twenty-two years. If I was prone to suicide, I'd have already done it. . . . The only thing in my favor is, I've never killed anyone. Since I was targeted as a Zodiac suspect in 1971, I've been fingerprinted, interrogated, made to give handwriting samples, and subjected to a ten-hour-long Justice Department lie-detector test. No way in hell could I go out and kill innocent teenyboppers—no way. But with them, I'm guilty until I'm proven innocent, and I figure the case will be around until I die. I did commit one crime, that was child molesting," he concluded. "I deluded myself into thinking that I wasn't hurting anyone, but I realize now that isn't true . . . and I've paid for it."

Allen told his friends and neighbors the police were hounding him unjustly. Some of them stuck with him. But onlookers would come into the neighborhood and yell obscenities at him in the house.

THURSDAY, AUGUST 1, 1991

ALLEN told the *Fairfield Daily Republic* that he had consulted with Mel Belli about retaining him as defense council. Belli had not spoken with Allen. That afternoon, Judge Dacy, after five months of secrecy, unsealed a search warrant that contained only partial information. The return affidavit offered precious little details about what police confiscated from Allen's house. Court Administrator Nancy Piano later blamed the lack of information on a clerical error. She said clerks did not know that the search warrant findings also were required to be made public.

WEDNESDAY, AUGUST 7, 1991

"OVER a Dozen Weapons Seized at Home of Local Zodiac Suspect," headlined the *Times-Herald*.

"VALLEJO: Police seized more than a dozen weapons ranging from pipe bombs to a 20-gauge automatic shotgun from the Fresno Street home of Arthur Leigh Allen, a retired Vallejo man who is once again being investigated in connection with the still unsolved 1969–70 Zodiac killings."

"I was amazed at how brazen Allen was," Bawart told me after watching Allen on television. "It's like he loved the attention all around him."

"And in his mind, he became the victim," I said.

"Oh, he did. He craved sympathy. He wanted to get some kind of stay-away order from the Vallejo P.D. and other departments, a restraining order. And yet he was giving interviews."

Why had no further action been taken against Allen? Police turned up a cache of pipe bombs and guns, pornography, and tapes of children being spanked. They had been looking for a manual typewriter linked to Zodiac correspondence and a 12-inch knife with rivets used in the Lake Berryessa stabbings. They uncovered a Royal portable typewriter, clips of news articles about the Zodiac, and "a hunting knife with sheath and rivets." No one could explain the department's reticence. "It's unlikely charges will be pressed against [Leigh Allen] in connection with the mysterious killings," said District Attorney Mike Nail. "I really suspect that nothing's going to come of it."

Why wasn't Allen arrested? "The reason they didn't take further action after the 1991 search," Toschi said, "is that they knew he was terminal. That was the excuse. He was close to death when they found these items. Some officer said, 'He's terminal. It wouldn't have meant anything.' You can believe that or not believe it."

"District attorneys want to be fairly sure of a successful prosecution when they charge anyone with anything," Conway said, "and the most difficult and controversial part of our suspect or any other suspect that's ever existed, we've never been able to reconcile the handwriting. It's a very specific, unique handwriting. George and I have a theory about how to reconcile it, but getting a district attorney to buy that theory is—if we get past the handwriting, then everything else is fairly simple."

Zodiac might be perverse enough to want to be captured; he left clues in his letters. However, experts thought differently. "No serial killer wants to get caught," said Vernon Geberth, author of

Practical Homicide Investigation, "because then he loses the control and power that he has."

Friction developed between the old-guard Zodiac detectives and new investigators. "Have I ever spoken to Conway?" said Toschi. "I never heard of the man. I first saw his name when Allen's place was searched and he was quoted all over the place. And this really annoyed some at SFPD. 'You never heard of him,' a detective told me. 'Armstrong never heard of him. And he talks too much. He keeps calling us every other week.' They're a little disenchanted, a little hesitant to trust Vallejo at this point because when Vallejo searched Allen's home they found enough evidence in the basement and where he lived that they should have charged him."

"I find it kind of amazing," said Bawart, "that the guys in San Francisco would in any way be upset with Conway. Conway has a raspy personality. I got along good enough because I knew him. I was his boss at one point. Sometimes it was difficult for me to tolerate the way he said things, but I knew it was Conway's way of doing things and so I discounted it. He easily grates on people. But! But he was the only guy that was authorizing any kind of investigation. He was the only guy getting any kind of money coming out of the city coffers to handle anything on the Zodiac case. Now that something comes up that may turn the tables one way or the other, all of a sudden for a few to bad-mouth Conway in any way is a big mistake."

Now an event, unintentionally humorous and tragic at the same time, relegated departmental feuding to the back burner. At the end of June, longtime criminal defense attorney William Steadman Beeman had presented a theory to retired Judge Bill Jensen. "I know who Zodiac is," he told the judge and, without giving a name, laid out his reasons why. Jensen was unconvinced. All the judge could learn was that the suspect was deceased and may have been a former client of Beeman's. Beeman also refused to share his suspect's name with D.A. Nail. The D.A's office called Jensen shortly after his meeting to learn the specifics of their conversation. They spoke with Darlene Ferrin's sister, Pam, to see if she had any ideas about who it could be. She said she suspected Beeman had discovered new evidence in confidential files obtained from an ex-client through probate.

Beemen didn't share his knowledge with Captain Conway and the Vallejo police either. "He didn't present any information," said Conway. "He wants to save it for the news conference."

Within months Beeman would call a press conference to reveal what he knew. The press, including Paul Avery, and police officials had been invited. The announcement would be made in Vallejo on Halloween.

"Before he had that Halloween Day press conference," recalled Bawart, "Beeman got hold of me and said, 'I'm going to do this exposé. I know all this stuff. I want you to investigate this.' So I went down and met him at his office. 'Do you have any documentation?' I asked. 'Well, no I haven't done any of that,' he said." Handprinting samples provided by Beeman had not matched those of Zodiac. But so far nobody's handprinting had, and probably nobody's ever would. I still believed that Zodiac might have been a different personality when he wrote his letters. No matter, we all had to wait until Halloween to hear what Beeman had to say.

31

JACK ZODIAC

TEARS welled up in Vallejo lawyer William Steadman Beeman's eyes. One tear coursed down a broad cheek, dampening his starched white collar. Shyly, the seventy-one-year-old man brushed a lock of straight dark hair from his glasses and peered over a podium crowded with microphones. Beeman, succeeding beyond his dreams, had attracted a multitude. Television cameras glinted in the light and cables snaked at his feet. He saw *Chronicle* reporter Paul Avery entering the Solano County Fairgrounds, and consulted his watch. They were a little late getting started. He had scheduled the press conference for 10:30 A.M. and spent almost $600 to stage the meeting, not including the cost of mailing invitations to reporters and investigators. He had a lot riding on this event. He let them stew a bit longer. After all, he was ready to reveal who Zodiac was—just about the biggest story there was.

"There is no apparent motive behind the timing of the announcement," said reporter Jackie Ginley, "but it dovetails with a Vallejo police investigation of Arthur Leigh Allen, a Vallejo man who was once a prime suspect in the still unsolved 1969–70 killings." Since Tuesday Ginley had worn out her dialing finger trying to reach Allen for comment on what Beeman might say. Was Beeman, like Spinelli, about to name Allen as the Zodiac?

For almost an hour Beeman presented the verification that led to his conjecture. "There are at least 101 points of circumstantial evidence," he said. "I have a real problem with revealing the identity of this person. I had to do a lot of soul-searching." Beeman began to build to his revelation, describing his suspect variously as "a recluse," and "a woman-hater." He was "so disordered that he could not hold down a job," said the attorney.

"He could not even face a woman in the unemployment office without flying into a rage. 'Women are subhumans,' he told me. 'They cannot think logically and they act on emotions,' he said. He had done occasional work for me and sometimes repaired television sets. He particularly hated Yellow Cab drivers."

Just before noon the big moment arrived. Beeman held up *Jack the Zodiac,* a two-part paperback book he had published under the pen name "Doctor O. Henry Jiggelance." Volume One of the set opened with the warning: "This story is entirely fictional." Light began to dawn in the eyes of the assembled throng.

" 'Jack the Zodiac,' was my own brother."

Jack Beeman, a long-haired, dignified sixty-six-year-old, had died in Phoenix seven years earlier. "Jack the Zodiac," Beeman said, "came close to killing me. If he hadn't been drunk, and I hadn't moved like a mongoose, he would have." In spite of the acrimony between them, Beeman had represented Jack in minor run-ins with the law. He also believed that his brother had been responsible for the 1983 death of a Vallejo prostitute. Beeman pointed out that Jack misspelled the same words as Zodiac. "He used the same phrasing as that in the letters," he said.

The audience was not persuaded.

"I feel you're sincere in this," said Avery. "It's a pretty heavy trip to be laying on your brother, but you've offered nothing more than circumstantial evidence."

"I wouldn't be wrong in saying there are one hundred people who have called with the same kind of generalities," Bawart later said. "We look into everything, but I'm not going to pay $58 for his book [the cost for the privately printed two-volume set]." Besides, Bawart had no time for reading unless he did it on a plane—he had just gotten a lead connecting Arthur Leigh Allen with Zodiac. That lead would take him to the other side of the world.

32

THE GERMAN
HIPPIE

"WHEN I RETIRED they kept me on the case—you know that,"
Bawart told me, "and anytime anybody would call, 'My brother
or brother-in-law's the Zodiac,' they called me in. However, the
department was totally satisfied that Arthur Leigh Allen is the
Zodiac. I used to use *Zodiac* like a Bible, because I could never
keep all the dates straight. I'd use your book to figure out when
stuff really happened."

"I always thought that would be the best value that such a book
could have," I said.

"There was a guy that was a friend of Allen's from high school
and college. His name was Robert Emmett Rodifer."

"Robert Emmett?" I said. That was the name anagramists had
deduced from the garbled last symbols of Zodiac's three-part
1969 cipher—ROBET EMET THE HIPIE or "Robert Emmett
the Hippie." Emmet was an Irish patriot who had been hanged. A
statue of him stood in Golden Gate Park in front of Morrison
Planetarium—a room full of stars and the hall of biology—
Allen's passions. Allen's father, Ethan, was named after Ethan
Allen, an American patriot who had been hanged. Robert Emmett had been born in 1803, Allen's father in 1903. "And was
Robert Emmett a hippie?" I asked.

"He was a hippie-type. Rodifer was a guy Allen knew at Poly
where he went to college in Southern California and stretching
back to the time of the earliest murder. Robert Emmett had also
been manager of the Vallejo High swim team. Later he became a
hippie attending the University of California at Berkeley and at
U.S.F. Apparently there was some really bad blood between the
two. I found Rodifer, but it wasn't any great sleuth work on my
part. Because of the search of Allen's house, Leigh's name came
out in the press. A woman in Vallejo saw it. She had gone to
school with Arthur Leigh Allen, bought your book, and read the

portion where it says [in the last line of the deciphered 340-symbol code of November 8, 1969], 'My name is Robert Emmett the Hippie.' And she said, 'My goodness, I know Robert Emmett. Emmy Lou—Robert Emmett Rodifer. She got a hold of me."

"They called him Emmy Lou?"

"I don't know why. Talented. Rodifer was a real outgoing guy. In fact he was a mime and he played on *The Ed Sullivan Show* and all that kind of stuff. Arthur Leigh Allen actually hated the guy. Maybe it was because Allen was an introvert and this guy was an extrovert, although they were friends—let's say, *had* been friends.

"We tracked the guy down. We found out about Rodifer through his classmate. We thought he might be working in concert with Arthur Leigh Allen. He was now living in Germany. Rodifer was around children all the time at the base where he worked. Jim Lang went with me. He was the chief deputy of the district attorney. Ironically, Jim Lang spent twenty years with the LAPD, the last portion of which was working homicide. He retired, but he was still a young enough man that he went to law school and got a law degree. He was the district attorney of a county up north. He came down here and worked initially in the public defender's office, then transferred over to the D.A.'s office for a number of years. Youthful-appearing, a real smart mind, and he knows the homicide business too because he worked in it. In any event he wrote all these letters of rogatory, and it started in August of 1991."

"This seems to be a very important time," I said. "Everything coming together."

"Right. It took a hell of a long time. We ended up in Germany in the dead of winter in February 1992. It was kind of a fun trip. We actually spent two weeks over there. One week we were actually working. One week we were touring. We made some very good friends. The captain in charge of the homicide division in Heilbraun, Germany, and his wife turned out to be good friends. They've been out here visiting us and we've got a big motor yacht and we took them out on the Delta. We had a great time with them.

"Basically, what happened in Germany was this—in order to speak with Rodifer, we had to go through letters of rogatory, which is requests of the German government to come over and interview a person within their country. Even though this guy

was an American citizen living on an American base, we still had
to go through the German laws. I brought my own copy of your
book, *Zodiac,* and a second copy. My German aide read English
and asked for one of the copies. The magistrate, who under German law determines whether it is permissible for U.S. officers to
speak with Rodifer, allowed it after some deliberation. Then he
looked over my copy of your book and asked if *he* could have it.
Of course I gave it to him. We met with the police in Heilbraun
and explained the whole situation, and they felt they had enough
to write a search warrant for Rodifer's place, which they ultimately did. We went there with about half a dozen German policemen, all of which were in plain clothes. They did a real
thorough search of his place. We didn't find anything connected
with the Zodiac. I found a bunch of kid stuff. They kinda thought
it might be important, but I wasn't sure of that either."

Bawart theorized Rodifer might have been aiding Allen. "I
didn't know if there were actually two killers, but there might
have been two individuals who got their jollies doing this. We
couldn't talk to him at the time of the search, although he did talk
to me quite a bit. He volunteered to. Rodifer was a small man,
five six at most. Kind of a bubbly kind of guy. He had been a
number of places. He worked with the Department of Defense
and he ran their Dependents' Activities Program. If you're a sergeant or something and you're going to be overseas long enough,
you get to bring your family over. The families sometimes don't
relate to the new country, so the Army has community centers
and he ran those community centers where your kids could go
there and learn to wrestle and play basketball and shoot pool and
just have different functions. It was so kids could occupy their
time while in a foreign country. He had been doing it a long time.
He was in Japan. In fact he was married while in Japan. I was
never able to locate his ex-wife.

"We had to ultimately go before a German judge. We served
the papers on him, and a day or two later we went to the courthouse and all the questioning [of Rodifer] was done before this
judge. It was an extensive questioning and he was under oath and
he had to answer truthfully. I don't know how much that means.
He gave us a story about him knowing Allen. He was never real
close friends with him. 'I was really popular in school and Leigh
was not,' he told me. 'He was jealous of me.' There was apparently some animosity between him and Allen because of this.

Then after that he volunteered to talk to me at length, and I jammed him pretty good. In fact he had a German-appointed attorney who got upset with me. I tend to believe him. I came back and I interviewed a lot of classmates who were in that era when they were together—junior college. We interviewed them and I'm satisfied that 'Robert Emmett the Hippie' is a guy that Arthur Leigh Allen didn't like."

"Did you get handwriting samples from Rodifer?"

"It was one of the things we went to talk to Rodifer about. We got samples of Rodifer's handwriting from the Department of the Army, where he was filling out requests to go here, there, and everywhere. There was both printed and cursive matter on it. He wouldn't be disguising his handwriting to fill out an application. We had our guy who was doing all our handwriting analysis, Cunningham from San Francisco, and he looked at it, compared it to the Zodiac letters, and said, 'No, he didn't write these.'"

"Where was Rodifer in 1968 and 1969? All those Zodiac letters then had had local postmarks on them."

"He was out of the country, I think. Oh, wait a minute. He was going to school in Berkeley."

"How about 1974–1977?" That had been the period when no Zodiac letters had been received.

"He was out of the country, but I don't want to say that for sure."

"Did Rodifer have a lie-detector test as well?"

"No," said George, "Germany doesn't allow it. And as for Rodifer, he was not useful to testify."

The detectives retooled and began once more looking for evidence. If they were to interview Allen again they would need some expert guidance from the FBI. When Toschi had gotten in trouble, Allen had said to his P.O., "Now he'll know what it feels like." Toschi had this to say about him: "Allen had a great resentment anyway, but after all that public humiliation—now he's really going to start hating cops."

TUESDAY, FEBRUARY 4, 1992

THE media storm blew over and Leigh went on with his life. His good friend, Harold Huffman, one of the first to offer solace after last year's search, visited to check on his health. "When he and

Leigh made contact again," his wife, Kay, told me, "they agreed to never talk about what he went to Atascadero for. If Leigh was going to speak about any of his perverted feelings or what had led him to do it, Harold could not be his friend. Those were the rules that were laid down. Harold said, 'I can deal with Leigh all right, but I do not want to know the particulars and I don't ever want to talk about it.' Leigh tried to discuss it a few times. He made a couple overtures, but was met with silence. When my husband said 'no,' people listened. The Leigh that Harold knew was not necessarily the Leigh I knew. When my son Rob got a little older he said, 'Mom, did you know Dad took me out with the Zodiac?' I said, 'Dad took you out with Leigh?' He said, 'Yeah, Mom.'"

Harold and Leigh went on day trips, shooting and diving around the North Bay. Though lame and legally blind, Leigh could still shoot accurately. In the water he was almost his old self. Harold told his son how Leigh had recently visited the coast to dive for abalone. A party of frogmen, decked out in expensive gear, were taking lessons. Before they could dive, Leigh appeared in his trunks, knife clinched between his teeth, and plunged into the surf. "In a few minutes," Rob recalled, "he returned with the legal limit suctioned onto his large belly. He loved to gloat in the surprise of bewildered spectators. He shined when the spotlight was on him." While Leigh even drove on occasion, he let Huffman take the wheel, only forbidding him to drive them near Blue Rock Springs or Lake Herman Road. "If the cops are tailing me, they might use it against me," he said. "They'll go, 'What were you doing cruising Blue Rock Springs with your friend?' I don't want to see you hassled."

Leigh was very familiar with Lake Herman Road. Once, he and Kay were driving around the outskirts of Vallejo when they stumbled on a bleeding man by the road. It was a scene much like the Lake Herman Road attack. "In 1956, Leigh and I were coming back on American Canyon Road," Kay elaborated, "and saw a man standing outside his little car pulled off the side of the road. He was waving his arms. We got out. He and his wife had been drinking a lot of wine out of a jug and some kids had come along and asked him for a match. When they rolled down the window, the kids pulled him out, called him a wino, and beat him up. So Leigh took the jug and he threw it far as he could out into the field. I never figured out how come I agreed to this—when you're young you do dumb things—I sat in the car with the doors locked with these two little people while he went and hunted for a highway patrolman. He drove up on Highway 40 and did all sorts of loops and illegal things before he finally attracted the attention of the Highway Patrol. They followed him back down to where we were parked."

33
ZODIAC

FOR THE LAST two years Toschi had been chief of security for the posh Pan-Pacific Hotel at 500 Post Street. As director of twenty-four-hour security he conducted discreet surveillance of the VIP's floor and coordinated with their security people—grueling work. "Many times computer companies asked me to meet with their own corporate security manager . . . do a walk-around of the hotel and the rooms where equipment is going to be," Toschi said. "Times people would call me and I would be so tense and exhausted—missing luggage and missing items from rooms." And yet, around each bend in the hotel's labyrinth of corridors, Toschi's nemesis still lurked. A stone's throw away Zodiac had flagged down Stine's cab that long-ago Columbus Day. Toschi recalled the legions of Zodiac suspects. Had there ever been a greater mystery? The legend grew. A new generation became obsessed.

As if he had never vanished, Zodiac turned up later as fodder for television dramas. One day location directors for the *Nash Bridges* television program arrived unexpectedly from Hollywood and checked into the Pan-Pacific. As Toschi inspected their five rooms, one asked him, "Are you familiar with the Zodiac killer story? That's our next project." He laughed, knowing how many years he had spent hunting Zodiac. "What was it like to be on the hunt for a serial killer?" they asked, and so he told them. When Toschi saw the completed show, he said, "At least they didn't make me a nut. I even got to save the life of Nash Bridges [Don Johnson] through the character of his former mentor. The plot is that Bridges hears his mentor in homicide, Dale Cutter, a retired inspector, is having family problems. After many years, he goes hunting for Zodiac again. The drama ends with the *real* Zodiac still alive and making a call to Bridges."

Unsolved Mysteries would profile Zodiac, and the Fox Network program *Millennium* filmed an episode in which the hero (Frank Black) approaches Zodiac's trailer through the brush in Santa Rosa. The climax occurs in a theater like the Avenue. In the darkened movie house Black comes upon Zodiac—gun pointed, one foot advanced, the square-cornered black hood with the crossed circle in stark contrast—the drawing of him in costume come to life. The figure, through, is a dummy that allows Zodiac to escape as effectively as the actual Zodiac had.

WEDNESDAY, MARCH 4, 1992

DETECTIVES had not yet given up on Leigh. Weary manhunters, realizing they were up against a wily and clever opponent, thought they had overlooked some clue. Painstakingly, they scrutinized items seized from the suspect's house, sought out the FBI for strategy. The bureau's thousand-page Zodiac file mentioned only Arthur Leigh Allen in detail, his dossier accounting for ten percent of the file. Agents studied periodicals recovered from Leigh's basement, especially an article on Dave Eastman, the "Bird Man of Eaton," that had seized the suspect's interest. The FBI ferreted out a second article on Eastman in *The Irregular,* a New Hampshire free periodical dated April 19, 1989. Of what import to Leigh Allen was Eastman, a former helicopter pilot and birdhouse builder? Leigh was a flyer (that association alone might have sparked his interest), but it made more sense if he had hidden something in a wilderness birdhouse. They noted that Eastman wore glasses like those in the Zodiac wanted circular. Detectives fine-combed their bounty again. Perhaps they already had that clue, but did it lie there unrecognized on a table heaped with other recovered articles?

"As an experienced homicide investigator," retired Detective Baker remarked, "I recognize that, for purposes of search warrants and for determining the validity of suspects' admissions/confessions, the existence of such items would not be made public. However, unless the mention of specific items was somehow redacted/deleted from the publicized versions of the warrants to search Allen's residence, this may not be the case (items not named with any specificity in the warrant may not be seized). This would lead me to believe that any souvenirs he may have collected may be more esoteric or abstract than would otherwise be recognized by the investigators. Then again . . . perhaps the investigators of that period may have lacked the present-day sophistication to have recognized the absence of such items from the scenes."

But what was there? A pile of recipe cards that had words humorously misspelled, a slip of yellow paper and a Zodiac Sea Wolf Watch the detectives had expected to find. They anticipated clippings on Zodiac; they were there. A serial killer who craved publicity would be compelled to keep cuttings of his newspaper appearances. He not only had videotapes of news programs mentioning Zodiac, but had retained a copy of the return of service of a search warrant Toschi had handed him in 1972. Allen had smiled then, as if he knew a joke that the police did not.

I thought of Lynch's anonymous tip in 1969. Without that tip, Leigh would not have been a suspect until he spoke freely to the three detectives at the oil refinery. He seemed to want to interact with the police, and enjoyed it when he was finally a suspect. What if Leigh had turned himself in? If not, who had been the tipster?

"I probably hadn't seen Leigh in twenty-five or thirty years," Kay Huffman told me later. "I hadn't kept in touch. I knew he had been down in Atascadero and I knew what for. And that blew me away because I had had no inkling of anything like that. Harold and Leigh had gone to an air show and he brought him home here. There was this little old man. I don't know what happened to the young vigorous person I knew, but he wasn't there anymore. Now the diabetes had made him look terrible and aged. I was devastated for days afterward. I couldn't believe it was the same person.

"My dad was very ill too and so I'd go up to Vallejo to visit him. I usually did that about every other weekend and if Leigh was in, I'd stop by and visit him a little bit. The first time I stopped by, he wanted to tell me about how he had burglarproofed the house 'cause there had been a break-in. Then he wanted to know if I wanted to see the guns and knives he kept in the basement room his mother built for him. We used to call it 'The Dungeon.' I looked at him and said, 'That isn't what I came to see. I came to see you.' And he says, 'You don't want to talk about my guns?' 'No, I don't want to talk about them and I don't want to see them ever.' "

MONDAY, MARCH 23, 1992

AN FBI special agent met with Conway while Bawart was following up leads. On Monday morning Conway advised the agent
they were reinitiating the Zodiac serial murder investigation.
"This was because of information concerning a possible suspect—Arthur Leigh Allen," the S.A. wrote of the meeting.

"Conway and Bawart were interested in designing an interview strategy for ALLEN should it become necessary to con-
front him," said the submitted FBI report [252B-SF-9447]. He
stated he "met on two separate occasions with Conway and
Bawart. . . . These two meetings lasted a total of approximately ten hours. These investigators were interested in an interview strategy for a possible suspect ARTHUR LEIGH
ALLEN. However, they indicated they had a considerable
amount of investigation to conduct prior to contacting
ALLEN." The memo mentioned the 1991 search and indicated VPD had subsequently interviewed him again twice. On
all occasions, ALLEN was "calm and cooperative," but denied
any involvement. This case was left pending because the
Vallejo police indicated that they wanted additional assistance
in their investigation as information developed. Therefore this
case was left open until 3/23/92, when Bawart was contacted
to provide a status report on the case. Because of SA caseload
during the last year with priority matters . . . no regular
memos have been placed in the [Allen] file explaining the reason to have the case remain open."

TUESDAY, MARCH 24, 1992

As Bawart and Conway prepared "Report, Case #243145," they
discovered more circumstances that indicated Arthur Leigh Allen
was in fact the Zodiac killer. "They got a lot of stuff that Mulanax
did, then went and talked to some of the same people," I was told.
"A lot of what the informants were telling Conway and Bawart in
the early nineties they didn't tell Mulanax. Maybe they were
afraid back then to come forward, but now in 1992 they're not so
afraid anymore. They just wanted to nail Zodiac."

Conway had advised the bureau that there "were two additional interviews to be conducted with people who had known the suspect for a long time . . . with a man who had known Allen at the time of the killings [Cheney]." Once these interviews were conducted, Conway indicated, he and Bawart "will present a full review of the case to the Sonoma County District Attorney's Office for an opinion regarding possible prosecution for ALLEN. If the D.A. refuses to fill charges against ALLEN, Vallejo Police Department will close its investigation on the 'ZODIAC' case."

Bawart located Cheney. "When George Bawart tracked me down," Cheney told me, "he contacted me by telephone, I talked to him. Then they had me come down to be interviewed by them in Vallejo. They flew me down to Sacramento, and George met me at the airport and drove me to Vallejo. We spent a couple of hours together with Roy Conway. What I had told Armstrong (and the other detectives) I told them. They recorded everything I said, and they pumped me for everything I could give them.

"Allen loved to outsmart the other guy, I told them. In a 1967 conversation Leigh asked me how to alter his appearance. We discussed theatrical makeup and what you could accomplish with it. I wasn't curious why he was asking me this. It wasn't unusual to talk about something like makeup." By the time Allen became a known suspect, he had already altered his appearance to an astonishing degree by burying his athletic physique in fat.

"With Leigh," said Cheney, "you just get into conversations about 'What if this' and 'What if that.' It was just more of knowledge for knowledge's sake. Leigh was always interested in all kinds of things. And I was too. Leigh enjoyed misleading people. He liked to trick people or influence them into things that they otherwise wouldn't do."

"In January 1969 Allen had a conversation with Donald Cheney, a friend of his," wrote Bawart in his report. "He guised this conversation as though he were going to write a novel. Allen indicated to Cheney that he would call himself Zodiac and use the Zodiac watch symbol as his symbol. That he would kill people in lovers' lanes by using a weapon with a flashlight attached to it for sighting at night, that he would write letters to the police to confuse and taunt them and sign them as the Zodiac. Allen stated he would get women to stop on the freeway indicating they had some problems with the tires, he would loosen their lug nuts so their tire would later fall off and he could take them captive."

Bawart arranged for Cheney to be polygraphed back in Washington State. "Bawart gave me a polygraph in his presence," Cheney told me. "It was so short I couldn't believe it. A month later, I went and took another one in the same police station in Kennewick, South Central Washington, one of the tri-cities here where I live, but without Bawart being present. I gathered that in the first they didn't have the right test questions. They flew a technician from Seattle over here to run the polygraph. It was a little on the dull side except for feeling some stress. They hooked me up so they could measure my respiration and blood pressure. It seemed to me there might be four to five responses—the number of needles on the paper.

"They asked questions that required yes-or-no answers. He told me to just answer in a calm and monotone way, no emotion. In the second test—I'll tell you why they gave me two tests. In the second test, when we had gone through all the questions—they start off with 'What's your name,' then they ask the questions about the case. Then when I thought he was finished with that, he kept asking me more questions. It didn't seem to matter what the answers were, but the questions were mainly rephrasing of things. I tripped up and made a misstatement. It wasn't a lie. I wasn't intentionally making a misstatement, but I just said something I didn't intend to say. All the needles made a jump, flopped around. Then he was satisfied. That was what he wanted. I guess that they were looking for something that would gauge." It turned out, as Bawart told me later, "Cheney was telling the truth."

The biggest obstacle still was that Allen's handprinting did not match the Zodiac's. "The experts explained that the only explanation for this would be if ALLEN would have been able to develop a 'false handwriting,'" Bawart wrote. Allen had once asked Cheney if books on how to disguise handwriting existed, and later studied books on fake handwriting. The FBI noted: "Vallejo has requested no further assistance on this case, and it is therefore *recommended that this case be closed at this time.*"

AT BAWART'S WORKPLACE, a cabinet shop, he was mulling over a possibility that had intrigued him for years—one that might explain everything. There might be two Zodiacs working as master and slave. That theory had been one of the reasons George had tracked down Allen's friend Robert Emmett. "I conjectured that there might be two Zodiacs, partners working together," he told

me later. "After that trip to Germany and seeing the man, I came
to believe there was only one. As for Donald Lee Cheney, he's
now a retired mechanical engineer in Washington. Panzarella is
wealthy, has sold his stock, and become owner of RKO Pictures
Film Library. I even went down to interview him. Panzarella was
just a regular guy, but he had all this money."

As for Ralph Spinelli, the other known tipster, he had reportedly been incarcerated 290 miles north of San Francisco on the
Oregon border. Allen, after the Stine murder, had kicked in his
door and beaten him a second time.

WEDNESDAY, AUGUST 26, 1992

ON a nice August afternoon about 3:00 P.M., George Bawart was
working in his garage, the smell of new lumber and sawdust
sweet in his lungs. A street cop phoned him at home and Bawart
hustled to the phone. It had a special attachment for his hearing
disability and made voices extra loud. "The cop was kind of a
joker," Bawart recalled.

"Are you still investigating Arthur Leigh Allen as the Zodiac?"
he asked.

"Yeah," Bawart said. "Arthur Allen."

"Well, I'm in his house and he's laying on the floor."

"What's he doing laying on the floor?"

"Well, he's dead and he's lying here with a great big bump on
his forehead."

George listened carefully to the rest.

He put the phone down. The room seemed to swim. They had
waited too long. He steadied himself. Had someone, perhaps Zodiac's partner or someone after revenge, gotten Zodiac before
they could?

34
ZODIAC

"A street cop got detailed there," Bawart told me. "Allen wasn't answering his door. He had a girl living upstairs. When they didn't hear from him for a long time, Allen's upstairs boarder found his body. The cops went there. They opened the door, got in the house, and there's Allen lying face down on the floor. I rushed over. I had to make sure he died of natural causes. His name has been published. He's been showing up on TV. He's been granting interviews and drawing all sorts of attention to himself. The Ferrin family had called me a number of times and said, 'Do you really think he did it?' I told them, 'Yeah.' And the Ferrin family can be kind of goofy. I thought, 'Jesus, did one of them do something?' So I went on down there and he was in fact dead."

Bawart stood in the dim basement, his intent face lit by the glow of Leigh's new computer. He steadied himself, looking thoughtfully at the big man in the bathrobe on the cold floor. The professional side of the detective took hold. Bawart began assessing the facts. He recalled Allen's words from television: "About the only way the heat will stop is if I die, that will cure it for me or if Zodiac himself confesses. . . . They haven't arrested me . . . *because they can't prove a thing*."

"He had fallen face down," Bawart told me. "I rolled him over. He had a little injury to his head that I was at first a little bit concerned with. He had been bleeding. Usually when you have a heart attack, if you die right away you don't bleed anymore. So I got the coroner and the medical examiner."

Thus, the prime suspect, with a lump on his head, his bathrobe open, lay with newspapers about Zodiac spread about him. In addition to clippings about the case, Allen possessed everything the experts had expected Zodiac to have—an arsenal of guns, bombs, a portable typewriter, a knife scabbard with rivets. . . . I recalled when Rita Williams had interviewed Allen the previous year, he had been dressed as he was today—in a flimsy bathrobe and rubber boots. He had attempted to shock her, waving his arms and shouting that the police had persecuted him. Bawart walked to the humming Epson Equity 1 computer. "The thing that interested me," he said, "is that when I got there there was a bunch of computer discs out on the table and they said 'Zodiac' on them and stuff like that."

Floppy discs were scattered by the printer. Bawart ejected a disc still in the machine. It was labeled "Zodiac." What was on the discs and in the computer and what was the significance of those particular Zodiac newspapers? Apparently the computers had been added since the last search—an Avstar computer, an Epson Equity 1 computer, and all accessories. Then Bawart spied a videotape marked with the letter "Z" lying on a bookshelf at the east wall. Bawart was excited over the tape. They would need a warrant to view that. As soon as they could, they played it. All the video showed was Allen mooning the police, cursing them, and complaining about the case—nothing incriminating.

For some time Bawart had known Allen had been ill—suffering from diabetes, heart troubles, severe arthritis, and kidney failure. So the end was not only expected, but might be easily explained. The detective consulted the coroner, and he established the facts of death: "Found August 26, 1992 at 3:10 P.M. Immediate cause of death: Arteriosclerotic Heart Disease. Other significant Conditions Contributing to Death But Not Related to Cause Given: Diabetes Mellitus, Cardiomegaly, heart disease." And the bump? "The coroner determined," said Bawart, "that when Allen hit the floor he banged his head."

D.A. Mike Nail had already scheduled a meeting on Arthur Leigh Allen sometime earlier. With the death, the parley would still proceed. "About a week before we went to meet with him, Arthur Leigh Allen dropped dead. So that at this meeting, this D.A., being kind of a half-assed comedian, said, 'We've got good news and bad news. We're not going to file on Shawn Melton'— they didn't want to spend the money on that—'but I'm going to file on Arthur Leigh Allen.' He was naturally joking because he knew he couldn't file on a dead man.

"Mike Nail," George told me later, "had political aspirations as a superior court judge [which he realized]. I've known Mike Nail my entire career. He started out as a rookie D.A. straight out of law school. He and I didn't socialize together, but we would joke and stuff. He probably would not have filed on Allen, to be honest with you, because he was going for a judgeship and would not in any way want that to be compromised. The gist of it is we were going to file on him and he promptly died on us. The problem was the district attorney didn't want to file on a dead guy. But they won't one hundred percent clear it.

"When we were getting ready to charge Allen with the case. I compiled a list so we could go to the district attorney's office. When Jim Lang and Conway and I met with Mike Nail. We were doing two things that day—there was a kind of infamous case from our county; a kid named Jeremy Stoner, a six-year-old, was abducted and ultimately found dead in the Delta. The responsible on that was a guy named Shawn Melton.

"Melton's father at one time alluded to the fact that Melton wrote letters to the newspaper [like Zodiac] and his terminology was somewhat similar to the Zodiac. Somebody came out with this harebrained idea that he was the Zodiac. But he wasn't, I can assure you of that! We were meeting with Nail, at that time, to see if he would refile on Shawn Melton. There had been two trials on him and there had been two hung juries. We were also meeting at the same time to see if he would file on Arthur Leigh Allen.

"Those thirty points were made to give to him to have something firm in his hand rather than us telling him each and every point. That report was actually made to present to the district attorney's office, but wasn't intended to be part of the case file per se. I don't remember all thirty of them. Some of them, when you're putting together something like that, I didn't intend for it to end up in the case file. It was more of a working file. One or two or three of those points a defense attorney could pick up on and really hammer because there was some supposition where I really didn't have a lot of background to back them up. But the meat of the thing I could back up."

THURSDAY, AUGUST 27, 1992

CONWAY signed an affidavit for a search warrant. "As you know," Bawart told me, "I wrote another search warrant and searched his house again even though he was dead. There was a computer system and the videotape. The purpose of the search warrant was to view that tape and, according to the affidavit, determine if it contained evidence related to the so-called Zodiac killings."

Vallejo police descended to the lower apartment at 32 Fresno Street—as dark, dank, and museumlike as it had been the previous year. In the Epson printer was Allen's partially completed "Polygraph Agreement" for the Vallejo police. Conway took possession of numerous videotapes and five containers of discs and manuals for the printer stacked there. Near the computer lay an index of computer discs labeled "Polygon" and a yellow disc catalogue with discs labled "Plolams" [Allen's intentional misspelling of "Programs"]. They discovered a "Fruit Juice Recipe" bomb formula and a box with blank notepaper. Strips of paper were covered with math. A last will and instructions for the computer were on the east wall bookshelf. The will and instructions read:

> "Being sound in mind, if not in body, I hereby put to paper my last will and testament. I will update this document as conditions warrant, so this computer version will always be the last and most current will and testament. In cases of printed copies, the date on the copy will determine whether it is the most recent version of the will. All pages must be signed and dated by me, as well as the end of the last page.
>
> "First and foremost I wish to have it known that, due to whatever circumstances, I enter a vegetative state, that all life support systems be disconnected and whatever of my body organs that can be used to help others be utilized for that purpose upon my death.

"The procedure for obtaining the most recent version of this will is as follows:" The detectives followed the procedure laid out—they turned on the monitor screen (the bottom roller on the lower right side of the monitor casing). They inserted the MS-DOS working copy.

"Diskettes are located in the yellow-loose-leaf binder next to the printer into the top slot of the computer," Allen had instructed. "This is known as the 'A' drive. With the elephant log on the top right toward you until it clicks. Push the 'push' button in so it clicks also. Push the power button in so the red light goes on. Insert the DATA disk into the lower slot (the 'B' drive) until it clicks, then push the 'Push' in as well. Now press the 'enter' key on the keyboard. A small light will appear on the 'A' drive and the computer will hum. Some printing will cycle onto the screen. When a request for the date or time appears, press the 'entry' key a couple times until the 'A Prompt' (A>) sign appears."

The instructions entailed seven complex maneuvers in detail to access the most current will: "I bestow upon my good friend, Harold Huffman, the duties of executor of this Will and Power-Of-Attorney. . . ." the document began. Allen left his Epson Equity 1 computer, all accessories, "porgrams" (as Leigh spelled it in his last will), and related literature to his tenant. Leigh concluded on a sad note and more lies.

"As for my Brother, Ronald Allen . . . I was very deeply hurt by the total lack of support by his whole family during my recent conflict with the law. I still love my brother very much, which made the hurt all the deeper. I was hurt (but not surprised at all) when my sister-in-law took pains to phone me several times to tell me they were so broke that I couldn't expect any financial help from them at all. Then they went right out and bought 3 Hondas, including a brand new Accord. Some poverty case! Still, if there is anything he wants for himself after all the above is sorted through, he is welcome to it. He'll be getting the house anyway, which should be worth a couple bucks."

Leigh had four more cars, including a Corvair. He wanted his dentist to get his Rolls, but Ron got that. The cops studied a letter to the Vallejo police on the computer. "In the letter," Bawart told me, "were references to letters he was gonna write about how he was gonna sue us for this, that, and the other."

"The return to the warrant says you found a knife and a knife scabbard with rivets," I said to Bawart.

"I don't remember the scabbard at all," he said. "I think we just took it because it had a knife. It wasn't anything really earth-shattering. As for the Royal typewriter we found, that pertained to the Riverside murder and I had discounted Zodiac for that." So had Conway. Riverside detectives were able to I.D. the typewriter used by the killer as a portable Royal typewriter, Elite type, Canterbury-shaded, such as found in Allen's basement. Morrill had ruled that Zodiac wrote the handwritten Riverside letters mailed, but if he typed the confession letters too, then Allen's typewriter might still offer a clue. I doubted it. The typewritten letters had been distant carbon copies.

"I got about four or five phone calls when Allen died," said Toschi glumly. "San Francisco was kind of curious why Vallejo didn't just close the case. They told an inspector that the Vallejo district attorney chose not to close the case because Allen was terminally ill and was expected to die within two weeks. They had already scheduled a conference to discuss that decision in the next month after his death, so they went ahead and had it."

SATURDAY, AUGUST 29, 1992

THE day before, a Vallejo police property report on Allen had been filed in the municipal court clerk's office. Now that the press realized who had died, they ran with the story. Erin Hallissy reported in the *San Francisco Chronicle*:

> "Man Once Suspected in Zodiac Case Dies—A man once suspected of being the Zodiac killer, who taunted police and terrorized Northern California with threats of murder, died Wednesday in Vallejo of a heart attack at the age of 58.
>
> "In 1971, attention focused on Arthur Leigh Allen when relatives and friends told police that he was acting erratically and that they feared he might be the sadistic slayer who killed at least six people and perhaps as many as 37 between 1966 and 1974. In his book "Zodiac," former *Chronicle* editorial cartoonist Robert Graysmith described Allen under a fictitious name as "the gut-feeling choice of most detectives" for the Zodiac killer. . . . Allen had reportedly told some people that he was the Zodiac killer."

THURSDAY, SEPTEMBER 3, 1992

"IN the mid-1970s Allen was convicted of child-molesting charges and sentenced to prison," Conway said publicly. "Last year, we searched Allen's home in Vallejo as a part of a follow-up investigation into the unsolved case. We found some writings, some pipe bombs, some illegal weapons. None of it was sufficient to make an arrest for him being the Zodiac. . . . It is still an ongoing criminal investigation. His death has not changed that. I can't discuss an ongoing investigation. I don't have any reason to believe that Allen's death was a suicide and there has been no preliminary evidence that foul play was involved."

In San Francisco, Dave MacHalhatton, KPIX-TV anchor, bannered the suspect's death on the evening news. He and his wife, Bonnie, had conducted the first hour-long show on Zodiac with me back in 1986. "Allen died this week," he said, "leaving behind the unanswered question, 'Was he really the Zodiac?' " Tomas Roman reported that "the only thing the police are certain of is that their case remains unsolved. His death has little effect on the ongoing investigation into the man known as the Zodiac, the man who taunted police by claiming to have killed as many as thirty-seven people. . . . But even after an extensive search, police still did not charge Allen . . . with any crime linking him with the Zodiac killings."

"I am not the Zodiac," Allen had told KPIX. "I have never killed anyone. They have me questioning myself. . . . The only way I could clear myself is for the real Zodiac to confess—if he's still alive. . . . All I can do is suppose on that. The only way I can get peace for myself is when I am finally dead and gone."

All Toschi could say was, "Mr. Allen was a very, very good suspect. We looked into Mr. Allen very closely." The FBI, on noting the death, said in a report, "The San Francisco case is closed at this time."

"This retired cop who was working on the case told me he's out of work now," Pete Noyes told me. "They found a lot of computer discs in Allen's house. They went in there and picked up a lot of stuff. The psychologist, Thomas Rykoff, apparently has some deal going with a guy down here to write a book. I don't know if that's ethical or not. Rykoff interviewed him at Atascadero."

Bob Woolridge, a good friend at *Time-Life,* called for an update on Zodiac. "Inspector Toschi called me at home for a chat," he said. "I've been tracking down all this stuff that's been going on in Vallejo. McCochran at the *Vallejo Times-Herald* has told me that the police apparently found a videotape after their second search warrant of Mr. Allen's house. I don't know what any of this means and I don't think Vallejo police are talking. I'm going to try and speak to Captain Conway at Vallejo a little later this afternoon. I hope he'll give me a hint at least. But if I hear anything I'll certainly let you know."

As soon as police could, they played the videotape. All it showed was Allen mooning the police, cursing them, and complaining about the case. Authorities hinted more was on the tape, but "nothing incriminating." Though Leigh had specified close friend Harold Huffman to be executor of his estate, the task fell to Ron Allen who "sort of took over." Karen "took first dibs on all his stuff, not Ron," a friend claimed. "Huffman only met her after Leigh's death, but quickly took a disliking to her. I've read how Ron cooperated with the police, helped gather some information. I got the feeling that Ron knew his brother was involved in this type of activity. They have people in the media who have tracked them down. Ron's a hard guy to reach. Usually, his wife won't let him near the phone. I thought, since the guy died suddenly, maybe he left something behind. Maybe he did. I thought, a good chance they found something in that house."

Leigh Allen was not embalmed. Though he was cremated, samples of his brain fluid were ordered preserved. It might allow future DNA testing. Leigh's ashes were to be scattered off the coast near San Rafael. The *Vallejo Times-Herald* headline a week after Allen's death said: "SUSPECT'S DEATH WON'T HALT ZODIAC INVESTIGATION." Death would not stop an investigation into the truth. We owed it to the victims to assemble the missing pieces. I could not stop. None of us could.

FRIDAY, OCTOBER 2, 1992

DARLENE'S sister, Pam, claimed that she had confronted Allen before he died and, after his death, was in his home. In his bathroom she claimed she had observed "a weird sexual device held with suction cups to the side of the tub."

"Of course, I'm not actively working on the case anymore," said Bawart. "I used to get all those letters, and since Arthur Leigh Allen died, nothing happens on it anymore. Someday down the road we ought to put our heads together. I've got every file that Fred Shirisago had. And all our files and all the original stuff on Zodiac. I've got it up in my attic along with a bunch of stuff of Allen's. It might be interesting to go over it someday down the road if you ever write a sequel. What was really interesting is if you read this report—from then-Sergeant Lynch, in the center of another report on a regular piece of paper—I don't think there are more than a hundred words in it. He talks about 1969 just after the Berryessa killings going and interviewing Arthur Leigh Allen as to his whereabouts at the time of the killing. Arthur Leigh Allen makes the statement about . . ."

"About the chickens? Two chickens . . ." I said.

"Yeah! And he was going to Berryessa on the day the killings took place, but he changed his mind and went to Salt Point. This was in 1969, before Toschi and Armstrong had even looked at him. I hadn't read that until I got reinvolved in it in early 1992. So I go back and Lynch is still alive. He has since died. I go ask him, 'John, you don't say in the report *why* you're talking to Arthur Leigh Allen. What prompted you to pick out this guy? You don't say—and he couldn't remember. Somebody—somehow, his name came up in 1969 just after the Berryessa killing.

"Usually—I'd write a report and say, 'Pursuant to John Doe telling me that Arthur Leigh Allen fit the description and claimed he was going to Berryessa on that day, I went by to talk to him.' Then at least I'd have John Doe to go back to and talk to later on. I'd ask him, 'Why did you accuse this guy?' Of course your book came out much before I went and talked to Lynch. When I talked to him, he had quit drinking. But he wasn't in the best of health. He just couldn't remember.

"John Lynch was a prince of a guy. He was a very honest, straightforward guy, but he had a hell of a booze problem. When John would get off duty—it was spooky—he lived in an old house in an old section of town. It wasn't really a Victorian. It was sort of a Tudor. If you had to go by and talk to him about something, he never would answer the phone. You go by and you knock and he'd come to the door and there were no lights on and it was musty. He would always talk to you on the front porch.

He'd be drunk from the time he got off duty to the time eight hours before he was to come on duty.

"My guess was this: Allen told a family member or friend he was going to Berryessa. Later that unknown person read of the murders. Allen must have said something or been acting erratically enough for them to tip the police. My money is on a family member." Would we ever discover who that early tipster had been?

"From our last two conversations, I'm truly amazed at your background information on Zodiac," said Toschi. "Some of the information you have on Arthur Leigh Allen in the Riverside area really got my attention, and I wish that the Riverside P.D. had given me the fact that Allen was actually known around their town. It would have given me a stronger case to discuss with our D.A. and the other detectives working on the Zodiac case."

SUNDAY, MAY 15, 1994

"**THERE** is one specific detective [Harvey Hines] who has since retired from a very small police department," Conway explained, "who is absolutely convinced that he solved the Zodiac case and it happens to be a guy who has a lengthy criminal history and he's living in Tahoe. Again there is no fingerprint match, no handwriting matches, there's nothing more than a whole bunch of coincidences."

The *Chronicle* ran a two-part story about Hines's suspect in its *This World* section. The article upset Toschi. "It was cheap journalism," he told me. "I wouldn't even call it journalism. I remember talking to Hines in the seventies, and he was very strange then. He had tunnel vision. He wouldn't even listen to other suspects and keep an open mind. Hines has had twenty years to find out where his guy was on the dates of the murders. It should be easy to prove one way or the other. Paul Avery called me, and he too was upset."

"Conway is equally certain that the Zodiac is someone else," reported the *Chronicle*. "I'll tell you what I told Harvey [Hines]," said Captain Conway of the Vallejo Police Department. "He's wasting his life barking up the wrong tree. [His suspect] is not the Zodiac. I can't tell you how much time I've given Harvey over the years, but he has nothing of any evidentiary value. I believe as I always have that the Zodiac was Arthur Leigh Allen. If I could show Harvey what evidence we have on Allen today, he would get off this kick immediately. Unfortunately, I can't do that for legal reasons." Added Conway about suspect Allen, who died in 1992, "If Allen were alive today, we would file charges against him as the Zodiac. Unfortunately, we ran out of time making a case against him and he died."

Judge Eric Udall, Superior Court Sonoma County, stood in the cool shadows of Lake Herman Road and discussed the case. "When Jim Lang spoke with Allen on the day of the 1991 search of his home," he told me, "he drew the big man out by discussing the recent death of his own father. Somehow he reached the suspect. Allen began to cry and slowly Lang began to draw a confession from him. Allen was on the brink of confessing that he was Zodiac when a patrolman boiled out of the basement and shouted they had found bombs. Allen regained his composure, the mood was broken. The moment was lost."

35

THE CONFERENCE

"THE subject today is the Zodiac killer," Judge George T. Choppelas said solemnly. A gray-haired, whip-smart Municipal Court magistrate, he looked like Fred Astaire, and kept as trim with regular workouts on his rowing machine. The perplexing case fascinated the judge, and he had called a special discussion on Zodiac to rethink the case and satisfy his own curiosity. The meeting convened at a San Francisco State auditorium at 1:30 P.M. in front of a large audience. Choppelas, acting as moderator, introduced Rita Williams, KTVU-TV newsperson. "She interviewed the person, the one suspect," he said, "that Vallejo and San Francisco investigators and Robert Graysmith, former political cartoonist turned author, and others believe to have been the Zodiac killer."

Choppelas then recounted Cheney's story of Allen's vow (a year before there was a Zodiac) to tie a flashlight to his gun barrel, shoot couples in the woods, and write taunting letters signed Zodiac to the police. He explained how Allen was in the Riverside College area when Bates was stabbed, and how Darlene Ferrin was stalked by a friend named "Leigh." He told how there were no letters from Zodiac while Allen was confined at Atascadero and how the Santa Rosa murders ceased during that time. Captain Roy Conway, immediately on the scene of the Ferrin murder in 1969, had been associated with the case ever since. "I was a patrol sergeant that evening and I was dispatched to a place that was in a remote part of Vallejo on July 4, 1969. Both victims were still alive at the time. The male survived, the female died. I tried to talk to her and talk to him both. She was unable to speak or do anything, and had been shot with multiple gunshot wounds. The passenger in the car had been shot multiple times and he has survived. He's still alive to this day.

"Because I was a patrol sergeant at the time, I was not initially assigned as the investigator on the crime. It was not till several years later when I got promoted to captain that I was given responsibility for the case. The primary investigator who's been working on this case the longest of all law enforcement personnel that's ever been involved is Detective George Bawart, who's sitting over there in the corner." George stood and waved. "What we've done over the years—every time there's any kind of media attention given to the Zodiac case, there's all kinds of information that flows into [the] police department, or departments, and other departments and [the] California Department of Justice. There's all kinds of people calling up who say I know who the Zodiac is."

Conway pointed out what he considered some of the misinformation about Zodiac. I didn't agree with all of it. "It's not intentional," he said. "One of the pieces of misinformation is the Riverside homicide. I'm here to officially tell you that the Riverside Police Department never believed that Zodiac was involved. We have since more than satisfied ourselves that Zodiac had nothing whatsoever to do with the Riverside killing." Riverside thought their local suspect had committed the homicide. But a handwriting examination had already proven Zodiac wrote letters to the Riverside press claiming responsibility for Bates's murder.

Captain Conway played his case conservatively, focusing unequivocally only on those cases where it was absolutely certain that Zodiac had been involved. "There are only three of them in that category. The reason we know the three are unequivocally the Zodiac is because he gives physical evidence or verbal evidence that only the killer would know." He pointed to the Paul Stine cab killing as most striking—Zodiac had swiped a portion of Stine's shirt, enclosing fragments with his correspondence. "In our case [the Blue Rock Springs murder] Zodiac went to a pay telephone right after the homicide. In fact, I would have had to have passed him because it's a long road out to where this homicide occurred. I probably passed him, although we went to great lengths to try and time everything. The people who discovered the people who were shot took a long time to get to a telephone— probably more than a half hour passed before we even got a phone call.

"Shortly after [12:40 A.M.], a male voice called from a pay telephone, which we subsequently located [traced to Joe's Union

Station at Tuolumne and Springs Road by 12:47 A.M.], telling that he just committed this homicide and how he did it and some other details to cause us to know this was really the guy who did it. One of the examples of misinformation is that we had no recording devices in the police department in those days. There was in fact no recording of that phone call." Former Vallejo Patrolman Steve Baldino disagreed. On *Now It Can Be Told,* with Geraldo Rivera, on July 14, 1992, he had said, "I heard the tape—the dispatcher let me hear it. I believe it was the next night. Apparently the tape is no longer here, but it did in fact exist, because I did hear it." Nancy Slover, the police operator, had heard it too.

"The other homicide we know positively for sure," continued Conway, "is the Lake Berryessa homicide. Again the killer gave some very pertinent information that only he would know. There's only three. The other killing, on Lake Herman Road, happened [seven months] before the Zodiac killing. We had some very good suspects in that case, and Detective Bawart and I are satisfied that the Zodiac didn't really do that case, although we don't have unequivocal proof on that.

"The other interesting thing about the Zodiac case is that there are several people who have become obsessed with solving the case. We have had several in our own department. There are private citizens who became obsessed with the case and have convinced themselves they have absolutely solved it. They are very absolute about it. Neither one of the suspects that they have are our suspect.

"All three have written lengthy documentation about it. One is an attorney in our city who claims his brother, his dead brother, is the Zodiac [Jack Beeman]. Another used mathematics to prove it. In his mind he is absolutely convinced he's solved the Zodiac case. He thinks it's a college professor at Boston University who now works for the University of California at Berkeley. If you talk to that man and give him any time, he is absolutely, unequivocally convinced. He says it's mathematically impossible for anybody to be the Zodiac except [his] suspect.

"We have two other individuals, both in law enforcement. One of them is now retired just recently . . . he's been working on it twenty years and he's absolutely convinced he knows who the Zodiac is. And his Zodiac is living in Tahoe. Then we have another person in another state agency that worked on the Zodiac for years. He happened to be on duty. He stopped and did a field interrogation of a person he believes to this day is the Zodiac. So everyone of these people, if you talk to them, independent of anything else, you would say he must be right. It's only logical that he's right.

"One of the major reasons that the Zodiac case has not actually been solved to the point of somebody being actually arrested and tried is that law enforcement didn't do a very good job of coordinating information. . . . One of the most telling points in Mr. Graysmith's book—he asks the question why the search warrant wasn't served at two locations, and only one location—and that was twenty years ago that happened. If they had served a search warrant at the right location at that time, they probably would have solved the Zodiac case. But they didn't.

"Twenty years later, Detective Bawart and I served that search warrant! And we did that a couple years ago. We found a lot of information that caused us to believe we were on the right track, but that person subsequently died and we don't have any legal mechanism to say we've solved the case because we can't bring the suspect to trial. He's referred to in Robert Graysmith's book as 'Robert Hall Starr.' His actual name is Arthur Leigh Allen.

"He's worked in Vallejo all his life. At the time [1971–72] San Francisco Police Department developed information that we subsequently backtracked and gone over every piece of it. That information would have allowed them to serve a search warrant on his primary residence in Vallejo, but at that point of time he was living part-time in a little trailer in Santa Rosa. And so they served the warrant on his little trailer in Santa Rosa instead of his home in Vallejo. I'm fairly convinced that if they had served the search warrant on that home in Vallejo, they would have found the actual smoking gun, but that didn't happen. It's primarily because they were working on their own and made no effort to coordinate information with our agency."

"There's a lot of instances that occurred in this case that happened in one area and the other area didn't know about it," added Bawart. "Those are the kind of errors in the case the various police departments made. Roy and I, in hindsight, taking all this stuff down twenty years later, put it all together and made us seem like we're real smart, but we're not. We had the benefit of all those reports."

The judge asked me how I came to write the book. "The way I

got interested in this," I said, "I was a political cartoonist for the *Chronicle* and every day you try to do a cartoon that's going to make a change in the world. I looked at the Zodiac case and thought, 'Here's a guy no one seems to be able to catch. If I go around the state and put together as many facts as I can and put a book out there, somebody's going to solve this.' It's pretty much what I decided to do, and I did over a ten-year period. At the end of that time I had a book of considerable length. An editor and I spent another three years taking out five hundred pages. Maybe we took the real suspect out. It's possible, but not likely. We did place Mr. Allen as a student at Riverside and in that library the night Cheri Jo Bates was slain. Perhaps, as Captain Conway believes, Riverside wasn't a Zodiac killing, but of all the 2,500 suspects in the case, Allen was the only one at the scene."

Conway discussed the prints in Stine's cab.

"Hundreds of people can be in a cab. There was emergency medical personnel at the scene, other officials at the scene. Nobody took any elimination prints at the time. They have a whole drawer full of fingerprints that came out of that cab, and it's an extremely arduous task and most of them are partial. I assure you the primary suspects have been checked. There's no fingerprint matches anywhere. . . . Ken Moses, one of the best print men in the state and SFPD has one of the best computer systems in the state. They certainly would have run that bloody print long ago had it worked out, but they didn't preserve the crime scene well enough, any of the prints, particularly the bloody print of the man believed to be responsible. There were ambulance people there, there were other cops there. They are saying, how come this print doesn't match up to the analyzer? It could have been the guy driving the ambulance got some of Paul Stine's blood on his hands and then touched it and that's the way of the bloody print.

"Incidentally, Allen wore size 10½ shoes, and that's the size of the Wing Walker shoe print found at Lake Berryessa," I said. I summarized the pattern of the murders: "They usually happened by a body of water on a weekend and usually involved a young couple who were enjoying all the things Zodiac did not enjoy—intimate, loving relationships."

"We interviewed everyone in this case," said Conway. "We interviewed Kathleen Johns. I'm at kind of at a loss as how to explain it, but I don't believe what she described even happened, let alone that the Zodiac did it." "Johns is the only one I thought was a little iffy," I said. "As years go by, I've come to believe more and more that the man who kidnapped her wasn't Zodiac."

"The only thing I put any stock in is a thing that I know for a fact," said Conway. "All this business about the phases of the moons and all these cryptograms in reality didn't have to do with anything. It was a way for the Zodiac to play with people's minds for his own perverse satisfaction. Those cryptograms, as it turned out, had no meaning." The ciphers did, however, explain his motive and revealed the clue of *The Most Dangerous Game,* which led to his family and friends turning Allen in."

We discussed my conversations with Allen. "It may have been because of the child molesting," I said, "but when you work in the arts you get a kind of intuitive sense about things, and literally my spine got chills when I was around him. There was something about him very wrong. I often used to go in and buy things—he worked in a hardware store—just a very scary guy, but highly intelligent. He had a degree in botany and biology."

"Biology," said Williams. "He said he didn't quite get his master's degree—he didn't finish his thesis; he had finished the course work for a master's. His bachelor's degree was in elementary education. And he said his I.Q. was—I wrote it down—in the 130s. 'Certainly no genius,' he said, 'but I am intelligent.'"

"He called himself gifted," said Conway. "That's the terminology he used."

"Really," said Williams. "'My mind,' he said 'I believe is 136.' I asked him about the cryptograms. 'I was in the Navy,' he said, 'and what I did there was chipping paint and then I was a third-class radioman. That certainly doesn't make me an expert on cryptograms.'"

We began naming his skills. "Scuba diver, marksman . . . airplane pilot," said Williams. "He knew explosive devices, cryptography, meteorology," I said, "charts (naval and pilot) and compass, writing, drafting, and graphics [his father was not only a Navy officer but a draughtsman]. Chemistry [he was a chemist], guns [he collected them], disguise and sewing [he was a Navy sailmaker]. He not only typed, but had the same kind of portable typewriter the Riverside letters were written on." "Phil Tucker," said Bawart, "had given us the information that as a child Allen had been forced to write with his right hand though he was naturally left-handed."

"Sailor, pilot," continued Conway. "In fact, he had some trophies for Hobie Cat. He was also a swimmer. The other thing he did, he was quite an avid cook. His living quarters were, as Rita could tell you, in the basement of his parents' house. And every part of this little room was covered with books from floor to ceiling. He was very well read and could converse on any topic you could think of."

"I heard Zodiac could quote Gilbert and Sullivan by heart," said the judge. "Could any of this be applied to Allen?"

"Absolutely," said Conway. "We confirmed his interest in Gilbert and Sullivan through his brother and other relatives. They also confirmed that he purposely misspelled words. It wasn't by accident. He'd write recipes for example and he'd spell 'eggs,' instead of 'e-g-g-s,' he'd spell it 'a-i-g-s.' And that was intentional just to get a chuckle out of people who would read it. He did that consistently with all kinds of things." I recalled that Allen in all his interviews referred to Zodiac as "The" Zodiac, just as the killer did in his letters.

"The most difficult part of this case is the handwriting issue," continued Conway. "There are at least two or three people in the area of handwriting analysis, and the one thing they say about the Zodiac letters is that they are consistent from the very first letter to the very last letter. All the letters and words, handwriting is an absolute match. It's one person who did those letters. That's not an issue. The interesting thing, to go back to the Riverside case, there's only one piece of evidence that Zodiac had anything to do with the Riverside killing, and that's the killer scratched some writing onto a desktop. The actual letter he sent that describes all the things that he said he did in this homicide is all typed. There was no handwriting or printing of any kind. The name signed on the bottom of the letter was 'Enterprise.'" Conway was in error here: The letter had been addressed to the *Riverside Press-Enterprise*. And Zodiac had also handprinted three Riverside letters.

"But the scratching on the desk of which a photo was taken, as Sherwood Morrill said, that matches the Zodiac letters. Since then George and I have gone to every expert there is and they unequivocally without hesitation say, he was wrong, these are not a match to the Zodiac handwriting. That, plus the fact that the Riverside police already have a suspect. From their point of view their case was solved. This so-called genius that wrote this other book with all the mathematical equations, his whole premise—

everything is built on the mathematics starting with the Riverside Case. When I tell him the Riverside case didn't have anything to do with it, his theory goes out the window. It didn't shake him. He still believes otherwise."

We all had our blind spots. Captain Conway was convinced that Allen had never been in the Navy in spite of his claims of having been "a paint-scraper." Various women and their daughters Allen had known over the years spoke of his time in the U.S. Navy. Reports showed the same. Leigh admitted to being "less than honorably discharged" and he had gone to college on the G.I. Bill. The Navy connection was unshakable. His father's twenty-five years in the Navy alone would enable Leigh to make periodic visits to Treasure Island, work at Travis AFB, and buy Wing Walkers at a base exchange.

"Judge," said Williams, "I'd like to ask a few questions of the other panelists that I've wanted the answers to. If indeed Arthur Leigh Allen were the Zodiac, I think both of you have indicated in the past that whoever was the Zodiac would someday prior to his death leave some message behind to let everyone know he was the Zodiac. If he was Allen, can you tell me why you think he didn't and why the killings stopped when they did?" I thought to myself, he might not have left any message because he died suddenly of a heart attack, one so sudden he bumped his head. "From my point of view," said Conway, "he did leave that message. One of Zodiac's letters talked about finding bombs in his basement. Well, in fact there were bombs in the basement of that house when we did the search warrant—there were pipe bombs. The other half of it is that he does leave that message by things that are in his basement and at the same time denying everything. There's so many lies I caught him in, his denying things that didn't have any relevance anymore. There was no letters whatsoever during the time he was in Atascadero state hospital. The last letter he ever wrote says, 'I am back.'

"There's several reasons why the killings stopped—this is from discussions with the FBI experts. There's a very famous FBI group back in Quantico, Virginia, that studies serial killers. My father used to be an avid deer hunter when he was a young man in his twenties and thirties. About twenty years ago he quit deer hunting and I asked him why he quit. It's not interesting to me anymore[, he said]. That explanation is really simplistic, but that's probably the explanation for Allen if he was Zodiac.

"The other thing is that he was a very ill man—he was fifty-eight when he died. He was extremely ill and knew he was dying and he'd had that illness for some time. Even though he could still get around he was not very mobile and there was a lot of focus on him as a suspect. Being a suspect, being ill, and losing interest—all adds up to the explanation as to why."

"Did you find fingerprints?" Williams asked Conway. "Allen says in the interview that police told him during the interview process with the Vallejo police that you have fingerprints on the pipe bombs under his house. He of course says it was some ex-con that had left them there before. He didn't even know they were there. Did in fact you find fingerprints?"

"Let me answer that this way—he first denied having any knowledge whatsoever of any bombs existing in his basement, and when we told him of his fingerprints on the bombs—which there wasn't, by the way. Then he had an explanation of how he was cleaning up the basement and moved them from one spot to another. That's the kind of stuff we went through with him all the time."

George Bawart spoke from the audience. "You have to understand that back in the sixties law enforcement was doing a pretty good job. They weren't really communicating with each other—they didn't have computers."

"Getting back to the fingerprints [on the cab], every single [Zodiac] suspect that ever existed," said Conway, "has been checked against those fingerprints and no one has matched. The other problem is that the Zodiac bragged in his letter how he wouldn't leave fingerprints anyway."

"Can I ask the captain and Robert, in your mind, who is the Zodiac killer?" said Williams.

"George, how do we answer that?" said Conway.

"Who is?" said Rita.

"I find," said Bawart, "so many coincidences that point in one direction, I feel it is no longer a coincidence, and I feel there are so many areas that point directly at Arthur Leigh Allen that I feel he is a viable suspect and in all probability the Zodiac."

"Robert?" said Williams.

"That's my opinion too," I answered cautiously. Allen had died all too recently. "All I can say is that of all the people who were ever brought to me—I conferred with Dave Toschi, he showed me files and files and files—Allen is the best I've seen. Zodiac could be some anonymous person who lives in the woods and has never been printed, but as far as I can tell, Allen is the best suspect they've come up with."

"First of all there's nothing wrong with circumstantial evidence," said Conway, "if you understand what circumstantial evidence is—leaving a fingerprint at the scene of a crime and denying you did the crime, circumstantially we prove that you did do the crime because of the fingerprints at the crime scene."

Rita Williams took out a letter Allen had mailed her. He'd scrawled a "Z" in the lower left-hand corner of the envelope. A similar "Z" had been written at the bottom of the 1967 Riverside letter. The postmark: "July 30, 1991 Oakland." He had dated the letter inside August 1. The typed letter began: "Dear Rita: Please pardon the informality, but I consider you a friend."

"So I guess I'm a friend of the Zodiac," said Williams, "if indeed he is the Zodiac. He just goes on to say that he appreciated the interview and he had a knot in his stomach and goes on and on with compliments. He says 'professionality'—interesting that he made up a word. 'I wonder if that word's in the dictionary,' he says. Certainly, he's the kind of person who would have a dictionary there and wouldn't use that word unless he really checked. I'm afraid I never answered the man."

THAT NIGHT SOME of the conference was briefly reported on KTVU: "Everything about the Zodiac is serious, giving the number of people he killed seemingly at random . . . perhaps as many as fifty. Who was the Zodiac?" Rita Williams asked. "This is the Vallejo man many investigators consider to be the notorious Zodiac killer, and is the first time his picture has been revealed. His name is Arthur Leigh Allen." As archival film ran, Williams asked Allen: "Are you the Zodiac killer?" "There would be nothing farther from my mind," he said. "I am certainly, most certainly, not the Zodiac killer."

"But at San Francisco State University this afternoon," continued Williams, "I was on a panel with people considered authorities on the Zodiac case and for the first time publicly they said this. Allen seems to be the best suspect they've come up with," she reported, quoting me. "There are so many areas," Bawart was seen saying, "that point directly at Arthur Leigh Allen that he is a viable suspect and in all probability the Zodiac."

"But investigators never charged Allen with any of the killings connected with the Zodiac," said Williams, "and last August Allen died. I interviewed him a year earlier. He was fifty-eight then, a diabetic and on kidney dialysis. But back in the later sixties, when the clever killer known as Zodiac terrorized California, Allen was in his late thirties, sixty pounds heavier, strong, and a biology graduate student. Police considered him a suspect almost from the beginning.

"The Zodiac killer taunted authorities and the media, sending complex letters and ciphers," Williams summed up. "Today Vallejo police investigators said they never charged Allen because they couldn't explain discrepancies in the Zodiac handwriting. Allen sent me this handwritten and typed letter after our interview."

Williams's 1991 interview, rerun that night, showed Allen collapsing and sobbing. What Rita Williams had observed stuck in my mind. "However," she said, "he didn't really cry. In looking at the tape, he kind of turned it on and turned it off. When Allen lifted his head his eyes were dry. I definitely felt he was pretending." "There are so many lies I caught him in, his denying things didn't have any relevance anymore," said Conway. Allen lied even when there was no reason to.

FRIDAY, FEBRUARY 14, 1997

SIX years had rushed by since the Valentine's Day search of Allen's home. Toschi rang me, sounding buoyant. "I've gotten calls throughout yesterday evening and today," he said. "Something is up. One of the inspectors, Rich Adkins, just inherited the Zodiac case. When a friend of mine was captain of investigations, he said that Rich really wanted to talk to me because he had gone through the files and just was a little curious about some things. He and his partner, a guy named Vince Repetto, paid me a visit Tuesday. I had some time, about a half hour, to talk to them about Zodiac.

"Vince told me he's never gone through everything that had been sent to Sacramento. He said, 'For some reason everything wasn't brought back.' They only had two boxes. That disappointed me. Sacramento should have returned everything that Armstrong and I accumulated. Remember, when they decided to bring everything up to Sacramento years ago, I felt that they had made a very, very serious mistake. I was extremely upset. A case of this caliber, known worldwide, and the work that Bill and I did on it (I have poor handwriting, but as I got older and more experienced I took better notes)—to do this, to shuffle it around in a cardboard box—you're going to lose something. Someone is going to put something in his pocket. You have to want to solve the darn thing! You have to!

"I hope they know where the rest of the files are in Sacramento and who's got them. Repetto and Adkins said this morning they were going to go up to Sacramento and have a look. What fascinated this Rich Adkins is that it is still a mystery—that the case is still active and that so many people are aware of it. So many other people have killed more people than Zodiac. Adkins asked why was there so much interest all these years later. I told him, 'It's a mystery—because of the letters, the ciphers, the codes. It's taunting, it's "Catch me if you can," and "I'm crack-proof." '

"Rich asked me if I had ever spoken to Conway. When Allen died, he was quoted all over the place. Now they tell me he told Adkins he was going to retire in December."

"Conway's just very enthusiastic," I said. "Some of his ideas are very good—such as paring the case down to its essentials."

"San Francisco was puzzled why Vallejo didn't simply close the case and this is what Inspectors Adkins and Repetto want to do," said Toschi. "What Rich Adkins asked of me is that if you—who are extremely knowledgeable—would be willing to talk with them. They're two pretty good guys. I said, 'Graysmith is one of the most honorable men I've ever met in my life. I think he would want to talk to you.' Adkins said, 'After all this time, we want to close it and we think we can.' They want to give Armstrong and I credit. 'What we want to prove,' Adkins told me, 'if it wasn't for you taking the initiative when Allen's brother called and going to Vallejo and talking to Allen's sister-in-law and brother . . . you guys made the case and did more work on Allen than any of the other jurisdictions who were closer to him.' "

"The one thing Vallejo can't understand is why John Lynch and Les Lundblad were on this guy so early in the case," I said. "Why? And this was long before the informants, Cheney and Panzarella."

"We never got that," said Toschi sadly.

"What brought them to Allen? Two guys in independent police

agencies both go right to Allen's front door. There's a little tiny piece missing. Lynch went out and talked to Allen after Blue Rock Springs and Lake Berryessa. And of course they have that knife story—'I've been killing two chickens. . . . ' "

"Yes. Adkins and Repetto even asked me if we could put Allen in Southern California. My memory was weak at that point, but I know you found some leads. The brother went and searched the basement of Allen's house himself, and he found cryptography books. I told this to Adkins on Tuesday and it blew him away."

That night I opened more mail from Zodiac buffs. "Look under the stamps and the envelope flaps for saliva and attempt a DNA test on it," Michael Hennessy suggested. "Also check the letter that had a bloody cross drawn on it for DNA. Check the skin and hair fragments that victim Cheri Jo Bates had under her fingernails when found." DNA, obtained from a variety of biological sources—blood, hair, semen, and saliva—had finally entered the Zodiac case, as I was about to find out.

SATURDAY, FEBRUARY 15, 1997

I called Repetto at 9:00 A.M. and he wanted to meet right away. "I'm going to be getting on the road here and heading toward the city," he told me. "I'll call my partner on the cell phone and I'll call you back with a time we could meet, say around ten-twenty, ten-thirty this morning." We set the place for the Mirabelle Cafe on Ninth Avenue, the site of the former Owl and Monkey Cafe, where I did all my writing.

I sat at my regular table in the front window and watched a light-rail car glide by. I recognized the two inspectors immediately as they crawled from their car and entered the cafe. Adkins, tall, broad-shouldered, and energetic, had a bruise on his left cheek from a fight he had just had with a suspect. Vince Repetto, older and more world-weary than his partner, squeezed into a chair. I soon wished they had canceled the meeting. Something had changed in the last hour.

The previous day Adkins and Repetto had gotten DNA results. Genetic markers on a Zodiac letter (they wouldn't say which one) had matched Allen's DNA! However, a call to Repetto after our conversation revealed a second run had showed no match. "I heard this bit of news just before I picked up Rich," he said.

Zodiac, with his knowledge of chemistry, even in the late sixties and early seventies, would hardly have been so foolish as to lick an envelope or stamp. While no such thing as DQ-Alpha DNA[18] testing existed back then, blood and saliva typing procedures did. In 1976, Dr. Richard Waller drew up the testing procedures and serology guidelines for secretor samples for the state crime lab in Santa Rosa. Genetic markers, a series of complex, energy-releasing molecules and enzymes present within the fluids of each individual's body, could be lifted from stains. They could be analyzed by various high-tech serological tests. ABO testing involved long-lasting, stable molecules, and PGM testing dealt with more perishable enzymes. Secretor samples found in ABO existed in saliva, semen, and blood.

Could the DNA false positive have come from a close relation? Had Allen had his mother lick the envelope for him? If so, under what pretext? Or had we been wrong all along? Toschi, Mulanax, Lundblad, Adkins, and Repetto and all the rest had believed that Zodiac was Arthur Allen. So did I. But Allen did not match the handwriting, did not lick the letter they had tested, and had passed a lie-detector test, albeit in a drugged state. What could be the answer? I thought back to the possibility of two Zodiacs working as partners, an idea that Bawart had considered. Now I had the unpleasant task of telling Toschi about the meeting. He was crestfallen.

"Tuesday," said Toschi, "they told me they were about a month away from hearing anything positive. I feel sorry for them. They were obviously positive in what was going on. Now one phone call that says no, it deflates you. It's a step backward."

"I remember Allen lamenting in 1975," I said, "that he hoped Zodiac would write a letter while he was at Atascadero to prove he wasn't Zodiac. If a confederate was writing the letters for him, why wouldn't he do so? The results of that DNA test is something I didn't see coming." I looked at my phone. From 1986 through 1991 I had gotten a steady stream of breathing and hang-up calls. They had stopped with Allen's death. I almost missed them.

---

[18]The FBI has been conducting forensic DNA (an acronym for deoxyribonucleic acid) testing since 1989.

SUNDAY, FEBRUARY 16, 1997

"I spoke with Inspector Repetto," I told Bawart.

"I know him," Bawart said. "Vince runs his own private security outfit. They had him assigned to this thing after Deasy. Deasy was handling it for the longest time out of the Pawn Detail. Then they turned it over to this Vince. Of course, he had his other cases to work within SFPD."

"SFPD got DNA results two days ago." I said. "And it came up it could be Allen. But by the time they got back to me—less than an hour, they had gotten a second report that said the sample *didn't* match Zodiac. Can you think of anyone who might have written the letters for Allen?"

"You know, we even compared Cheney's handwriting," said Bawart. "And Sandy Panzarella and Ron Allen, a pretty straitlaced guy."

"Robert Emmett was teaching school in Germany when the letters stopped. I'm thinking they might want to test his DNA."

"This is something that Conway had pressed for before he retired," said Bawart. "As for the samples on Allen, I don't know where San Francisco would have gotten them. I have the Vallejo coroner holding that stuff and he's supposed to notify me if and when they get a request from San Francisco. I haven't heard anything. Maybe Allen had his dog licking his stamps. . . ."

"No, it was human DNA," I said. I mentioned Andrew Todd Walker,[19] the third important suspect in the case.

"I don't dislike Walker," said Bawart. "I just don't think there's enough definitive information on him to make it really viable. These guys [a Naval Intelligence officer and two CHP officers] pursue it as a hobby and that's wonderful. They apparently have gone to the expense of stealing some of his silverware. They paid for a DNA check, at least they told me they did. They have Walker's DNA. You know, I'll bet you Walker and I bet you this guy that Harvey Hines likes—I bet you both of them, just to get everything off their backs, would submit to a DNA test."

"Well, sure. I sat down with Morrill in the seventies. He studied some of Leigh's printing I got from Ace Hardware. It looks

---

[19]This name has been changed.

fine—the three-stroke *k*, all the rest. If they're going to run a genetic test, then they should at least do all of the suspects."

"I just wish that back in '71–'72 Toschi and Armstrong would
have followed up further. I wish they'd searched the home. I talked
to Prouty, who was a handwriting analyst who worked at DOJ that
worked under Morrill. And Prouty said he was losing it toward the
end. I looked at that [desktop printing] stuff and I couldn't make it
[as Zodiac writing]. He died shortly after his retirement. I'm not
sure Repetto or Adkins have ever viewed any of my reports . . . but
nobody's pounding on their door. Stine's family isn't there every
day saying what are you doing about the death of my husband,
son, or whatever. And the same thing happens in Vallejo. The Ferrin family's not pounding on the door. It's the old adage—the
squeaky wheel gets the oil. I don't blame Vince at all. He's probably got a half-dozen cases where people are pounding on his door."

All in all it had been a stunning development. Lieutenant Tom
Bruton, SFPD homicide investigator, called me. He had inherited
the Zodiac case, an heirloom passed down from generation to
generation. Bruton wondered if I could provide some originals of
the missing letters.

"Well, what do you have missing?" I asked.

"The three-part-cipher letter," he replied. That would have
been the first Zodiac letter San Francisco had received.

"I have FBI reproductions of that. Would that do?"

"No. We thought maybe the original had been passed on to
you. Kathleen Johns said that she received a *second* Zodiac Halloween card and mailed it on to you. Do you have that?"

"No. She means Paul Avery. However, you're welcome to anything I have. I want to see this thing solved." We spoke for a
while longer, and then I thought to ask a favor of my own. "I've
been thinking about that DNA test done on Allen and I have two
questions."

"Go ahead."

"First, where did they get a sample of Allen's genetic material?
He was buried in 1992."

"We got it from the Vallejo coroner. They kept a sample of
brain fluid or a brain fragment that they'd kept refrigerated."

"That clears that up."

"And the second point?"

"*Which* letter did they test?" I had in mind one of the early letters that contained squares of Paul Stine's shirt. That blood-

stained swatch would authenticate the sender as Zodiac.

"We used the 1978 letter," he said.

"The forgery?"

Once, I had believed in that letter. But in 1978 one thing had troubled me. "Excluding Zodiac's greeting cards, desktop, and car door, his handprinted communications have all been written on 7½-inch-by-10-inch bond in letter-sized envelopes. The 1978 letter was on 8½-inch-by-11-inch bond in a *legal*-sized envelope." I knew now that not only was the 1978 letter a fake, but the SFPD knew it.

"What are the chances of a second test using one of the older letters?" I asked.

Bruton said nothing.

I called Toschi. He asked incredulously why they didn't test a letter that contained a swatch of Stine's shirt. "Since they wanted to know if I had any original letters," I said, "I suspect they've either misplaced some or they've been stolen. The truth is, there's not enough DNA on the remaining letters for them to evaluate. They had tested for saliva in 1969–71 and found none. Only the 1978 fake had enough cells for a test." The SFPD later prepared a chart of available Zodiac DNA:

"Zodiac letters and envelopes for 10/13/69, ENVELOPE PROCESSED FOR DNA—FEW CELLS. 11/8/69 Card: 'Sorry I haven't written' Pen dripping, ENVELOPE PROCESSED FOR DNA—FEW CELLS. 12/20/69, Contained piece of cloth from Stine's shirt (per keel), ENVELOPE PROCESSED FOR DNA—FEW CELLS. 4/20/70 'My name is . . .' (Cipher), ENVELOPE PROCESSED FOR DNA—FEW CELLS. 4/28/70, Card: (Sorry to hear . . .) 'Blast . . . Buttons . . .' ENVELOPE PROCESSED FOR DNA—FEW CELLS. 6/26/70 Handwritten note & map: 'I shot a man with a .38 . . .' ENVELOPE PROCESSED FOR DNA—FEW CELLS."

The lab found some cells in these communications:

"Handwritten note: 7/24/70 'Woman & baby in car . . . ' ENVELOPE PROCESSED FOR DNA—CELLS FOUND. 7/26/70 'I will torture my 13 slaves waiting in paradice,' ENVELOPE PROCESSED FOR DNA—CELLS FOUND.

1/29/74 'saw the Exorcist,' ENVELOPE PROCESSED FOR DNA—CELLS FOUND."

Among the lost and unprocessed by the lab were these:

The 11/9/69 handwritten note: "This is the Zodiac Speaking,—LOCATION OF ENVELOPE UNK." Also apparently missing were the original three letters and ciphers of 7/31/69, the letter of 8/7/69, the 10/27/70 Halloween Card, the 3/13/71 "Blue Meanies" letter to *Times*, the 3/22/71 postcard, "Sought Victim 12," the 5/8/74 note signed "a citizen" and the 7/8/74 "Red Phantom" letter.

The report concluded with the tested letter: "4/24/78 Handwritten note 'that city pig Toschi . . .' DNA SAMPLE OBTAINED/*NOT AUTHENTIC ZODIAC LETTER.*"

Arthur Leigh Allen had *not* been ruled out as the Zodiac after all. Soon after Zodiac returned from the grave.

36
ZODIAC III

AFTER Zodiac II, no one ever expected Zodiac's murders to be emulated again. A Zodiac copycat had been horrific—a third Zodiac, inconceivable. But for a third time the killer's undying persona reached out to bring death, this time some three thousand miles away. Kobe, a well-to-do suburb 270 miles west of Tokyo. Kobe lay complacent in its relative safety, almost as murder-free as the rest of Japan. Hammer attacks against two girls in the neighborhood on February 10 had rocked the community from its slumber. Today, Ayaka Yamashita, a ten-year-old, was bludgeoned and killed by stab wounds to the head. Less than an hour later, a nine-year-old was stabbed and nearly bled to death.

SATURDAY, MAY 24, 1997

ON a stormy morning, rain beaded on a plastic bag left at the green iron front gate of Kobe's Tomogaoka Junior High. Though a light fog had formed on the underside of the bag nearest the pavement, a human head was visible inside. A pitiful lock of black hair splayed and fanned out against the plastic. A schoolboy's clouded face peered out. Only moments before, neighbors had glimpsed a stout man staggering under the weight of two black garbage bags as he rushed down a narrow street. "He was about forty years old," they told police summoned to the junior high. The victim's head had been severed at the jawline with a hacksaw and sharp knife. The killer had gouged his eyes out and stuffed a message in his mouth. Written in red ink, the words ran with rain. Zodiac's crossed-circle symbol was starkly legible. The killer was strong and had used only his right hand to strangle the boy. A search for the rest of the body began. The corpse, discovered in the wooded area of a fenced-in television transmission station, had been undressed, then redressed. The victim was Jun Hase, a mentally challenged eleven-year-old last seen three days ago. Just after lunchtime, he had set out to visit his grandfather. Now neighbors recalled a suspicious vehicle had been parked near the boy's home.

"JAPAN KILLER MAY IMITATE 'ZODIAC'" read the Associated Press headline. "Note on beheaded boy similar to those of infamous Bay Area murderer decades ago . . . a cross-like symbol found on notes left by the Kobe Killer." The murder and contents of the killer's message shocked the Japanese people as no crime in memory. Prime Minister Ryutaro Hashimoto pleaded with police to capture the killer as soon as possible. "So this is the beginning of the game," read the letter. "I desperately want to see people die. Nothing makes me more excited than killing. Stupid police, stop me if you can. It's great fun for me to kill people."

The message was hardly more than a rephrasing of Zodiac's: "I like killing people because it is so much fun. It is more fun than killing wild game in the forest. . . ." Several English words in the communication had apparently been misspelled on purpose. A black-bound translation of my book on the Zodiac slayings had been published in Japan two years earlier. Perhaps the killer had identified with Zodiac's obsession with the *Mikado*.

I heard banging at my front gate. A team of newsmen from Japan International Network were there to speak with me. Masahiro Kimura offered plane tickets to me. "We want you to come to Japan to look over the crime scene." Though I had lived in Tokyo for six years, I saw no way I could help. Instead we drove to Julius Kahn Playground, the last place Zodiac had been seen. Kimura showed me copies of the letters. We ended the day riding in a taxi along the same route as Stine had taken, an unsettling trip for the Yellow Cab driver who was eavesdropping. Kimura said neighborhood watches in Kobe had been organized.

In Japan hundreds of police cordoned off the school site. Teachers stationed stress-guidance counselors at local schools and children left for school with electronic alarms inside their backpacks. The killer had threatened to take revenge on the "compulsory education system." The tragedy in Japan brought back horrible memories of how armed guards had been stationed on Bay Area school buses when Zodiac had threatened:

"School children make nice targets, I think I shall wipe out a
school bus some morning. Just shoot out the front tire & then
pick off the kiddies as they come bouncing out."

THURSDAY, JUNE 5, 1997

THE Japanese Zodiac's rambling, partially incoherent 1,400-
word letter was published. In handwriting that matched the message stuffed inside the head, Zodiac III took responsibility for the
schoolboy's murder. He threatened to kill "vegetables," a word
police took to be the writer's disparaging term for people. "From
now on, if you misread my name or spoil my mood I will kill
three vegetables a week," he wrote. The original Zodiac had
threatened to kill if he did not see his name in the papers. "If you
think I can only kill children you are greatly mistaken." It was
signed *Seito Sakakibara* [Apostle Sake Devil Rose]. Zodiac III
claimed this was his real name.

Like Zodiac, Devil Rose had presented a name by which he
wanted to be known. Like Zodiac, it infuriated him when the press
misinterpreted his words. They had taken *"oni-bara"* ("devil's
rose") on the note as a coded message. Amateur sleuths also noted
a chilling connection between the beheaded child, Zodiac, and
The Exorcist. In January 1974, Zodiac had mentioned the wildly
popular movie. Nine years later William Peter Blatty, author-
producer of *The Exorcist,* wrote a sequel, *Legion.* In uncorrected
proofs, Blatty named the villain Zodiac. In a film, *Exorcist III,* he
was called the "Gemini Killer." Gemini decapitated a twelve-year-
old boy just as the Tomogaoka Junior High killer had.

Neighbors in Kobe noticed that a local fifteen-year-old boy
had recently turned "a bit gloomy." The physically small ninth-
grade student, eldest of three sons in a middle-class family, was
killing and mutilating pigeons and cats in the neighborhood. The
boy had beaten a friend for telling on him to schoolmates. The
same classmates tipped police he killed two kittens.

SATURDAY, JUNE 28, 1997

POLICE raided the boy's home, seizing horror videos, a knife,
and "a book about the San Francisco killings" in his room. In his

journal the youth wrote of a god, "Bamoidooki," and called his
attacks "sacred experiments." They dredged a hacksaw from a
close-by pond and arrested him for beheading his neighbor and
classmate, Jun Hase. He confessed he had also bludgeoned a ten-
year-old and attacked three other girls, two with a hammer the
previous February and March. Under Japanese law the boy was
not identified because of his age. Convicted on October 18 of attacks on all five children (two of whom died), he was sentenced
to a juvenile prison to be treated for mental illness until he turned
twenty-six.

SUNDAY, OCTOBER 19, 1997

THEY finally located Stine's lost bloody shirt in the Bryant Street
property room. It had been checked out, listed as a miscellaneous
item, and abandoned in a cardboard box in the official coroner's
office—a blunder probably indicative of past performance. The
SFPD had recently tossed out evidence in the Charles Ng serial
killings. They thought the case had been completed, but after
decades Ng was just coming to trial. Bawart feared the San Francisco investigation of the Stine murder had been "very sloppy."
"For instance," he told me, "the names of the fire crew [at Cherry
and Washington] were not taken to eliminate them as donors to
the bloody print." Toschi reassured me, "The cab had already
been taken away by the time the fire crew arrived."

37
ARTHUR LEIGH ALLEN

SUNDAY, OCTOBER 11, 1998

THE first words out of Toschi's mouth were bitter as ashes: "I got up this morning and the first thing I realized was that it's been thirty years since it all began." San Francisco celebrated Fleet Week. Jets buzzed downtown skyscrapers. Outside the Golden Gate, a Navy plane, guided by an angled crossed circle—a huge Zodiac symbol—coasted featherlike onto a carrier's deck. Frustrated detectives from San Francisco, Vallejo, Napa County, and Solano County had gathered, possibly for the final time, to discuss Zodiac. The last of the original Zodiac trackers, Ken Narlow, had retired in 1987. "I have a place on the coast where I attack the salmon and abalone," he said. "I needed something to occupy my time besides golfing and fishing so I took the job of transportation director for our local Catholic high school." And Zodiac? "I'd like to think that if we had some of the technology in those days that we have today, we'd be a lot closer to this guy,"

"The old Zodiac—that thing will never die," said another. When Toschi spoke to Avery, Avery said, "That's history, that's all in the past, Dave." "That kinda saddened me a bit," Toschi told me, "because for me it was *the* case of a career."

SUNDAY, AUGUST 29, 1999

"**IT** always surprised me that Ken Narlow knew hardly anything about Allen," Tom Voigt, who ran a Web page on Zodiac, told me. "I brought him the Bawart Report on the reasons why Allen is the Zodiac and copies of Mulanax's report. We went over to his house and he started reading it. He was not impressed with how the report looked—the first thing he said was, 'It's not on official letterhead, but the content makes up for the way it's presented.' He read a bit more. He turned red, and was swearing quite a bit by the time he finished. He was very angry. 'If even a couple of these things are true,' he said, 'then Allen's the Zodiac!'

"Narlow was upset because he hadn't known anything about this when it was going on. He had been invited to the search in 1972, but couldn't go because he had a hernia operation. He was relying on Mulanax, Armstrong, and Toschi to clue him in. He's really angry because he's reading all this for the first time and knew nothing of the facts in the report. At that point he started trying to track down Bill Armstrong. He was tough to find, but Narlow eventually talked to him. They had a long conversation. Armstrong had put it all behind him. When Armstrong quit, he really quit. He didn't realize that Allen had ever been searched again. He didn't know that Allen had died. Basically, it was just like he was living in a cave."

"As far as I could tell," Voigt told me, "the Vallejo police had put all their Zodiac records on microfilm and destroyed the originals. Mel Nicolai told me—we talked in May—he told me they placed Allen in Riverside and they know for a fact he was there. He wasn't a student and he didn't work there. At the time Bates was murdered he was a schoolteacher at Valley Springs Elementary School in Calaveras County, and every weekend Allen would go to Riverside. Drive all the way down to Riverside because he was a member of this racing club."

TUESDAY, OCTOBER 19, 1999

"I decided last week I was going to retire," Toschi told me. "I wasn't feeling too good—I was kind of dragging. I was working an average of ten hours a day. I'm sixty-eight now. I'm still doing a little security and bodyguard work at Temple Emmanuel since around 1987. I was doing a lot of things and it was beginning to take its toll. I'm going to do a little P.I. work. I've had my license since '86. You've got to have your weapon, state firearms certificate, a book test. Because of my background they'll waive the firing test. 'I think you still know how to shoot,' they said. I had my 'CCW,' carrying concealed weapon, from the chief, which made me legal."

As I spoke with Toschi, it had occurred to me I had interviewed many of the witnesses the police had not, seen files long since destroyed. I knew facts they did not. Perhaps the case against Arthur Leigh Allen could still be made. I tried out some of the new intelligence on Toschi.

"Did you know," I asked him, "that Allen had his trailer repaneled just before you searched it in 1972? Who knows what was hidden in those walls? He had another trailer by Bodega Bay. No wonder you didn't find anything. Then Zodiac signed his murder of the San Francisco cabbie."

"How is that?" asked Toschi.

"Stine, undeniably a Zodiac victim, did not fit the pattern of attacks against couples, though he qualified by being a student. He may have been chosen for another reason. Stine did not die at a water-related site, though his original destination had been Third Avenue and *Lake*. After Allen told Spinelli he was going to San Francisco to kill a taxi driver he chose a specific cabbie and specific destination. Paul Stine's middle name was 'Lee,' and his birthday, December 18, the same as Leigh Allen's. Yellow Cab dispatcher LeRoy Sweet gave Stine his last scheduled trip destination at 9:45 P.M.—to 500 Ninth Avenue, Apartment #1—an apartment complex, the *Allen* Arms. Tom Voigt pointed that out to me. Zodiac had given us his first name, 'Lee,' his birth date, 'December 18,' and his last name, 'Allen.'[20] But how Zodiac knew Stine's birth date and middle name and how he snared that specific cab, I can't imagine. Did this mean he knew Stine? Additionally an 'Arthur Allen, student,' was renting an unfurnished apartment at 320 2nd Avenue, only four and a half blocks from the murder site."

Stine began pushing his hack at 8:45 P.M., his only completed fare—from Pier 64 to the Air Terminal. His incomplete way-bill read Washington and Maple Streets in Presidio Heights. "He never arrived at the 9th Avenue location," said Sweet. "At 9:58 P.M. I assigned the 'no-go' dispatch to another cab." Responding officers at Washington and Cherry discovered the cab meter still running, indicating Stine had picked up a fare en route. At ex-

---

[20]Other Zodiac victims and relations seemingly fit this name game: *Arthur* David Faraday, first Northern California victim; *Arthur* Dean Ferrin, husband of the third Northern California victim; Bill *Leigh*, her boss, Santa Rosa students Lori *Lee* Kursa, Maureen *Lee* Sterling, Kim Wendy *Allen*.

actly 10:46 P.M. the meter read $6.28."[21] That enabled Armstrong and Toschi to backtrack to where Zodiac had gotten into the cab—Geary and Mason. Witnesses observed Zodiac wiping down the left-side doors of the cab prior to his escaping, leading Toschi to believe that this was the side from which he entered downtown.

Stine, who drove a motorcycle, had been selling insurance to pay his way through SF State. Could he have previously met Zodiac as an insurance client or at a motorcycle club? Zodiac shot Stine from the backseat, then entered the right front door. Three teenaged witnesses across the street observed Stine being "jostled" by Zodiac who was "seated in the right front seat at the time." Stine generally kept his cab fares and tip money in his pocket and would separate it at the end of his shift. His wife, Claudia, said he had only $3 to $4 of his own money when he left home for work. Zodiac took Stine's wallet (where he kept all his registration papers) and some keys to the cab. Was Zodiac looking for something that would link him to his victim?

"If Stine was taking his cab out to the Richmond [District]," theorized Toschi, "Zodiac may have flagged him down and said, 'I want to go to Washington and Maple.' Stine might have said, 'That's almost in the same area. I can do two at once. I can drop you off and get over to Ninth Avenue in five minutes. I've got a guy jumping in the front seat. I can take you and handle the other one. I get two fares for one.'" Toschi had suspected Allen was left-handed, but never been able to prove it.

"In his last will," I said, "Leigh requested that a Clear Lake friend, Mark, receive 'my *left-handed scissors* and all my archery equipment.' So, he was ambidextrous after all, as you suspected. Eyewitnesses confirmed that Leigh wore unique Wing Walker shoes the same size as Zodiac's. He fits Zodiac's physical description in every way—six-foot height and over two hundred and thirty pounds. The lumbering walk. Leigh, by his own words, placed himself at the Berryessa and Riverside scenes. He had the

[21]"The theory holds that Stine's murder occurred one block further [than Washington and Maple Streets]," wrote John Douglas, "because the killer needed him at a precise point on the map. That's why the Zodiac switched his victim choice from couples to a cabdriver. Whom else could he get to a precise set of coordinates so easily?"

technical knowledge to write codes, diagram and build bombs, and the skill to shoot various weapons. He and Zodiac share the same birthday. He misspelled the same words as Zodiac on his menu cards. And what about Don Cheney? When he took a lie detector test, he passed. His comments in 1971 about Allen saying he wanted to hunt people and call himself the Zodiac were true."

"That doesn't surprise me at all," said Toschi.

"Now Phil Tucker says Allen told him the same things. Leigh confessed he was Zodiac to a variety of people—a Sonoma Auto Parts employee; Spinelli, of course. Police referred to the criminal as 'Zodiac.' However, Zodiac referred to himself as 'The Zodiac.' Allen, in his taped interviews with television crews, always said 'The Zodiac.' On his analyst's tapes Allen reportedly sobbed and admitted he was 'The Zodiac.' He claimed he spoke for Zodiac, and explained the origin of the Zodiac ciphers as having originated at Atascadero."

"How do you discount remarks like that?" said Toschi. "Allen was a very sick, disturbed, and dangerous man—a frightening person. It was unfortunate that the Vallejo P.D. didn't charge him even though they knew he was Zodiac. It would have put closure on the darn thing. It would have brought relief to those who survived. And made a lot of peace officers happy. The case is closed. That's all I wanted to do was close the case. Tap him on the shoulder and say, 'Let me advise you of your Miranda rights,' and then handcuff him. To this day, I still say Leigh Allen was 'my man.' Guys would tease me and I'd say, 'I think the case will be solved someday.' I think it is solved. If you're comfortable on what you've done on this one, then I would go with it."

Could I find eyewitnesses placing Allen at the scene of the murders? Only two Zodiac crimes offered that potential. I began to re-examine them in depth, including all that I had recently learned. I commenced with the stabbings at Lake Berryessa on September 27, 1969, on a lovely Saturday afternoon.

38

THE CITY AT THE BOTTOM OF THE LAKE

As BRYAN HARTNELL and Cecelia Shepard had over thirty years earlier, I went by way of Pope Valley, rushing past old stone wineries and hot springs until I reached the twisting shoreline and inlets of Lake Berryessa. At this tree-shaded resort east of Napa, Zodiac had become Count Zaroff at his hunt—stalking his victims in the twilight. Riverside had a connection to this attack too. After two years at Angwin College, Cecelia was transferring to U.C. Riverside to study music. She had just driven up from San Bernardino with her friend Dalora Lee. They planned to drive back the next day. I got a permit from Park Headquarters and turned left to drive two miles along the meandering shoreline of oak-studded groves and coves. Twenty-five miles long, several miles wide, Berryessa was man-made. It had been created with the construction of Monticello Dam in 1957. In September the surface of the clear blue lake is warm. Two hundred and seventy-five feet below the temperature plunges to a frigid 40 degrees. At the bottom schools of black bass swarm among the ruins of a town sacrificed for the dam. Somewhere in those submerged houses, where only a scuba diver could go, Zodiac might have hidden trophies.

The clearing where Bryan and Cecelia had been attacked by Zodiac on September 27, 1969, lay 510 yards from the parking lot on a promontory of the lake's west shoreline. Behind burbled Smittle Creek. Beyond, sun flashed off placid water near an island. The wind lifted dust, blowing it among the groves and stretch of deserted shoreline. Shrubbery covering the bank isolated it even more. A sign nailed to an oak read: "Dangerous Area—no open fires or firearms." I heard, as Zodiac must have, the stillness of the forest, the wind sweeping solemnly across stretches of deserted lake, and the bite of Wing Walker boots in the sand. The killer had imprinted deep tracks all around the Kar-

mann Ghia. Aerial police photos shot from a fixed wing aircraft
eerily marked his path, each step covered over with a little cardboard box. As I studied the secluded lake, I realized I had underestimated how few people were visiting Lake Berryessa that
terrible day. There had been virtually no one around. Zodiac had
to have been seen without his hood.

Here's who was at the lake: Bryan Hartnell and Cecelia Shepard (the victims), Park Rangers Dennis Land and Sergeant
William White (both in a patrol car three miles away when the
call came in), Ronald Henry Fong of San Francisco and his son
on the lake fishing (who saw the couple and rowed for help),
Archie and Beth White at Rancho Monticello (who arrived at the
crime scene with White and Fong by boat, Land drove to the
scene from park Headquarters), Cindy, a waitress, a patron at
Moskowite Corners, and a father and two young boys across the
lake shooting BB-guns. They were all removed from the scene.
At the scene were Dr. Clifton Rayfield and his son, David, three
PUC college girls, and a stocky man who walked oddly.

Originally I had discounted a description of a heavyset man at
the lake because he had dark hair and Zodiac did not. That had
been reinforced two weeks later when Officer Fouke described
Zodiac as blondish, balding, and "graying in back." An anonymous typewritten letter[22] on Eaton bond (like the Zodiac letters)
sent to the *Chronicle* and bearing an FDR stamp read:

> "Dear Sir: With the popularity of hair pieces today it would be
> a logical masquerade to remove whatever was the usual hair
> style if the Zodiac killer intended to strike. It would be normal
> to resume the hairstyle he usually appeared in for daily ap-
> pearances. To illustrate my point, I have cut the hair styling
> from the picture of the victim [Cecelia Shepard], and superim-
> posed it on the composite. . . . Anything to help. I would as
> soon remain anonymous."

Had Zodiac as far back as 1970 been telling us (as he mentioned a Zodiac watch) that he had worn a wig at Berryessa? Now
I recalled Hartnell had gotten a sense of that before he was
stabbed. "I remember a kind of greasy forehead," he told me.

---

[22]Mailed November 17, 1970, from Aptos, California, at 1:00 p.m.

"The attacker had sweaty dark brown hair—which showed through dark glasses covering eyelets in the hood. And it's not impossible the guy was wearing a wig." If Zodiac had been the dark-haired man, then eyewitnesses had seen him without his hood, had observed events *preceding* the crime.

Three college seniors, all twenty-one years old, saw Zodiac unmasked. They attended the same college as Bryan and Cecelia—Pacific Union College at Angwin. The Seventh-day Adventist campus perched loftily atop an extinct volcano, Mt. Howell, about eight miles from St. Helena. They had traveled the same route as Bryan and Cecelia, coming into Berryessa from Angwin via Pope Valley and Knox Valley Road. At 2:55 P.M., they pulled into a parking spot two miles north of the A&W at Sugar Loaf. Before they could exit, another car, a Chevrolet, "silver or ice-blue in color," a 1966 two-door, full-size sedan, slid alongside. As the driver pulled past them, they saw the auto's California plates. The stranger then backed up until his rear bumper was parallel and off to the side of their car. Zodiac had performed a similar maneuver at Blue Rock Springs. The man sat there, his head down as if reading. The girls got the impression he wasn't.

"We had pulled in at a gas station and this man pulled up beside us," Lorna,[23] one of the students, told me. "He was scooted way down, his eyes just kind of looking over at us—watching us. And he followed us to the parking place back maybe a hundred feet where we parked and walked down to the water's edge." At 3:00 P.M. the trio had walked to the lake shore and settled under the oak-studded cover. Half an hour later, they were in their swimsuits sunbathing when they noticed the stranger again—smoking cigarettes and watching them. Twenty minutes later he was still there, his T-shirt hanging out at the rear of his trousers.

"And within a few minutes he was in the trees watching us," said Lorna. "My two girlfriends didn't pay any attention. 'I'm not going to look at him,' they said. 'He's just a creep.' But I watched him a lot, and over a period of almost an hour he watched us from various trees. He was between us and the car so we couldn't leave. He was not distinctive, just an average, normal

---

[23]This name has been changed by request.

plain person, other than he gave us the creeps. And he obviously
followed us and obviously watched us. I remember his face as
being square, all sides symmetrical. I don't remember him at all
being pudgy, just compact . . . stocky, solid. The minute you
mentioned the suspect was a swimmer, that felt so right about his
body type. I wouldn't say he had a limp, but he favored one leg
when he walked. He was clean-cut, nice-looking, and wearing
dark-blue pants, pleated like suit pants, and a black sweatshirt
with short sleeves, knitted at the ends." Fouke had seen Zodiac
wearing brown pleated pants.

The women estimated the man to be six feet to six feet two
inches tall and between 200 and 230 pounds. Hartnell thought Zodiac weighed between 225 and 250 pounds. "I don't know how
tall Zodiac was," he told me, "maybe . . . six feet, somewhere in
there. I'm a pretty poor judge of height because of my own
height. . . . He was a sloppy dresser." Allen, then thirty-five, stood
six feet and weighed between 200 and 230 pounds. "I would say
older than thirty-five—middle thirties," Lorna said. "He was
clean-cut and had hair that was too perfect."

"You mentioned his shirttail was hanging out," I said, "and I
realized how inconsistent that was with neatly parted hair."

"I know," Lorna replied, "and it was exactly parted and combed
and probably was a wig in such a breezy place. Other than in the
gas station, I don't remember any other people up there. I think
the only reason we were safe is that we faced a marina. There was
no activity, but there were mobile homes and boats at least parked
there. We felt like there were people around, but I don't think we
saw people. There were none on the beach. We were the only
ones—none on the parking area. None on the road."

At 3:50 P.M., the women looked up. The stranger was gone.
When they didn't see him again, they waited almost forty minutes to be sure it was safe. "At one point he disappeared and at
that point we made a run for the car," Lorna told me. "When we
got to the car, Bryan and Cece's car was parked behind ours.
They were directly around the corner from us probably within
three hundred yards. Later we were in one little cove and they
were right around the corner. We didn't know it at the time, but
their car was parked right by ours. Cecelia and I were maybe four
or five rooms apart [at PUC] on the same dorm floor. She was our
floor monitor. We weren't close friends but I knew her well. She

was a singer and I worked in that department. She was incredible and the tiniest, most fragile person."

When Ken Narlow and Deputy Land later asked the women to provide details, they were "very sure and positive of what they had seen." "All three said they could identify the man if they saw him again," said Narlow. "However, only [Lorna, the principal witness] felt confident enough to work with an Ident-a-kit artist. This particular sketch was drawn with the assistance of the three young girls who had seen this particular individual in a car acting suspiciously, but this wasn't near the scene of the crime. To the best of my recollection, it was probably four or five hours prior to the actual crime."

"It was a terrifying experience for me," Lorna said. "At Cece's funeral, the FBI had me outside with them thinking he might show up. When I was interviewed by the police and the FBI, it was with the understanding no one ever knew who I was. It was probably irrational, but I had a lot of fear about this man knowing who I was and trying to find me. I think at the time, because my description was so different, the police had a tendency to discount what I had to say. It's so coincidental that we were right there and this happened right there. What are the chances someone else would have followed us that day?"

Amazingly, after March 1971, before Leigh Allen became a suspect, no policeman ever spoke with Lorna or showed her photos of suspects. Thirty-one years later she was still frightened. I provided her with photos of Leigh Allen. After first consulting with the Napa P.D., she insisted on consulting her attorney before giving me her evaluation. I waited.

Moskowite Corners General Store stood across from Pearce's Chevron Service near the lake. At noon the day of the stabbings, a round-faced man rushed into the cafe and asked anxiously for directions on the "fastest way out of the area." A patron eating lunch found him suspicious, followed him out, and watched him drive off in an ice-blue Chevy. He matched Lorna's description of the man watching her and her friends sunbathing. In 1974 the patron spoke with police and "tentatively" identified a middle-aged suspect as the man leaving the cafe. Within two weeks, the witness was killed in an explosion.

"We have better witnesses," Narlow had told me, "people who had seen the suspect closer to the scene of the crime both geographically and time-wise than that sketch there, but it could easily have been the guy. We have evidence that about a quarter mile down the road, about forty-five minutes earlier, Zodiac was seen without his mask by a doctor and his young son." Dr. Clifton Rayfield, an ophthalmologist, and his son, David, had parked their car four-fifths of a mile further up the road from Hartnell's Karmann Ghia and toward Oak Shores Park and Rancho Monticello. "Rayfield reported to me," continued Narlow, "that at approximately 6:30 P.M. he and his son had parked their vehicle north of Park Headquarters . . . in the general area of the crime scene and walked down toward the beach. While en route Rayfield observed a WMA described as five feet ten inches, heavy build, wearing dark trousers and a long-sleeved dark shirt with red coloring."

David Rayfield had seen Zodiac unmasked. Thirty-two years had passed since anyone had asked him about the man he had seen. I tracked him down.

"How many people would you say were up at the lake that day?" I began.

"There were like zero," Rayfield said. "There was no one up there—it was really desolate. I walked all around and was shooting my gun, a .22 with a scope. That's why my dad and I went to the lake, because I could shoot my gun and not be bothered, wouldn't be scaring or hurting anyone. My dad never saw him. He was fishing down at the lake. I saw Zodiac at a distance of about one hundred yards, so I wouldn't be able to comment on his face. He was walking along the hillside about halfway between the road and the lake. But I remember him as being a stockier person. He wasn't nimble when he was walking. And when he turned to walk away he wasn't like a smooth, athletic person. To me he seemed a little overweight and on the clumsier side. Not having followed the story or ever having been re-interviewed by the police, I didn't realize Zodiac came upon us just before he stabbed the young couple. I sort of assumed I saw him making his getaway. I'll tell you one thing, he didn't like the fact I was carrying a gun. He turns and looks at me and my gun (which with its scope was pretty intimidating) for probably five, six seconds, and then turned and went up the hill in a southerly direction. I said to myself, 'That was funny. This guy wasn't carrying a fishing pole. There's no camping equipment. There's no gun. What's he doing out here?'"

"What you're telling me fits the prime suspect. Everybody remarked how he lumbered, how clumsy he was. The reason his friends thought this was so interesting is that Arthur Leigh Allen was gorgeous in the water. When he'd go up to the diving board and waddle out, people would say, 'Oh, my God, he's so ungainly.' The minute he was in the air or in the water he was fine. But on land everyone commented on how awkward he was."

"That's what jumped out at me about the picture you sent of him walking. . . . He has the same body language of the guy I was watching from a distance. While I'm not sure I was close enough to say that much about his face, this is the same-size guy that I saw. I remember thinking that guy is not a small guy. His body type matches what police said at that time—two hundred pounds or more. He was pretty big and built, but he didn't move like he was a real coordinated, smooth-walking guy. He didn't move up the side of the hill easily."

"I can't understand with the limited number of witnesses who had seen Zodiac, the police didn't come back and speak with you at every opportunity," I said.

"I can't either," said Rayfield. "It continues to shock me. I came to think what I saw at the lake wasn't related or they would have been all over me. They never came back or called me. I said, 'Jesus. What's going on that they would never want to talk to me again? It must not have been the guy. It must not have fit the scenario for them that he would have been there.'

"It's funny you should mention the composite sketches. 'Cause I saw the sketches with the hair on them and I didn't remember black hair, neatly trimmed hair, on the man I saw."

"What did you see?"

"I didn't remember him having a full head of hair. The suspect in the driver's license you sent would have been only thirty-six at the time, so of course he wouldn't be bald." Rayfield was telling me Zodiac was almost bald. Since he was wearing the same clothes as the man Lorna had seen, it meant he had taken off his wig. "Leigh Allen was almost bald at that age," I told him. "He shaved the sides of his head close."

"Wow," said Rayfield. "In retrospect, how could the man I saw not be Zodiac? I can't believe the case was never solved and police had all those leads."

Zodiac had written, "I shall not tell you what my descise consists of when I kill." Zodiac's disguise consisted of hairpieces:

October 30, 1966—a false beard on a stocky man at Riverside Library.

February, 1969—"curly, wavy dark brown hair."

July 4, 1969—"combed hair up in a kind of pompadour, short curly, light brown hair." Second description: "light brown hair in a military crew cut."

September 27, 1969—three girls see stocky man wearing an obvious wig, "dark straight hair parted neatly." Rayfield sees him soon after, remarks he's so young to be bald. Hartnell saw "dark brown sweaty hair" through the eyelets of Zodiac's hood. ". . . it's not impossible the guy was wearing a wig."

October 11, 1969—"reddish or blond crew cut" and "short, curly light brown hair in Military-type crew cut." In the 1960s, crew-cut wigs were available for military men with long hair who did not want to cut their hair short. Long hair was then fashionable.

"The kid had a .22 rifle," Narlow summed up, "and Zodiac came down within one hundred yards of them across an inlet. The kid saw the guy over there and he was wearing the blue windbreaker jacket. But evidently this wasn't what he was looking for because it was a father-and-son deal. So the killer went a quarter mile up this road, went back up to the road, and evidently came down the road this way and saw this single car parked here, and then pulled in behind it. Rayfield and his son both stated that they had not observed a vehicle parked in the area of their car, and had only noticed the subject at a distance of approximately one hundred yards. Rayfield did report that there was a man with two young boys in the area shooting BB guns, but didn't know whether or not they saw the subject.

"I think their time was off a little bit 'cause I think Rayfield actually saw the Zodiac killer just prior to him going south four-fifths of a mile to where Shephard and Hartnell had their car parked. It sure looks like he stumbled on them and had not followed them. I'm convinced that Zodiac was just stalking any singular parked cars along the route. And that's why he stopped when he saw Rayfield's car there. When he saw the father and son and they saw him, he decided to go back up to his car. Then he drove down the road a little ways and saw the white Karmann Ghia. Then he came down here and saw a boy and a girl laying on this blanket under this oak tree, and this is what his game was, to kill the boy and the girl. This is why he struck here and not further up the road."

When I talked with Bryan Hartnell in the 1970s he had already gone through considerable anguish trying to recall all he could about Zodiac.

"When Zodiac left he must have thought we were dead," said Hartnell. "I was extremely fortunate to survive. I quit breathing! I just froze! What I heard was him walk away in a non-hurried fashion. And then after that there's a little dead spot I don't remember. In fact I don't think I went out, but there is a slight haze in my memory. There was no way I could hear his car starting. It's really some distance to the road up there. You're going to get some white noise that may blur that out. But I remember starting to get untied and moving around. I had a ways to walk. It's not impossible that first time I blacked out or something. All I had made it up to was the jeep trail when I saw a [pickup] coming. The toughest part was yet to go, but the way I was going, I would have made it [to Knoxville Road].

"Now while I was in the hospital a couple of weeks," he said, "it was basically to confirm I was all right, and in fact was. The stab wounds I received missed all the organs. Obviously they hit my lungs, and I needed some time for the lungs to heal up, and I had some scarring. But that's nothing. A surgeon deciding he was going to make seven or eight holes in my back couldn't have done it better. The guy I probably liked least in the whole mess was that psychiatrist Narlow got. He had an idea that I should do some hypnotism. That was such an abortion. I told him, 'I don't know if I'm going to be able to do this. My church [Seventh-day Adventist] has kind of a taboo on those kind of things. I'm willing to give it a try, but I think it's going to take more than a slambam, thank you, ma'am, to get me to go under. I think I'm fairly suggestible, but I don't think this is going to work.' He does his thing and I said, 'I'm not under.' 'Don't argue,' he says, 'just answer these questions,' and had me run through it.

"One question he asked me to answer was describe the arm. 'Do you want to experience it or see it on a television screen?' I'm looking and I'm seeing a man with bare arms, but there was no question that guy was wearing a jacket. OK, I'm looking and I'm seeing bare arms. . . . 'Tell me about the bare arms.' 'Well, they are fairly heavily haired.' [Allen was not.] He thinks this is great shit. But the guy had a jacket on. I could be way out of line and I was hypnotized and really seeing it, but you know one of the early things I screwed them up on is that I had this guy as being really fat. I said either the guy was moderately heavy and wearing a windbreaker, or he was skinny and wearing a lined jacket . . . kind of a cotton poplin, crew collar, and gathered around the sleeves, ordinary garden-variety short jacket. How much he weighed depended on whether that was lined or unlined. If I went through all that kind of cerebration over a jacket, I know he didn't have bare arms."

That evening I spoke to Toschi. After the stabbings, Zodiac had come down from the 440-foot elevation fast. A Vallejo police officer told me that another policeman had ticketed Allen speeding down from Lake Berryessa the day of the stabbing. On the seat of his car lay a bloody knife. Leigh caught the officer's gaze and said, "I used that to kill a couple of chickens."

"Remember that on September 27, 1969, Allen was supposed to be going to Lake Berryessa," I said, "and had a bloody knife in his possession?" I read Toschi part of an FBI report:

> "Conway indicated to the FBI that 'a surviving victim of the ZODIAC series of murders had positively identified ALLEN as the ZODIAC killer.' Lake Berryessa victim Bryan Hartnell thought Allen's voice and build were compatible with Zodiac's."

"I was never told that," said Toschi. "To this day I've never heard any detective tell me that."

"First Hartnell went into Sonoma Auto Parts, to hear Allen's voice," George Bawart explained. "DOJ was working on it. This guy Jim Silver, the investigator for the DOJ, had him go in, make a purchase, and have him listen to Allen's voice." Hartnell looked at him and told Silver, 'He could have been. There is nothing about what I saw or heard that would rule him out as the killer. His physical size, mannerisms, and voice are the same as the person who stabbed Cecelia and wounded me.' "

Zodiac's voice to Hartnell was "some type of drawl, but not a Southern drawl . . . [it] sounded uneducated, moderate in sound, not high or low pitched." Others had heard Zodiac's voice. Napa Officer David Slaight thought the "barely audible" caller sounded in his "early twenties." Vallejo switchboard operator Nancy Slover heard an "even but consistent, soft but forceful" voice with no trace of accent. It sounded "mature, deepened and became taunting toward the end." All these voices were Zodiac— were there several Zodiacs or did he have multiple personalities?

FRIDAY, JUNE 23, 2000

I continued to wait for Lorna, who was undergoing considerable anguish over the photos I had given her. Could Arthur Leigh Allen be placed on the day of the murder at Lake Berryessa within yards of the crime scene at a destination he had announced to friends? Finally, at 10:00 A.M., Lorna called to give me her answer.

"When I looked at the older man," she said, "my instant sort of response was fear by looking at his eyes, but I couldn't say I recognized the face.

"When I look at the young version, in the picture in the 1950s, that is exactly the way I remember the man looking that we saw at Berryessa. Even to the point that I never saw him fully face on, but a little in profile, and that's how the photo was taken. So if I had seen this photo back then I would have said—absolutely!"

Thus, Leigh Allen, wearing a wig, could be placed at the crime scene the day of the stabbings. "I do not always look the same," Zodiac had said. He had spoken the truth.

"Leigh told me he was at Lake Berryessa the day of the murder, hanging around hunting for squirrels," Leigh's friend, Jim, told me. "He told me he was there flat out. No question about it. And he had gone to an area of Berryessa with trees, but kind of open and remote. It wasn't a high-visibility area, so that nobody would have seen him up there in that area of Berryessa. He would have been all alone. He did say it was the same day the kids were attacked. And he said that if anyone had seen him they would have seen he was off in a different area of the lake and had left before before it happened." He later wrote Jim that he recognized Hartnell when he came into the parts store and "disappeared in the back of the store where cops were waiting. Hell, if I once got tired of all this crap and said I was the one, there'd be no way I could prove I *wasn't*."

SUNDAY, DECEMBER 10, 2000

AFTER leaving the *Chronicle,* Paul Avery wrote for the *Sacramento Bee,* then returned to San Francisco to report for the *Examiner* until his retirement in August 1994. For years he had suffered with emphysema and heart problems. Ironically, the reporter had fallen ill at the same time as Leigh Allen. He often visited the M&M, a famous Mission Street newspaper watering hole, dragging his oxygen tank with him. "The image that I'll keep forever," *Examiner* Editor Phil Bronstein said, "is of Paul, police radio attached to one ear, cigarette in his hand, oxygen supply hooked up to his nose, arm around my shoulder, sharing the scandalous details of the latest story he'd broken." This morning on Orcas Island, Washington, Paul had died at age sixty-six at the West Sound home of the grandfather of his wife, Margo St. James. He had died without unlocking the riddle of Zodiac. But for many years the reporter had been divorced from his biggest story, and by 1980, when I visited him in Sacramento, he had forgotten most of the details.

Harold Huffman died on June 19, 2001. "Leigh would write Harold from Atascadero," Kay Huffman told me, "and include letters that were stamped and addressed and ask Harold to mail them on. I never figured out why if he could mail out to Harold why he couldn't mail out to other people. I never saw the insides of them. Actually, I found one while I was going through some of Harold's stuff. Harold never forwarded it on. Whether he ever sent the others on or not I have no idea. It sounds like something my husband might not have done. I never opened that letter. I figured if Harold wasn't going to forward it, it wasn't something I wanted to see either." In Harold's opinion, the contents of those letters were harmless. One of the unforwarded letters was a request for aviation charts and addressed to the Distribution Division (C-44), National Ocean Survey in Washington, D.C.

"I get awfully lonely when I am ignored," Zodiac had written. If "obsession" best described Zodiac's hunters, "lonely" was a word that Zodiac had made his own. In that loneliness, the shape of Zodiac's crimes unfolded like fireworks in the copper-colored sky above Vallejo. The secret lay with Darlene Ferrin on that long-ago July Fourth. Her murder held the secret of Zodiac's identity. Zodiac had known Darlene, known her well, and more importantly, she had known him in his true identity and without the concealment of that hideous black veil.

39
UNMASKED

"**I** spoke with Don Cheney," Zodiac buff Tom Voigt told me. "Cheney, as you recall, had fingered Leigh Allen as Zodiac in 1971. He was up in Washington when I suggested we meet. He was willing to drive down here to Portland to the Hood River, which is about an hour from me, but four hours from him. We met at the Hood River Inn, which is right on the Columbia River. We had a whole section to ourselves. It was a beautiful view of the Columbia and he sat facing it. He was very relaxed and a nice pleasant guy, probably six feet tall."

"Was Leigh homosexual," Voigt asked Cheney, "or did he have an interest in women? Was there ever a girl he really liked?"

Cheney thought. "In the time that I knew Leigh," he said, "there was only one female that Leigh ever mentioned and she was a waitress."

"Was this in Vallejo?" Voigt asked.

"Yeah."

"Where did she work?"

"At a pancake house. I don't remember her name or anything, and it was the only time Leigh ever mentioned her. We went to an International House of Pancakes, right around the corner from Leigh's house. We had dinner there after a hunting trip in 1967. I was still living in Concord then. Leigh pointed out the waitress, a girl with brown hair. She was pretty and she was young. Leigh liked her."

"If you saw a picture of that girl would you recognize her?" said Voigt, his interest up.

"Naw, it's been too long," Cheney told him.

"I don't know if Allen ever went to Terry's," Voigt said with a laugh. "Allen liked IHOP, I don't know about Terry's. Why would you go to Terry's when you've got an IHOP just around the corner?"

Cheney told me the same thing. "The IHOP was close to the house there," Cheney said, "a couple blocks away at the bottom of Fresno Street. Leigh and I made a right turn on Tennessee. We were going someplace for an outing when we saw the girl there. Leigh indicated he was interested in her. 'What do you think of that waitress?' he asked. 'I think I might be able to make some headway with her.' But nothing ever happened with it. It was a girl of very similar appearance to Darlene Ferrin. She could have been the girl that he pointed out at the IHOP, but I couldn't say from my memory that it was the same girl. This happened in 1967."

Cheney could have said that the waitress was Darlene and that the restaurant was Terry's Waffle Shop at Magazine Street and Interstate 80. That Darlene had waitressed at Terry's from April 24, 1968, until her murder on July 4, 1969, was well publicized. But I knew Cheney had told the truth because of something he did not know.

After Darlene filed for divorce from her first husband, Jim Phillips, she spent six months in Reno, making four round trips to maintain residency. She returned to Vallejo in 1967 to work with her friend, Steven Kee, *at the International House of Pancakes on Tennessee Street* at the foot of Fresno. Darlene *had* been the woman Leigh pointed out to Cheney. He had even gotten the year right. Dean Ferrin had been the cook at the IHOP and eventually he and Darlene were married and she began to work at Terry's. "Why do I meet all the sick ones first?" she had written Dean from Reno.

"Darlene and I first met in '65 at the phone company in San Francisco," said Bobbie Oxnam, Darlene's friend and coworker at Terry's. "Six girls came into the phone company together. Three of us lived in an apartment house and three of the others lived in the residence quad just next door . . . some strong ties built there. Whenever I would have some of the group up, Darlene always had the invitation to come over. And so a lot of times when we talked, we were talking about the other girls. Unless she was really down or really depressed, Darlene seldom talked about her personal problems. She had to be especially down to burden you with her own problems.

"She worked at the phone company about nine months, then

her and Jim, her first husband, took off to the Virgin Islands.
Then when they got back they got hold of Mel and I for a place
to stay. They stayed with us two or three weeks. One of the reasons why we kicked them out of the apartment was because Jim
had a small handgun and we didn't want that. That's when we
told them to get out; otherwise they would have stayed with us
longer while she was looking for work."

"Darlene's first husband had a .22-caliber handgun while in
Vallejo," Sergeant Mulanax told me. "Because a .22-caliber
semiautomatic had been used in the two murders out on Lake
Herman Road, I went looking for him. I picked him up in Santa
Cruz [February 2, 1970] and checked it out then."

"Jim was into horoscopes," continued Oxnam. "I was scared of
him and he scared Darlene. This guy who brought her a silver
purse and belt from Mexico was down there while Jim was. I was
always under the impression that Jim bought it and sent it up to
her through this guy. I moved back to Vallejo. By this time she
and Jim had split and she was going with Dean. It was sweet.
She'd buy twenty-five chocolate mints for Dean, put them under
her pillow, and forget about them. She was always there to listen
to you, but would make a statement every once in a while that she
was terrified of 'this guy.' She would never go into any sort of
depth. If you questioned her she would clam up, but I know Darlene was afraid of someone. She never verbalized precisely what
made her afraid. He had something on her, but what he had I
don't know. I have a feeling it was connected with the Virgin Islands, but that's just a hunch. From some of Darlene's conversations, Jim and her got into trouble while they were in the Virgin
Islands skin diving for shells." It was rumored they had seen a
murder there.

In 1966 Dean Ferrin had moved to a back apartment of Vern's
Bar at 560 Wallace Street. After he and Darlene married, she
moved there too. Their daughter, Deena Lynn, was born January
24, 1969. Just over a month before Deena's birth, David Faraday
and Betty Lou Jensen had been shot out on remote Lake Herman
Road. The next day Darlene told her coworker Bobbie Ramos,
"This is scary. I knew the two kids who were killed on Lake Herman Road. The girl more so. I'm not going up there *again*." Darlene told her baby-sitter the same thing: "That was really spooky.
I knew that girl who was killed on Lake Herman Road. I'm not
going out there anymore."

"It all started after her baby was born," said Oxnam. "I mean, we talked about her fears a couple of times. Darlene was scared of somebody, had been for quite some time . . . she would make a statement every once in a while that she was having trouble. I think a lot of us know the man she was afraid of, but can't place him. Darlene was the type of person who had a lot of friends and was friendly toward anyone. That was one of the problems between her and Jim. Every week there was somebody new, a new friend. They'd be her friend for a week, but after that wouldn't be the topic of our conversation. People were her whole interest in life. She really enjoyed mixing and just being around people."

"What about this guy in a white Chevy who had been bothering her at Terry's?" I asked. "According to one of Darlene's baby-sitters, she had complained of a stocky man coming to the restaurant early in the morning to talk to her."

"Yeah, that's true," Oxnam said, then added surprisingly, "You know, in all the years since her murder the police never talked to me."

In February and March 1969, Darlene's baby-sitter, Karen, observed a man in a white car staking out their ground-floor apartment. Around 10:00 P.M. the man lit a cigarette or momentarily turned on the interior light, and she got a glimpse of his face: "He was heavyset, middle-aged, and very round-faced," Karen said. "His hair had a curl to it. I told Darlene about it when she got home. 'I guess he's back checking up on me again,' Darlene told me. 'I heard he was back from out of state. He doesn't want anyone to know what I saw him do. I saw him murder someone.' Dee [Darlene's nickname] sometime during this conversation mentioned the man's name, and that first name was very short, three or four letters. His second name was just slightly longer. A common name. Dee appeared to be genuinely frightened of this individual, and mentioned that he had been checking up on her at Terry's Restaurant. . . ." Karen was so upset she quit in May.

A strange man left packages for Darlene at her home—a silver belt and purse from Mexico, a flower-print fabric, and a package the size and shape of a bundle of money. "About the time I took that package from him that looked like money to me," reported Darlene's sister, Pam, "Darlene started paying me for baby-sitting in ten-dollar and twenty-dollar bills. Before that she was giving me quarters, her tip money." Darlene's sister, Linda, described the man who brought Dee presents from Tijuana—"large forehead

and close-cropped hair"—like Leigh Allen's. Leigh and his
chums had made a trip to Mexico about that time, feasting on lob-
ster on the beach. Around the same period, a man Darlene referred
to interchangeably as "Robbie" and "Lee" moved from his residence near Hogan High, about two blocks from Darlene's friend
Mike Mageau's home, to directly across from the Ferrins' home.

"About the beginning of June 1969," Bobbie Ramos said,
"Darlene told me of a man in a white car watching her." I asked
about her "new friends." "Darlene's new friends were Mike
Mageau and a man in a Mercury Cougar named Robbie or Lee. I
never spoke to him, but I definitely know how he looks. He drove
Darlene over and she had her laundry with her." However, Bobbie recalled a slender and much younger man than Zodiac, with
black hair and horn-rimmed glasses.

Evelyn Olson, another Terry's waitress, said a man named
"Lee" had "some kind of hold on Dee [Darlene's pet name]."
Linda Del Buono, Darlene's sister, also named Darlene's closest
friends for me: "They were Sue Gilmore [Dean Ferrin's cousin],"
she said. "Bobbie, a blonde down at Terry's, and this guy named
Lee who used to bring gifts to her from Mexico. Darlene met this
Lee by Franklin School at a laundromat. He told her he lived
above the laundromat. I wonder if that's when she got her laundry stolen—uniforms, baby's diapers, everything." Leigh Allen,
who also spelled his name "Lee," worked part-time at the
Franklin School as a janitor.

Though Dean saw no change in Darlene's demeanor, her
friends did. "Darlene became more nervous than ever. She rarely
smiled now," they said. They attributed her weight loss to diet
pills. "I seen a change in my sister the last four months before she
died," said Pam. "Very nervous, losing weight. I don't think it
was drugs. She was just frightened of this guy who was constantly following her."

"Towards the end, that last year, we weren't that close," said
Carmela Leigh, Dean's boss at Caesar's Palace Restaurant and
his landlord. "She had a whole new group of friends—never
mentioned names—she was just never around. We'd have barbe-
cues and everything and Dean, who everybody just really liked,
he'd come over for the barbecue and we'd say, 'Where's Darlene?' and he'd say, 'She went to the laundromat about 4:00,' and
this would be about 9:00. She'd go to the laundromat, and five

hours later he'd be at the party by himself and he just didn't know anything."

On May 9, 1969, Darlene purchased a new house at 1300 Virginia Street, and reported that a former neighbor was watching her. Darlene organized a painting party and invited a few of the many policemen she knew from Terry's. "Lots of the cops knew her," Sergeant Lynch told me. "They used to stop in at the coffee shop out there. She worked the 3:00 A.M. late shift on weekends, and she'd get off work and run off to San Francisco. She used to like to take off her shoes and stockings and run through the surf, and this is at four in the morning. She dated all kinds of guys. She was a goer."

"Among [Darlene's] companions were men," the *Times-Herald*'s Gene Silverman later wrote, "men who were not necessarily her husband. Dean Ferrin was reportedly unconcerned. He considered her association with male friends just an aspect of her being young and lively." "You got to understand how cops operate, especially back in those days," Detective Bawart added. "If you're working the swing shift, the graveyard shift, and a new waitress came on, it would be a contest to see who could get in her shorts first. That's the way cops were back then. There were a lot of cops pursuing her. She was a pretty loose gal, Darlene was."

"Darlene had a rep as being pretty fast and loose," Mulanax elaborated. "She was dating a lot of different guys. Certainly during the time she was working as a waitress out at Terry's. Prior to Terry's I have no knowledge of Darlene dating. Before her death she saw three Vallejo cops, one 'a drive-in Romeo' and another a deputy in the sheriff's office. According to our reports, Blue Rock Springs was Darlene's favorite hangout to take her boyfriends. So regardless of who she was with, that's where she would go." And yet she had turned down the lonely older man in the white car. How must he have felt?

Saturday, May 24, was the day of the painting party. "How many people showed up at the party?" I asked Linda. "There were about fifteen. The party lasted a long time." "Who was there?" "The Mageau boys. Steven Kee. They were there. Steve went directly into the Navy after graduating from Hogan High in 1965. His friendship with Darlene goes back to about 1963, I think. He was worried about Dee during her year-long absence and was stationed on the U.S.S. *Rook*. He was very shy. I recall he had a little red car at one time and a green Olds pickup. He was also very jealous of Dee, you've got to keep that in mind. He moved to San Diego just after the Lake Herman murders, and so was not there for her." I was more interested whether he had seen someone bothering Darlene at IHOP.

"George was there." Linda continued. "I know Howard was there." "Howard 'Buzz' Gordon?" "Yeah." "How about women?" "Only one or two." "How about Baldino?" "Steve? Yeah." Another Vallejo cop. Vallejo Policeman Richard Hoffman, though on the guest list, had not attended. Among the other guests were: Jay Eisen (a San Francisco friend of Darlene's); Rick Crabtree; Darlene's female friend Sydney; Linda, Darlene's sister; Pam, Darlene's younger sister; Ron Allen; and *a stocky man in a business suit and tie.*

"Darlene called me and told me to come over to the party," her sister Linda said, "and Darlene was scared to death. She didn't expect for this man to show up. I got there at one in the afternoon. He showed up when I was on my way over. He was the only one dressed neat. Everyone else had old jeans on and was painting the house that she had just put a down payment on. . . . And so the police assumed that this was Bill Leigh, who was Dean's boss, and they just left it at that. But it was 'Lee,' and it was not his last name. I never spoke to him, but I definitely know how he looks . . . and Darlene was scared to death. This guy at the painting party was the Zodiac. I know Zodiac is the person I saw at the party. The way she was acting. This guy had no business being at her house.

"Dee got into something and she was afraid and wanted to back out of it. And she begged me, 'Linda, don't go near him. Just don't talk to him.' He was overweight . . . this guy scaring the heck out of her. I mean, she couldn't eat. I noticed how much weight she had lost. When something was bothering her she couldn't hide it. She wasn't smiling. . . . She begged me, 'Just go, Linda, just go.' She asked me to leave 'cause she didn't want him to know any part of the family.

"The way she acted made me fix this man's face in my mind. I can see him sitting there in the chair. There were still fourteen people left at the party when I left, and more coming. I wish I would have stayed. I do believe that she got into something and was afraid and she didn't know how to go about getting out of it. I think she did want to get out, and the Zodiac said, 'Well, we'll just do away with her 'cause she'll probably go to the police.' He was also the one at Terry's. When I walked into Terry's this one particular day with my dad, this man was sitting there and he was constantly watching Dee all the time. And as I walked in he held the paper up above him 'cause he noticed me. Later somebody [a tall, lean, black-haired man] shot four holes in the ceiling at Terry's."

After Linda left the painting party, Darlene's younger sister, Pam, arrived. She also noticed the man in the suit. "He was so out of place," Pam told me. "He was a pretty well-dressed guy. Yeah, very well-dressed, an older man. I saw him only the one time. He never did get out of that chair. Everybody was a little scared of him being at the party and a little nervous because he was there. . . . This guy was asking about her at work, prying into her finances . . . he is the same man who was sitting at the bar, the counter, this was the same man that was asking me questions. He was asking me about her little girl and what was her relationship with her husband, Dean. 'What did she do with her tips?' he asked. 'She really got her head together.' 'I understand Dean never wants to watch the baby.'

"The stranger had a short common nickname—Lee. It was 'Lee,' L-E-E, not 'Leigh,' and it wasn't his last name. There was this guy at the party who I think is Zodiac. The same guy who was at the party was the one who delivered a package to the doorstep of Wallace Street one day that I was baby-sitting. I saw him at the door and took a package from him. He told me under no circumstance was I to look in that package. He was the same man I remembered seeing leave a package on the doorstep at Wallace Street."

"And the age of the man at Terry's harassing Darlene—"

"I would say between thirty-five and thirty-eight." She estimated him to be almost six feet tall. "I can picture this man. . . . I remember seeing him at the door and I remember seeing him at the painting party and he liked to talk to me because I was a pretty honest person. Dee got upset with me because she thought I was telling him too much. 'Well, he would ask me something so I answered.' Dee said, 'Pam, I'm going to stop asking you to my parties if you don't stop talking to him. There are some things I don't want people to know about me.' I said, 'I thought you were dating this guy the way he talks.'" Ron Allen's name had been on the guest list for Darlene's painting party. After Cheney moved to

Southern California in 1969, Leigh's brother and sister-in-law paid him a visit.

"Ron and Karen were at my house for dinner," Cheney told me. "This was before my purchase of my new house [at 1842 Berkeley Avenue]. We were sitting around the kitchen table chatting, and Karen told us about Leigh going to a painting party in his suit. Ron and his brother were at the party and Leigh was dressed in a suit and tie. Karen was using that as an example of him being unadjusted to social things. She was ragging him on that. She was a little afraid of her brother-in-law because she recognized he was not squared away with the world at all. With her education in social work she had been exposed to such things, and I don't think Ron had."

Two Lees were crossing paths in Darlene's life. "Robbie" or "Lee" (she apparently called him by both names) lived close enough to see into Darlene's house on Wallace Street. Thus, he had no reason to park out front to watch her. That had to be a second "Lee." I asked Mulanax about him. "Assuming that Zodiac is one of Darlene's new friends, did you ever put together a list of her new acquaintances? Did you come across a Robbie?" "The people interviewed were her family basically and her coworkers," he answered. "There are numerous people there she was associated with, but whether they were her new friends, I don't know."

On June 29, 1969, Darlene confided to her friend Bobbie Ramos, at a county fair, that "Lee" was the name of a man who had lived across the street from her. A Terry's waitress had also observed a man in a white car, its vertical grill bars blacked out like a Mustang, following Darlene. She had jotted down his license number, and this enabled me to track the car down. The vehicle was a 1968 white hardtop Cougar Mercury coupe (only hardtops were made until 1969). I was disappointed. That car could not have been the one Zodiac used at Lake Berryessa. His worn tire tracks showed two different-size tires and a width between the wheels of 57 inches. The Cougar had the widest wheelbase around—111 to 123 inches. Its wheelbase width was closer to the white four-door hardtop 1959–60 Chevy Impala seen at the murder site on Lake Herman Road. Coincidentally, the Cougar's owner had traded in a 1960 Impala sedan in April 1969 for the Mercury.

Only one apartment building, 553, stood on Wallace Street. After a long search, I found and interviewed the Cougar's registered owner, a Robbie Lee Moncure, who had once lived at the Wallace Street apartment house and worked at Kresge's and Mare Island Naval Station. In 1971, he had moved to Fresno, California, and in April 1977, sold and junked the Cougar. However, he was black-haired, too thin (165 pounds), and too young (twenty-five at the time of the murders) to be Zodiac. My hope was that if he had been watching Darlene, he might have seen the older man named "Lee" who was watching her.

"We were real close . . . friends," Robbie told me, "and that was it! She didn't share the names of her friends with anybody. Each was sort of separate. I didn't pry. . . . I was just into her. These little games she played with different people were like you could see on TV or in a movie. A series that was going on and on. Darlene was petite. Full of devilment. She was on Wallace Street and flying a kite one night. But I remember that she called me another night from the Coronado Inn to come out and pick her up. She didn't trust this guy—an older man. The guy I saw was stocky. At the time I wasn't paying too much attention to him because she told me she wanted to come home right away." Robbie could recall no more.

A year after this encounter, a Vallejo resident, Marie Anstey, vanished from the Coronado Inn parking lot on Friday the thirteenth. Anstey, bludgeoned, then drowned, had not been sexually molested and was found near water—like the Santa Rosa victims. I believed Robbie Lee had seen Zodiac unmasked.

Leigh Allen could be linked to Darlene through the painting party and her friends who knew of a shadowy figure named "Lee." Could he now be connected to Darlene on the night of her murder? I had sought Lynch's advice. He was not totally unaware that a man named "Lee" might be Zodiac. He had searched out tips on a variety of men with the middle name Lee. One owned a .22-caliber gun, a .45, and a 9-mm gun. "There was a guy here who thinks he's Zodiac, a local nut," said Lynch. "He's been in and out of Napa. In fact I knew him. I didn't think I knew him when I got that tip by letter from out of state by his ex-wife. He was a sadistic two-hundred-pounder, six feet tall, with a fetish for leather. He told his wife, 'You will be my slave in the hereafter,' a phrase similar to Zodiac's 'slaves in the afterlife' remark. You can't really pin anything down with those guys. None of them will ever talk to you."

"Who tipped you to Leigh Allen as Zodiac?" I asked the last time we spoke. "Was the informant anonymous?"

"I think the information came through the local sheriff's office . . . Les Lundblad, he's dead now. I think the information came through him. Yeah, everything was coming second-hand. You could never talk to anyone directly."

"You talked to Darlene's sister, Linda, in San Jose."

"I did talk to her—many times."

"Did you ever speak to this 'Lee' from the painting party?"

"No."

"They dug a perfect bullet out of the car," I said, "one that wasn't smashed. It probably went through the fleshy part of Darlene's body and had just enough momentum to penetrate the upholstery. That copper-coated ammo was pretty new. It had only been out for six months. Did you ever get a lead on that?"

"No," said Lynch. "I admit I don't know much about guns. A guy on Skyline Boulevard south of San Francisco was firing his gun and he had that kind of ammo. I had that guy in, trying to find out how he got that. Nothing came of it. I never thought that Zodiac chased Darlene and Mike to Blue Rock Springs. I believe that guy just came upon them at random. He was just out there to shoot somebody and he found them." I disagreed with that. Zodiac had to have stalked them to some degree. At last I came to that fatal Fourth of July.

"**IT WAS AN** exceptionally hot Fourth," Bobbie Oxnam told me. "Everyone was down by the waterfront." The sky was filled with a spectacular display of pyrotechnics. The staccato pop-pop-pop of firecrackers was like gunfire. The smell of gunpowder was in the air. Earlier in the day Darlene had her hood up by a bowling alley when she had an altercation with a man driving a white van. He was later described to police as thirty years old, six feet tall, 180 to 185 pounds, with hair "the color of champagne combed straight back."

"Darlene was all excited when she came into Caesar's that evening," Carmela Leigh told me. Caesar's stood at 1576 Vervais Street, near Elmer Cave School, where Leigh Allen worked. "All I knew was she was going to get to ride on a boat in the parade. When Darlene left at 7:00 P.M., she said, 'I'm going to have a party,' and wanted me to come. I said, 'Yeah, OK, OK,' but she knew I wouldn't be there."

Darlene and her sister, Christina, went out to Mare Island for a ride on a decorated and lighted boat, the *General French Genora*. Leigh Allen's boat reportedly was also in Vallejo's Traditional Boat Parade on the channel. "A friend of hers had a boat," Mulanax told me. "There were two guys on a boat and two guys flying that Darlene knew." At 10:00 P.M., after the Mare Island parade, Darlene and Christina stopped by Caesar's again. Darlene had planned a small party at her house after the restaurant closed. Fifteen minutes later she called her sitters and learned Bobbie Ramos wanted to talk to her. At 10:30 P.M. Darlene and Christina arrived at Terry's, and Darlene went inside to talk to several waitresses. "Darlene did not speak to anyone other than some of the girls who work at Terry's before she took me home," Christina recalled.

But outside the restaurant Darlene had a second confrontation. She argued with a man in his "thirties or forties" in a blue car with out-of-state plates. Earlier in the evening, Deputy Ben Villareal had seen a blue 1967 Ford sedan sitting out at Blue Rock Springs. Christina (the "most stable and honest member of Darlene's family") said she "sensed a tension in the air and in the conversations." Darlene came away "very upset." She asked Darlene, "What's going on?" "Don't worry about it," Darlene answered, "you'll read about it tomorrow in the papers." Only a day or two before, Darlene had told her the same thing. "Really, something big is gonna happen. . . . I can't tell you yet, but it's going to be this week." Christina later mentioned the out-of-state car, the stranger, and her sister's odd remarks—none of which appear in the final VPD report—to a detective:

> "DEE and CHRISTINA went to Terry's Restaurant where DEE talked with several waitresses and, outside the restaurant, talked to a man (nfi) parked outside in a blue car with out-of-state plates (nfi). CHRISTINA claims to have sensed a tension in the air and in the conversations and reportedly asked DEE what was going on to which DEE allegedly replied, "Don't worry about it—you'll read about it tomorrow in the papers." Her description of the car was later modified in a notation made by Lt. Jim Husted in the left margin: The car was "1) all white. 2) larger than Dee's Corvair. 3) Older than Dee's Corvair (1963)."

Pam also confirmed the argument in Terry's parking lot. "All I know was when she came back to the car," she told me, "the story

I got was that he wanted to take her out. She didn't want to go out with him because she was married . . . he was between thirty-five and thirty-eight years old." One argument had been in daylight; the other an hour and a half before the shooting at Blue Rock Springs. Investigators had confused the nighttime argument with a morning confrontation. Just like Robbie and Lee, they were two different things at two different times. At 10:45 P.M. Darlene dropped Christina off at the family Vallejo home. The sitters, Janet Lynn Rhodes and Pamela Kay, were anxious to go. They had been sitting since early afternoon. Janet Lynn had sat for Darlene only that Fourth of July. The girls told Darlene "an older-sounding man" had been calling her repeatedly. Darlene changed from her patriotic jumpsuit of red, white, and blue stars. Quickly, she donned blue shoes and a white-and-blue flower-patterned slack dress, a pattern Zodiac would later describe.

"Dee knew the teenagers killed out on Lake Herman Road," Janet Lynn confirmed to me. "She had said that. 'He's back from out of state. I once saw him kill somebody.' " Later, from his hospital bed, a heavily sedated Mike Mageau told police what happened next.

> "Dee came [via Georgia Street east] to MAGEAU'S home at 864 Beechwood [west of Hogan High where Betty Lou Jensen had attended]," read the official statement. "At approximately 11:30 P.M. . . . and picked him up in her car. Since both were hungry, he said, they headed down Springs Road and went toward Vallejo. However, at approximately Mr. Ed's Restaurant, Dee said she wanted to talk with him about something."

An eerie parallel here—Betty Lou and David had stopped at Mr. Ed's Drive-In too just before being shot. The teenagers had visited Sharon, a friend, on Brentwood Avenue at 8:20 P.M., and remained until 9:00 P.M. At 10:30 their Christmas concert was over and they went from there to Mr. Ed's, then Lake Herman Road. Mr. Ed's phone number was later found scrawled on a photo envelope in Darlene's purse along with the words "hacked," "stuck," "testified," and "seen." Had Zodiac, December 20, 1968, mistaken Betty Lou for Darlene? Betty Lou Jensen bore an uncanny resemblance to Darlene Ferrin at age seventeen

(I had two photos of them at the same age). The odds of Zodiac happening upon two women who could be twins in pitch blackness and in widely separated, remote areas were incalculable—unless he trailed them. On several occasions Betty Lou had cautioned her older sister, Melody, to close the blinds. On occasion, their mother found the gate leading to the side of the house open and tracks in the garden.

Did Zodiac mistake the teenagers for Darlene and her friend Steven Kee, whose parents lived on Cottonwood one street over from Jensen's friend, Sharon? Did he trail them to Mr. Ed's, Darlene's hangout? Or was Betty Lou's murder meant as a warning to Darlene, who claimed to know her?

"They turned around and at his suggestion," continued Mageau's report, "drove east on Springs Road to Blue Rock Springs where they could talk."

"The minute they drove off, Mike told Dee they were being followed," Linda said. "Just that phrase, 'We're being followed.'"

"How did you hear that?" I asked.

"I heard that through Sergeant Lynch and Sergeant Mulanax. Darlene started just going down any side streets and this car just kept following them. . . . I don't know what made her go toward Blue Rock Springs." Linda had also spoken to Mike in the hospital after Zodiac shot him, and I was anxious to hear what else she had learned.

"They knew they were being followed?" I asked her.

"Yes."

"And Darlene thought it was someone named Lee."

"Yeah."

"She did say that?"

"Yes."

"Did the police understand that Zodiac's name was supposed to be Lee?"

"I don't think so, but Mike knows who Zodiac is. He does."

Pam agreed. "Zodiac knew Darlene," she told me, "because he called her by name . . . *she was known by 'Dee' and he called her 'Dee.'*"

"He did this when he shot her?"

"Uh-huh."

"And this is something Mike told you."

"And this is something Mike told me in the hospital." His acute tongue injury had prevented him from providing a description to police for two days.

> "One unconfirmed source states that MAGEAU claimed they were followed from the time they left his house by a similar suspect car."

Was this true? Sue Ayers, a legal secretary and friend, talked to Mike in the hospital. "Dee and the shooter," he told her, "had an argument at Terry's on July 4. They drove away and the man followed them to Blue Rock Springs where the argument continued and shooting followed." The daughter of the caretaker at Blue Rock Springs reportedly witnessed the argument in the lot, and seconds before shots rang out told her father there was going to be trouble. Mike's offical statements continued the story:

> "After five minutes there," MAGEAU said, a car [reportedly a 1958–59 brown Ford Falcon with old California plates] pulled in from Springs Road, the driver turned off his lights and pulled around to the left of their car (east of their car) some six to eight feet from Dee's car. The car remained there for about one minute.

Mike said he asked Dee if she knew who it is and she stated, "Oh, never mind. Don't worry about it." Mageau said he did not know if this meant she knew who it was or not. The car left after one minute at terrific speed, hurtling toward Vallejo on Springs Road, and they were left alone in the darkened lot overlooking the golf course. About five minutes later the man returned. He parked on the passenger side and to the rear of their car, headlights still on. A man came up to them carrying a flashlight with a handle on it. Were Darlene and Mike followed to Blue Rock Springs? I asked Mulanax. "I wouldn't have that feeling because my thought is these Zodiac killings are not planned," he said. "They're opportunity things. That's my feeling."

"But Zodiac did describe what Darlene was wearing and it was pretty dark."

"He was also shining a heavy big flashlight in there too."

"That's true."

"It's a flashlight that has a handle on it like you'd use in a boat. The kind that floats."

"MAGEAU said they thought it was the Police and they started to get some identification out of their purse/wallets when suddenly the man started shooting. MAGEAU said it sounded like the gun had a silencer on it."

This was a fact never reported, something only Zodiac would know. In 1991, after the search of his home, Leigh Allen told a friend, "They missed a few things—like the silencer I had hidden in my socks in the dresser." Had Zodiac turned away, not to re-load, but to install a silencer? Darlene, Mike, and the stranger had already attracted the attention of George R. Bryant, twenty-two, a Selby Smelter employee and son of the Blue Rock Springs caretaker. "The groundskeeper's son saw three people arguing," Mulanax told me. "Bryant was in a two-story house looking out the window and trying to get some shut-eye. Fifteen minutes later, he heard gunshots." Bryant was some eight hundred feet from the lot lying on his stomach when he heard "one shot, a short interval, another shot, a pause, then rapid fire." Finally he heard "a tire screeching as a car left the scene." Bryant's recall of the number of shots was insufficient. Zodiac fired a total of seven shots.

"After firing repeatedly the man turned to walk back to his car, but MAGEAU believes he cried out and the man returned and fired two more shots at him & twice more at Dee."

Mageau, wounded in his neck, left leg, and right arm, was thrashing his legs when Zodiac fired a second time. "Mike got the door open," Lynch told me, "and fell out of the car, and the only time he even looked at the guy was when the guy got back into his car and he opened the door and he got a clear profile view of him. You know, where some people kind of comb their hair up in a kind of pompadour and then back." Mike described Zodiac as having "a large face, thirty years old, with short curly light-brown hair worn in a military-style brush cut. As for his build, he was beefy, heavyset without being blubbery fat, 195–200 pounds and had a slight potbelly."

Sergeant Richard Hoffman, responding to the crime scene, took up the story from there. "I was working juvenile division as a plainclothesman in a plain car when the call came out that night," he told me. "It was dark at Blue Rock Springs, elms swaying in the wind, the wild cries of strutting peacocks roaming the grounds coming to my ears. Roy Conway and I had been the first officers to reach Blue Rock Springs [four miles from downtown Vallejo and two miles from the site of the earlier Lake Herman murders]. Mike Mageau had originally been in the backseat, but I found him outside on the ground on his back. His eyes were wide and he lifted his arms upward as if imploring me for help. When he opened his mouth to call for aid, blood gurgled out. CPR had just come in, and the doctor removed Darlene's sweater and began applying pressure to her chest. With each downward pressure the little tag on her bra fluttered as air exited the bullet hole. The M.E. took this probe and put it in each of Mike's wounds—he was staring upward and fully conscious—feeling every bit of it."

Lynch and his partner, Ed Rust, arrived next. "Mike was lying at the rear of the car," said Lynch, "and she was still behind the wheel. I remember she was trying to say something, and I put my ear over her like this to try to understand, but I just couldn't." "First came firecrackers, then gunshots," Rust added. "One patrol got there before us—around midnight. It took us ten to fifteen minutes to get there. She died at 12:26 A.M. She kept trying to talk, but we couldn't distinguish anything. In fact, we sent one of the officers with her in case she could say something. I think it was Dick Hoffman. He was the patrol officer who was there first. Mike said he thought it was a police officer come up to check. He pulled up behind them at sort of an off line from their car. He said that he had been parked in the same place before, and Darlene had a police officer that came up the same way [a cutoff technique] and shined a light just the same. It had happened before that way, and he had the impression it was a police officer when he first came up. Mike got out after the guy left, pushed out the right side of the two-door car. He said he had climbed over the seat trying to get away. The guy shot him several times. This was the only avenue he had was to get in the backseat."

"Shortly after, the ambulance arrived," Lynch said, "and I helped the driver take her out of the car. Then Dick Hoffman followed the ambulance to the emergency hospital."

"We took Mike up to the Queen of the Valley Hospital," concluded Rust, "Lynch and I saw that out front of the hospital they've got a little monument . . . it's got a zodiac sign on it."

When she was shot, Darlene had been reaching for her quilt-pattern leather drawstring purse on the rear floorboard. It was as if she was getting identification out for the police. With the photo envelope inside her purse was a notebook with two names, "VAUGHN" and "LEIGH," underlined. I consulted Darlene's three personal directories and, under *M*, found the following entry crossed out: "MT. Shasta SK. Bowl Inc. (NRT) (VAUGHN) Area Code 916/ Mt. Shasta Ski Bowl NR 1." Leigh was not listed. Police dismissed it as the name of Dean Ferrin's employer, Bill Leigh.

The time of the murder concerned Darlene's sitters. "What time did they say she was murdered," Janet Lynn said, "12:05 P.M.? [Darlene was shot at 12:00 A.M.] Because that was a big discrepancy. At one point we figured that she couldn't have had time to even get to that parking lot. We kept telling the police that she didn't leave the house until then . . . 'cause we were watching some program that doesn't come on until almost midnight and she hadn't even left the house yet. And then they are telling us she was murdered like five minutes later, when how could she get out to Blue Rock Springs in five minutes? And we kept telling this police officer [Lynch]. That was the biggest thing I never liked about that was the time discrepancy. It was right before midnight and you just can't get out there that quick. And we did mention that time thing again to them. I do remember them asking us to come in. They didn't even write it down."

"I was at Berryessa that day [of her murder]," Steven Kee told me. "I was to meet her that night, but when I got home I learned that Dee was killed." Why had Mike rushed out and left all the lights in his house burning, the television blaring, and front door standing wide open? In the aftermath investigators asked themselves other questions:

"Why was Mike wearing three pairs of pants and three sweaters? What about the alleged argument in Terry's restaurant parking lot shortly before the shooting and then being followed by the same man to Blue Rock Springs where an argument continued and ended in shooting? Other Questions: Did Mageau not, in fact, know the man who committed the at-

tacks. Did he witness Darlene arguing with a middle-aged
man either at the crime scene and/or earlier that evening at
Terry's . . . 'There was an *argument between occupants of
DV's car and another individual* at Blue Rock Springs park-
ing lot *minutes before her murder*.' DV argued with likely
Suspect in presence of SV *several hours* before her murder.
(SOURCE: SV [Mageau] as related to family friend.)"

At Blue Rock Springs that night, Officer Hoffman admitted he
feared the killer might return again any minute and shoot him
too. But at 12:40 A.M. Zodiac was busy elsewhere. He was calling
switchboard operator Nancy Slover, VPD, from Joe's Union Station (which closed at 8:25 P.M.) at Tuolumne and Springs Road to
report what he thought was a double murder. "They were shot
with a 9-millimeter Luger. I also killed those kids last year." This
booth was two thousand feet to the south from Leigh's house.
At 1:30 A.M., fifty minutes later, four phone calls were placed
through the operator from a booth at Broadway and Nebraska. This
booth was three thousand feet northwest from Allen's home. One
call was to Dean Ferrin's parents, Arthur and Mildred. They heard
"only deep breathing . . . no one said anything, we were certain
someone was on the line." The Dean Ferrin household got two
phone calls. The sitter answered and heard only "breathing or wind
blowing." Next a call was placed to Dean's brother, Gordon (who
was in Thailand). Zodiac must have known Darlene in order to
place these calls to her in-laws. News of the shooting and who the
victims were had not yet been either on the radio or in the papers.
When I made a map of Allen's neighborhood I saw how close
he was to all the Vallejo victims and how close they were to each
other. Zodiac victim Mike Mageau's house was four and a half
blocks from the home of another victim, Betty Lou Jensen. Since
the murders, Criminal Geographical Targeting has become a
valuable police tool. Geographical Profiling is based on the theory of criminals' spatial behavior. Criminals strike close to home
just as the average person chooses stores where he shops daily.
They operate close to areas they are familiar with and have previously scouted. A murderer has a tendency to hunt prey in identifiable areas and the impulse to disguise his home location. Thus,
the sites of his crimes tend to radiate on all sides of the offender,
like a spider in his web.
As Zodiac roared away from the Blue Rock Springs lot, he

would have reached a fork in the road. Narrow Lake Herman Road to his left offered no place to hide until he reached Benicia. Columbus Parkway (Leigh's brother lived at the midpoint on Columbus Parkway) to his right led back into Vallejo, but offered the possibility of police cars coming at him on Springs Road. To avoid being trapped, I believe Zodiac took a small road, just off Columbus Parkway, so hidden I had to make an abrupt turn to reach the road. It led me in a dead straight line into the heart of Vallejo. At the end of twenty-four blocks I arrived at a familiar doorstep—the home of Arthur Leigh Allen.

As far as finding Zodiac's weapons and hood—the opportunity had long passed. One reason Zodiac used a new weapon each time was that he was discarding them as he went. Surely, after each of the ill-starred searches in different counties, he had destroyed his hidden souvenirs. But as Detective Baker had reasoned, the things he had taken might still be in plain sight, having a symbolic significance to Zodiac alone.

The *Napa Sentinel*'s Harry V. Martin long afterward speculated:

> "Darlene knew a terrible secret . . . because of that secret she was murdered—not randomly, but deliberately . . . planned and executed by a person she knew very well, a person who bought her gifts, a person who visited her place of employment and even her home."

Carmela Leigh, pregnant and due three days after Darlene's murder, was so afraid she had a peephole put in her door. "We didn't know if this guy was going to get rid of her husband, her friends," she told me. "We didn't know if it was one of her goofy friends. It's too bad they never found him. We were all afraid for a long time. We didn't know whether this person knew Dee— that's what everybody thought because she knew so many people. Then we thought Dee knew something about a narcotics bust or something, and the person who killed her knew she knew and got her before it all came out. And then we thought maybe she knew she was going to be murdered, and maybe some of the people in the occult, you know, they'll sacrifice their life or something.

"Then we thought maybe she knew. Maybe she did. Maybe she knew the guy was going to kill Mike and that's why she wasn't scared. From what Mike said in the paper, she wasn't a bit nervous."

"There was the hint of drugs at the paint party—drug dealings there," said Cheney. The sitters disagreed. "There were no signs of drugs in the house," they told me. "There's no indication of drugs in any of the police reports," said Mulanax. "Some of the people that she associated with were, I think, involved in drugs, but there's nothing in any of the reports that I have that would indicate that she herself was a user." "I've had investigators come out every year," said Bobbie Ramos, "to see if I've thought of anything. They'd ask if she was selling drugs. Did she make more tips than you? Sure she did. I might have made twenty, she might have made thirty-five. They were kind of maybe saying she sold drugs. . . . I'm not saying she didn't smoke pot or anything. Smoking and selling is different."

"She might have taken marijuana once in a while," Bobbie Oxnam told me, 'but selling was strictly taboo to her. The implications that were put into the paper after she was murdered really made a lot of us mad. People forget the good about Darlene. She was not a tramp. She was no angel, but she was not a tramp either."

SERGEANT LYNCH AND his partner Rust later interviewed Linda at 400 Brandon Avenue in San Jose. As with many of Darlene's friends, she had been difficult to find after the Blue Rock Springs shooting. "And they talked to me for over seven hours," Linda told me. "Lynch thought there were drugs involved. He gave me a typed list and he said, 'Any names that look familiar to you, circle them.' Of course I circled all the names I've mentioned to you as being at the painting party."

"Was Lee's name on there?" I asked her. "Yes, there was another name on the list spelled different—'Leigh.' I circled the ones that Darlene knew. And when I had circled this particular name they wanted, they go 'mm-huh,' as if they had already made up their minds. When I had circled the one, they said, 'That's enough.' " Linda had circled the name of a middle-aged, round-faced local man who resembled Leigh Allen. And it was at this moment that the police went wrong. Lynch had yet to interview Leigh Allen.

"Then I helped the police prepare a composite of the man at the party," Linda told me, "a middle-aged man with a peculiar stare, a cold stare. I sat there with the police and the artist did the drawing from my directions. I kept asking for them to show me photos, but they never did. When the drawing was done, Lynch asked, 'Do you think she's ready?' I say, 'Ready for what?' And they open up this black real thin binder. It had cellophane on it and it was another composite drawing. The only thing I had different from it was the chin. It just blew me away."

This was a sketch prepared from Mageau's description from his hospital bed. He had seen Zodiac's profile clearly when he shot him, and was able to speak in two days after the shooting. Officer Baldino said it was "probably the same individual" who had been frequenting Terry's, a man he had picked out of "a social situation."

"Steve Baldino picked out a guy he saw at the restaurant," Linda told me. "Steve was pretty shook up over all this. He knew the family and he used to come by. I sat in the cop car one time and he let me feel his club, touch a gun. He was a really good cop and when Dee died he kind of went overboard. I think he might have made a mistake." The man Baldino eyeballed at an A.A. meeting admitted to visiting Terry's, but he was not the man at the painting party. Lynch had the right picture, but the wrong name. Zodiac must have felt invulnerable after this. He had grown increasingly bolder.

"But you know," Linda continued, "I think Zodiac wears makeup, and has got to be from Vallejo 'cause he knows how to get away. The strange thing is everyone left Vallejo [Mike and his brother, Steven Kee, Robbie Lee, Linda herself, Christina, Darlene's younger sister]. I would think if the guy was from San Francisco they'd stay. They'd be a lot safer in Vallejo. But they all left the city and got effectively lost."

Linda's composite did some good. It was accurate enough for Cheney to later recognize it as his friend, Arthur Leigh Allen.

"Of course I've never doubted that Zodiac was Leigh," Cheney told me. "And I've always been astonished that they never tripped him up. I couldn't believe it. I kept waiting for something to turn up, to read that Zodiac was arrested. Nothing happened. I believe that the Lake Herman Road and Lake Berryessa were just window dressing, but he killed Darlene Ferrin on purpose.

"When I finally read your book, *Zodiac*, and I had purposely not done so until now in order not to affect my recall, I got an idea. Darlene was certainly not a lovers' lane random killing. I think Darlene was killed on purpose. I suspect she was the target and he threw the others in for confusion. There was the business about Darlene saw him kill somebody, or he just may have wanted to close her mouth. Darlene may have been blackmailing him."

George Bawart, at the Zodiac conference, stated he believed Allen to be Zodiac. Captain Roy Conway said in a published interview: "I believe as I always have, that the Zodiac killer was Arthur Leigh Allen." I asked Toschi the same question. "There is no doubt in my mind," he concluded, "that Arthur Leigh Allen was, in fact, the Zodiac." I had written the same in 1977 (when we had an army of suspects) because Allen had offered to help catch himself.

I recalled the Zodiac Conference and a question Rita Williams had asked: "If Arthur Leigh Allen was the Zodiac, why didn't he leave some message behind to let everyone know he was the Zodiac? If he was Allen, can you tell me why you think he didn't?" I remembered that when police showed Allen bomb plans on lined yellow paper with a menu for making bombs, he said, "I've never seen that piece of paper before. . . . I've never seen these documents before." And yet it was in his own handwriting.

"Did he leave some message behind to let everyone know he was the Zodiac?" repeated Conway thoughtfully. "Allen does leave a message by things that are in his basement and at the same time denying everything. From my point of view, he did leave that message. One of [Zodiac's] letters talked about finding bombs in his basement. Well, in fact, there were bombs in the basement of that house when we did the search warrant—there were pipe bombs. He talked about a particular way of making the pipe bombs, and we found handwriting evidence of him having written that formula that he denied even making. Ultimately, the only handwriting match we have is to him in his writings of Zodiac's bomb-making formula. So in his own way he did, as far as I'm concerned, leave that message."

Conway had indicated to the FBI that he and Bawart would present a full review of the case to the Sonoma County District Attorney's Office for an opinion regarding possible prosecution for Leigh Allen. "If the D.A. refuses to fill charges against ALLEN," he wrote, "the Vallejo Police Department will close its investigation on the 'ZODIAC' case."

"Once these interviews have been conducted," the FBI wrote in 1992, "Conway indicated that he and Bawart will present a full review of the case to the Sonoma County District Attorney's Office for an opinion regarding possible prosecution for ALLEN. If the D.A. refuses to file charges against ALLEN, Vallejo Police Department will close its investigation on the 'ZODIAC' case. Vallejo has requested no further assistance on this case, and it is therefore recommended that this case be closed at this time." The FBI, on noting the death of Arthur Leigh Allen, said in a final report, "The San Francisco case is closed at this time. . . . Vallejo has requested no further assistance on this case, and it is therefore recommended that this case be closed at this time. . . ."

But who was that first tipster, the one who alerted Lynch so many times in 1969? "I got that tip *by letter*," Lynch told me without thinking the last time I saw him. In the absence of that anonymous tip, Allen wouldn't have been a suspect until 1971. The Vallejo P.D. suspected that Allen's own brother or sister-in-law had turned him into the police as a Zodiac suspect. They did later on. "Lynch told me he was tipped to Allen more than once, maybe three times, by some woman," I told Toschi. "She was calling up and tipping him. So I'm thinking it's possibly the sister-in-law."

"You're reading my mind," said Toschi. "I'm thinking it's Karen too."

If Allen had not died, the saga of Zodiac would have had a different ending.

On Tuesday, March 24, 1992, upon his return from Germany and shortly before Leigh Allen's death, George Bawart conducted an important interview.

"What I'm referring to is where I am finally able to recontact victim Mike Mageau," he told me, "and I show him a six-photo spread. It included Harvey Hines's suspect. I had a picture of Arthur Leigh Allen in there; the rest were not INS, NIS, and CHP officers, they were just fillers. My wife Jan was down in L.A. at the time for a company she was working for. I had to meet with Mike Mageau at some point in time, so I dovetailed this when she was down there for a week. I visited with her while I was there, stayed at the same hotel room, and saved the city some money. Now this is some twenty years after the Blue Rock Springs thing, so I'm not real hyped up about meeting Michael Mageau and showing him this photo spread. I'll tell you how much credence I took to it—normally if I went down to an airport, I'd get ahold of airport security. They'd give me an office and I'd sit there and talk to the witness and show 'em a photo spread. I thought so little of this, thinking I was going to be there about ten minutes, that I just located him and found a small corner of the airport.

"There were people milling around and everything, but it was fairly quiet. And that's why I showed him this lineup. 'Cause I just knew that he'd look at this lineup and say, 'There's nobody in there that I recognize.' Well, I pulled this lineup out and they were driver's license pictures from 1967 or '68. Anyway, they were from the era when Zodiac started. They were of Arthur Leigh Allen and of 'Larry Kane' and fillers, all fat-faced people. And these were the old-style photos. They were black and white. You got them from DMV in those days. These were blown up larger than a regular license picture. A regular license picture is about maybe an inch and a half square. These were maybe two inches or three inches square. They were not huge pictures, but they were fairly large pictures.

"I give Mageau the lineup admonishment, 'Just because I'm showing you pictures, you don't have to identify anyone as the responsible, he may not be in here—blah, blah, blah.' So I hand him them.

"He looks at them for twenty, thirty seconds. Points to Arthur Leigh Allen and says, 'That's the man! That's the man who shot me at Blue Rock Springs!'

"I was absolutely flabbergasted that he picked out Arthur Leigh Allen. I didn't expect him to pick out anybody at all!"

EPILOGUE

DAVE TOSCHI IS now with North Star Security Services as a vice-president and member of the board. Retired detective lieutenant Mike Ciravolo, a chief investigator on New York's Zodiac case, now runs a private investigation company in suburban New York City. He left the department when Zodiac II first vanished, arguing that the Zodiac Task Force should not be abandoned. He helped train Detective Sergeant Joe Herbert who recognized the hand of Zodiac II in Seda's handwriting. Bryan Hartnell, married and the father of two sons, is a probate lawyer in Southern California.

"The Santa Rosa murders were never solved," Sergeant Steve Brown, Sonoma Sheriff's Department, told me. "In fact, we're working them pretty hard right now. One was never found, but of the six that were found I only have evidence on one of the girls, Kim Wendy Allen. What I'm still trying to do is find the rest of the evidence. We're clearing out the archival evidence that's out at our Juvenile Hall facility. These old cases are tough because who knows where the evidence goes. Hopefully, I'm going to find some more. I especially want to find the rope used to strangle Kim Wendy that they submitted to the FBI. They tested this rope in every possible way and there was nothing special about it. It was a nylon regular rope that you could buy anywhere."

On the Presidio, where Zodiac was last seen and nurse Donna Lass once worked, ten-story Letterman Hospital and its five-story annex remain only as desolate hulks. The hollowed-out concrete buildings will be demolished and replaced by a digital movie production campus, Lucasfilm's Industrial Light & Magic. Sandy Panzarella sold Science Dynamics. With that money he purchased the RKO-Radio Pictures film library which he later sold to Ted Turner. "It was a tough decision," Panzarella told me, "to give up a library which not only included *Citizen Kane*, and other beloved films, but *The Most Dangerous Game*." The movie-obsessed Zodiac would have appreciated the irony.

By May 2002, SFPD was reeling from a blistering expose in the *Chronicle*. Reporters David Parrish and Jaxon Van Derbeken's three-part investigation was headlined: "SFPD LAST IN SOLVING VIOLENT CRIME. Inspectors function poorly in flawed system." The SFPD ranked last among the nation's biggest city police forces, on average solving only 28 percent of violent crimes between 1996 and 2000—the lowest violent crime "clearance rate," among the nation's twenty largest cities. The series spotlighted murder cases in which investigators failed to interview key witnesses, left vital leads unpursued and lost critical evidence.

As the Board of Supervisors moved to create an investigative panel, the SFPD was under fire. Buried beneath an avalanche of new cases, the current inspectors on the Zodiac case took the unusual step of attempting to clear a suspect developed by their predecessors over thirty years earlier. They set out to prove by DNA that Arthur Leigh Allen, convicted child molester, was Zodiac. But the letters (kept in an old cardboard box from 1969 until May 14, 1981, when SFPD Inspector James Deasy drove them to Sacramento) had never been refrigerated to preserve DNA. It's hard to beleive any had survived. Years later they returned.

In June 2000, Dr. Cynde Holt, a criminalistics supervisor, had been hired to oversee the SFPD's DNA lab. Her three-person team, she said, barely had the finances to investigate outstanding recent crimes that had occured before the use of DNA-typing technology. The best lab in the region, in Berkeley, refused to process its DNA findings. Though that facility had opened nine years earlier, no San Fransico case had ever had a "cold hit." The reason was simple, Dr. Holt told the *Examiner*. Cases weren't sent because the Berkeley DOJ's Convicted Felon Databank only accepts DNA profiles from acccredited labs, which SFPD's was not.

Dr. Holt told the media that she was able to replicate a DNA sample (saliva traces beneath a stamp on a bona fide Zodiac letter large enough to test a "partial print of DNA." On October 15, 2002, the *Chronicle* reported: "DNA seems to clear only Zodiac supsect." But, said detectives, 'it is not enough at this time to submit [to DNA databases], but other new evidence may yield more usable DNA within weeks or months." They seemed intent upon clearing Allen though he had known and stalked many of the victims, been placed at the crime scenes and had been identified by surviving witnesses. The point that was the inability to match him to the letters was the *only* reason Allen had not been arrested as Zodiac—witness the investigation of the German Hippie, the tall, black-haired young man, and the deceased art teacher as possible letter writers. "I've always wondered if there wasn't more than one person involved," I told the *Chronicle*, "someone running interference for Allen. It's what makes the Zodiac case one of the great mysteries of all times." Stirring up people, getting things accomplished, making a difference, isn't that what books should be about?

APPENDICES

RETURN TO SEARCH Warrant Served on Arthur Leigh Allen, February 14, 1991. The following personal property was taken from 32 Fresno Street, City of Vallejo, Solano County, California.

1. Four pipe bombs.
2. One primer Cord.
3. Seven Impact devices Railway Torpedo.
4. Two Safety fuses, green, two rolls ea. 98½'.
5. Two rolls of safety fuses (orange).
6. One cardboard box w/Mrs. E. W. Allen on label.
7. Two *Vallejo Times-Heralds* dated 060382.
8. Two *San Francisco Chronicles* dated 060182.
9. Two glass bottles of black material.
10. Nine Non-electric blasting caps.
11. Two 1" galvanized pipes with one end cap.
12. Five pipe thread compounds.
13. Six pipe vises.
14. One cardboard box with fireworks, safety fuse (green), bottles of potassium nitrate, two bottles of sulfur, miscellaneous fireworks.
15. Brown plastic bag covering Item #6.
16. One can of black powder partially full.
17. Euroarms .44-caliber black powder #13357.
18. Ruger .22 revolver #85655 and six live rounds.
19. .22 Revolver #N31025.
20. Ruger .44 Blackhawk #8155788 and five rounds.
21. Colt .32 auto #216374 and seven rounds.
22. Winchester, Super and miscellaneous ammo for .32, .22, .44, and .30-caliber.
23. .22 automatic clip with three rounds.
24. Zodiac Sea Wolf Watch #26894.

25. Miscellaneous papers and news clips "Zodiac."
26. Marlin .22 rifle with scope #24373783.
27. Inland .30-caliber rifle #5044680.
28. Sears electric typewriter.
29. Royal manual typewriter.
30. Cut letter from DOJ and miscellaneous news clips.
31. Zippo lighter engraved "D. E. Brandon."
32. Small flashlight.
33. Hunting knife with sheath and rivets.
34. Four boxes of videotapes, one box audio reel tapes, one cassette recorder.
35. Remington .22 short caliber rifle.
36. Stevens Model 835 12-gauge double-barrel shotgun.
37. Winchester Model 50 20-gauge automatic shotgun.

ARTHUR LEIGH ALLEN'S TRAILERS, CARS, AND BOATS

Universal trailer (off wheels), license, AP 6354, parked at the Sunset Trailer Park, 2963 Santa Rosa Avenue. Slot A-7. Owned since 1970.

Trailer ME8636, special construction. Registered 10/31/79.

Trailer GS8803, special construction camper, 12/31/75.

A Trailer in Bodega Bay.

A Trailer rumored to be parked in a neighbor's tract of deep woods.

Car #1. DXW 186, 1962 VW Karmann Ghia, registered 7/18/80. An exact duplicate of Bryan Hartnell's car at Lake Berryessa 9/69.

Car #2. MLZ 057, 1965 Buick sedan, Gray Skylark, registered 4/20/80.

Car #3. XAM 469 tan station wagon.

Car #4. 1964 dark Ford. On the night of the July Fourth murder, a deputy had seen a blue 1967 Ford Sedan in the Blue Rock Springs parking lot earlier in the evening.

A two-seat Austin Healey.

A white Buick.

A white 1965 Mercedes, 220SB.

LDH 974, 1958 Ford sedan.

Allen had use of Tucker's 1965–66 brown Corvair. Whether or not he used it without permission on July 4, 1969 is not known.

Small blue and white Sailboat: a twenty-two-foot-long sailboat on a trailer, partially draped by a blue tarp. California license number, NE3725.

Open sailboat ten feet long. CF 9127 FD license. Sticker #HI07782. Fuel Unknown.

THE BAWART REPORT

Vallejo Detective George Bawart's confidential 1992 thirty-point report was prepared, not as part of the official Zodiac case file, but as an introductory outline for Vallejo District Attorney Mike Nail to facilitate his decision whether or not to arrest the prime suspect. Cheney had used Allen's dismissal from teaching and his subsequent move home as a date to place the conversation in his room. He knew that he moved from the Bay Area to his new Southern California job on New Year's Day. That was in fact, January 1, 1969. In later conversations Cheney corrected this. I have left the inaccurate date, 1968, in Bawart's report. Leigh's conversation with Cheney still predated the creation of the Zodiac persona and his M.O. by eight months. The report read as follows:

CIRCUMSTANCES WHICH INDICATE ARTHUR LEIGH ALLEN IS, IN FACT, THE ZODIAC KILLER.

1. In 1966, Riverside, California, Cheri Jo BATES, WF, is stabbed to death. The Riverside Police Department received a typed letter from the killer. On this letter, the killer identified himself as "Enterprise" [actually, this was to direct the letter to a Riverside newspaper of that name]. The brand of typewriter used in this letter has been identified as Royal with an elite type. An older Royal typewriter with elite type was found during the service of the search warrant at ALLEN's residence on 02/91.

2. In December of 1967, ALLEN was given a Zodiac brand watch as a Christmas present from his mother. The company

symbol for their Zodiac watches is exactly the same symbol as later adapted by the Zodiac Killer. This watch was taken during the service of a search warrant in February of 1991.

3. In January 1968, ALLEN had a conversation with Donald CHENEY, a friend of his. ALLEN guised this conversation as though he was going to write a novel. ALLEN indicated to CHENEY that he would call himself "Zodiac" and use the Zodiac watch symbol as his symbol. That he would kill people in lovers' lanes by using a weapon with a flashlight attached to it for sighting at night. That he would write letters to the police to confuse them and taunt them and sign them as the Zodiac using the Zodiac watch symbol. ALLEN stated he would get women to stop on the freeway indicating they had some problems with their tires, and that he would loosen the lug nuts so their tire would later fall off, and he could take them captive. ALLEN told CHENEY that he would shoot children as they got off school buses.

4. On July 4, 1969, Darlene FERRIN was killed, and Michael MAGEAU shot numerous times at Blue Rock Springs, Vallejo. On July 31, 1969, a letter was received by the *Vallejo Times-Herald* describing the killing and shooting incident at Blue Rock Springs, signed only with the symbol of the Zodiac watch. August 7, 1969, a letter was received, wherein, an individual identified himself as Zodiac indicating many facts about the shooting in Vallejo. He indicated he sighted with a flashlight attached to his gun. The letter was signed with the Zodiac watch company's symbol.

5. In early October 1969, Sergeant Lynch of the Vallejo Police Department interviewed ALLEN as to his whereabouts on 092769 (the date of the Napa County Sheriff's Department killing at Lake Berryessa). ALLEN said that he had planned to go to Berryessa on that date but had changed his mind and had gone to the ocean instead. This same conversation was confirmed by Captain [Roy] CONWAY and myself during the service of the search warrant on 02/91.

6. In 1969, a Philip TUCKER of the Greater Vallejo Recreation District indicated that ALLEN, who was a close friend of his, often talked about the Zodiac case. TUCKER indicated that ALLEN had previously talked about shooting with special sights for shooting in the dark. TUCKER indicated that he saw the Zodiac symbol at ALLEN's house and also some type of cryptograms.

7. A Zodiac letter received by newspapers dated 101369 alluded to "shoot the little darlings as they came bouncing off the bus." Almost the same verbiage given to CHENEY in 1968.

8. A Zodiac letter dated 110969 described making his bomb for blowing up buses by using ammonia nitrate, stove oil, and gravel. A formula in ALLEN's handwriting was found during the service of the search warrant at Allen's residence on 02/91, as well as completed pipe bombs.

9. A Zodiac letter dated 110969 stated, "You don't know if the bomb is at the site or stored in my basement for future use." During the service of the search warrant of ALLEN's residence on 02/91, pipe bombs were found in ALLEN's basement, as well as formulas for ammonia nitrate and stove oil bombs.

10. A Zodiac letter dated 110969. It indicated that the killing tools were bought through mail order. During the service of the search warrant at ALLEN's residence on 02/91, mail order catalog pages were found regarding bombs, booby traps, and guns.

11. On 032370, Kathleen JOHNS was stopped by an individual flashing his headlights. This individual indicated that her tire was loose. He, in fact, loosened the lug nuts on her tire causing her tire to fall off, and then took her in his vehicle for quite some time. A letter sent to the news media on 072770 by the Zodiac claimed he was responsible for this incident. This is almost exactly the same as told to CHENEY in 1969.

12. During this conversation with CHENEY in 1968, ALLEN asked CHENEY how to disguise his handwriting, and he would wear makeup to change his appearance. Note—The Zodiac handprinting has never been matched to that [of] ALLEN. This could explain this match not being made. This premise has been discussed at length with Terry Pascoe, Questioned Document Examiner, DOJ retired. He originally worked on some of the Zodiac letters. He agrees that a person with high intelligence could study the methods used to examine handwriting and fool a document examiner.

13. During the conversation with CHENEY, ALLEN indicated he would have fun hunting people.

14. ALLEN told CHENEY that he would send letters to the police to confuse and antagonize them.

15. ALLEN told CHENEY that he would attach a flashlight to a weapon for sighting in the dark. This is referred [to] by the Zodiac in a letter he sent to the news media on 080769.

16. Shoe prints found at Lake Berryessa by the Napa County Sheriff's Department belonging to the killer are size 10 1/2. ALLEN wears shoes size 10 1/2.

17. The description of the killer in Vallejo at Blue Rock Springs and in Napa County Sheriff's Department jurisdiction at Lake Berryessa is a heavyset white male with a potbelly. ALLEN is a white male, heavyset with a potbelly.

18. Letters received from the Zodiac by the media had what appeared to be intentionally misspelled words. ALLEN intentionally misspells words. One example would be in documents found during the search warrant of 02/91, ALLEN spelled the word eggs "aigs." This intentional misspelling of words was confirmed by his brother Ron ALLEN who says that Leigh ALLEN did that to be funny.

19. ALLEN denied any knowledge about making bombs and denied ever making any formulas for making bombs. ALLEN's handwriting has been matched to the formulas found for making bombs during the search warrant of 02/91.

20. ALLEN was reported to the Sonoma County Sheriff's Department on 092374 as having molested a boy in that city. He was arrested in late September or early October 1974. The last letter received from the Zodiac in this time frame was 070874. ALLEN was released from Atascadero State Prison in September 1977. No Zodiac letters were received while ALLEN was in Atascadero Prison.

21. In 1969, Ralph SPINELLI had a conversation with ALLEN. ALLEN admitted he was the Zodiac. ALLEN claimed he would do a killing in San Francisco to prove that he was the Zodiac killer. On October 11, 1969, Paul STINE, a cabdriver in the City of San Francisco, was shot to death. This shooting differs from the July 4, 1969, killing in Vallejo, and the September 27, 1969, killing in Napa County inasmuch as those were both men and women in secluded areas. On 101469, a letter from the Zodiac

took credit for the STINE killing and sent part of STINE's shirt to the newspaper.

22. In May of 1991, ALLEN gave an interview to the *Vallejo Times-Herald*. In that interview he indicated a "Man from Lake Tahoe" had recently given Vallejo Police Department information regarding him (ALLEN). It should be noted that SPINELLI owned a restaurant in the Lake Tahoe Area in the early 1980s. It is apparent that ALLEN must have kept track of SPINELLI as he was never told by us that SPINELLI had any connection with Lake Tahoe.

23. Reference Item #6 in this list of circumstances—On 061191, Captain Conway and I re-interviewed Phil TUCKER. The excerpts from Item #6 were from a 1971 interview by Detective Dave TOSCHI of the San Francisco Police Department. During our interview Phil TUCKER was unable to remember that Arthur Leigh ALLEN had told him that he had special sights for shooting in the dark. He did, however, indicate that Arthur Leigh ALLEN told him he was proficient in shooting and proficient in shooting in the dark.

Most significant new information revealed by Phil TUCKER was the following: The book [Allen had mentioned] was about hunting people with a bow and arrow. ALLEN was fascinated with this. He indicated a number of times that it would be more sport to hunt people as they had intelligence. This conversation took place while ALLEN and TUCKER were discussing hunting trips while [en route] to the ocean to go diving. ALLEN was fascinated with the concept of stalking people rather than game. TUCKER indicated that he felt that ALLEN wanted TUCKER's reaction to these statements. TUCKER told ALLEN that he would never consider hunting people. TUCKER indicated he thinks ALLEN told him the name of the book he had read. After some time I asked TUCKER if the name of the story was "The Most Dangerous Game," and TUCKER said he did not think that was the name of the book. TUCKER indicated that this conversation took place prior to September of 1966 as that is the month and year he married his first wife, and he did not see ALLEN to any great degree, nor go out on hunting and fishing trips with him after his marriage.

It should be noted this is almost exactly the same as part of the conversation he had with Donald CHENEY on January of 1968 and almost exactly the same as alluded to by the Zodiac in his letters to the press, as well as in his cryptogram. TUCKER was asked if he knew Donald CHENEY, and he advised he did not.

TUCKER was asked why he did not give this information to TOSCHI and MULANAX in 1971. He indicated he only answered their questions and was not asked about any fantasies ALLEN may have related to him.

TUCKER also indicated that during the span of this conversation, Arthur Leigh ALLEN had a Zodiac brand watch with a Zodiac symbol which consisted of a circle with lines horizontally and vertically through it.

TUCKER also indicated that he has seen Arthur Leigh ALLEN write with both hands, and that he uses both hands equally well when handwriting. TUCKER describes his handwriting as not real good.

TUCKER also indicated that ALLEN had an interest in codes, and that he had seen a handwritten Zodiac-type cryptogram at ALLEN's house prior to any cryptograms being published in the newspaper. TUCKER also indicated that ALLEN loved to try and outsmart the other guy.

TUCKER indicates that in 1969, he owned an older brown Corvair that was beat up, and that ALLEN had driven this Corvair. He could not specifically indicate whether ALLEN drove this Corvair on July 4, 1969. It should be noted that witnesses at the killing at Blue Rock Springs on July 4, 1969, described an older brown vehicle, possibly a Corvair, as being the responsible vehicle.

24. In the mid-1970s D.O.J. Investigator SILVER accompanied by Bryan HARTNELL, the victim in the Napa Sheriff's Department Zodiac Case, went to a hardware store where ALLEN was working. HARTNELL was directed to make a purchase from ALLEN. HARTNELL then informed SILVER that ALLEN's physical size and voice were the same as the person who had killed his girlfriend and badly wounded him, HARTNELL, in Napa. HARTNELL did not see the face of the responsible [assailant] in this incident as he was wearing a hood.

25. While Arthur Leigh ALLEN was incarcerated at Atascadero State Prison, D.O.J. Investigator SILVER had a polygraph examination given to ALLEN by D.O.J. Polygraph Examiner Sam LISTER. Sam LISTER indicated that ALLEN had passed this polygraph test, and he felt he was not, in fact, the Zodiac killer.

We had our polygraph examiner JOHNSON examine the charts used by LISTER on ALLEN. JOHNSON indicated that after examining the charts, it was his opinion that ALLEN was on some type of drugs while he was taking the polygraph for LISTER, and that it was also his opinion that ALLEN did not pass the polygraph examination, and that it was inconclusive. It should be noted that Atascadero is a mental hospital, and many of the inmates are on different types of tranquilizers.

26. During the search warrant in February of 1991 at ALLEN's residence, a letter was located that indicated it was from Investigator SILVER at the Department of Justice. This letter was to "Whom It May Concern" and indicated that ALLEN had passed the polygraph examination, and law enforcement should no longer consider him as a suspect in the Zodiac killings. Also found was the master for making this letter. ALLEN subsequently admitted that he had printed this letter while working in the print shop at Atascadero Hospital. However, ALLEN maintained that this letter was authentic.

Contacts with SILVER indicated that the signature on the letter was authentic, but it was not D.O.J. letterhead, and he would never write such a letter. SILVER did indicate that he had written letters to ALLEN to obtain his permission to do a polygraphic examination, and this may have been where his signature was found and used in this bogus letter.

27. In mid-1992, Michael MAGEAU, the victim in the Zodiac killing in Vallejo, wherein Darlene FERRIN died, and he was badly wounded, made a positive identification from a photo lineup comprised of driver's license photos, one of which was Arthur Leigh ALLEN's picture from a 1968 driver's license, that ALLEN was the responsible who shot him on July 4, 1969, at Blue Rock Springs.

28. One of the cryptograms sent by the Zodiac had a line on it that indicated, "My name is," and it was a different cryptogram at

this location. This cryptogram was finally broken, and it was determined to read, "Robert Emmett, the Hippie." No one was able to locate "Robert Emmett, the Hippie." In August of 1992, information was developed that ALLEN was an associate with the manager of the swimming team at Vallejo High School whose name was Robert Emmett RODIFER, and this person later became a hippie attending University of California, Berkeley, and U.S.F. in San Francisco.

Robert Emmett RODIFER was located in Germany. He confirmed that he did, in fact, know Arthur Leigh ALLEN although he indicated they were never friends. RODIFER indicated that he was very popular when in school, and that Arthur Leigh ALLEN was not, and there was apparently some animosity between him and ALLEN because of this. He was given the information about "Robert Emmett, the Hippie," and the only explanation he could have was that ALLEN was jealous of him, RODIFER.

29. Information was developed that when Arthur Leigh ALLEN was born, and as a youngster, he was left-handed, and that he was forced to write with his right hand by his parents. Thus, he became ambidextrous. ALLEN steadfastly denied this [ability], indicating he was only able to write with his right hand. However, his brother indicated that, in fact, Arthur Leigh ALLEN could write with either hand. Also, we interviewed Arthur Leigh ALLEN's best friend, Glen RINEHART, who was very defensive of ALLEN, but confirmed that ALLEN was able to write with his left hand.

The handwriting of the Zodiac killer has never been matched to the handwriting of Arthur Leigh ALLEN. Our handwriting expert, CUNNINGHAM, confirms that if ALLEN had the ability to write with his left hand, that this could explain the inability to match the handwriting to Arthur Leigh ALLEN.

30. In August of 1992, Arthur Leigh ALLEN was found dead in his residence of a heart attack. A search warrant served at ALLEN's residence revealed more bomb formulas, and a videotape of all the TV interviews related to the Zodiac. Also, a letter that was to be opened upon his death indicating that he was not, in fact, the Zodiac, and that he had been persecuted by the Vallejo Police Department.

THE ZODIAC LETTERS

ZODIAC'S RIVERSIDE, CALIFORNIA WRITINGS

1. November 29, 1966 (Tuesday). Two typewritten carbon copies of a "confession" letter sent to the press and Riverside police. Zodiac typed on a sandwich of Teletype paper and carbon paper and mailed the faintest, the fourth and fifth impressions. The original typed top page was never sent. He entitled the letter "THE CONFESSION By————" and typed at the bottom: "CC CHIEF OF POLICE, ENTERPRISE." The confession had the same mocking tone Zodiac used in a later letter he began "My Name is————." The threat of more killings to come is also Zodiac-like. Both envelopes were addressed in heavy-felt type printing to the "Homicide Detail, Riverside" and the *Daily Enterprise*, Riverside, California." He flagged them "ATTN; CRIME." The two letters had no postage, only the stamped reminder: ALWAYS USE ZIP CODE. Postmark: RIVERSIDE CALIF. NOV 29 PM 1966.

2. April 30, 1967 (Sunday). Zodiac's handwritten letter on 8 1/2-by-11-inch lined three-hole note paper and envelope in pencil to the *Riverside Press-Enterprise*. Note the "Z" at the bottom of the letter (the FBI agreed that this was a "Z" and not a numeral "2" and double postage—two four-cent Lincoln stamps, on the envelope and lack of postmark. "Bates had to die . . ." FBI Specimens Q66 and Q67. SFPD Item #16. Includes the three letters and envelopes postmarked April 30, 1967.

3. April 30, 1967. Zodiac's letter in pencil to the Riverside Police Department. Two four-cent Lincoln stamps, on the envelope and lack of postmark. "Bates had to die . . ." FBI Specimens Qc68 and Q69.

4. Zodiac's letter in pencil to Joseph Bates, April 30, 1967. Two four-cent Lincoln stamps, on the envelope and lack of postmark. "Bates had to die . . ."

5. Circa January 1967. Desktop poem, found in the Riverside City College Library around the same time as Letters 1, 2, and 3, but probably written three and a half months earlier, then stored in

an unused basement. It was discovered by a janitor. Ballpoint pen, "Sick of Living . . ." Photocopy of ten line poem of crude free verse. The message was written on plywood board study desktop with a ballpoint pen. Four fingerprints and three partial palm prints (Latent Case #73096) on the top remained unidentified. They did not match the three local suspects that Riverside P.D. had under investigation. This poem measured a mere five inches deep by three-and-one-half inches wide, no bigger than a file card. Zodiac sent cards through the mail of the same size. By writing so tiny, Zodiac was able to further disguise his handprinting.

The FBI Lab, working only from photos and photocopies, reported that "Portions of the material, particularly the three Riverside letters, may have been disguised or deliberately distorted . . . the handprinting examination of these letters was inconclusive. However consistent handprinting characteristics were noted the Q85–Qc100 letters which indicate that one person may have prepared all of the letters including the Riverside letters and the message found on the desktop in the Riverside case."

ZODIAC'S NORTHERN CALIFORNIA WRITINGS

1. July 31, 1969 (Thursday). Zodiac's letter to the *San Francisco Chronicle* contains one-third of a cipher. "This is the murderer . . . brand name is Western." Page Two of Zodiac's blue felt-tip pen letter to the *Chronicle*, July 31, 1969 is on back. Paper is so thin that overleaf shows through. The letter we received at the *Chronicle* measured 7 1/8-inches-by-10 1/2-inches. Letters mailed to the *Examiner* and *Times-Herald* measured different sizes and indicated the killer was using remaindered paper bought in lots. One-third of Zodiac's three-part cipher enclosed in his letter. Envelope, slip of cipher, envelope flap and both pages of Zodiac's letter fingerprinted. Police mistakenly marked photocopy sent to FBI as cipher to the *"Examiner."*

1A. August 10, 1969 (Sunday). Typewritten envelope addressed "Sergeant Lynch, Vallejo Police Department Vallejo, California. Accompanying damaged white three-inch-by-five-inch card (the same size card used later) bearing typewritten note, "Dear Sergeant Lynch I hope the enclosed key . . ." Sheet of paper bearing handprinted letters and symbols beginning "A-G-S-(backwards) L . . ." No indented writing found. Postmark: San Francisco Calif. 3A PM 10 AUG 1969.

1B. Salinas schoolteacher Donald Gene Harden's original work-sheets for decoding the first part of Zodiac's three part cipher sent to Bay Area's papers on July 31, 1969.

2. July 31, 1969 (Thursday). Letter to *San Francisco Examiner*, contains one-third of a cipher which measured 7 1/16-inches-by-10 3/8-inches. Envelope postmarked "SAN FRANCISCO, CALIF PM 31 JULY 1969," bearing handprinted address "S.F. EXAMINER San Fran, Calif." On flap are the large, scrawled words: "PLEASE RUSH TO EDITOR." First page of handprinted letter: "Dear Editor This is the murderer of the two teenagers . . ." Back of letter begins: "Here is part of a cipher . . ."

3. July 31, 1969 Zodiac's letter to the *Vallejo Times-Herald*. "I am the killer . . . print this." Police exhibit includes front and back of envelope, one-third of a Zodiac cipher measuring 7 1/16-inches-by-10 7/16-inches, a letter measuring 7 1/8-inches-by-10 9/16-inches and photo of the cipher after being fingerprinted. Police in marking exhibit confused the partial cipher with one sent to the *Chronicle* on the same day. On August 2, police fumed the letter with Ninhydrin, a chemical that develops prints, but causes the handprinting to run and blur.

Of the three ciphers mailed July 31, 1969 and marked QC 32, the FBI wrote, "The ciphers are hand drawn and not normal handprinting. For these reasons not definitely determined whether specimens submitted and others in this case written by one person. However, all threatening letters may be one writer."

4. Page Two of Zodiac's three-page letter to the *Vallejo Times-Herald*, August 1969. First use of name Zodiac. "In answer to your asking for more details." Police date this letter as August 7, 1969. It may have been sent on the first or second of August as an article in the *Examiner* reproduces it on August 4, 1969 and "buries it" on Page Four. Zodiac never wrote the *Examiner* again. "If Zodiac mailed the first three letters on July 31, 1969 and they were published August 1 he wrote that second letter because the cop asked for more details. "It looks like he jumped right on it," police said.

4A. September 27, 1969 (Saturday). Writing on Bryan Hartnell's Volkswagen Karmann Ghia car door at Lake Berryessa. It can be seen in a crime scene picture in the photograph section and close-up in *Zodiac*. The printing on Hartnell's locked car (white with a black vinyl top Oregon license, #4U2040) as described by Deputy Dave Collins on 9/29/69: "At the top of the door panel and to the center was a circle and an even sided cross, running completely through the circle on all four sides. Below the circle and the cross which is described as a cross hair symbol the word 'Vallejo.' Below the word 'Vallejo,' the date '12/20/68.' Below that date '7/4/69.' Below that word 'Sept. 27, 69-6:30.' Below that in printing 'by knife.' This was written in black ink that appeared to be put on with a felt pen."

5. October 13, 1969 (Monday). Front and back of the envelope to Zodiac's letter to the *San Francisco Chronicle* . . . about the Stine killing. Envelope contained a bloody square of Paul Stine's gray and white shirt. In custody of the SFPD Lab, #1 and FBI Q85. Postmark: PM 13 OCT. 1969 1B.

6. November 8, 1969 (Saturday). Front and back of the envelope to Zodiac's letter to the *San Francisco Chronicle*, Envelope contained a 340-symbol cipher and a greeting card ("Sorry I haven't written . . .") with a dripping fountain pen from the Gibson Company with dripping pen. SFPD Lab #2. Includes square of Stine's shirt. Postmark: PM 8 NOV. 1969 4A.

7. November 9, 1969 (Sunday). Seven page letter, "Change my way of collecting . . ." SFPD Lab #2. FBI Specimen Q86. No postmark.

7A. December 7, 1969 (Sunday). Copycat letter addressed to "*San Francisco Chronicle*," postmarked Fairfield. "I will kill again . . . I will turn my self in O K." FBI marked documents Qc34 and Qc35. "Some of the threatening letters in this case, particularly Qc34 and Qc35, contain some distortion and were not written as freely as other threatening letters in this matter," reported the FBI lab.

8. December 20, 1969 (Saturday), "Dear Melvin . . . Help me . . . can not remain in control much longer . . . Happy Christmass . . . [Zodiac's way of spelling Christmas]." Marked FBI Specimen Qc43 (envelope) and Qc44 (letter). Piece of Stine's

shirt per keel. Location of envelope unknown. SFPD Lab #3, FBI Specimen Q87. Postmark: PM 20 Dec. 1069 no mark, CA. at bottom center.

8A. December 3, 1968 (Tuesday). Analysis of bank robbery note to Sutter branch of Wells-Fargo Bank in San Francisco to see if matched Zodiac's printing. It did not. "This is a Bank Robbery if you dont do as I say I will shot."

9. April 20, 1970 (Monday). "My name is . . ." and bomb diagram. Zodiac's envelope, front and back, to the *San Francisco Chronicle*. SFPD Lab #4. FBI #Qc45 and Q88. Postmark: AM 20 APR. 1970 4A.

10. April 28, 1970 (Tuesday). Front of overposted Zodiac's envelope to the *San Francisco Chronicle*. Man on dragon greeting card. "Enjoy the blast . . . buttons . . ." SFPD Lab #5, FBI Q89. Postmark: H. P.M.

11. June 26, 1970 (Friday). Single-stamped Zodiac envelope. Postmarked San Francisco, California "1A 26 JUN AM 1979," to the *San Francisco Chronicle*. Enclosed, a torn portion of a Phillips 66 road map (FBI Specimen Qc51 and Q90). Darlene Ferrin's first husband was named Phillips. With a single line of crypto. Phillips 66 road map had symbols indicating Contra Costa County and specifically Mount Diablo, aka "Satan's Mountain." The killer now claimed twelve victims. The back of Zodiac's map has never been reproduced in print and contains a visual clue linking the killer to his earliest murder near Santa Barbara. Envelope to Zodiac's letter of June 26, 1970 which contained the threat "to punish them if they did not comply by anilating a full school buss." SFPD Lab #6. Postmark: AM JUNE 1970 1A.

12. July 24, 1970 (Friday). Envelope, Zodiac's letter to the *San Francisco Chronicle*, a mention of kidnapped woman and baby, a reference to Kathleen Johns and her infant. SFPD Lab #7. Marked Qc53 and Q91 by FBI. Postmark: PM 24 JUL. 1970 6B.

13. July 26, 1970 (Sunday). "Got a little list . . ." The rarest of all Zodiac letters—never reproduced, never seen outside police

headquarters. I was fortunate to see it when it arrived at the *Chronicle* in 1970. Zodiac paraphrased Gilbert and Sullivan's *The Mikado* in his letter (FBI Specimens Qc54 and Qc55). Envelope marked Qc52 by FBI. Only Zodiac's lengthy letter of November 9, 1969 contained more clues. SFPD Lab #8, FBI Q92. FBI document photocopy Qc55 began "As some day it may hapen that a victom must be found . . ." Qc56 began "This is the Zodiac speaking Being that you will not wear . . ." The FBI lab noted that "Some of the photocopies [provided to them by SFPD] including Qc52-Qc56, are not sufficiently clear to permit detailed handprinting comparisons. However, characteristics indicate that all of the threatening letters, including Qc52–Qc56, were probably prepared by one person." The Lab further suggested, "The reference to billiard players in Qc56 may have been taken from a song sung by the Mikado in Act II. . . ." No code or cipher material was found in Specimens Qc52 through Qc56. Postmark: PM 26 JUL. 1970 no mark.

14. October 5, 1970 (Monday). A three-by-five-inch card addressed to "Paul Averly"—"Pace isn't any slower . . ." Front of Zodiac's montage postcard to the *San Francisco Chronicle*. The card is generally regarded as a fake, but Zodiac's Los Angeles letter of March 15, 1971 also uses the phrase "Crackproof." The three-by-five-inch card (with thirteen punch holes symbolizing victims) contains a bloody cross. It is not human blood. Don Cheney said, "Leigh had a three-hole punch," but Zodiac used a single-holed punch. Toschi advised me that the cross under the numeral 13 was made of thin red paper pasted on the postcard as was other printing. Back of Zodiac's montage postcard to the *San Francisco Chronicle*, Monday, October 5, 1970. Postmark: PM 5 OCT. 1970 1A. It was published on October 6, the one year anniversary of Lynch's interview with Arthur Leigh Allen.

14A. October 17, 1970 (Saturday). Copycat letter postmarked "BERKELEY, CA 17 OCT PM 1970." Bearing message cut out of newspapers or other publications beginning "Mon, Oct 12, 1970 . . . the Zodiac is going to . . ."

15. October 27, 1970 (Tuesday). "Your secret pal . . ." Contained a threatening twenty-five cent (Gibson Greetings) Halloween card to Paul Avery, claiming fourteen victims. The brush lettering

spelling "Averly" is the same as on a March 23, 1971 postcard. Zodiac's postcard, hole-punched like the October 5, 1970 card, was done with brush lettering. Zodiac demonstrated art skills and practice with a brush. He misspells the reporter's name here and on a the October 5, 1970 card as "Averly," a common Zodiac touch. SFPD Lab #9. FBI Specimens Qc60–Qc6s and Q93. Postmark: PM 27 OCT. 1970 6B.

16. March 13, 1971 (Saturday). Postmarked Pleasanton 94566, to *Los Angeles Times*. "Blue Meanies . . ." SFPD Lab #10 FBI Specimen Qc94. Originals in possession of the Los Angeles Police Department. Postmark: PM 13 MAR. 1071 Pleasanton 94566.

17. March 22, 1971 (Monday). Zodiac's letter to the *San Francisco Chronicle*, Four-cent postcard. "Peek through the pines . . ." Cut out and pasted letters, holes punched. One reader, Mike Hopkins, studied the lone punch hole in the upper right-hand corner of the card. "It's at approximately the 11:00 position," he explained. "When the card is oriented so the words 'Sierra Club' are upright, there is the suggestion of a face in the foliage. Did Zodiac sketch himself into the picture and is that what he meant by 'peek through the pines'?" The author obtained the original elaborate brochure which Zodiac used to manufacture the postcard and studied it inch by inch. The killer had added no additional artwork to the pen and ink landscape. Postmark: Canceled Lincoln stamp in which the president is shown in left profile and mourning, which is another indication that someone in Zodiac's life had recently died.

18. January 29, 1974 (Tuesday). Zodiac's letter to the *San Francisco Chronicle*. Exorcist Letter. SFPD Lab #14. FBI file #Qc62 and Qc63. "Qc59–Qc61 being forward to Cryptography Section for evaluation," reported the lab, "you will be advised on the results." Postmark: AM 29 JAN. 1974 940. Three contact palm edge prints were found in 2001 which did not match Allen's palm print.

18A. Copycat card and envelope marked "SLA" to *Chronicle*, postmarked 14 February, 1974. SFPD Lab #11.

18B. Copycat postcard marked May 6, 1974. SFPD Lab #12.

19. May 8, 1974 (Wednesday). Zodiac's letter from Alameda to the *San Francisco Chronicle. Badlands* Letter, signed "A Citizen." Postmark: 8 MAY 1974 Alameda County.

20. July 8, 1974 (Monday). Zodiac's "Red Phantom" to the *San Francisco Chronicle* from San Rafael. SFPD Lab #13, FBI Specimen Q97. Postmark: PM 8 JUL. 1974 San Rafael 1B.

21. April 24, 1978 (Monday). Hoax Zodiac letter to the *San Francisco Chronicle.* "I am back with you . . ." San Francisco Police notation: "DNA SAMPLE OBTAINED/NOT AUTHENTIC ZODIAC LETTER." SFPD Lab #15, FBI Specimen Q99. Postmark: PM 24 APR. 1978 8B.

ZODIAC COPYCAT LETTERS

22. October 29, 1987 (Wednesday). A Zodiac copycat, probably the true author of the April 1978 letter (21), writes the *Vallejo Times-Herald.* "Dear Editor This is the Zodiac speaking I am crack proof. Tell herb caen that I am still here. I have always been here. Tell the blue pigs . . ."

23. June 19, 1990 (Tuesday). Anne Murray, a reporter with the *New York Post* received a letter from Zodiac II. "They faxed me a copy," Ciravolo told me. "It's our guy—it's obviously the same handwriting—claiming responsibility for three prior shootings. He says he shot a man with a cane in the street on March 8."

24. June 21, 1990 (Thursday). "In the letter I left," Zodiac II said later, "I used the phrase I read from the encyclopedia. It was to throw you off the track. . . . I just wanted to increase the fear."

25. June 25, 1990 (Monday). Zodiac II wrote, "Only Orion [The Hunter] can stop Zodiac and the Seven Sister. No more games, pigs."

26. August 5, 1994 (Saturday). Mike Ciravolo told me, "I get a call saying 'Zodiac shot people. He's writing notes [and codes].' It checks out. He's out there again."

27. May 24, 1997 (Saturday). "So this is the beginning of the game," read the letter from Japan's Zodiac III. "I desperately

want to see people die. Nothing makes me more excited than killing. Stupid police, stop me if you can. It's great fun for me to kill people."

28. June 5, 1997 (Thursday). The Japanese Zodiac's rambling 1,400-word letter is published and signed Seito Sakakibara [Apostle Sake Devil Rose]. Zodiac III claimed this was his real name.

BOOKS, FILMS, RADIO, AND TELEVISION SHOWS THAT INSPIRED ZODIAC

"The Most Dangerous Game," printed in *Variety* and published by Minton Balch & Company in 1924, won the O. Henry Memorial Award for that year. Richard Connell's short story has been included in numerous adventure anthologies over the years.

The Most Dangerous Game. In 1932 RKO-Radio Pictures, Inc. filmed a 63-minute-long black and white film version of "The Most Dangerous Game" with executive producer David O. Selznick, producer Merian C. Cooper, and directors Ernest B. Schoedsack and Irving Pichel (dialogue director). Screenwriter was James Ashmore Creelman. The film starred Joel McCrea (Bob Rainsford), Fay Wray (Eve Trowbridge), Leslie Banks (Count Zaroff), Robert Armstrong (Martin Trowbridge), Noble Johnson, Steve Clemento, and Dutch Hernian. Max Steiner, music. RKO Production #602.

In 1945 RKO re-made *The Most Dangerous Game* as *A Game of Death* directed by Robert Wise and starring John Loder and Audrey Long. Edgar Barrier played General Kreigner. The following year, *Johnny Allegro* used elements of Connell's story. Nina Foch and George Raft. George MacCready emulated our old friend Count Zaroff as a sportsman killer, who liked to claim his victims with bow and arrow.

In 1956 came the third retelling of Connell's yarn. Bob Waterfield, former L.A. Rams quarterback, produced the film. United Artist's *Run for the Sun* starred Richard Widmark, Trevor Howard, and Jane Greer as a magazine editor who goes to Mexico to ferret out a reclusive novelist. Rather than an island, this time the action was set on a jungle plantation. Widmark and Greer crash-land on the estate of a Nazi war criminal who hunts wayward travelers with a pack of blood-hounds. Long after the film was completed, Greer learned she had been exposed to a rare virus contracted during the grueling waterfall and swamp scenes, Coxsaci B, that lay dormant in her body for years. Only a heart operation in the 1960s saved her life.

In 1961, Robert Reed starred in *Bloodlust*—another variation. Cornel Wilde's *The Naked Prey* was filmed five years later. *The Perverse Countess* was released in 1973, *Slave Girls from Beyond Infinity* in 1988, and *Deadly Game* in 1991—all versions of *The Most Dangerous Game*.

Follow Me Quietly. Directed by Richard Fleischer, RKO. Starring William Lundigan, Dorothy Patrick, and Edwin Max as "The Judge." 1949, 59 minutes. "The Judge" is a Zodiac-like character who carries on a deadly chess match with a police inspector.

Charlie Chan at Treasure Island. The 1939 20th Century-Fox film. Directed by Norman Foster and John Larkin. Original Story and Screenplay by John Larkin. Based on the character Charlie Chan, created by Earl Derr Biggers. Sidney Toler, Cesar Romero, Pauline Moore (Eve Cairo), Victor Sen Yung (Number Two son, Jimmy Chan), Douglas Fowley (Pete Lewis, *San Francisco Chronicle* crime reporter), June Gale (Myra Rhadini, Rhadini's wife and a professional knife-thrower), Douglass Dumbrille (Thomas Gregory, an insurance investigator), Sally Blane (Stella Essex), Billie Seward (Bessie Sibley), Wally Vernon (Elmer), Donald MacBride (Chief Kilvaine), Charles Halton (Redley), Trevor Bardette (the treacherous Dr. Zodiac's Turkish servant), Gerald Mohr (voice of Dr. Zodiac), Louis Jean Heydt (Paul Essex). 72 minutes. All the magic props from this film were later re-used in *A-Haunting We Will Go* (Fox, 1944), a Laurel and Hardy comedy.

The Boston Strangler, the first docudrama about a real-life serial killer, starred Tony Curtis, 1968.

No Way to Treat a Lady. A psychotic killer, Christopher Gill (Rod Steiger) disguises himself as a policeman, a woman, and a priest. He chooses to play a cat-and-mouse game with a police detective, Morris Brummel (George Segal). The killer calls him after each crime, leaves clues in taunting letters, and draws his mother's lips on his victims' foreheads. The cop and killer both have mother complexes. Detective Brummel says to the killer of his victims, "But they all had lipstick, didn't they? The very shape of your dear mother's lips. The very lips on all those portraits out in your lobby." Zodiac conceivably took ideas from this 1968 movie in which Steiger portrayed what has been called "the perfect fictional serial killer . . . intelligent and egotistical who never changes his pattern until suitable motivation is provided." Gill is a "psychotic master of disguise." From the novel by William Goldman.

The Exorcist. William Peter Blatty's book and 1973 film, influenced Zodiac as shown in his written critique of the movie on January 29, 1974 in which he deemed the film "the best saterical comidy" he had ever seen. Perhaps demonic possession as a factor in serial killings intrigued the Cipher Slayer.

Badlands, a movie based on the Charlie Starkweather and Caril Ann Fugate 1950s murder spree, aroused Zodiac to write the *Chronicle* again on May 8, 1974 to express his "consternation concerning your poor taste" by running ads for the film.

"The Most Dangerous Game" appeared on the radio on *Suspense* on September 23, 1943, as the most famous audio adaptation of Connell's short story. The fifty-eighth episode of the series, the program starred Orson Welles and Keenan Wynn. Jacques A. Finke wrote the script for producer-director William Spier. The radio show was still sustaining (without a sponsor) and had just moved from Saturday nights to Thursday the month before.

On February 1, 1945, Finke's script was used for a second *Suspense* broadcast, but this time starred J. Carrol Naish and Joseph Cotten. Two years after that Les Crutchfield adapted "The Most Dangerous Game" as a half-hour show for producer-director Norman Macdonnell's *Escape*, on October 1, 1947, starring Paul Frees and Hans Conried. *Escape* had begun its irregular run on CBS radio in July.

A 1950s *Alfred Hitchcock Presents* starring Myron McCormick and adapted from a story by William C. Morrison—featured a young man with a flashlight taped to his rifle. "Just shoot for the dark spot in the light and you will hit your target," he said—exactly as Zodiac wrote. Hunting small game at night, he chanced upon two lovers—result: accidental murder and the man's imprisonment. His vengeful father says at the conclusion, eyes glittering: "The excitement of a manhunt—the most dangerous game."

The Man Who Never Was, starring Robert Lansing and featuring the crossed-circle symbol. This ABC television show debuted Wednesday, September 7, 1966.

FILMS AND TELEVISION SHOWS THAT ZODIAC INSPIRED

Zodiac, a minimum-budget, 84-minute color film in which Zodiac is highly fictionalized. The film features a penlight on a gun barrel and lovers' lane murders. Shown exclusively at the RKO Golden Gate Theater at Golden Gate Avenue and Taylor Street for a single week. Police staked it out in case Zodiac should attend and fill out a card explaining, in twenty-five words or less, why they believed Zodiac killed. The person who answered best would win a free Kawasaki 350cc motorcycle. One review: "A movie disguised as a warning sneaked into the Golden Gate this week . . . the print is flawed, but this is expected to be improved. Less easily remedied is the script and its dialogue . . . the picture ends limply, despite a few remarks in the narrative that Zodiac may be the man behind you in the theatre." The cast includes Hal Reed, Bob Jones, Ray Lynch, and Tom Pittman. Produced and directed by Tom Hanson, with a screenplay by Ray Cantrell and Manny Cardoza. The film was advertised in the *Chronicle* with the lines, "Who is he . . . what is he . . . when is he going to strike again??" and "Zodiac says . . . 'I Lay Awake Nights Thinking of My Next Victim.'"

Dirty Harry. While *Zodiac* was low-budget, Don Siegel's 1971 *Dirty Harry* was shot in Technicolor Panavision and starred Clint Eastwood as an Inspector Toschi–type searching for a ski-masked sniper named "Scorpio" (Andy Robinson) who signs himself with a crossed-circle symbol. Like *The Most Dangerous Game*, Scorpio fired a 30-.06 rifle with a sniper scope such as Zaroff used in the movie. Interestingly, Scorpio wore the military shoes worn by Zodiac. In *Dirty Harry* police used the personal column of the *Chronicle* to communicate with him. I suspect that the real Zodiac also used the paper's personal column to communicate with a confederate or instill fear in people who suspected him. "Dirty" Harry tracks the serial killer through the underbrush of Mt. Davidson and corners him near Golden Gate Park at Kezar Stadium close to Stanyan and Haight Streets, not far from Paul Stine's house. Faithful to the facts, the movie diverges in making Zodiac's threat to kidnap a school bus filled with children a reality. Written by Harry Julian Fink, R. M. Fink, and Dean Reisner, photographed by Bruce Surtees. First choices for the role were Frank Sinatra (an injured tendon in his hand made it painful to hold a gun) and Paul Newman (who objected to its politics and suggested Clint Eastwood). The name of Eric Zelms, Fouke's partner the night Zodiac escaped into the Presidio, is shown on a memorial plaque to San Francisco police officers. Zelms died in the line of duty in 1970.

Lured, directed by Douglas Sirk, a "lost" film from 1947. Black and White, 105 minutes and starring Lucille Ball, George Sanders, Boris Karloff, and Charles Coburn. Produced by James Nasser with screenplay by Leo Rosten. This film concerned a serial killer preying on young women in London.

The January Man, starring Kevin Kline.

Exorcist III: Legion. The "Gemini Killer" is based on Zodiac.

Millennium. This Fox Network series featured a realistic drama about Zodiac. The scene where Agent Frank Black approached Zodiac's trailer is especially authentic as is the climax in the darkened theater where Agent Black is fooled by a statue of Zodiac in costume.

Nash Bridges. Featured an "Inspector Toschi" character and an encounter with Zodiac. At the conclusion, Bridges (Don Johnson) implies that Zodiac will return.

A 1978 *Lou Grant* episode, starring Ed Asner featured a police inspector obsessed with a Zodiac-type serial killer, the Judge, who has apparently returned and is writing letters to press and police again. Inspired by fake Zodiac letter of April 1978.

The Limbic Region with Edward James Olmos, and to a lesser degree, *Copycat* with Sigourney Weaver, *The Mean Season* with Kurt Russell, and *Seven* with Brad Pitt.

FACTUAL TELEVISION PROGRAMS ON ZODIAC

Rolanda Show. "The New York and San Francisco Zodiac." Tuesday, September 6, 1994.

Hard Copy. "Zodiac [Hines's suspect]." May 10, 1994.

America's Most Wanted. "America Fights Back: The Zodiac Killer." Saturday, November 14, 1998.

Sally Jesse Raphael. "Zodiac." Taped on Thursday, August 16, 1990.

Unsolved Mysteries. "The Zodiac Killer. (Episode #2324.)

Crimes of the Century. "Zodiac." Syndicated program.

The History Channel. "Zodiac." Taped 1999.

The Learning Channel. "Case Reopened." A 1999 episode with host Lawrence Block.

ZODIAC'S INSPIRATION FROM LIGHT OPERA, CARTOONS, AND COMICS

Gilbert and Sullivan's *The Mikado*.

The Yellow Submarine. Zodiac mentioned the "Blue Meannies," a reference to the music-hating "Blue Meanies" who terrorized the Beatles in the 1968 cartoon feature. The submarine aspect made sense. Since Zodiac was obsessed with water and Allen was a skin diver, all of his souvenirs might be hidden in watertight containers underwater. *Sgt. Pepper's Lonely Hearts Club Band* referred to the killer's loneliness.

Mad magazine: Zodiac adapted the "fold-ins" on the back cover to conceal messages in one of his letters; Mad #170's parody of *The Exorcist*, "The Ecchorcist," written by Larry Siegel and drawn by Mort Drucker. The lampoon appeared in the October 1974 issue (published in August), cover captioned, "If the Devil Makes You Do It," and showing Alfred E. Newman costumed as Satan.

Whiz Comics #2 [#1]. A mention of the "Death Machine." "This, my friend, is the life machine. With it I can restore the dead to life. But first I must kill you, so—the death machine!" says a mad chemist, a dead ringer for Count Zaroff. "I place these cyanide pills in the cup. When the door is closed they will drop into the bucket of sulfuric acid, forming a deadly gas."

The *Dick Tracy* comic strip ran daily in the *Chronicle*. Zodiac was a longtime reader of the strip since he recalled various Tracy's tips to avoid leaving prints and other clues. On August 17, 1969, Chester Gould's story line introduced the Zodiac Gang, a group of astrological killers who drowned an astrology columnist. Their leader, Scorpio, had an astrological symbol of Scorpio tattooed across his face. Light-haired and round-faced, he closely resembled both Allen and Mageau's description of Zodiac at Blue Rock Springs.

VISUAL INSPIRATIONS FOR ZODIAC

The Most Dangerous Game. Count Zaroff's costume.

Ku Klux Klan hoods and black robes of Klan officials.

Black Mass Symbols and hoods used by Anton Le Vey's Church of Satan.

A cattle brand used on Fred Harmon's Pagosa Springs, Colorado ranch.

Carrying a cocked bow and rifle, Zodiac resembled not only Zaroff, but the hooded killer, a staple of painter H.L. Parkhurst's fortics *Spicy Mystery* pulp covers one of which showed a nighttime scene with a powerful hooded killer firing a .45 at his pursuers and clutching a struggling woman under his arm. Is that how Zodiac visualized himself?

The cross within a circle was the mark of Cain, the killer-*teth* in ancient Hebrew. The word *tav* stood for the righteous.

The cross-haired symbol is found in ancient American Indian carvings in the Nevada caves.

SOURCES

FEDERAL, STATE, AND LOCAL LAW ENFORCEMENT FILES, INTERVIEWS

A special Confidential Report: *UNSOLVED FEMALE HOMICIDES, An Analysis of a Series of Related Murders in California and Western America*, California Department of Justice, Division of Law Enforcement Organized Crime & Criminal Intelligence Branch, February 1975.

Special Report: *ZODIAC HOMICIDES*. Confidential. California Department of Justice, Division of Law Enforcement / Bureau of Investigation, 1971. 1972 corrected edition. The author also studied the rough draft of this report as corrections were being made by the detectives involved.

Dr. Murray S. Miron of the Syracuse Research Institute, Confidential FBI psycholinguistics report, working from Zodiac letters, May 31, 1977.

Federal Bureau of Investigation File Number 2528-SF-94447-1. The complete 900-page FBI file on Zodiac. One hundred pages of the file are on Arthur Leigh Allen.

FBI report 9-49911-88 (January 14, 1970). Quotes conversation between Belli's housekeeper and Zodiac, December 18, 1969.

FBI report, December 31, 1969, noted Belli letter "not been written as freely as the other threatening letters in this matter." Enciphered Airtel, 12/29/69.

FBI file #32-27195, Latent Case #73096.

FBI Lab, May 19, 1978. Questioned Documents Q85 through Q99. Riverside letters, including the desktop, studied separately in photographic form and labeled Qc100.

FBI report 252B-SF-9447, March 23, 1992.

Officer Donald Foulk's SFPD Intra-Departmental Memorandum, November 12, 1969.

Napa County Sheriff's Office, Case #105907.

Bawart and Conway Report, Case #243145.

Detective George Bawart of Vallejo P.D. A seven page report to the FBI, Case #243145. "Circumstances Which Indicate Arthur Leigh Allen Is, in Fact, the Zodiac Killer," 1992.

Allen Search Warrant #1970, 22 pages, by Roy Conway, dated February 13, 1991.

Return to Allen Search Warrant, filed February 21, 1991 by Roy Conway. Return lists 37 items recovered including pipe bombs, fuses, guns, and rifles.

Inspector William Armstrong, Affidavit for Search Warrant, Santa Rosa, 6 pages, September 14, 1972, 12:00 P.M.

Jack Mulanax Officer's Reports, July 28, 1971, August 3, 1971, August 9–12, 1971, personal interviews with the author.

Mulanax and William Garlington: July 29, 1971: Exemplars for Arthur Leigh Allen, report from A.L. Coffey, Chief of the Bureau.

Manhattan Beach Police Department: "Information: Possible Zodiac Suspect," July 19, 1971, Chief Charles W. Crumly.

Riverside Report, October 20, 1969.

John Lynch, Vallejo P.D. Report on Arthur Leigh Allen, 4:05 October 6, 1969.

SFPD Report. Two pages: Suspected Zodiac Correspondence and DNA Testing.

San Francisco Police Department, Vallejo Police Department, Napa Sheriff's Department, Benicia Police Department, Vallejo Sheriff's Department, Santa Rosa Police Department, and Riverside Police Department incident reports and files. Included in these reports are ballistics and crime lab results, autopsy reports, fingerprint comparisons, and suspect files.

Personal Interviews by author with Vallejo Detective George Bawart, Detective Sergeant John Lynch, Detective Jack Mulanax, Captain Ken Narlow of Napa Sheriff's Department, Homicide Inspector David Toschi (Toschi's interviews ran to almost three hundred hours over a thirty-year period), Detective William Baker, Lieutenant Tom Bruton, and Inspectors Vince Repetto and Rich Adkins. Police investigators' personal case notes and reports, including rough drafts of local and state reports.

Psychiatric studies of Arthur Leigh Allen.

Unpublished crime scene photographs and maps.

Unreproduced Zodiac letters and potentially authentic typewritten letters from the killer. Photos of the killer's shoes, watch,
and actual samples of the prime suspect's handprinting. All
newspaper and television accounts of the Zodiac case, including computer files and unpublished stories.

Various stories, internal memos, and unpublished notes for stories including personal observations by reporter Paul Avery to
the author between 1969–1976.

Cablegrams and reports by phone from Melvin Belli from Rome
and Munich, December 1969.

San Francisco State Zodiac Conference: Attended by author,
Captain Roy Conway, Detective George Bawart, and Rita
Williams. Author worked from his handwritten record of the
meeting and a tape recording that he made. Follow-up questions were asked of Conway, Bawart, and Williams after the
meeting, and in the weeks following. Additional detailed interviews with Williams by phone and in person were conducted by the author in 2000 and 2001.

The original tip letters received at the *San Francisco Chronicle*
1969–1983.

Letters and phone calls from readers to the author 1969–2001.

Employment records, phone logs, and academic files of some
suspects.

Hypnotic interviews conducted with witnesses and suspects.

Suspect's letters from Atascadero State Hospital for the Criminally Insane.

California Department of Motor Vehicles and some insurance
records.

CI&I Handwriting reports and numerous interviews with the
State Questioned Documents chief.

Discarded files on the case.

Xerox photocopies made from the originals of all of the Zodiac
letters.

Interviews with Donald Lee Cheney, January, February, May
2001.

Interview with Sandy Panzarella. The full story of Cheney and
Panzarella's tip to police is also enclosed in the 1991–92 requests for search warrants for Allen's home. These court documents are now on file at the County Courthouse.

January 29, 1981, interview with Darlene's close friend, Bobbie
Ramos.

Interview with Linda Del Buono on November 8, 1980, January 29, 1981.

Bobbie Oxnam, a close friend of Darlene's, interview, June 15, 1981.

Interview with Mary Pilker, Donna Lass's sister, April 7, 2001, July 7, 2001.

South Lake Tahoe Police File, Case #70-6436-Donna Lass, RN.

Douglas County Sheriff File, Case #70-3120-Donna Lass, RN.

Sonoma County Probation File No. 62892, Court No. 7588-C.

Technical advice: Dave Toschi, Mary Ontano, Wendy Manning.

Penny Donaly, Sonoma County Coroner's Office.

Santa Rosa Sergeant Steve Brown, August 2001.

NEWSPAPERS AND PERIODICALS

Blum, Walter. "Zodiac." *San Francisco Examiner*, November, 1968.

Clark, Mark. "Dangerous Games." *Scarlet Street Magazine*, No. 27, April 1998, pp. 33–37.

Dorn, Norman K. "Putting the Right Sound into Silent Movies." *San Francisco Chronicle*, January 4, 1972.

Ginley, Jacqueline. "Local Attorney Claims to Know Zodiac." *Vallejo Times-Herald*, October 30, 1991, p. A-1.

Hackler, Timothy. "Can We Blame It on the Moon?" *San Francisco Examiner*, December 13, 1978, p. 24.

Hedger, Matthew. "Was the Zodiac Killer a Local Teacher?" *Calaveras County Ledger Dispatch*, June 2, 2001.

Holt, Tim. "The Men Who Stalk the Zodiac Killer." *San Francisco Magazine*, April 1974, pp. 34–36.

Jennings, Duffy. "Step by Step with Two Detectives." *San Francisco Chronicle*, April 1, 1974, p. 4.

Lieber, Dr. Arnold L. "The Lunar Effect and Dade County." Report culled by Dr. Arnold from *Florida Homicide Records*, 1955–70.

Lyons, Corey. "Zodiac." *Contra Costa Times*, December 3, 2000.

Martin, Harry V. "Zodiac." *Napa Sentinel*, December 17, 1991.

McCockran, Robert. "Suspect's Death Won't Halt Zodiac Investigation." *Vallejo Times-Herald*, September 3, 1992.

O'Flaherty, Terrence. "The Police: Reel vs. Real." *San Francisco Chronicle*, August 21, 1975, p. 46.

Peterson, Dave. "Zodiac Link to Santa Barbara Murders." *Vallejo News-Chronicle*, 1969.

Starr, Kevin. "The City's Supercop." *San Francisco Examiner*, August 13, 1977, p. 11.

Silverman, Gene. "Zodiac." *Vallejo Times-Herald*, January 19, 1986, p. 1.

Stark, John. "The Man We Loved to Hate." *San Francisco Examiner*, January 20, 1980, Scene Section, p. 1.

Stienstra, Tom. "Zodiac." *San Francisco Examiner*, March 17, 2000.

Weir, Tom. "The Cop Who Hunts Zodiac." *Oakland Tribune*, July 13, 1976.

Zellerbach, Merla. "My Fair City." *San Francisco Chronicle*, September 11, 1968.

SOURCES FOR THE NEW YORK ZODIAC [ZODIAC II]

Associated Press. "Attacks by 'Zodiac' Gunman Linked to Book." July 1, 1990.

Celona, Larry, and Bowles, Pete. "Shooter Foils 'Zodiac' Author's Intent." *New York Newsday*, June 24, 1990, p. 1.

Bunch, William, and Gordy, Molly. "Trying to Chart a Gunman's Moves." *Newsday*, June 22, 1990.

Crowley, Kieran. "Breaks Zodiac Code." *New York Post*, August 8, 1994, p. 5.

Crowley, Kieran. *Sleep My Little Dead*. New York: St. Martin's Press, 1997.

Frankel, Bruce. "Zodiac Killer Stalks NYC." *USA Today*, June 27, 1990, p. 3A.

George, Tara, Breen, Virginia, and Mooney, Mark. "He's Nailed." *New York Daily News*, June 19, 1996.

Lyons, Richard D. "Zodiac Detectives Turn to Computers and Stars." *New York Times*, June 28, 1990.

Marzulli, John. "Zodiac Knew Signs of Victims." *New York Daily News*, p. 3.

McNamara, Joseph. "New York Zodiac Copies S.F. Killer." *New York Daily News*, June 24, 1990.

McNamara, Joseph. "Frisco Killer Unrelated to Stalker." *San Francisco Examiner*, June 24, 1990, p. 43.

McNamara, Joseph. "Zodiac Fires on 4th Man." *New York Daily News*, June 22, 1990, p. 7.

McAlary, Mike. "Cop's Net for Maniac." *New York Daily News*, June 28, 1990, p. 34.

McAlary, Mike. "Following the Stars." *New York Daily News*, June 24, 1990, p. 2.

McQuillan, Alice, Marzulli, John, and Siemaszko, Corky. "Gunman Admits Serial Shootings." AP, June 19, 1996, p. 30.

Miller, Alan. "Killer May Be Copycat." *USA Today*, June 27, 1990, p. 5A.

"Zodiac II—the New York Gunman." *New York Times*, June 23, 1990.

"Zodiac." *New York Times*, August 13, 1994.

Rashbaum, William K. "Confession of Murderous Terror Spree." *UPI*, June 20, 1996, p. 34. Source for first-person confession of Zodiac II.

Shain, Michael. "Subway Trap for Zodiac." *New York Daily News*. July 12, 1990, p. 5.

Smith, Greg B. "Son of Zodiac Creates Climate of Fear in New York." *San Francisco Examiner*, July 2, 1990, p. A-6.

Weiss, Murry. "He Warned Police Before First Attack." *New York Post*, June 22, 1990, p. 5.

SELECTED REFERENCES

Belli, Melvin, and Kaiser, Robert Blair. *My Life on Trial*. New York: William Morrow & Co., Inc., 1976.

Douglas, John, and Olshaker, Mark. *The Cases That Haunt Us*. New York: Scribner, 2000.

Fallis, Greg. *A Murder*. New York: M. Evans and Company, Inc., 1999.

Gardner, Earle Stanley. *The Court of Last Resort Handbook*. Privately published.

Gilliam, Harold. *San Francisco Bay*. Garden City, New York: Doubleday & Company, 1957.

Goldner, Orville, and Turner, George E. *The Making of King Kong*. Ballantine Books, New York, 1975.

Hanke, Ken. *Charlie Chan at the Movies*. McFarland & Co. Inc.

Huffman, Rob. "Camping with the Zodiac." 1997, 2000.

Kessler, Robert. *The FBI*. New York: Pocket Books, 1993.

Lunde, Donald T., M.D. *Murder and Madness*. New York: W.W. Norton & Company, Inc., 1979.

Time-Life, editors. *Serial Killers*. Alexandria, Virginia: Time-Life Books, 1992.

Zinman, David. *Saturday Afternoon at the Bijou*. New York: Arlington House, 1973.

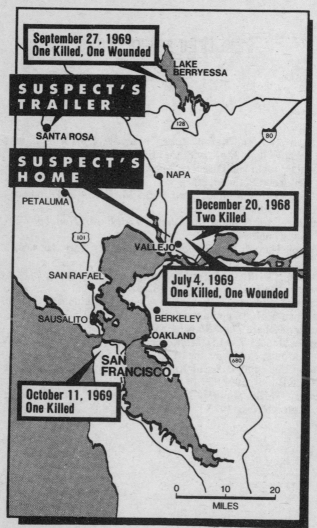

September 27, 1969
One Killed, One Wounded

LAKE BERRYESSA

SUSPECT'S TRAILER

128

80

SANTA ROSA

SUSPECT'S HOME

NAPA

PETALUMA

December 20, 1968
Two Killed

101

VALLEJO

SAN RAFAEL

July 4, 1969
One Killed, One Wounded

SAUSALITO

BERKELEY

OAKLAND

SAN FRANCISCO

680

October 11, 1969
One Killed

0   10   20
MILES

Map by Robert Graysmith

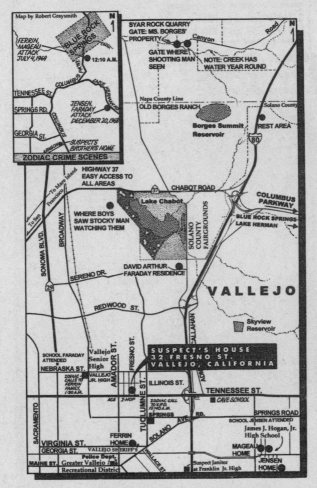

Map of Vallejo Showing Prime Suspects's Close
Proximity to the Victims, Witnesses and Crime Scenes.

INDEX

and timing of murders, xi, 105, 288
Tropical Zodiac analysis, 288
Atascadero State Hospital for the
    Criminally Insane, 160,
    161, 163–170, 174,
    180–181, 263, 272, 309
Automobiles. *See* Cars
Avery, Paul, 94, 340
    health, 88, 92, 404
    meeting with Riverside P.D., 96
    retirement, 404
    suggestion for information
        clearinghouse, 226–227
    theft of Zodiac files from, 88–89
    theories on Zodiac, 89, 144, 147,
        193
    threats to, 91, 96, 190
    witness to stabbing, 92
Ayers, Sue, 420

Badlands, 156, 450, 453
Baker, Detective, 125, 131–132,
    349, 425
Baker, William, 14, 73
Baldino, Steve, 368, 412, 427
Balmer, Thomas D., 103
Barca, Charles, 110, 112, 140
Basement. *See* Allen, Arthur Leigh,
    Vallejo home
Bates, Cheri Jo
    and Allen, 11, 188, 372, 389, 435
    evidence, 84, 236–237, 269
    murder, 37, 76–78, 435
    surveillance at burial, 153
    Zodiac letters about, 84, 94, 372,
        435, 443
Bates, Joseph, 81, 84, 443
Bawart, George
    case summary, 369–370, 374,
        428, 436–444
    and death of Zodiac, 354,
        355–357
    during DNA analysis, 380
    and Emmett, 342–345
    on Ferrin, 411

interviews, 18, 23, 201–202,
    234–235, 327–328,
    429–432
investigation, 18, 23, 201–202,
    234–235, 262–263,
    298–299, 327–328
    on jurisdiction issues, 62, 338
    on polygraph test by Allen,
        165–166
    re-opening Zodiac investigation,
        351–354
    report of 1992, 388–389,
        436–444
    retirement, 342, 363
Beeman, William Steadman,
    338–339, 340–341, 368
Behavioral Science Unit, 191
Belli, Melvin, 12–13, 52, 152,
    238–239, 296, 317–318,
    319–324
Benecia, Calif., 102–105, 216, 232
Benecia Police Department, 103,
    104, 124
Bennallack, Nancy M., 90
Berkeley, Calif., 97
Berkowitz, David (Son of Sam),
    215, 280, 310
Berryessa. *See* Lake Berryessa
Betts, Sandy, 315
Bianchi, Kenneth, 133, 197
Bidou, Pierre, 103
Black hood. *See* Hood and
    executioner's costume
Blocker, Dan, 75, 129
Bloodlust, 247n.10, 452
Blood tests, 275, 378, 379
Blue/black felt tip pens. *See* Letters,
    blue/black felt tip pens
    used
"Blue Meannies," 9, 383, 413, 456
"Blue pigs," 39
Blue Rock Springs
    murder/shooting. *See also*
        Ferrin, Darlene; Mageau,
        Mike

Robert Graysmith is the national bestselling author of *Zodiac* and *The Sleeping Lady*.